'D-DAY' DAKOTAS

'D-DAY' DAKOTAS

DAKOTAS

6TH JUNE, 1944

MARTIN W BOWMAN

Pen & Sword
AVIATION

First published in Great Britain in 2019 by
PEN AND SWORD AVIATION
an imprint of
Pen & Sword Books Limited
Yorkshire – Philadelphia

Copyright © Martin W Bowman, 2019

ISBN 978 1 52674 615 3

Printed and bound in the UK by TJ International

Typeset in Times New Roman 11/13.5 by
Aura Technology and Software Services, India

Pen & Sword Books Ltd incorporates the imprints of Pen & Sword
Archaeology, Atlas, Aviation, Battleground, Discovery,
Family History, History, Maritime, Military, Naval, Politics, Railways,
Select, Social History, Transport, True Crime, Claymore Press,
Frontline Books, Leo Cooper, Praetorian Press, Remember When,
Seaforth Publishing and Wharncliffe.

For a complete list of Pen and Sword titles please contact
PEN & SWORD BOOKS LTD
47 Church Street, Barnsley, South Yorkshire, S70 2AS, England
E-mail: enquiries@pen-and-sword.co.uk
Website: www.pen-and-sword.co.uk

Or

PEN & SWORD BOOKS
1950 Lawrence Rd, Havertown, PA 19083, USA
E-mail: Uspen-and-sword@casematepublishers.com
Website: www.penandswordbooks.com

Contents

In fifty-one they tried to ground the noble DC-3
And some lawyers brought the case before the C.A.B.
The board examined all the facts behind their great oak portal
And pronounced these simple words "The Gooney Bird's Immortal.
The Army toast their Sky Train in lousy scotch and soda
The Tommies raise their glasses high to cheer their old Dakota.
Some claim the C-47's best, or the gallant R4D
Forget that claim, their all the same, they're the noble DC-3.
Douglas built the ship to last, but nobody expected
This crazy heap would fly and fly, no matter how they wrecked it.
While nations fall and men retire, and jets go obsolete
The Gooney Bird flies on and on at eleven thousand feet.
No matter what they do to her the Gooney Bird still flies
One crippled plane was fitted out with one wing half the size.
She hunched her shoulders then took off (I know this makes you laugh)
Only wing askew, and yet she flew, the DC-3 and a half.
She had her faults, but after all, who's perfect in every sphere
Her heating system was a gem we loved her for the gear.
Of course the windows leaked a bit when the rain came pouring down
She'd keep you warm, but in a storm, it's possible you'd drown.
Well now she flies the feeder lines and carries all the freight
She just an airborne office, a flying twelve ton crate.
They patched her up with masking tape, with paper clips and strings
And still she flies, she never dies, Methuselah with wings.

Tribute To The DC-3; Anon

Acknowledgements

Much information has been gleaned from *'Airborne Operations in World War II, European Theater; USAF Historical Studies No.97*, produced by the USAF Historical Division, Research Studies Institute, Air University by Dr. John C. Warren, published at Maxwell Air Force Base, Alabama in September 1956. 'Men of D-Day' website provided excellent first-hand accounts of troop carrier and glider pilots, 82nd and 101st paratroopers.

I am indebted to Mike Bailey; Paul Wilson; Nigel McTeer; *The Pegasus Archive* and *Silver Wings Museum*.

Chapter 1

'Devils in Baggy Pants'

There are eighteen men in the plane, nine facing nine on the chromium bucket seats. The plane is that valuable dray horse of war, the twin-engined C-47. Scores of other planes, still in formation, fly through the night and the wind and in all of them sit the quiet men, heavy with equipment, rifle or Tommy gun, ammunition, grenades, land mines, first-aid packets, rations and maps, perhaps a radio, a bazooka, or a light machine gun as well - one hundred pounds or more to carry to the ground. This is the long last waiting and their faces and their eyes are blank. What concerns each man now is entirely private and his empty face guards him, where he lives alone. The lucky ones sleep. After all there is nothing to do but wait, everything that can be known is known, the mind only uses itself looking backward or forward; it is good to sleep if you can.

No man was forced into these planes. Paratroopers are volunteers. There had been months of preparation for this ride and there was a time, before a man earned and accepted his parachute wings, when he could reconsider and choose some other way to war. In the beginning, at jump school, they were driven through a course of training which was not only intended to harden them and teach them their new trade but was also meant to discourage them if possible. For weeks, from sunup till sundown, they ran until their lungs ached, did push-ups and sit-ups and twirled Indian clubs until their muscles knotted with pain, tumbled from platforms into sawdust pits until they were numb, stumbled and dragged on the ground behind opened chutes, blown by a wind machine, jumped from 35-foot towers and from 250-foot towers and learned to pack their chutes, with the chilling knowledge that they would use these same chutes on their first real jump. Finally, as one of them said, 'preferring certain death to any more training,' they were taken up in C-47s

1

and twice a day they spilled themselves out; having overcome this daylight hazard, they tried it again at night.

After they got their wings, the training was no less rigorous, but at least there was some praise mixed with the punishment. Nothing that could be taught was left untaught; they were also told that one paratrooper was worth five of any other kind of man. Their confidence in themselves and their units and their division grew to be iron hard and they were prepared to pay for this pride.

The time for payment had come. They had been briefed; each man knew what was expected of him and knew the plan that directed them all. They also knew what can go wrong. They knew that a chute can fail to open, a 'streamer' they call it. They knew a man can land and break his legs, his back and his neck for that matter. They knew a man can be shot as he floats to earth, or hang in a tree as a helpless target. They knew there is no guarantee that they will be dropped where they expect. They knew for certain that wherever they dropped the enemy will be all around them, waiting and they can only hope that darkness and surprise will give them that edge of time they need. The moment for thinking and knowing is past; the red warning light has flashed and the jumpmaster gives the command that belongs to them alone: Stand Up and Hook Up!

Seventeen men rise and fasten their static lines to the main cable. Check your Equipment! Sound off for equipment check!

Number ten okay!

Number nine okay!

The voices count off, above the motor and the noise of the wind. Are you ready? There is a full, roaring shout. Then the final words: Let's go! The officer disappears into the wide loud night; men shuffle fast down the length of the plane; hurry, hurry, the faster you get out the nearer you will be to your buddies when you land; the plane is empty. In seconds which cannot be measured in time, men have descended into battle.

Stand up and Hook up! by Martha Gellhorn describing the start of Operation 'Husky' in 1943. Martha had grown up in St. Louis, an only daughter in a family of four children. Spending much time in Germany in the 1930s acquiring background material for a new novel she had observed 'the strutting storm troopers and frightened people with despair.'

The first combat airborne missions in history were flown by the Germans in 1940. Recognizing the possibilities of such operations, the British and Americans followed suit. The first British mission was flown in February 1941 and the first American mission was flown from England to Oran, Algeria, on 8 November 1942 as part of the Anglo-American invasion of North Africa. Other, later missions, principally in the Mediterranean region, provided the American troop carriers with an apprenticeship in airborne warfare. Foremost among the transports in US and RAF service, the military C-47 'Skytrain', an outgrowth of the DC-3 (Douglas Commercial model 3), which was in turn an outgrowth of the DC-2, was flown in troop carrier operations in all theatres, but it is best known for its combat roles in North Africa, Sicily, Italy, Normandy, Holland and Germany. These were the glamour missions, the ones that earned medals, but many other missions were flown carrying tons of critical freight wherever needed. Return trips often carried the injured and the wounded. Most of the preliminary design work was carried out in the early thirties at the request of the airline industry. Shortly after the war began, scores of commercial DC-3s were hustled into the Army, Navy and Marine air arms, until a high-level production of military versions could be obtained. This was quickly done and the C-53 'Skytrooper' soon began making its appearance on the extending routes. Externally similar to the C-47, but without a reinforced floor or the double doors for loading cargo it was designed to carry paratroops and tow gliders and they would also see service transporting wounded and carrying cargo. The C-47 was equipped with a single static line and one exit door for eighteen paratroopers. The C-53 was equipped with two static lines and two exit doors for eighteen paratroopers arranged into two nine-man sticks. In practice, two nine-man sticks will exit quicker and land closer together than the C-47s single stick. The C-53 also substituted the bucket seats for the more luxurious reclining seats.

Conversion of the DC-3 to a true cargo plane, involved many changes. First, it called for a reinforced bottom and floor and a wide loading door capable of admitting heavy machinery and weapons. Also numerous changes in production were necessary if these aircraft were to be turned out in volume. Hand riveting was replaced by automatic riveting wherever possible. Fibre replaced aluminium in many parts of the aircraft interior. Forging was used on certain parts instead of gas welding and flash welding was introduced extensively. All this was accomplished with no loss of strength and frequently with greater ease of interchange or replacement of parts. The interior of the C-47 was so rigged that litters could be installed quickly; transforming it into what was, in every sense, a hospital plane. Soon it was found that the C-47 was a fine glider tow-plane because of its robust construction and if became the first aircraft ever to tow a glider across the Atlantic.

By September 1943 more than 2,000 C-47s had been built at the Douglas Long Beach, California plant. By February 1944 more than 2,500 C-47s were being flown by Air Transport Command alone, to say nothing of another two thousand by Troop Carrier and other Army units and by the Navy and Marines. Over 1,900 Dakotas were supplied to the RAF under Lend-Lease.

Written doctrine for airborne operations scarcely existed on 10 July 1943 when the Allies invaded Sicily (Operation 'Husky'). 'Husky 1' was preceded by US bombing attacks on Sicilian airfields in the landing area, the drop of dummy paratroopers at scattered locations and the use of radar-jamming B-17s to blind Axis radars. The 226 C-47 transports had to take a convoluted route to the drop zone to avoid being fired on by the Allied fleets and flew at 500 feet over the sea to avoid radar detection. The remnants of a summer storm disrupted the approach as the airdrops began around midnight on 9/10 July and only about fifteen percent of the paratroopers landed anywhere near their intended drop zones. The leading 3/504th PIR [3rd Battalion/504th Parachute Infantry Regiment] landed near its objective but were badly dispersed. Some groups coalesced near Castel Nocera and were able to beat back Italian counterattacks. The main objective, the Niscemi road junction, was captured by 'Item' Company, but most of 'George' Company landed three miles away near the Acate River and the remainder of the battalion was scattered ten to fifteen miles from the drop zone near Vittoria. Much of the 1/505th PIR landed in the British sector almost fifty miles east of the Niscemi road objective. 'Able' Company landed about two miles from the Niscemi objective and attacked Italian pillboxes along the Niscemi road. Much of the 2/505th PIR unintentionally landed in front of the 45th Division beachhead.

Jack Thompson, *Chicago Tribune* correspondent, who jumped with the First Lift, wrote: 'One group of the 1st Battalion, including Lieutenant Colonel Arthur Gorham, of Wichita, Kansas landed four miles south of Niscemi, about 2½ miles from the scheduled DZ. They were just east of a very sturdy, thick-walled farmhouse, which had been converted into a military fort held by sixty men with four heavy machine guns and six lights. It was well wired in with trench defences. Gorham ordered an assault on the house and it was organized and led by Captain Edwin Sayre and 22 men. Their first attack was launched at 2 o'clock in the morning. They were held up then, but attacked again just before dawn, with rifles, grenades, one 60 mm mortar and a bazooka. They forced the Italians back out of the trenches and into the house and attacked the house with grenades. Sayre led the assault, carrying one hand grenade in his teeth and another in his left hand, with his carbine in his right hand. It was after they had taken the farmhouse that he discovered that the man who was covering him was armed only with a trench knife and not a Tommy gun as he had thought. A rifle grenade fired at about ten feet blew open the door, but the door swung shut again. Sayre walked up, threw open the door and pitched a hand grenade inside. They found a total of fifteen dead and took 45 prisoners, some of whom were Germans. Four paratroops were wounded, one of whom later died. The house soon came under fire from an 88 and Colonel Gorham withdrew his men back to another hill.'[1]

'Husky' included the first large-scale use of airborne troops to support an Allied amphibious assault. The American mission was codenamed 'Husky 1' and was conducted by Colonel James Maurice Gavin's Combat Team 505, consisting of the 505th PIR reinforced by the 3/504th PIR and totalling 3,405 paratroopers. Its mission was to seize key road junctions and bridges to shield the 1st Infantry Division landings near Gela. In contrast to the American mission, the British mission, under the command of Brigadier Philip Hicks, was specifically aimed at seizing the Ponte Grande Bridge and four other objectives. As there were insufficient transport aircraft for all three brigades to conduct their operations simultaneously, it was decided that the first operation would be 'Ladbroke', whose objective was the capture of the bridge just prior to the amphibious landings on the night of 9 July, while the remaining two operations, that of capturing Syracuse harbour and the urban area that adjoined it and either destroying or confiscating a coastal artillery battery that was in range of the amphibious landings, would take place on successive two nights.

The final troop carrier group carrying the regimental headquarters and specialist troops had the most severe navigation problems and scattered its hapless paratroopers from Syracuse across south-eastern Sicily. Even so, 'Husky 1' was largely successful. The paratroopers were able to secure many of the objectives owing to the weak resistance of the Italian coastal units. Units that landed away from their targets used their own initiative and

---

1 This group later made contact with the 1st Division and joined the 2nd Battalion, 16th Infantry, with which they fought two days until relieved. Colonel Goreham was killed in action.

began attacking targets of opportunity all along the Sicilian coast. These sporadic and scattered outbursts of fighting convinced the Italians that they were facing a much larger and more powerful force and this contributed to the confused Axis reaction to the landings in the American sector on the morning of 10 July. By 27 July the Axis commanders had realised that the outcome of the campaign would be evacuation from Messina. Full-scale withdrawal began on 11 August and continued to 17 August.

In 'Husky' the routes selected for the troop carriers had been much too complicated and difficult. The planners resolved to make them as simple as possible for 'Overlord'. Fire from Allied guns had disrupted two airborne missions to Sicily in spite of the establishment of safety zones and in spite of warnings to the surface forces. Henceforth the necessity for ample precautions against such mishaps and particularly for keeping as far away as possible from convoys and naval vessels was consistently stressed. The principal glider mission in 'Husky' had been a fiasco, largely because the gliders had been released at night over the open sea. Because of the glider's ability to deliver men and materiel in concentrated packets, COSSAC had hitherto favoured it over the parachute and had planned to use 350 gliders in the initial assault. However, all agreed that the initial airborne assault in 'Overlord' would require the protection of darkness and 'Husky' had confirmed earlier opinions that glider missions should not be flown at night except perhaps in fair weather under a full moon. Chances of getting fair weather and a full moon simultaneously for 'Overlord' were less than fifty percent. These circumstances explain why responsibility for the initial assault came to rest with the paratroops.

Faulty navigation at night in the Sicilian missions caused dispersion of the paratroop drops over the entire south-eastern portion of the island. These errors stimulated a search for means to guide the troop carriers to their objectives in spite of darkness or bad weather. One remedy was the dropping of pathfinder troops before the arrival of an airborne mission to mark drop or landing zones. Some experimentation with pathfinder teams using visual aids had been done and the need to provide guidance for formations which otherwise might pass many miles outside visual range led to consideration of radio and radar beacons for pathfinder use. Most promising of these was the 'Eureka', a simple, light, durable radar navigational aid which could be dropped by parachute and be put into operation within five minutes. Its responses to the signals of an airborne interrogator called 'Rebecca' an airborne interrogator gave an accurate bearing and a fair indication of distance at ranges which varied considerably with conditions but were generally over ten miles. After pathfinder teams equipped with 'Eureka' proved effective in guiding airborne missions during the invasion of Italy it was generally accepted that pathfinder tactics would be employed in 'Overlord', the invasion of Normandy, in June 1944.

Many of the C-47s flown in the invasion of Normandy were from a special order known as the 'Urgent 400.' These were extra aircraft that General Arnold requested the Douglas Company to produce over their full schedule - specifically for Invasion needs. These were given a top manufacturing priority over and above all other aircraft in production - including fighters, medium bombers and heavy bombers.

IX Troop Carrier Command would have 13½ groups with 986 aircraft and over 1,100 crews available for 'Overlord'. In England 46 Group, RAF Transport Command created in February 1944 for the purpose of transporting and supplying the Airborne Forces, consisted of five Dakota squadrons: 48 and 271 Squadrons at Down Ampney; 233 Squadron at Blakehill Farm and 512 and 575 Squadrons at Broadwell. 512 Squadron had formed on 18 June 1943 at Hendon in 44 Group Transport Command. Amongst routine internal flights, its first duties included the movement of freight and passengers to Gibraltar and then to Maison Blanche near Algiers. Later these flights were widened to include internal flights in North Africa and long-haul journeys to Bombay, India. On 6 October the Squadron suffered its first fatalities when Flying Officer Robertson's Dakota struck barrage balloon cables over London, killing all nine people aboard. More losses followed in December, one aircraft crashed on take-off and another was forced to ditch on Spain; who were a neutral power in the war and so the crew was interned.

On 1 February a number of Dakotas and their crews were removed from 512 Squadron to form the basis of 575 Squadron and during this move some of the ground crews travelled to their new home at Broadwell in Horsa gliders towed by the Squadron's Dakotas. In the same month 48 Squadron returned to England, exchanging its Hudsons for Dakotas. The rest of the winter and the spring of 1944 were spent training intensively for the invasion of Normandy. In particular they concentrated on formation flying and navigation over long distances, by day and night. Until the end of May they participated in numerous large-scale exercises alongside various units of the 1st and 6th Airborne Divisions. 'Exercise Mush' carried out between 21 and 25 April over an area stretching from the Severn estuary to the borders of Wiltshire and Oxfordshire was a typical example; nineteen of 512 Squadron's Dakotas dropped 248 paratroopers at dawn and within the hour eighteen of these aircraft had returned with gliders. 512 Squadron flew its first operational sortie during the night of 24/25 April when their Dakotas flew over France to Sainte-Lô and Vire to drop leaflets to gain experience. Throughout May training with Airborne Forces intensified and by the end of the month the Squadrons were ready to play their part in the imminent invasion. In the weeks before 'D-Day' the Dakota squadrons were used on leaflet dropping missions over France.[2]

The Allied commanders, particularly AVM Sir Trafford Leigh-Mallory the commander-in-chief of the Allied Expeditionary Air Force for the Normandy invasion, had been anxiously aware of the danger presented by German aircraft and anti-aircraft. It was estimated (correctly as it turned out) that the Germans would have at least 850 usable aircraft in northwest France on 'D-Day' and that over 200 of them would be first-line fighters.[3] It was hoped to cripple the Luftwaffe forces by pounding their airfields, but there was little expectation of knocking them out. It was anticipated that as many 1,000 sorties a day might be made by the Luftwaffe. Since German warning radar was capable of picking up the troop carrier formations more than two miles off the coast, the risk of fighter interception in daylight missions, particularly glider missions appeared great. Enemy night fighters were not numerous in Normandy but the whole tip of the Cotentin north of a line from les Pieux to Quineville was known to be infested with light and heavy guns and intense fire was to be expected all along the east coast. To protect the airborne operations against these perils the Allies relied on avoidance, deception and powerful air support. By 12 April IX Troop Carrier Command had planned and won approval for a route which avoided most anti-aircraft concentrations by entering the Cotentin through the back door.

Unlike the British landing zones, those around 'Utah' would be in the hazardous Norman Bocage; countryside marked by small fields bordered by high hedgerows. Leigh-Mallory felt that the area was unsuitable. A combination of terrain, flak concentrations and anti-invasion defences were expected to inflict casualties as high as 50 per cent among the paratroopers and 70 per cent among glider-borne troops. He felt that

---

2 437 Squadron RCAF formed at Blakehill Farm on 4 September 1944, but did not officially come into operation until two days before Operation 'Market Garden'. It then had the distinction of being the only Royal Canadian Air Force squadron in Transport Command.

3 On 5 June Ninth Air Force calculated that the Germans had 1,099 usable aircraft, including 634 fighters, in position for employment against 'Overlord' by 'D+1'.

losses would be excessive - certainly far more than the gains were worth. General Bradley, though told Eisenhower that 'much as I favour the Cotentin assault... I would sooner see it go by the boards than risk a landing on 'Utah' without airborne help.' Eisenhower finally decided that the possible benefits outweighed the risks. Both the troop carrier and airborne commanders' protested to Leigh-Mallory that they were once more being committed to night landings and that such landings on the small fields of the Cotentin might cost half the force in crashes alone. (The glider training programme of IX TCC had not included tactical landings at night). On 27 May, to protect the glider missions from ground fire, the take off times were changed to an hour or so before dawn.[4]

The preparations of IX Troop Carrier Command for 'Overlord' were favourably affected by a strong transfusion of experienced officers into it its headquarters and adversely affected by an influx of new and green personnel into its flying units. Most important of the personnel changes was the assumption of command on 25 February by General Williams, former chief of XII Troop Carrier Command, in place of General Giles. When Williams took command the field strength of IX Troop Carrier Command was growing fast. What had been little more than an advance party in 1943 was being built up to a point where it could undertake large-scale training in March 1944. In the first two months of the year the 436th, 437th and 438th Troop Carrier Groups, part of the 439th and Headquarters, 53rd Troop Carrier Wing had come from the United States. In addition most of the air echelon of the 61st, 313th, 314th and 316th Groups and Headquarters, 52nd Wing, which commanded them, had flown up from the Mediterranean. By the end of March the rest of the 439th, the 440th, 441st and 442nd Groups had arrived from the United States and all of the 52nd Wing and its four groups had come from the MTO, as had 47 aircraft and crews for the 315th Group. The command had attained its full complement of 13½ groups and three wing headquarters.

The groups from the United States brought with them their T/O complement of 104 glider pilots apiece, Of the aircraft themselves over three-quarters were less than a year old as of 1 June and all were in fine condition. All old engines had been replaced, thus eliminating a prime

---

4 Even as late as 30 May, Leigh-Mallory went to Eisenhower's Headquarters at Southwick House and made a final, last-ditch plea to prevent was he was convinced would be 'the futile slaughter of two fine divisions'. Eisenhower deliberated into the night before deciding to side with Bradley. See C. J. Masters, *Glidermen of Neptune: The American D-Day Glider Attack* (Carbondale, IL: Southern Illinois University Press, 1995).

cause of abortive sorties. During the winter, supply shortages had been frequent, but by late May, time, effort and high priorities had given the troop carriers all the items they needed for their aircraft with one exception, self-sealing fuel tanks. The command had asked in February for personnel armour and self-sealing tanks. Thanks in part to lend-lease assistance from the British they got armoured seat-pads for their pilots and co-pilots and flak helmets, armoured vests and aprons for all crew members. Seat-pads and armoured clothing were also procured for the pilots and co-pilots of the gliders. The request for self-sealing tanks was turned down; General Arnold, himself, ruled in February that they could not be spared for troop carrier use. Information in April that about 75 such tanks might be available roused IX Troop Carrier Command to new efforts to get at least enough to equip its pathfinders, but these attempts, too, were in vain.

Throughout the winter training period, the 52nd and 53rd Wings were closely paired with the divisions they were to carry in 'Neptune'.[5] When the 53rd moved to its southern bases it found its partner, the 101st 'Screaming Eagles' Airborne Division (motto: 'Rendezvous with Destiny'), already established close by. Divisional headquarters was at Greenham Lodge only a mile or so from wing headquarters at Greenham Common. The divisional commander, Major General William C. Lee, one of the pioneers of airborne warfare, was incapacitated by illness in March. His place was taken by Brigadier General Maxwell D. Taylor, Divisional Artillery Commander of the 82nd Division, an officer who had won much experience and a fine reputation in the Mediterranean. In mid-February the 82nd 'All American' Airborne Division whose troopers proudly wore the 'double A' shoulder patch (a double entendre also indicating they hailed from all 48 states) had moved from Northern Ireland to the Leicester area within easy commuting distance of the bases into which its partner, the 52nd Wing, was then moving. Divisional headquarters was set up at Braunstone Park in Leicestershire. The 82nd's commander was Major General Matthew B. Ridgway who had directed the 82nd throughout its campaigns in the Mediterranean.

The 53rd Wing had been selected to specialize in glider operations but would have to be ready for possible paratroop commitments. To aid its preparation for this dual role, it was given the only four groups in the

---

5 'The 50th Wing was able to work with the 82nd Division until it moved south in April, but its southern fields had been acquired too late to make good arrangements for training there with the airborne.

command which were intact and fully operational at the end of February. Of these, the 434th and 435th Groups had already flown many paratroop and glider exercises in the United Kingdom. Initially stationed at Langar in Nottinghamshire, in February the 435th TCG had moved to Welford airfield in Berkshire so that the Troop Carrier squadrons could be closer to the airborne troops that they would carry during the invasion. Training intensified with regular flights in both the CG-4A and Horsa gliders. The 436th and 437th were well qualified for paratroop work but had had only rudimentary training with gliders. By 3 March these four groups had been assigned to the wing and moved to their tactical bases, Aldermaston, Welford, Membury and Ramsbury. Shortly after its arrival at Fulbeck, the 437th Troop Carrier Group at Ramsbury, five miles east-northeast of Marlborough, Wiltshire was reassigned to RAF Aldermaston west of London in the Salisbury Plain area to co-locate with 101st Airborne Division in preparation for the invasion of northern France. The 438th Group, which joined the Wing at Greenham Common on 16 March, was not operational until April. During early March the 53rd Wing put its fliers through a series of paratroop exercises with simulated drops and on the night of 12 March executed a successful drop of a parachute regiment. The wing made a spectacularly good drop on 23 March in the presence of General Dwight D. Eisenhower the Supreme Allied Commander, Lieutenant General Lewis H. Brereton, Ninth Air Force commander and Winston Churchill and a still better one on the night of 12 April. These performances won the confidence of IX Troop Carrier Command in spite of the fact that in a night exercise on 4 April heavy clouds with bases at 1,000 feet had caused three out of four serials of the 53rd to abort and the other to disperse and to drop inaccurately. The wing ended its work with paratroops on 18 April, because its partner, the 101st Division, decided its troops had jumped enough.

All groups of the 53rd Wing did some training with gliders during March and the 434th and 437th Groups, which were picked to specialize in glider operations, reached the point where they could fly glider formations at night. After some experimentation the 437th concluded that the most satisfactory formation was the pair of pairs in echelon to the right. Glider training in the 53rd Wing rose to such intensity during April that the wing logged 6,965 hours of glider towing that month. The effects of this work were shown in an exercise on 21 April when pilots, most of whom had towed a Horsa for the first time less than seven weeks before, released 241 out of 245 Horsas at their proper landing zones after a long flight. For the first three weeks of May the wing continued glider training with increasing emphasis on night formations and on landings at dawn in areas less than 400 yards in length. The final verdict of IX Troop Carrier Command was that it was fully qualified for its coming role.

Between 11 February and 5 March almost all the air echelon of the 52nd Wing, including the flying personnel of the 61st, 313th, 314th and 316th Groups flew from Sicily to England via Marrakech and Gibraltar with a loss of only one out of 221 aircraft. The rear echelon arrived by boat on 18 March. The remnant of the 315th Group in England was assigned to the 52nd Wing on 17 February. In March the 315th's two squadrons in North Africa returned to the ETO and the group also received 26 aircraft with experienced crews transferred from troop carrier units in the Mediterranean to bring it up to strength. These crews later were organized into two new squadrons. Attached to the 52nd Wing in May for operations and training was the 442nd Group, which had arrived from the United States between 26 and 29 March and had been assigned to the 50th Wing.

During the training phase the groups of the 52nd Wing were concentrated within a fifteen-mile radius of Grantham, except for the 315th, which was at Spanhoe 22 miles away. Wing headquarters and the 316th Group were at Cottesmore, the 61st at Barkston Heath, the 313th at Folkingham, the 314th at Saltby and the 442nd at Fulbeck. All bases were connected by good English roads and when completed had all necessary facilities including hard-surface runways in the 6,000-foot class. The notoriously bad spring weather of northern England often interfered with flying. However, enough time had been provided so that the training of all but the 315th and 442nd Groups was completed with time to spare.

The quality of the 315th and 442nd Groups was very different from that of the other four. The others had flown so much that there was a danger they would go stale. Their pilots had an average flying time of well over 1,500 hours when training began. Most of them had been overseas for more than ten months and had flown paratroop missions. The fliers of the 315th Group had equally impressive amounts of overseas and flying time, but its two original squadrons had been employed for ten months on routine transport work and never had had much training for airborne operations. Also, the group, having been built up from various sources, needed time to develop teamwork. The 442nd was a very green unit. Activated in September 1943, it had had only one or two C-47s per squadron until December. Its training in the United States, hampered by winter weather and curtailed to meet the schedule for 'Overlord', had included almost no night formation flying or dropping of paratroops.

The 52nd Wing had been selected to fly the paratroops of the 82nd Division into Normandy. Since its bases were too far north to be suitable for glider missions, the wing concentrated on paratroop work. Nevertheless, it spent 4,207 hours in April and May towing gliders and demonstrated in a daylight glider exercise on 29 May that it could fly glider missions if necessary.

The 61st and 316th Groups were able to make actual drops of paratroop battalions on 18 March. The 313th and 314th Groups, hampered by construction at their fields, flew no exercises until April. By the end of that month all four were considered ready, although the 313th and 314th had done badly in three night drops.

Meanwhile the 315th and 442nd had not begun training programmes until 3 April and had spent the month mostly in formation flying. They flew exercises and dropped no troops until May. By then the American airborne divisions had almost wound up their jumping programme and were eager to risk accidents by further parachuting. Fortunately, the 82nd Division had some men who had not completed their quota of jumps and additional exercises were scheduled for the nights of the 5th and 7th of May. In the former both groups had loose formations and the 315th drifted off course. In the latter, flown in cloudy weather by the 315th, assembly, formation and drop were unsatisfactory. During April each of the groups had a different programme. The 439th specialized in glider towing and became skilful enough to fly night formations with gliders. It carried out four glider exercises by daylight with good results. In its only paratroop exercise everything went wrong and the drop was far from the DZ. The 440th flew one successful daytime glider exercise and executed four paratroops drops, the last three of which were very good. The 441st Group, which had dropped paratroops only twice in its short life, carried none in April. It concentrated on day formation flying until the tenth and on night formations thereafter but did make a very accurate resupply drop on the afternoon of the 21st.

Last of the troop carrier wings to enter intern training was the 50th. During the winter it had been at Bottesford in command of the groups subsequently given to the 53rd Wing. In their place it received the 439th Group on 25 February and the 440th and 441st Groups on 21 March.[6] None of these groups had been in existence for more than nine months. All had arrived from the United States within a few days of their assignment to

---

6 'The 442nd Group was also assigned to the 50th Wing its training has been discussed in connection with the 52nd Wing.

the wing. The 439th was stationed at Balderton, the 440th at Bottesford, the 441st at Langar. The three fields were in the northern group and were all within about five miles of IX Troop Carrier Command headquarters at Grantham. Some formation flying was done in daytime during March, despite wintry weather, but the wing's training programme did not really get under way until the beginning of April. At that time an inspector observed that all groups in the 50th lacked practice in night formation flying and that most of the navigators were inexperienced and ignorant of all radar aids, even 'Rebecca'.

During the last week of April the 50th Wing moved to southwest England. Wing headquarters and the 440th Group went to the former Battle of Britain airfield at Exeter, the 439th to Upottery next to the village of Smeatharpe, Devon about fifteen miles northeast of Exeter and the 441st to Merryfield (also known as Isle Abbotts) ten miles northeast of Upottery, the last of the three airfields to be built on the Blackdown Hills during 1943. Robin Gilbert had been born in the small Devon village of Newcott a few years before the war and as a boy stayed regularly with his grandmother three miles away in the nearby village of Smeatharpe where the airfield had been built. He had watched it grow out of virgin farmland and develop into the bustling home of the 439th Troop Carrier Group under the command of Colonel Charles H. Young. Upottery, Exeter and Merryfield were fine large bases with long hard-surface runways. Although some construction was still going on at all three fields, they were ready for use and Robin would witness the peak of Upottery's wartime use when it dispatched the C-47s and their cargo of men from the US 506th Parachute Infantry Regiment to Normandy. The 442nd TCG was still in Nottinghamshire so did not arrive in the south west until a few days after 'D-Day' having operated on the same mission under the umbrella of the 52nd Troop Carrier Wing, they then moved onto Weston Zoyland airfield near Bridgwater to rejoin the rest of the 50th Wing.

May brought an increased activity level with a sense that something 'big' was coming. Newly assigned pilots were given maximum flying time on three practice missions, including two simulated wing paratroop drops at night. On the 10th and 11th of May 'Eagle', a command rehearsal involving a 72-plane paratroop mission, a troop re-supply mission dropping bundles and a glider exercise, went ahead with the take-off of seven pathfinder serials from North Witham half an hour ahead of the main serials. Four pathfinder serials got excellent results; two did well; one lost its way in a haze which in places limited the visibility to three miles. When it did reach its zone it was so late that the troops it carried were unable to get their equipment into action in time to direct the 315th Group, which was the first scheduled to drop there. After the pathfinders came nineteen paratroop serials spaced at six-minute intervals. The parachute echelon of the 101st Division was flown by 432 aircraft in ten serials, half from the 53rd Group and half from the 50th. The first jump took place at 0033. The serials of the 53rd Wing were uniformly successful. Those of the 50th also did creditably, except that one flight from the 440th Group fell out of formation, missed its drop zone in the haze and returned without making a drop.

The paratroops of the 82nd Division were carried by 369 aircraft of the 52nd Wing in nine serials. Unlike the 101st Division which, having prepared the operation long in advance sent over 6,000 jumpers, the 82nd was able to provide only token loads of two jumpers per aircraft. One serial - that of the 442nd Group - broke up on the way. Only sixteen of its 45 aircraft got to the vicinity of the drop zone and dropped troops. The rest, lost in the haze, returned to base on orders from group headquarters and tried again at dawn. The 'Eureka's and lights on the zone were off at the time and the 442nd, baffled, dropped its paratroops ten miles away. The other serials reached the drop area approximately on course and on schedule and six did well. However, the aids on the zones of the 314th and 315th Groups were not on when they arrived. Most of the 314th made a second pass; saw the 'T', which by then had been lighted and dropped troops on it. However, nine pilots had given up and gone home and another nine made drops by guesswork far from the zone. The 315th Group, although it finally received some signals, was too disoriented to make use of them and returned without making any drop.

Only two glider serials were flown in 'Eagle'. They were spaced ten minutes apart from head to head and consisted of 52 aircraft each from the 434th and 437th Groups, towing a mixture of Wacos and Horsas. The first glider was to be released at 0529, ten minutes before civil twilight. Seven pilots in the 434th lost their way in the dark, but the 437th released all but one of its gliders at the proper point. The landings were considered good.

These training missions were used as an opportunity to test new equipment like 'Rebecca' receivers, the 'Biscuit Bouncer' (used to toss door bundles) and a glider pick up system and devices that would be used to guide the missions across Normandy. Much reliance was placed on navigational aids to be set up on the zones by teams of pathfinder troop flown in half an hour ahead of the main serials. The pathfinder aircraft were to locate the zones by conventional navigation assisted by 'Gee' (PPF)[7] and SCR-717C (PPI), an American airborne radar sender-receiver, which scanned the landscape with its beams. The reflected beams produced on the scope a crude outline map in which water seemed black, while land and shipping appeared lighter. It would thus provide a recognizable map of the Channel Islands and the Normandy coast.[8]

Not all of these new systems were well received as a crewmember in the 61st Troop Carrier Group at Barkston Heath recalled: 'One of the big disappointments in airborne tactics was that navigating with the brand new hush-hush radar navigation facilities turned out to be of little help. All our planes had the 'Rebecca' receivers which were supposed to react to signals from the 'Eureka' radar transmitters which pathfinder troops carried down with them. When many planes in a large formation switched on 'Rebecca' however, the 'Eureka' transmitters got swamped and tended to send out misleading signals, sometimes three and four miles away from the actual DZ. Our flight leaders' planes, in addition, had the overly sophisticated, hard to interpret SCR-717, called the 'belly-button radar' because of its exterior housing under the fuselage. The SRC-717 mapped out a crude image of the landscape over which we travelled and was practically useless for navigators except when we were passing over bodies of water like the Channel or large rivers. Finally, a few of us had 'Gee', meant to show you through 'triangulation' (three intersecting beacons) where you were. All these sets sat on the navigators' compartment, but in actual flight you would usually find the sets turned off and the navigator standing behind the pilot trying to match what he saw unrolling before him through the cockpit window with what he had in his briefing notes and what he read on his maps. This was the equipment that the crews had to use for finding the drop

7 The first experimental installation of 'Gee' on an American troop carrier aircraft was made in mid-January 1944. By the end of the month the command had decided to use it and by 23 February the 9th Air Force agreed to equip 108 troop carrier aircraft fully and 44 others partially with 'Gee'. On 25 February General Williams, who had no experience with 'Gee' in the Mediterranean but was full of confidence in 'Rebecca', offered to give up all or most of the 'Gee' equipment if it were needed for bombing. This concession was not called for and IX Troop Carrier Command got its quota of 'Gee' sets.
8 On 8 January 1944 IX Troop Carrier Command had requested samples of SCR-717 and on 4 February the War Department promised to give it sixteen sets by the middle of March, including five which were already installed on aircraft of the 52nd Wing. More were to be sent thereafter as they became available. However, because of production difficulties IX Troop Carrier Command had only eleven aircraft with this equipment on 9 April and only about fifty sets arrived in time for use in the Invasion.

zones in the missions to come. Despite the technology available, their basic navigation skills would prove crucial.'[9] The brand new hush-hush radar navigation facilities would turn out to be of little help. All C-47s had the 'Rebecca' receivers which were supposed to react to signals from the 'Eureka' radar transmitters which pathfinder troops carried down with them. When many aircraft in a large formation switched on 'Rebecca' however, the 'Eureka' transmitters got swamped and tended to send out misleading signals, sometimes three and four miles away from the actual DZ.

The effect of 'Eagle' was to induce a mood of optimism as far as troop carrier capabilities were concerned. Williams, who had already declared that, barring unexpectedly heavy flak or failure by the pathfinders, ninety -100 percent of the paratroops in IX Troop Carrier Command's Normandy missions would land in the correct area, was confirmed in his opinion. Even Leigh-Mallory stated that he was highly impressed.

Intended as the final exercise of the training period, IX Troop Carrier Command recognized that the 315th and 442nd Groups needed more work and felt that the 314th had not yet proved itself in night operations. The performance of the three groups in 'Eagle' bore out this opinion. Accordingly the 314th was given another night paratroop exercise on 14/15 May and the training periods of the 315th and 442nd were extended to 26 May at which date they too made night paratroop drops on a token basis. The exercises were so completely successful as to indicate that even the least experienced groups would be ready for 'Neptune'.

Although the 50th Wing did well in 'Eagle', it was considered to be in need of further practice. Since there were no paratroops to drop, it flew four more night exercises with simulated drops between 18 and 29 May. These were carefully designed to resemble actual operations and lights were flashed to indicate when the jump signal would have been given. The results were good. Besides these exercises a heavy schedule of other flying training was continued until 29 May. By then the 50th Wing, too, was rated as ready for action.

Final troop carrier preparations began with the completion by IX Troop Carrier Command of Field Order I, 'Neptune-Bigot' at 1500 on 31 May. Although as yet few knew it, 'D-Day' had been set for 5 June and the first aircraft were to be on their way over the Channel before midnight on the 4th. The 52nd Wing at Cottesmore was so close it could

---

9 *Blackjacks At War 53rd TCS* by Major Steven C. Franklin.

pick up the orders almost immediately and have its own order out next day. Copies for the 50th and 53rd Wings were flown to them, those for the 53rd arriving at Greenham Common about 2300 on the 31st. Working continuously the staff of the 53rd Wing issued the first part of its order at 0800 on 1 June. The 50th Wing issued its field order at 0800 on 2 June. By 1400 that afternoon the 53rd had the last annexes to its order ready for distribution. Group held orders, being hardly more than extracted copies of the command and wing orders, came out almost immediately after the wing orders. Some groups relied on wing orders and issued none of their own.

On the evening of 'D-1' final briefings were held from which in most cases the crews went directly to their aircraft. Formal briefing of flying personnel was done on a group basis, although additional briefing was done by squadrons. Each group had its own schedule and procedure. Some began briefing on 3 June, some on the 4th and some, learning that operations had been postponed 24 hours, set back their schedules accordingly and began briefing on the 5th. Not until those last meetings was the time of the mission announced. The briefings were generally rated as very good and the information in them thorough and accurate, as might be expected considering the unparalleled time and effort devoted to collecting it. During the last two or three days General Williams flew from group to group giving short talks to staff members and flight leaders. These however were 'pep talks' rather than briefings.

Between 28 May and 1 June the airborne divisions moved onto the airfields from which they were to be flown. There they bivouacked in the most isolated spots available behind heavily guarded barbed wire. The service troops keeping house for them were also isolated. On the arrival of the airborne units the troop carrier men were restricted and so were the large numbers of British civilians living in the base areas. Current business provided pretexts for a surprising number of special passes, but the movement of military and civilian gossips and possible spies was successfully halted. Before briefing began, the bases were sealed to almost all personnel. Personal phone calls were prohibited and all calls were monitored; pay phones were discontinued and personal mail was put in special bags and stored until after 'D-Day'. All briefed personnel were segregated in special quarters under officer guards who escorted them even on trips to the latrine. Wing and group war rooms were also put under 24-hour guard and so were the marshalling areas during the servicing and loading before take-off.

'On 1 June the 101st paratroopers had already begun to arrive at our base - and they were promptly sealed off' wrote Sergeant Boris 'Marty' Wolfe, a C-47 radio operator in the 81st TCS, 436th TCG at Membury in the parish of Lambourn, Berkshire about 4½ miles north-northwest of Hungerford.[10] 'They bivouacked in wooded lots away from the runways and their tents were surrounded by barbed wire and guards. Rumours were flying fast and furious throughout the camps but security measures paid big dividends because most men were not even aware that on many Troop Carrier bases over 1,000 paratroopers were secretly bivouacked on post until they were seen on the 5th, lining up for showers.'

---

10 Martin Wolfe authored *Green Light! A Troop Carrier Squadron's War From Normandy To The Rhine*; Centre for Air Force History Washington DC 1993.

Chapter 2

The Pie-eyed Piper of Barnes

The Allied commanders agreed that the British Airborne operation east of Caen could be handled by 38 Group and 46 Group commanded by Air Vice-Marshal Leslie Norman Hollinghurst DFC and Air Commodore L. Darnell respectively. However, because of the small size of the RAF troop carrier force, IX Troop Carrier Command might have to assist it if further missions by the British airborne were undertaken. Later it was planned that the Troop Carrier Command might help carry the British Airborne Division in an operation after 'D+6' or make an emergency drop of a British paratroop brigade to reinforce the beachhead. However, it was never called upon to carry out those missions.

In the winter of 1944 a freshly trained flight mechanic, Leading Aircraftman Alan Hartley, sat on his kit bag in a crowded train corridor to join 271 Squadron in Doncaster. He was travelling from Locking in Weston-Super-Mare where for four months a group of trainees had specialised on the new Napier Sabre engine being fitted to the latest fighter, the Hawker Typhoon, so they were looking forward to joining a Typhoon squadron to service these 'monster fighters'. 'Imagine our chagrin when reporting for duty at Doncaster to be told that the aircraft we would be servicing would be the new transport aircraft, the Douglas DC-3 or Dakota as the RAF named it. So we spent the next few days familiarising ourselves with the large Pratt & Whitney radial engines and the 95 feet wingspan of these fat green elephants of aircraft. But on 29 February our 271 Squadron moved to an airfield in the Cotswolds near Cirencester and a little village called Down Ampney. Although we had never heard of it, apparently it was the birthplace of the well-known composer Ralph Vaughan Williams. On arrival we were briefed on our future role which was to train to fly all aspects of airborne Operations, Glider towing, paratrooper dropping, air despatch, the dropping of supplies to ground troops and air ambulance, for at Down Ampney we had a large Casualty Air Evacuation Centre fitted with a fully surgical hospital and we were told that between airborne operations we would be bringing back casualties from the European war fronts.'[11]

Towards the end of 1942 when the Allies were beginning to think in terms of an offensive war and a possible invasion of mainland Europe, 271 Squadron was brought into contact with the Airborne Forces and during the following year they carried out numerous exercises with these troops to give them flying experience whilst at the same time improving the navigational skills of the aircrews. The Squadron became a part of Transport Command when it was formed on 25 March 1943 and in August they began to replace their Harrows with Dakotas, a greatly superior aircraft for the airborne role. Even so a Flight of Harrows was retained and converted into air ambulances, capable of supporting stretchers, with the intention of evacuating casualties from France when the invasion began.

271 Squadron became a part of the newly formed 46 Group and their establishment of thirty Dakotas were moved to Down Ampney, which they shared with 48 Squadron, but the Harrow Flight remained behind at Doncaster. From March until the end of May, all Squadrons in the Group trained intensively with the 1st and 6th Airborne Divisions and the 1st Polish Parachute Brigade, in preparation for the forthcoming invasion. In this way they became familiar with the deployment of both gliders and paratroopers and also they practiced large scale formation navigational exercises at night.

'Shortly after settling into our corrugated iron Nissen huts we were joined by another Dakota Squadron, No.48. Later on, we were advanced in our training we had both Squadrons taking off towing the wooden Horsa gliders and circling the village. The noise was horrendous and I often felt sorry for those 280 or so villagers torn out of their rural serenity by all of these aircraft and over 3,500 airmen and WAAFs who had taken over their village, particularly when the village bakery opened at 8 am and was sold out of every crumb by 8.15, the long queues at the tiny Post Office and the sole telephone box, the never-ending hunt for beer in the local pub which soon became carefully husbanded by the publican for the locals, whilst we could only buy a liquid paint stripper which they called 'scrumpy' or 'rough cider'.

'In March we soon learned a lesson about the dangers of war and flying hazards when whilst practicing close formation flying, the wing tip of one Dakota contacted the elevators of another, which plunged to the ground

---

11   *It's Only A Number* by Alan Hartley.

killing all of the aircrew and some of our mechanics who had gone up for a joy ride. By coincidence the pilot whose wing tip caused the accident was killed himself a month later when the glider he was towing got out of control and brought his Dakota down. By now it was April and training and exercises became more intense. It was most exciting to go on some of these exercises which we mechanics were encouraged to do, flying to Salisbury Plain with a plane full of heavily equipped paratroopers. We always flew without doors in the Dakotas and it was quite exciting to experience the howling rush of air from the slipstream and the noise of the throbbing Pratt & Whitney engines. Over the door aperture there were two lights, a red and a green and as we approached Netheravon the red light would suddenly flash. Immediately five or ten paratroopers (depending on the size of the 'stick' as they called it) would clip their static lines to the cable in the roof of the aircraft and then check the clip of the comrade in front. They would then close up very close to each other until the red light changed to green and then with a clatter of Army boots like a huge centipede they moved rapidly down the centre aisle, sharp turn right out of the door and the only evidence of where they had once stood were the static lines and parachute bags which we had to haul back in the aircraft before we dropped the next stick. It was quite remarkable, the speed of leaving the aircraft for not only were the paras heavily equipped with arms and ammunition pouches, entrenching tools, grenades but they also had an equipment bag which fitted on a leather side strap on their left legs. A long pin and eyelets kept this bag firm until just before the para landed, he would pull the pin and the bag would fall away on the end of a 60 feet length of rope. This enabled the para to keep his equipment bag handy when he landed but would not be encumbered by the weight of the bag on touchdown.[12]

'Again, one of these exercises was marred by an unfortunate and avoidable lethal accident. One para's chute had become entangled in a tree whilst his

---

12   The US High Command looked into the possibility of using the British 'leg bag' designed to carry a variety of items including radios, medical gear, machine gun tripods and extra ammunition and were attached to the soldier's leg. A quick release strap was operated just after the parachute opened and the bag, which was attached to a 20 feet coiled rope, dropped beneath the paratrooper and hit the ground first. To evaluate these bags, a small number of paratroopers from the 3rd Battalion, 506th PIR were asked to perform a test jump. The group took off from Ramsbury in a C-47 aircraft that initially headed east before turning through 180 degrees and making its way back toward the village. As the plane flew low over the West End, the soldiers jumped, all landing safely in fields just west of the village. This was the first time the British 'leg bag' had been used by US airborne forces. The trial was judged a success and the bags were employed by the 101st on 'D-Day'. *Tonight We Die As Men* by Ian Gardner & Roger Day (Osprey 2009).

bag was in another. So there he swung between the two trees, suspended about forty feet above the ground, shouting quite happily to his mates below and receiving some friendly but derisory banter. The fire brigade engine arrived from Devizes and a telescopic extending aluminium ladder was raised. A fireman climbed up the ladder to the para but unfortunately he hadn't been briefed on the para's harness, for instead of cutting the rope to the bag, thus allowing the para to swing to the tree, he pressed the release knob on the harness with the result that it dropped off and the whole weight of the heavily equipped para and the fireman were suddenly transferred to the top of this flimsy ladder and to our horror it collapsed. Both men plummeted to the ground and the fireman fell on top of the para who was killed by the impact. It was a very sombre bunch of mechanics that flew back to Down Ampney after witnessing this tragic event. On the same exercise a para became tangled in the tail wheel of his Dakota and despite frantic efforts to get him back in, they failed. So they decided to fly to Poole Harbour where they flew low and cut his strap for him to fall in the sea but he was unfortunately dead when he was recovered.

'Shortly after this, I also had a salutary lesson in the dangers of glider towing. I was sitting on the grass beside the Horsa glider and chatting to the glider pilots prior to a cross country exercise called 'Balbo', when one of the glider pilots asked me if I had ever been up in a glider, when I answered negatively, he invited me to join them. Several times I had watched these black gliders swoop silently over the hedges, apply gradual flap and gently land on our airfield on the grass between our runways. So I had no hesitation in racing over to our dispersal flight hut to ask 'Chiefy' (our Flight Sergeant) if I could go. He expressed his policy of not interfering with suicidal aspirations and acquiesced. So I stepped into the cockpit and stood between the two green tubular seats of the glider, the only sound being the thumping of my heart. We took off very smoothly, being airborne well before the Dakota became unstuck. So there we were, swaying gently from side to side or up and down in the slip stream at the end of this long thick rope entwined with the telephone cable which enabled the glider pilot to talk to the tug pilot. High tow, low tow - we went through the lot until we reached Oxford and turned for base which we reached after a short time of flying. We circled the airfield but to my surprise our glider cast off its rope at about 3-4,000 feet and our Dakota flew away trailing our rope. Suddenly the glider pilot barked 'Hold tight son' and puzzled, I wondered where we were going. I soon found out for the pilots pushed the control column onto the floor of the glider and placed their Army boots on it. The nose dropped and diving vertically, it plummeted earthwards. My knuckles became white as my terror stricken grip tightened on the green tubes of the seats and my eyes started to bulge as I looked at the tiny 'Matchbox' model of the black and white control van at the end of the runway getting bigger by the second. The Horsa had been described as a 'Silent Sword' but I can refute this for there are gaps between the separate sections of the glider and as we gathered speed a banshee wail screeched from these gaps. Thoughts tumbled through my addled brain - one, that the whole tail unit was held on by four bolts for rapid exiting, another was that I had made a terrible mistake and lastly the heap of strawberry jam that would be sent to my mother with regrets.

'By now all or my internal organs had assembled in the nape of my neck. Compared to this stomach-wrenching experience of a seven ton glider's descent everything else pales into insignificance. Then, when I thought that all was lost, the gliders pilot shouted 'right' and they both hauled the stick back and we levelled out. As we touched down the huge barn door flaps were dropped and it was like running into a huge rubber block. As I tottered away from the glider, I had the thought that whilst I was fully fit, the experience left me mentally and physically exhausted but in battle our glider pilots would be expected to fight. When I arrived at dispersal the NAAFI wagon was serving tea.

'What was it like?' I was asked.

'A piece of cake' I replied with my shaking hand slopping tea from my mug. From that day on, I grew a tremendous respect for the glider pilots. Think of a glider pilot landing in pitch darkness in a plywood box and a Perspex screen, the only thing between you and perhaps a wall, a barn or tree, at up to 80 mph.

In the meantime life proceeded at Down Ampney and late in April, 271 Squadron flew several sorties to drop leaflets over France. 'Living conditions improved enormously' recalled Alan Hartley. 'We had a superb gymnasium built and our Sports Officer was Flight Lieutenant Len Harvey who used to be British Heavyweight Champion, who refereed all our boxing matches for which I had been 'volunteered' into becoming the Station welterweight. We had a concert party organised by our Entertainments Officer, Flight Lieutenant 'Jimmy' Edwards. 'Jim' had a favourite RAF officer's cap which he had had since taking his commission, the peak of which had frayed and a piece of black rubber hung down over his forehead but he wouldn't change it. We also had RAFDA players the Drama Section who used to put plays on to entertain our group. Then occasionally we had visits from ENSA, the Forces Entertainments, which we quickly named 'Every Night Something Awful' after their initials.'[13]

Born in Barnes, London (then Surrey) on 23 March 1920, the son of a professor of mathematics, James Keith O'Neill Edwards was educated at St. Paul's Cathedral School, at King's College School in Wimbledon and at St. John's College, Cambridge, where he acquired a taste for comedy and the stage while performing in the 'Footlights Revues'. His aptitude for the footlights was confirmed with the staging of concert parties at Down Ampney. He had also his own personal Dakota which rejoiced in the serial number KG444 and which he had nicknamed *The Pie-eyed Piper of Barnes*. This had been painted in large yellow lettering on the nose. This was a wheeze that Wing Commander Booth had borrowed from the Americans and it certainly gave one much more interest and pride in the job. Tim Beddow [another pilot on the squadron] had called his *'Boozer's Gloom'* and everyone else had concocted something 'jolly'. Edwards also had complete confidence in the Dakota, so much so that he had become very casual about details such as the distribution of load. 'The slide-rule provided in each aircraft for the calculation of such things remained firmly wrapped up in its container. Besides, we had a Freight Section whose job it was to sort these things out and - from sheer idleness - I had complete confidence in them. The Dak was wonderfully adaptable. When the freight door was opened wide, it was amazing what could be squeezed in, from jeeps to motorcycles and ammunition and [much later when the advance was going so deep into enemy territory] we began taking thousands of brand-new battledress uniforms for prisoners-of-war who were being released. And always the canvas harness was there for slinging stretchers on the return journey.[14]

It was at Doncaster, in an overcrowded crew-room that the CO, Wing Commander M. Booth DFC, a tall, fair-haired man finally put the aircrews in the picture, as Edwards, who had recently been ferrying Wellingtons to North Africa, was to recall:[15] 'I am in command of 271 squadron of which you are all now members. The 'Sparrow' flight will continue to operate from here, but we shall be equipped with a new American Transport plane,

---

13   *It's Only A Number* by Alan Hartley.

14   *Six of the Best; the spirited 'war memoirs of ex-Flight Lieutenant Edwards. J. 123886* DFC (Robson Books 1984).

15   Ibid.

which the RAF is calling the 'Dakota'. As soon as they arrive, we shall learn to fly them and the whole effort will then move to an aerodrome which is being built in the south-west. There are too many of you to be accommodated in this Mess, so most of you will be given a billet not too far away. I suggest you go there now, unpack and get back here in time for the squadron party, which begins at seven.' A cheer went up at this last piece of news and I staggered off with my kit to get acquainted with my new landlady, Mrs. Moon. She was very north-country and very kind and also had two very pretty daughters. 'Come upstairs,' she said. 'I've moved out of our best room so that you can have a large bed.' Such luxury, after that ghastly tent in Algiers. I told her about the party so she gave me a door key and said, 'I'll leave a light on in the hall and see you in the morning.'

'I walked cautiously back to the Mess, memorizing the route and pitched into the beer with a will. There were so many old faces; so much to talk about. Our morale had soared sky-high. We were members of a squadron at last. Transport Command had only just been formed and we were in on the ground floor. I don't think any of us knew what we were going to be called upon to do, but it didn't matter. Booth and his flight commanders very sensibly saw that a good get-together at this stage would pay dividends later and the bar stayed open until only a few stalwarts like myself were left. Then I set course for my billet, head spinning with a mixture of beer and a natural elation.

'At Doncaster 271 Squadron was up to strength, both in aircraft and personnel; but what was this I noticed in the Mess? - a 'Brown Job'. A short, wiry, swarthy individual in the uniform of a Major in the South African Air Force was introduced to me.'

He was Major Piers Simon Joubert, who had flown in the 1914-1918 war and wore World War I ribbons. After service in the First World War in South, West and East Africa, he transferred to the Royal Flying Corps and gained his wings in the last few months of the war. After the war he flew mail and other civilian flying roles but was still on the reserve with the South African Air Force. In June 1940 he was re-commissioned into the South African Air Force but owing to his age (he was born in South Africa in 1896 and was 48 years of age) he had been farmed out to Transport Command and for the first years of the war he was assigned to ferry duties. Joubert again met up with the RAF and was based at RAF Uxbridge as a ferry pilot. He then trained on Wellington bombers but it was not a bomber squadron he was posted to but a Transport Command Squadron 271, part of 46 Group, as a flight commander on the 29 February 1944. His crew was the same for the whole of 1944; Flight Lieutenant Ralph Fellows, Flight Lieutenant David Grant and Flight Sergeant David Butterworth. With his crew he followed an intense few months of training, consisting of towing gliders, dropping paratroopers, supplies and on odd occasion leaflet dropping over France. In September 1944 he was awarded the Air Force Cross.[16]

'I soon found out that he had been a commercial pilot for donkey's years in South Africa, but had joined the Services in his own country as soon as the war started and had immediately applied for a posting to Europe. All he wanted to do was to see some action, but, as he was well over fifty at this time, he had to be content with us and a Dakota. He had been put in charge of 'C' Flight, of which I was a member and I subsequently got to know him well. His voice had that distinctive guttural quality that belongs only to the Afrikaner and his impish sense of humour made him well able to cope with the ribbing he got from us. But, although we ribbed him mercilessly about his uniform and his voice and his total lack of knowledge of things administrative, we all loved and admired him for joining in a war which he could so easily have avoided. He was a good drinker and devilish keen on the WAAFs and we soon established that easy rapport that is founded on respect, but allows familiarity in the right places, at the right time. To us aircrew he soon became known as 'Jouby', but in his office every morning he got a salute and a 'sir' without any prompting.

'Soon after this, the first Dakota arrived, flown across the Atlantic by Ferry Command and picked up from Prestwick by Wing Commander Booth. He quickly familiarized the flight commanders with the machine and as more and more of them came in we all made our acquaintance with this gentle lady of the air. The dear old 'Dak' was a twin-engined, low-winged, monoplane, designed in 1931 as an entirely new concept in passenger aircraft and known as the DC-1. Two years later it went into service with slight modifications, as the DC3 and had been flying in the USA ever since. It came to us with all the internal refinements removed - no sound-proofing, no posh seats, no bar (more's the pity!). Along each side of the fuselage there was a line of bucket seats, designed especially for paratroops to sit in on their way to their target and extremely uncomfortable for anyone without a parachute strapped to his bottom. There was a large cargo-door at the rear and with any luck a jeep could be coaxed up a ramp and into the fuselage. The mollycoddled air-traveller of today would be astounded by the two propellers, driven by Pratt & Whitney piston engines, amazed by

---

16 See *Air Battle for Arnhem* by Alan W. Cooper (Pen & Sword, 2012).

the absence of a nose-wheel and confused by the fact that when you entered you walked up quite a slope towards the nose. At the top of the slope was a metal door which led into the crew compartment and here we just had room for two pilots, a navigator and a wireless operator. There wasn't a machine-gun anywhere. The great luxury for myself and Mac [the co-pilot] was the dual control. Each pilot had a control column and his own panel of flying instruments and the engine controls were placed between us. On the Wimpy there had been only one stick, so that, if I wanted Mac to take over, he had to slide into my seat as I slid out, while the not-very-good automatic pilot did the flying.

'At last came the day when, after a farewell binge in the Officers' Mess, we said farewell to Doncaster and left it for the Harrow Flight to continue their mercy runs with greens for the Scottish Islands. We headed south to look for the tiny Cotswold village of Down Ampney, where our own aerodrome was supposed to be ready for us. It was not difficult to find, with Cricklade and its distinctive church tower a mere two miles away and the beautiful old town of Cirencester less than ten. The operational part of the aerodrome - the three runways, set as a triangle and the hangars and control tower - were all laid out neatly on the flattest piece of land in the neighbourhood. But the rest of it - the living quarters, the Messes, the Headquarters buildings - seemed to have been jumbled up with the village in a most haphazard manner. The Officers' Mess for example had been plonked into the orchard just behind the largest farmhouse and there seemed to be Nissen huts scattered higgledy-piggledy everywhere. But we soon settled down and the villagers got used to our frenetic comings and goings at all times of the day and night.

'Down Ampney held two squadrons, ourselves and 48 and just the other side of Cricklade, Blakehill Farm held two more. Nearer to Oxford was RAF Broadwell, which accommodated a further two and these six squadrons, all equipped with Dakotas, made up 46 Group. Each squadron was divided into 'A', 'B' and 'C' Flights, all with six 'Daks' each, so the entire group comprised just over a hundred machines and there were plenty of Horsa gliders to go round. This meant that we now housed a good number of members of the Glider Pilot Regiment and so at last 'Jouby' was not the only 'Brown Job' in the mess. These chaps had a wonderful leavening effect on what might have become a very stodgy RAF loaf and they also provided a colourful addition to our Mess nights, when each of them turned up in his own regimental Mess kit, complete with tight trousers and spurs. Major [Burton Henry 'Peter'] Jackson [commanding 'E' Squadron GPR], who was in charge of them, was an ebullient eccentric who drove about in a vintage Bentley with huge headlights and gave forthright and down-to-earth briefings. One of his classic remarks was: 'If you do have to make a crash-landing, make it as near our gliders as you can and then march back with us. But - don't forget - bring your own water-bottle'.[17]

'Late in April we knew that the invasion could not be far off, for we were briefed to do a 'nickel raid'. This was a code name for dropping pamphlets over France, warning them of their imminent liberation and advising them what to do when our forces arrived. Up to now, these raids had only been carried out by operational aircraft, like the older types of bomber, which could defend themselves if attacked. But some brain in the higher echelons of command now decided that things were so quiet over France at night, that we could usefully and safely perform this function. At this stage our bomber offensive was mainly directed to targets in Germany, so most of the Luftwaffe was engaged over their own country. Even so, it gave us an eerie feeling to realize that we were going straight over the Channel to wander about trying to find the right place to distribute our reading matter. All our 'Daks' had by now been equipped with the latest navigational aid, a thing called a 'Gee'. 1 had only the sketchiest knowledge of its workings, but gathered that strong signals were sent out from various transmitting stations in England and they made a sort of pattern which was then superimposed on our maps. With the aid of a receiver the navigator could get two separate signals and where their lines crossed on the map was our precise position.

'Harry Green reckoned that he had mastered this by now, so, on the appointed night, we set off for our target, which was in Tours in the Touraine district of France. By now 'Mac' MacNeil had left my crew and was a skipper in his own right and in his place I had been given Flight Lieutenant 'Daddy' Wallis, who earned his nickname by being older than all of us and by wearing a long-service medal. He was amiable enough and had spent so long instructing on Oxfords that he found the Dak a bit of a handful and I had not had much time to let him try his hand. This 'Nickel' raid was only

---

17   'Major Jackson and his band of glider pilots walked back to the beaches and in company with one Dakota crew were ferried home in an empty landing craft. They were itching to be ordered into the air for further adventures, but they too now kicked their heels in the Mess for a matter of four weeks.' Born in 1919, 'Peter' Jackson was one of the first pre-war regular officers to transfer to the Glider Pilot Regiment at its inception on 24 February 1942.Under his command 'E' Squadron's 47 Horsa gliders carried the main body of the 1st Battalion Royal Ulster Rifles of 6th Air Landing Brigade to the landing zone immediately north-east of Ranville on the evening of 'D-Day'.

my first trip in 'Treble Four' and I did many more before it came to a sticky end. Mind you, I did my best to get rid of it on this sortie. We set off with our cargo of bundles of bumph for the French and climbed, on a pitch-dark night, to 8,000 feet over the Channel. We saw nothing of the French coast, but I assumed that Harry had things under control. However, after an hour he came forward with the dismal news that 'the Gee was jammed' and he couldn't get any signals from it. 'Never mind,' I said in my most press-on mood, 'Carry on with normal navigation and we'll drop the stuff on ETA.'

Harry looked crestfallen at this and two sergeant pilots who had been sent along for the ride and to help chuck out the literature, both begged me to turn back. But I would have none of it. 'I shall do as I say,' I said sternly, 'and if you mention it again, I shall report you when we get back.' A terrible silence settled over the cockpit as we chugged on over France, seeing absolutely nothing. Harry was just staring at his maps so I maintained the course he had given me with great and I thought, admirable, resolution, until at last he said miserably, I reckon we're about there now.'

The paperwork was duly thrown out of the open door as I made a slow left-hand turn and when it was all gone, in the absence of any help from my own dejected navigator, I set course due north. I calculated that wherever we were in France, as long as we hung on to a northerly course, we must eventually see some part of England. How the time dragged. Daddy Wallis was asleep, Harry was gazing hopelessly at his 'Gee' set, 'Bill' Randall was maintaining a discreet silence and the sullen antagonism of the two sergeants could be felt all through the cabin. By this time I knew I had been a damned fool in pressing on for so long and one could tell by the painfully slow way in which the occasional light on the ground grew nearer, that our groundspeed was desperately low. Now there was literally nothing to do but hang on to that course. We had been in the air about five hours and not a word had been spoken for the last two, when the bright lights of an aerodrome appeared straight in front of us. Inch by inch, it grew nearer and moment by moment the crew began to come alive.

'I know what...it's Hurn' said one. 'No, it isn't, it's St. Mawgan' said another; it's bloody Lyneham... It's Brize Norton...' - they were all guessing now. 'Wherever it is, I'm not landing until we've called them up,' was my firm answer. We could see the whole place lit up now and there were three searchlights set around the perimeter, whose beams met together over the runways at about 2,000 feet. This was standard practice in the UK for aircraft who had perhaps had their radio knocked out and who were completely lost.

'The runway lights were on, too and the whole thing looked very inviting. But I was uneasy. If it was an English aerodrome - and after all that time flying due north it could even be somewhere in the Midlands - why wasn't there a light anywhere flashing a code signal? I continued to circle, calling out: 'Darky, Darky' on the emergency frequency. But there was no reply. 'OK chaps,' I said, 'we've got a fair amount of petrol. I'm going north a bit further until I'm positive we're over England.' There was a groan from the entire crew, but I swung on to 360° and maintained my altitude. By now the same thought was in everybody's mind. When dawn comes, if we are still over France, we'll be a sitting-duck for any fighter who cares to take off. The night was still as black as your hat, but when we had been airborne for fully six hours, the horizon began to lighten and we could at last make things out beneath us. And there it was... the coast of England! But where? Suddenly there was an airfield and as I rapidly lost height, we could all clearly see the large white letters by the control tower... TR. 'Tarrant Rushton!' we all chorused and, with a turn to port, dear old Down Ampney was soon in sight. It was daylight now, so without bothering to call them up on the RT, I dived down and swept past the tower almost at ground level. As we pulled away, up came a green Very Light and in a matter of minutes we were on the ground. Six and a half hours, it says in my log-book. Where the hell had we been? All the others had been back ages ago.'

'At the end of May' wrote Alan Hartley 'an order came confining us to camp. The phone box was sealed, all letters left open for the censors and all leave cancelled. The invasion loomed near. Then came the order on 4 June to paint black and white stripes round the fuselage and wings of all our Dakotas and Horsa gliders to help our anti aircraft gunners on 'D- Day'. At about 0600 on the morning of 6 June someone cried 'Christ, look at this lot!' and marching round our perimeter track were the 3rd Canadian Parachute Regiment. They had cropped their hair to the bone leaving a tuft of hair in a 'V' shape like the Cherokee Indians. They had black and white war paint on their faces and in addition to all of their equipment; many of them carried butchers' meat cleavers in their belts. They looked fearsome and we were all delighted that we were helping them to depart rather than have them arriving. Our Dakotas had actually flown on the night before to drop gliders and paras on crossroads, bridges and gun batteries before the actual invasion. They took off at precisely 2235 on the night of 5 June so in effect the invasion started at Down Ampney.[18]

---

18 *It's Only A Number* by Alan Hartley.

Chapter 3

'We're Goin' Over; Over There'

American troops, or 'GIs' as they were known because of their own derisive term of 'Government Issue', began arriving in war-weary Britain in the months immediately after Pearl Harbor. The 'Yanks' came from the big cities and the backwoods, upstate and downtown: from California to Connecticut, Delaware to Dakota, 'Frisco to Florida; Midwest to Maine, the mighty Mississip' to Missouri; New York, New England, Ohio and Hawaii; the Pacific, Philly and the Rockies to the Rio Grande; from Texas to Tallahassee; Wyoming, Wisconsin, the Windy City and way beyond. The English locals and the Americans themselves were in for a culture shock. From all they could hear the English said that the 'Yanks' were 'overpaid, overfed, oversexed' and 'over here'. Aside from the 'four overs' the Americans said that the British were 'underpaid, underfed, undersexed' and 'under Eisenhower'. Some things though never change. Boston, Cambridge, Ipswich, Manchester and Norwich were the same in any language, on both sides of the 'pond'.

Wild Blue Yonder by Martin W. Bowman.

Eighteen-year old Marvin Litke signed up for the USAAF in January 1942 before he graduated from Roosevelt High in Chicago, Illinois. In Primary flight school at Cimarron Field outside Oklahoma City he flew the PT-19 open cockpit plane and then the BT-13 Vultee 'Vibrator at Enid Basic Flying School. At Aloe AFB at Victoria, Texas he completed single engine advanced training in AT-6s. He 'was in heaven' he wrote 'because I thought that I was a sure thing for fighter aircraft on graduation.' He did well, scored expert in ground and aerial at Matagorda Island Gunnery School and even rode back seat to help his instructor while he tried to qualify in aerial gunnery. Feeling sure that he was going to be posted to a fighter school he was devastated to be given a troop carrier assignment; 'What the hell is Troop Carrier?' He later found out that he had graduated just when plans for 'D-Day' were being finalised and the planes and pilots for the airborne drop had top priority. Not long after he was sent to Bergstrom Field at Austin, Texas for transitional training on C-47s. As he remembered, the course was sixty days long. 'We were taken up in groups of four and traded off flying the bird. It seemed enormous to me. The problem was that I got only one touch and go landing and takeoff. No one kept track of who had what and just before graduation I got my first chance at landing and taxiing it to the tarmac. It was with great shock and dismay that I found I did not know how to taxi a twin-engine airplane that did not have a steering system. Someone had to take my place and bring it to the ramp.

'I was posted the 434th Troop Carrier Group at Alliance, Nebraska; a town of 17,000 civilians. There were two just forming Troop Carrier Groups, each with four squadrons and the 507th Airborne Regiment, (later called the 507th Provisional Regiment) of the 82nd Airborne Division. There was also a regiment of glider infantry on the base. The base had not yet been brought up to full compliment; in fact the 434th Troop Carrier Group was nowhere near being a full unit. The four squadrons all had only about six aircraft each. Most of the pilots already in the squadron had graduated from multi-engine school. We did some interesting work while at Alliance attempting to gain expertise and also to work the bugs out of the SOPs that were new. We flew formation at fifty feet and then climbed to 700 feet at a simulated drop zone. Later we maintained 1,200 feet and pulled back the left throttle to lower the air speed. It was always SOP to pull back on the left engine, as that was the side the jump door was on and prop wash would play havoc with the paratroopers as they jumped. No one really thought it was crazy, as none of us knew better. We brought large bunches of wheat and prairie grass back in our wheel wells while flying the fifty foot formations. The one thing that never changed was having to fly night formation off of hooded, blue 'Blitz' lights and damped exhausts in 'V of V's formation. The blitz lights could only be seen when in exact position in the formation. We were the only pilots who flew tight night formations in any air force in the world.[19]

In September 1943 it was time for the C-47 crews in the 434th Troop Carrier Group to start on their overseas journey to the European theatre. In October the Group was ordered to Baer Field, the staging area at Fort

---

19 *Flying With The 71st Troop Carrier Squadron, 434th Troop Carrier Group*, an autobiography by Marvin Litke.

Wayne, Indiana. The move was made by flying the entire personnel and equipment by air, so they had to make a number of trips back and forth from Alliance to Baer Field. Twenty-seven year old 1st Lieutenant (later Colonel) Alvin E. Robinson's wife Beryl left to go to Fort Wayne and got a room at a hotel there along with other wives of the pilots. 'At this time' recalls Robinson, Major 'Ace' Parker, the former airline captain, got sick and he was removed from command. Captain Ralph Strean was assigned CO and I was assigned the duty of Operations Officer. I didn't want this assignment, but figured I'd get out of it sooner or later.' Alvin Robinson had spent four years in the Navy and fourteen months in the Hawaiian Area aboard the heavy cruiser *Astoria*. He then joined the Army Air Cadet programme. After graduating from Lubbock Army airfield and further training on the DC-3 he was assigned to the 435th Troop Carrier Group stationed at Bowman Field near Louisville, Kentucky. The 435th was moved to Sedalia, Missouri to prepare for further training in night and day precision formation flying.

After Sedalia Alvin Robinson was reassigned to the 74th Troop Carrier Squadron in the 434th Troop Carrier Group at Alliance where the Group finished training in preparation to going into combat. Then they went to their final base at Baer Field for outfitting in preparation to the long trip to the European Theatre of Operations. We spent our time in getting the aircraft in top shape for the trip and getting our gear that was necessary for the overseas assignment. My wife Beryl stayed in the hotel and I would come up there when I could. She had a chance to be with the other wives and I hope she enjoyed it.'

The first three Squadrons of the 434th would fly the northern route and the 74th the Southern route. The ground echelon went over on the *Queen Mary*. Alvin Robinson recalled: 'We took off on 30 September on a seven hour 48 min flight to Puerto Rico. The now twelve ships landed at Barenquen airfield. We stayed all night and took off the next day for Georgetown in British Guiana landing at Atkinson airfield. The mosquitoes here were terrific and we had to have mosquito netting to sleep and it was HOT. The next day we took off on a six hour and 48 minute flight for Belem, Brazil. This was another hot humid place and I was glad we didn't have to stay over but for one night. We then left next day on 3 October for Natal on the eastern bulge of the South American continent. We didn't get a chance at any of these places to get off the airbase, so we didn't see much.

'On 5 October we took off for the longest leg of the journey so far. It took ten hours to arrive at the small island of Ascension in the South Atlantic. We were hoping the homer beacon at the island would not go out as it was a hard place to find in the old C-47. My navigator, Walt Lamb was keeping track of our progress by astral navigation just in case the lead navigator in Captain Strean's ship had trouble. We had cabin tanks with 1,200 gallons of gas, which with our load, gave us about twelve plus hours flying time. It was a fine sight to see the island come into view. The runway was a most peculiar one with a sharp drop at each end and high in the middle. The tower call was 'Wideawake': named after the birds that lived on the island there and who had priority for morning take-off and for evening landings! The ground was all volcanic and we slept in tents with no floor. They grew their vegetables hydroponically. There were no WACs on the island. The commanding officer said that he had been offered a couple to come over, but he said unless they could send enough for all the men not to bother.

'On the 6th we got our usual briefing on the weather for our next stop at Accra in West Africa and took off on an eight hour and eighteen minute flight. Briefings always included pictures of the next airfield at which we would be landing. Upon arriving in the vicinity of Robert Field there was one of those tremendous tropical thunderstorms. It was like a sheet of rain pulled down and we had to go to our alternate field up the coast; which I think was in what is now Liberia on the Gold Coast. The runway was metal planking laid in the grass and no hangars or ground crews. The nearest military was a British radio station and rescue unit nearby.

'The natives turned out to see us and us to see them. It was interesting to walk a jungle trail and see the many kinds of trees and grasses. That night the natives threw a 'party' for the crews. I didn't go as I surely was not going to drink any of their brew. I did get a kick out of visiting the village and watching them work. There was one girl about 18 that was beating up corn or something in what looked like a churn with a long stick. I went over and looked into it, but that was not what I was looking at as she didn't have on anything but a grass skirt.

'The next stop took four hours and twenty minutes on 7 October up the coast to Dakar. This was about as filthy a place as I had ever been at that time. The heat was around 120° and flies and human manure all over the streets made it a sad place. It was desert-like also and we stayed in square twenty feet by twenty feet houses raised off the ground with screens to keep the mosquitoes out. I went down to the town of Dakar this time with some of the pilots and to a place called Madame Tussauds. It was a house of prostitution, but had drinks and a floor show that was horrible.

'We then took off on a ten hour plus flight time from Dakar, with no fond farewell, for Marrakech in Morocco. On the flight we flew over desert and saw some small walled villages with narrow streets hidden in the foot hills. It was hard to believe they could find food out there to live on. Here at Marrakech John Ramsey and 'Ty' Robinson, when they arrived at this stop, made a name for themselves by shooting flies off the ceiling with their 45 automatics. The only trouble was that an officer and his wife living in the apartment up above him! The airfield was interesting as there was a number of old aircraft of the oddest sizes and structure I had ever seen. Some of the wheels were about six feet tall.

'Our squadron (and other airplanes) was flying up to England by going around Spain, as France was occupied by the Germans and then cutting in to England after passing France. We had to take off at night and at intervals of about two minutes and went up different longitude lines. We took off on the night of 11 October. It was a long nine hour flight. We had 1,200 gallons of gas aboard giving us twelve hours flying time. On the way up we could see the lights of Spain in the distance and they looked closer than they were. All went well, but we couldn't get a decent weather report, as there was no way to receive the changes that could happen in nine hours. Walt said, 'It was a horrible night for me. I got a couple of star fixes before the storm hit, but resulting positions showed us right on course and making faster ground speed than predicted by weather briefing in Africa. In spite of course corrections we stayed right on course. Along the way we picked up a high overcast and then a lower undercast so we were flying on dead reckoning alone. Of course we didn't want to cut into England too early and thus go into France and become prisoners of war before we even got a chance to get started. We broke out over the Irish Sea at about 400 feet and then I homed into the Newquay transmissions and was the second ship to arrive, even though I had taken off about twenty-first. This day (12 October) we found that our squadron was mostly all at Newquay although we and other squadrons, had ships scattered all over England and Scotland. It took us eighteen days for the trip, which was about ten days longer than we had predicted due to weather hold ups.

'Newquay was the terminal of the Great Western Railway from London. The town being blacked out totally was a new experience for us. We were put up in a nice hotel called the Great Western Hotel. We now had a chance to walk around the streets. It was interesting to go through a blanket to get into a pub and see dart boards on the walls. They served 'warm' beer instead of the cold beer we were used to. I also enjoyed the different way the English ate. There were six meals during the day if you call the 'teatimes' meals. With the tea they served small sandwiches and cookies. We stayed five days and had a good chance to rest up and enjoy a taste of England.

'We wanted to fly directly to our base at Fulbeck just south of Lincoln and East of Nottingham. The English said we would have to be led there by a RAF pilot that knew the way (as if we couldn't find our way after all the flying and training we had had). Anyway we got our airplanes in the air and headed for Fulbeck and arrived all OK on 18 October. The base was still under construction and of course muddy and very crude living conditions, although metal buildings were there. We called Fulbeck 'Pneumonia Valley' as it was so cold and damp. In the mornings it would be solid fog and visibility about twenty feet and the ground would have Hoar Frost about six inches thick. There was only a peck of coke (burned out coal) to use for our heaters for a week. I know the farmers are still mad at us for burning up their fences for heat. I would sleep in my clothes and fur-lined flying suit and about five blankets and still be cold. The only time we got warm was when we took a bath in some bath tubs with hot water. The only trouble was that the building where the hot water and tubs were located had no roof and it was odd to be in a tub and looking at the sky at the same time. When I got out of the tub I was chilled by the frigid air.

'We didn't have a regular cook so we had to assign different crew members to cook for us. We would have powdered eggs for breakfast and they tasted terrible as of course our mechanics didn't know how to cook them. I was fortunate as I had the 'K' rations off our ship under my bed and I would eat off them.'

'Since the support elements did not arrive for some time' adds Marvin Litke, 'we were fed from an RAF unit. The English had developed a method of cooking food until it no longer could be identified as such. We longed for our squadron mess. Since we were also the assigned mess for group headquarters, we always had the best of food. Three things about England caught my attention immediately; a people who were literally still living with their past history; the beauty of the land; and the unusual slang wording of their language. To find out what time we wanted to be awakened we were asked: 'When do you wish to be knocked up'? Another saying that got our attention was 'Keep your pecker up', which was slang for keep a stiff upper lip. A cookie was a biscuit, but a 'bum' was the 'centre of one's sitting cushions'. A 'nappy' was a baby diaper. A horse race was run by the 'galloping gee gees.' However, as in all of my overseas postings I found the population to be generous and forthcoming, wanting to like and be liked.

'After adjusting to the country and the intense training, I was settled in and feeling comfortable. On leave I envied the bomber types with the three waves under their 'class A' jacket lapel indicating that they had bailed out and been plucked from the Channel. And, the fighter types with the obligatory top button on the jacket always unbuttoned. I was also fascinated with the variety of uniforms from numerous organizations and countries.

'We started off with an attitude that youths need to prove that the boundaries for each us were less than for everyone else. The squadron immediately lost two ships and their crews in a mid-air collision stemming from 'cutting it to close.' The two pilots were the favourites in the unit and sobered every one up for a short time. I have never ceased to be amazed at how casual war time stupidity is accepted compared to the everlasting investigations, boards, meetings, directives, etc that come out of minor incidents in peace time. It was wartime and everyone got a little crazy. The glider pilots for want of something to break the boredom of waiting started a bicycle ski ramp, peddling their bikes at high speed off of a dirt ramp. A after a couple of broken bones and many sprains the flight surgeon put a stop to it. He also stopped the volleyball games as jumping high enough to have your head clear the net invited a fist in the face. But the business of flying got serious. We trained hard and often. Flying was a part of most nights and days.

'We flew a heavy schedule: Lots of night formations, night paratroop and glider drops; also, lots of forming up a stream at night. This called for groups, usually with 52 aircraft each, hitting a mark to the minute in order to fall into place in the stream. There would be about 400 planes when the stream was formed. One night in the process of flying one of these I thought I saw shadows flitting across the night sky. At that point someone really saw something and flicked on his running lights and landing lights. The group that was to fall in behind us arrived early and was flying at 90° through the middle of our formation. Everyone took evasive action and there were aircraft all over the place for about two minutes and then the there was no one and I and most everyone else was alone. The gods of crazy people brought everyone back safely. About ten minutes after this incident, as I was trying to find my way back to our blacked out field I caught a flicker of light to my left and made an almost past the vertical right turn trying to dodge…a star.

'Early in our preparation we would sometimes form up with the red and green running lights on until the formation was fully formed. Flying at the usual low altitude, looking at the formation coming at you looked much like a Christmas tree laying flat. The folks in the area we were flying in called us the 'Flying Christmas Tree'. We had three pilots from somewhere in the group request being removed from flying status during this time. As I look back after many more flying hours I am still amazed that 19-24 year old kids with very little flying experience (most had only about 200 hours of flying time, counting flight school) were doing the impossible and doing it well, with a minimum of mishaps.

'Bad weather often got us into difficult situations. One evening the weather closed in as we were returning with a full group after a formation practice. The new group CO made us circle and land one squadron at a time. We could normally put 52 aircraft on the deck in three second intervals or shorter if needed. The way this was handled we only got one squadron down before the field socked in. There were no radio aids at that time and all facilities were completely blacked out except for perimeter lights, which could not be seen in the soup. We broke up and found fields on our own. I was fortunate enough to request and gained what was called 'FIDO'. This process consisted of pipes with jets in them down each side of a runway that carried fuel and was lit up just long enough to burn off a few feet of fog so an aircraft could land. It was so expensive and a glaring breach of the blackout that it was only used when the result made the cost and chance worth it. As it was the RAF tower crew thought I was a formation so they allowed it. They were fairly put out when only one ship landed. A more usual method was to fly in a pattern and call 'Darky' which was a signal for requesting help, usually a direction to the nearest field. Another signal was 'May Day' called over the radio. It was an anglicized version of the French for 'Help Me'. The only problem was that the radios we were using were the new version of UHF which were great for line of sight but did not carry far so one had to be within range if in trouble. I had a great need for this service later on.'[20]

'We got in some training at Fulbeck' remembers Alvin Robinson 'but the weather was so bad it prevented our activities in that area to a great extent. On 11 November we moved to Welford so that we could work with the 101st Airborne Division on practice parachute jumps and glider tows. The next two months were spent at Welford. Then we moved back to Fulbeck where we did a lot of flying during January and February when the weather would allow. Several interesting things happened at this time. The weather was so bad most of the time I decided to do something about it so I could

---

20 *Flying With The 71st Troop Carrier Squadron, 434th Troop Carrier Group*, an autobiography by Marvin Litke.

get in some flying time. I contacted Marion ('Radar') Huggett as he was our officer that handled the maintenance on the 'Eureka' and 'Rebecca' sets that we used to drop paratroops at night. The set had a radar scope at the navigator's position. When homing into the beacon on the ground there was a blip that could be centred and it showed the distance. When the aircraft got over the beacon it of course showed zero mileage. I wanted a parallel scope put up in the cockpit where there was room just to the left of the instruments on the pilot's side. We had to get the machine shop to cut a five inch hole in the panel and then we installed the parallel scope. It worked fine, although it did throw the scope in the navigator's compartment off to the left a little.

'The weather was still very bad with almost no ceiling and visibility. I told Huggett to get a man with a Eureka set and put it out on the end of the runway and put one a mile out in line with the runway. He did as I was to try some night landings using the system that night. I had drawn out a system of flying a square around the outer set and letting down to 500 feet and then homing into the one at the end of the runway letting down to field elevation so I could land, I just hoped the equipment would not fail in flight. Well, I had a time getting someone to fly with me. My co-pilot would not do it and my navigator said no. I finally got another pilot as crazy as me by the name of David A. Whitmore (the one who had flown formation with the airliner in Nebraska).

'We went out to the aircraft and got it running and took off into the night fog. I made four landings using my system and it worked just like I had predicted. So I taxied in and parked in front of the operations building and who was there but the CO of the Group (later replaced by Colonel William B. Whitacre.) The CO asked how in hell I was flying under those conditions, as he was really confused. I had to show him what I had done to my airplane and I thought I had had it now. Well, he looked at me and said, 'I have been looking for a pilot to be the pathfinder to lead the group in on 'D-Day' and now I have found him.' I was told to then get ready to leave soon for pathfinder training. So, I had to turn my plane over to another pilot and go to pathfinder school at Cottesmore just south of Fulbeck. The Squadron moved to Aldermaston near Reading on 5 March. I never found out what happened to my 'invention' I had put in my airplane.

'While at Fulbeck another interesting thing happened to me. I was towing gliders for practice along with the rest of the squadron. We would pick up a glider and take off and then cut him loose at about 2,000 feet and he would fly back to the runway and land. I was in David Whitmore's aircraft as my aircraft was in inspection. As I took off this time and was towing the glider, the airplane started doing funny things and felt real odd. I didn't know until later that the colonel of the base was flying the glider and that he had a British general with him. He was showing him how it felt to go up and down through the prop wash. Well, anyway I cut the glider loose and then went up to about 6,000 feet to check out the plane before I went back to get another glider. The plane flew fine and I had it going at about 170 mph to see if anything was wrong when a Spitfire aircraft buzzed me off the left wing missing me about a foot. In the past they would do this for practice. I decided to play with him a bit and when he chandelled off to the left I turned into a chandelle myself and turned inside of him to show him the C-47 could turn sharper than even a Spitfire. This would have been fine except there were two Spitfires and they were making a double pass and I got between them. The first I knew about it was a spat through my left wing and the Spitfire going off in a spin without his rudder and elevators. It took off about fifteen feet of my left wing and cut his aircraft in half. He did bail out but broke both of his legs. He was a Turk training with the RAF.

'As I was trying to get the airplane back in a level flying condition to scan my damage my co-pilot, Otis McLendon got hold of the wheel and tried to turn it over so he could see the Spit go down.

'Mac' said, 'Rack it over so I can see him go down' and I said, 'if you don't watch it we will be with him.'

'About this time the navigator, Walter Lamb, came running up to the cockpit.

'Our wing is coming off and it is peeling off up to the engine! Walt cried.

'I said, 'Yes, I know that and I am trying to get it back to the airfield.'

'Walt said: 'I am leaving this airplane' and took off for the back end. In just a few seconds he was back up front and said there wasn't a parachute on the plane (it was David's plane) so I told him he had better stay aboard then. I called the airport for a direct landing and told them the emergency and had no trouble making the ten miles to airport. It flew a little lopsided, but the big old rudder held it fine. After landing and I alighting from the plane I had my first feelings about the incident when I went out and looked at the damage. I suddenly got weak-kneed. The base CO came up about that time and looked at the damage and said, 'What have you been doing; buzzing?' I was in no mood for criticism so I said, 'Yes Sir, backward.' As any fool could see the metal was all pushed up forward. He then asked what happened and I told him a Spitfire had hit me and he said that I surely couldn't catch a Spitfire so he turned and walked away. I never told him all the details and when they had an inquest I sent Mac to handle it as I said I was too busy.

'Another interesting thing happened here in Fulbeck. We were putting on a show for the British generals. Our Squadron was to make a low pass over the runway at the end of the show and I was leading the third flight. We were tucked in real tight, the lead ship about three feet off the runway; and I was only about ten feet off the runway. So here were nine ships coming down the runway and all of a sudden the wing men of the front flight of three peeled off. The right aircraft climbed to the right and the left wing man climbed to the left. The wing men of the other two flights also followed the first and it left just the three leaders flying in trail down the runway. I told 'Mac' that I must have been asleep in the briefing because I didn't remember this manoeuvre. Later when I landed they told us that the lead flight had hit a flock of teals (birds).One had gone through the windshield of the right ship and hit the pilot in the face and another bird had gone through the windshield of the left wing man and hit the co-pilot in the face. Outside of some cuts and coverings of blood and guts they came out OK.

'I didn't stay long at Cottesmore; just long enough to get a new aircraft that had PPI-717 radar on board. The antenna was on a large barrel like object on the belly of the C-47. It gave a drag and could not go as fast as the other ships, nor could it pull two gliders. I wish I knew more of the other pilots' names at the pathfinder's school, but I have forgotten them as they were just in passing. I do remember one incident when a couple of pilots took their aircraft for the first time. They were practicing instrument and had a black hood over the pilot and the co-pilot had to watch for aircraft. One of the engines quit and the pilot checked the gas gauges and they read OK so he went and feathered the engine (stopped the engine by turning the blades of the prop into the wind). He thought that the other pilot had given him a practice single engine. Then the other engine quit and he came out of the hood but it was too late and they had to belly land in a field. The co-pilot thought that the pilot was giving himself a single engine for practice. The gauges of the four tanks were turned upside down. The full ones read empty and the empty ones read full. It was a stupid mistake all around and it washed out one of our brand new aircraft.

'Shortly after that we were transferred to the newly activated Pathfinder Unit at North Witham. I was assigned a new navigator, name of Lieutenant Don Caldwell. So with my crew of McLendon, Caldwell, Fisher and Wiser we started to train for our 'D-Day' activity. Colonel Joel Crouch was the Squadron CO. We made many flights using the radar and 'Rebecca' and 'Eureka' sets and also very intensive training for night flights on seeing (wearing red glasses all day so we would have good night vision). I got to see a lot of England from the air as well as Wales, the Isle of Man and The Wash. We would have games of trying to see who came the closest to a 'Eureka' set that was on the ground in the middle of the night by dropping a bag of something on it.

'I remember one training mission very vividly that occurred at this time. Several of our ships were to go to Land's End in the far western part of the British Isles and then out over the chain of islands to get practice for the navigator on his radar. It would be similar to going in on 'D-Day'. I flew down to Aldermaston where our group was now getting ready for the invasion. I went in to get my weather briefing. The weather at Land's End was terrible. Although it was about 1,000 feet at Aldermaston the ceiling at Lands End was very low. The weather man would not clear me and I should have let it go at that. I wanted to make the flight even though it was bad as I figured that I could always let down over the water and come in with our radar to hit the airfield. So I went to the Group Commanding Officer, Colonel 'Bill' Whitacre and asked him to clear me. He said he would be glad to do so and if I could not get in then he didn't want me to be leading his group on 'D-Day'. So we took off into the lowering clouds. I had my crew (co-pilot and navigator) trained real well on reading a map at low altitude. I had drawn a line the way I wanted to go and had checked the route for any known obstacles. The further we went the worse the weather got until the clouds were occasionally hitting the ground. At this time we had the radar altimeter that had three lights that could indicate when we hit a certain altitude over the ground. I had set the green light for 400 feet and the yellow one for 200 feet and the red one at fifty feet as near as I can recall. So when we ran into a cloud that was on the ground I would pull up real sharply to 200 feet and wait to break out in a couple of seconds. This only worked because we knew exactly where we were all the time almost to the foot. The maps were excellent, even showing the houses and forests. One time as I pulled up sharply the three lights all came on right down to the 50 foot red light. We must have come real close to someone's house.

'When we arrived at Lands End it was raining and visibility about half a mile. We hit the airfield right on the head and I started to circle with my wing staying inside the airfield all the time so I would not lose sight of it. I finally found a runway and got the gear down and came in on a turning approach. I got my wheels on the wet runway and really rode the brakes and stopped just short of the end of the runway, as we were landing down wind. At the end we looked down and 400 feet down was the Atlantic Ocean. Well, we taxied in and when I went into the operations office the weather man came over and said, 'I say old chap, do you know what the weather is?' I said 'no' but it was sure bad. He said, 'Yes, it is measured fifty foot ceiling and one half mile in rain.'

"Mac' my co-pilot stated 'Yes, I can believe it because I was in the soup all the time while he was turning around the airfield,'.

'Well, as you can imagine we were the only ones to arrive at Lands End. We spent five days at the Officer's Club in a big house overlooking the sea. It had been taken over for the duration of the war. It was real nice for visiting officers as well as staff officers stationed there and in the morning I would be awakened by a WAAF with hot coffee in bed at 0600. Then we had breakfast and around 0900. We would have tea and crumpets and lunch at noon and again tea in the afternoon; then dinner at 1700; and then another snack at around 2100. It was so foggy we couldn't see across the street so we just stayed in and rested. We never did get to do the practice over the islands west of Lands End and I headed back to Aldermaston.

'Time went by rapidly as we were very busy and then my crew and I were sent back to the 434th Troop Carrier Group to lead them in on 'D-Day'. I didn't know until I arrived that we were to be the lead group of the whole glider formation. We did a lot of work practicing leading the group on practice drops in all types of weather. There are a lot of little incidents that happened such as dropping Polish paratroops and their system of wicker baskets on a rail they would put down on the floor of the C-47. They would all be up toward the front until they got ready to dump them out and then they would push them to the rear and all go back there to jump out. This would throw the airplane into a stall due to the fact we were already at low speed and in the propwash of other airplanes. I noticed that Colonel Whitacre flew with me as much as he could but I didn't know why (not knowing he had planned to fly with me on 'D-Day'). He had me do my 'Sunday Best' short field landing and I really gave him a good one.

'When not flying, everyone kept their spirits up with the movies at the base theatres, weekly Red Cross dances with the local girls and the arrival of American flight nurses [in the 818th MAETS (Medical Air Evacuation Squadron]. May ended with a payday, typhus injections and talk of 'invasion' as everyone waited that fateful hour. The Red Cross dance and off post passes were cancelled and intelligence officers returned to Wing Headquarters under armed guard and 'carrying innocent looking barracks bags that contained enough information to wreck the Nazi war machine. The barracks radio was reporting that the French coast was taking a pounding from Allied bombers in an attempt to soften up the coast for future invasion and of course RAF Bomber Command and 8th Air Force were still carrying destruction to the heart of Nazidom.'

On 3 June C-47 crew chiefs and radio operators were briefed together with navigators and pilots. After months of the wildest speculations, the secret was out. However, 'some horrible flaws remained in 'Neptune's planning' wrote Sergeant Marty Wolfe. 'But no-one can deny that the harassed and anxious planners at COSSAC did what they could to put together an operation that most of them thought at least had a good chance. They certainly intended to protect the extremely vulnerable troop carrier planes and gliders from a 'friendly fire' disaster like the one in Sicily. 'Friendly fire' was even more of a potential danger over Normandy.'

Major Benjamin F. Kendig CO, 44th Troop Carrier Squadron, 316th Troop Carrier Group at Cottesmore recalled: 'It was common knowledge that our Group was transferred from Sicily to England to participate in the invasion of the European continent. Even the German radio announced our arrival and welcomed us to the UK. Of course, they also promised that we would all be shipped home in wooden boxes. At the time of the Normandy Invasion we had been overseas for about a year and a half. Our group participated in the Sicilian landings with two night paratroop drops. The second drop was met by heavy fire (mostly so called friendly). Our group lost twelve airplanes out of 36. Even though it didn't show on the surface, we were all somewhat apprehensive about the invasion plans that we all knew were in our future. After arriving in England we soon adapted to our new country and in some ways because of the many similarities we almost felt as though we had gone home. Our days and nights were filled with flying supply missions in England and Scotland and many night formation training flights.

By mid-May 1st Lieutenant Julian 'Bud' Rice and his fellow C-47 pilots in the 316th Group were shut down for the night, wondering what their next mission would be. They all knew something big was about to happen but were not sure what or when. 'Bud' had been born and raised in a small town in Panama where his grandfather had settled and built a brewery. Following the Great Depression era people accepted work anywhere they could find it. Many American families migrated south in response to jobs offered during the Panama Canal construction. 'Bud' spent his early childhood in Panama but was sent away to school in New Orleans. Plans to go to Notre Dame were thwarted by the Depression of the 1930s and instead he went back to Panama to work for the Canal Department. 'Bob' Broom, 'Jimmy' Day and I were best friends all through school. We played in the Canal when it was still a ditch in the dirt and later grew up to work Canal office jobs. During the afternoon of December 7, 1941 'Jimmy', 'Bob' and I were enjoying *Gone with the Wind* at the one movie theatre in town when suddenly the house lights came up. The theatre manager announced, 'Attention everyone! Pearl Harbor has just been attacked.' The possible bombing of Panama Canal was a threat the military took seriously when a Japanese submarine was spotted off the Panama Coast. My two buddies and I handed in our job resignations the following morning and headed for the local Army Recruitment Centre. We passed the test for flight school and were on our way to boot camp. Although 'Jimmy' and 'Bob' were excellent pilots, I would lose both my best friends within the year.

'Bud' had been assigned to the in the 37th Squadron at Cottesmore after eighteen gruelling months of intensive technical and academic training and 400 flying hours. By 'D-Day', each pilot had acquired over 800 hours of flight training hours including supply missions, day and night formation flying, paratroop drops, glider tows, short field landings, instrument flight training, etc. 'We all knew the Invasion of Europe was coming so we concentrated on perfecting our skills. We were rigorously trained and tested to maintain eligibility for our 'Instrument Rating Card' - the official military license then required of all 1st pilots.

'One afternoon all pilots and their crews were ordered into Operations Room at 0700 hours for an important announcement. In standing room only in a cloud of nervous cigarette smoke you could hear a pin drop. Then our group commander Colonel Burton Fleet walked in. 'Gentlemen,' he began. 'As you know, we've been training you pretty hard for many months. We knew something big was in the planning but didn't know precisely where or when. Now that we have more information, we need to run a special five-hour training flight. This rehearsal ['Eagle' on the night of 11/12 May] is critical because it isn't just about flying at night in blackout with radio silence. You know all that. You probably also know there are eleven other squadrons like ours, 72 planes in each group, at eleven different airfields around England. All eleven squadrons will be running the same practice mission from their individual airfields. The purpose of the practice is to learn how to meet up and blend together mid-air and still maintain your diamond formations.

'We will break ourselves down into two sub-groups at this airfield… 36 planes in Group 'A' and 36 planes in Group 'B'. We'll be flying at midnight with the usual blackout and radio silence orders. It is imperative you maintain an EXACT seven-minute separation between your two groups.

A minute off could mean disaster, so let's all synchronize our watches right down to the second. Now all of you go back to your barracks and report back here in Operations at 2200 hours prepared to board to your aircraft with your crews. Thank you gentlemen; I expect to see you here on time and I expect you to do a good job.'

'At 1100 pm my 36-plane Group 'B' was given the signal for takeoff. We blended mid-air, met all of our checkpoints on time, then across the Irish Sea, and over the Island of Wales. By then all the pilots were pretty tired. We'd flown practice missions all day and hadn't been to sleep yet. Still, we did our best to keep our formations intact and still maintain the seven-minute separation rule.

'Eventually my group reached the end of our flight and readied ourselves to turn around. Just before turning around I noticed little red dots in the distance. As I focused more closely, the red dots steadily grew bigger and bigger. I suddenly realized these red dots were the wingtip lights of Group 'A'. My stomach caved, because this was not good. Red wingtip lights were located on the front of our planes, not the back. Somewhere in the first group the seven-minute rule had failed and they were heading back too soon. We were no longer following Group 'A'. We were flying straight into them!

'Within seconds, planes were close enough to bump noses. As one guy came directly at me I could see his face looked as scared as mine. With no time to think, I shoved down on my yoke and by some miracle he decided to pull up on his at the same time. We nearly skimmed each other's fuselage, passing so close that the air compression bounced my plane downward about 500 feet. It felt like a violent earthquake.

'Then the unthinkable happened. The sky lit up like high noon. One explosion after the other. Head-on collisions sadly took the lives of 30% of our squadron, including our beloved Squadron commander, Major James R. Farris, our group Chaplain and one of the jump masters for the 82nd airborne. It was another hard lesson learned. The plan was perfect, but luck plays no favourites.'[21]

'This accident naturally affected us all continues Major 'Ben' Kendig. 'There was deep sorrow for the loss of our friends and also the heightened

---

21   The lead plane flown by Farris with Colonel Burton Fleet the Group Commander flying as an observer was hit by the C-47 flown by 1st Lieutenant Joseph L. Sharberof the following element at a turn-around beacon. All personnel on both planes including the Group Chaplain, Captain Floyd N. Richert, who was also riding along as observer and passenger on Farris' aircraft were killed. Lieutenant Colonel Harvey A. Berger assumed command of the 37th Squadron two days later.

awareness that the night formation flying, required for the invasion, could be even more dangerous.

'In addition to the many practice night formations, we had gas drills and night vision training. For the gas drill, we had to don our masks and walk through smoke filled tents. The night vision training consisted of wearing dark-tinted red goggles (in a darkened gym) and playing catch with a large white ball. We also trained to identify aircraft and read text that was faintly projected on the wall of a darkened room. On the mission, we wore impregnated coveralls, carried gasmasks and wore tin helmets. We certainly did not look like aircrew members.'

'One day we received visitors. They were members of the 82nd Airborne who set up camp on our field at Cottesmore. There was no doubt now that we would be participating in the invasion! We would be taking them on a one way trip to some undisclosed location someplace on the continent. We certainly did not envy their position. Their camp was isolated and we didn't get to talk with them until just before they boarded our planes. The less any one individual knew about the whole operation, the better the chance to keep the secret from the enemy.

'Because I was a squadron commander, I was briefed on the operation sometime before the rest of the squadron. I don't remember the exact sequence of the activities prior to the invasion. We did go to a nearby airfield to listen to a talk and receive a send off by General Eisenhower. Then came the postponement of the mission for a day due to the weather. I breathed a sigh of relief but realized it only meant another day of anxiety!'

Staff Sergeant Maurice E. 'Speedy' Smith was a nineteen-year old radio operator on Lieutenant Colonel Leonard C. Fletcher's crew in the 37th Troop Carrier Squadron at Cottesmore. 'Around the first of June' he wrote 'the field got its first word of the up-coming invasion. All leaves and passes were cancelled. Everybody was restricted to the base. Then a few days later paratroopers of the 505th PIR started arriving. Something was definitely going on. Then we finally got the official word that the 'D-Day' invasion was on for the following morning, the fifth day of June and we would be jumping paratroopers over Normandy on that day before daylight as part of the invasion. Sometime during the day we were informed that the invasion had been postponed for 24 hours.'

'D-Day' had been set to be 5 June but it got pushed backward by General Dwight D. Eisenhower the Supreme Allied Commander. June 4th had been the designated 'Departure-Day,' but meteorological forecasts for 5 June predicted winds of 17 to 22 knots, thick clouds below 500 feet and a four-foot surf on the Normandy beaches, the waves so high that the landing craft would be swamped and winds so violent that paratroopers would be in danger of getting whipped right out of their chute shrouds when they jumped. The low visibility would make the towing and landing of gliders next to impossible. Troopships were already being loaded with heavily equipped and mightily apprehensive soldiers. From the more northern ports some ships actually put out to sea on 4 June - the waves in this rough weather adding to the misery of the soldiers. Even amphibious landings would be hazardous in the high surf. Then at 0415 on 4 June only twenty hours before the troop transports planes were scheduled to takeoff, the bad weather forced Eisenhower to postpone 'Overlord' - at least for twenty-four hours.' Troop carrier schedules were changed accordingly and briefings continued on the 5th.

Private Edward C. 'Bogie' Boccafogli in 'B' Company, 3rd platoon, 508th PIR in the 82nd Airborne wrote: 'On the night of 4 June we loaded into C-47s at Folkingham. Everyone was very nervous, very tense. We took off, being as we were in the first lead group. We flew around for about an hour and then word came that the invasion was called off for twenty-four hours due to the bad weather. They said that there was one of the worst storms in many years in the Channel. When we landed back at the airfield it was really a let-down. It just seemed to take everything right out of your stomach. That night there were very heavy rains and a couple of tents collapsed: one was hit by lightning. Next morning, the fellows were trapped underneath the canvas because of the weight of the water.'

Sergeant 'Marty' Wolfe wrote: 'Francis Farley, the Operations Officer, came around to our barracks to tell us 'Neptune' was off. That news was received with extremely mixed feelings.' Meanwhile, the troopships already at sea had to turn around and steam away from Normandy. No amount of imagination and sympathetic understanding can capture the agony in Eisenhower's mind at that time. If he cancelled the ponderous invasion, secrecy as to the actual landing beaches - given all the people who were now in the know - would have been impossible to maintain. He had been advised that the beach tides and other factors would not be favourable again for another two weeks. Battle commanders, whipped up to high levels of mental readiness, might have reacted negatively to a cancellation. The Soviet Union, pressing so stridently for a 'second front' to take the pressure off her own armies and reduce her huge losses on the eastern front, might have concluded that the Allies were untrustworthy and even might have tried to work out a separate peace with the Nazis. Six hours after its postponement, however, the invasion was back on. The beach landings would take place one day later, the morning of 6 June. Meteorologists had been able to predict a definite but limited easing of the bad weather for the two days of 6 June and 7 June to be followed by another bad turn after 8 June.

'This foul-up because of weather may have had unexpected good results. Weather patterns in this part of Europe move from northwest to southeast; thus, while the weather was getting steadily clearer over southern England and the Channel, to the southeast, in Normandy and most of northern France, the weather on the night of 5/6 June was terrible. Most German garrisons relaxed in their barracks, confident that no invading planes or ships could be expected in the very near future. The German commanders were caught with their Channel patrol boats at anchor and most of their reconnaissance planes in hangars.

'Securing the base during all the planning and theorizing, we in the 81st TCS were bringing ourselves up to the highest possible level of preparedness. The more pessimistic fellows in our outfit were voicing their fears: compared with what we faced in the coming invasion, they said, missions of Eighth and Ninth Air Force bombers would look like Sunday school outings. This was only the wildest sort of guessing. What we did know was that we had benefited from fifteen months of the most thorough training: in tight formation flying, day and night, in glider tows (even double glider tows), in paratrooper drops simulating actual missions, some of which were reported as unqualifiedly successful and in navigation and communication exercises. We were convinced that the entire outcome of the invasion, perhaps that of World War II itself, might well hinge on whether troop carrier succeeded in delivering the airborne troopers to where they could head off German counterattacks against the beaches. All of our training, all of our indoctrination and all of our pride in our own efficiency and dedication were on the line. No matter how devastating the enemy's fire, we were told, our job was to drop the paratroopers and tow in the gliders. No matter how badly we were hit, as long as our planes were flyable, we were to keep on toward the DZs. We believed we could and would do just that. Those of us in the 81st TCS regarded ourselves as expendable, in the best sense of the word. If any among us felt that it was unjust that we should be expendable, or that we could not live up to such high standards, he kept that idea to himself. We believed we were not only a good outfit but also a lucky one. We had lost not a single one of our crews during our training in the US and in Britain. Our feeling that we were not only good but lucky was reinforced by many close shaves during the last months of training. For example, in Operation 'Bumble Bee', one of the invasion training manoeuvres back in late May, Arthur Swasey crashed his plane while landing; his ship exploded and burned on the runway but none of the crew was hurt. There seems no question about it: morale in the 81st Troop Carrier Squadron just before 'D-Day' was high.'

Then, as the weather cleared General Eisenhower gave the order to proceed - high waves notwithstanding - starting with the pilots and paratroopers, 50-75 percent of whom were not expected to survive. Meanwhile off the coast of Normandy, thousands, their uniforms drenched, jammed into 1,500 windswept and water-soaked flat-bottomed craft and continued to wait. Big steak dinners, coffee and doughnuts were served to the paratroopers - too spun up to sleep - while jazz bands played tunes like *Tiger Rag* to keep spirits high. But mostly they sat pensively as B-17s were loaded with thousands of leaflets for scattering over the countryside in the early morning prior to the invasion, warning the French citizens to stay away from railways and roads, along with essential information for identifying their Allied rescuers.

Thus the invasion was set to take place on 6 June unless some new and extraordinary difficulty arose. The paratroops, its advance guard, would set out on the night of the 5th. The Troop Carrier Command operations officers had carefully devised an extremely complex plan to assemble 821 C-47s into a workable formation. This needed to be loaded and launched and assembled precisely into a pattern that would deliver troopers and gliders to their specific drop zones and landing areas - on time and on the button for 'Overlord' was the equivalent of moving the Wisconsin cities of Green Bay, Racine and Kenosha - every man, woman and child, with every vehicle - across Lake Michigan in one night.

Chapter 4

'Rendezvous With Destiny'

'When I met him they told me he was going to do a very important job on 'D-Day' and although I had no idea it was going to be that important, I instinctively knew it would be something very brave.'

New York Journal-American reporter Lorelle Hearst (onetime women's editor and Follies girl; second wife of publisher William Randolph Hearst Jr.) in a story published on 7 June. She had met Colonel Joel Crouch a week before the invasion, at a time when the plan was still very much top secret.

In the 434th Troop Carrier Group at Aldermaston eight miles east of Newbury in Berkshire C-47 pilot, twenty-year old Lieutenant Marvin Litke felt and treated the task ahead with deep feeling. 'On about 3 June we were suddenly briefed, placed behind guarded barbed wire and began to check the aircraft and figure loads. About half of the 71st was sent to Greenham Common, a nearby field to be tacked on to the 438th Troop Carrier Group. The only reasons that I can think of for augmenting the 438th was to drop a maximum number of paratroopers for the lead group, or to add some specialized unit to the drop. Due to the British double summer time it was just dusk as the pathfinder aircraft took off. It had become dark as we took off at about 2330.'[22]

Corporal Richard M. Wright hated the killing, the death and the carnage of war. He lost some of his closest of friends such as Terrence 'Salty' Harris, who was killed on the green fields of Normandy by a German sniper bullet and Walter L. Moore, who was severely injured by a demolition explosion that sent him back to the States even before 'D-Day'. But Wright faithfully did his

---

22 *Flying With The 71st Troop Carrier Squadron, 434th Troop Carrier Group*, an
    autobiography by Marvin Litke.

job and his duty. Wright was a Pathfinder in the 2nd Battalion, 'Easy' Company in the 506th PIR of the 101st Airborne. As a paratrooper he had volunteered to become a Pathfinder, acknowledging, 'It was probably the quickest way to get into the fight against the evil tyranny of Nazi domination that had overwhelmed and brutalized most of Europe.' The Pathfinders were destined to be the first paratroopers into combat. Wright added, 'They explained to us that it was a suicide mission and I just felt that I had to volunteer for it.'

An hour before the operation commenced, experienced all-volunteer paratroopers would jump into the Cherbourg area. Their mission: Designate the zones for the drop; cut all telephone lines, preventing the German units from communicating; and divert the enemy as the warships moved into position. The main combat jumps would be preceded at each drop zone by three teams of pathfinders that arrived thirty minutes before the main assault to set up navigation aids, including top secret 'Eureka' radar transponder beacons and Holophane marker lights and brightly coloured panels to help guide in the vast armadas of C-47s carrying tens of thousands of American and Allied paratroopers and gliders to their selected drop and landing zones in the dark. Being a Pathfinder was not an easy job. It meant being out in front of the pack and facing most of the German army head-on and alone, thus being in a dangerous and costly position. The development of a separate pathfinder organization seems to have been a gradual process. The success of RAF bombers led by 'Gee'-equipped pathfinders inspired the command to begin training navigators at Bottesford in the use of 'Gee' about the end of January 1944. The school had one radar officer, a second lieutenant and four instructors with one 'Gee' ground trainer, three 'Gee' ground sets and two 'Gee'-equipped aircraft. Early in February the arrival of five aircraft from the MTO equipped with SCR-717C made it possible to begin training with that instrument. By 12 February IX Troop Carrier Command had decided to include both 'Gee' and SCR-717 training in one Command Pathfinder School.

To secure more room and better facilities the school was moved to Cottesmore. On 26 February 33-year-old Lieutenant Colonel Joel L. Crouch, of Riverside, California who had planned and led pathfinder operations in Italy, was named as Commandant (one of General Williams' first appointments in IX Troop Carrier Command). On the 28th the school officially opened. Cottesmore, which also housed the 316th Group and 52nd Wing headquarters, proved to be too congested, so on 22 March the pathfinders were moved to North Witham airfield deep in the heart of Twyford Wood, off the A1 about ten miles south of Grantham.

Early plans for large-scale radar training had to be whittled down for lack of equipment and instructors. Aircraft with SCR-717 already installed trickled in one by one from the United States. Men trained to use or repair the SCR-717 were scarce and tools with which to repair it were scarcer. Although 'Gee' was more plentiful and the British had provided instructors and mechanics to help the Americans get started, test equipment and parts for it were hard to get. Consequently the first class had to be limited to 24 crews, three from each of the eight troop carrier groups then in England. A few more were included after the course started. These were to be trained intensively for sixty days. If time and facilities permitted, another class would be trained later in the spring. Whole crews were enrolled on the grounds that much better results could be attained by a team working together than by a trained navigator whose comrades were ignorant and perhaps sceptical of his new techniques.

By the end of March the students had completed ground training and had an average of sixty hours flight instruction and practice with the new instruments. Most of them were deemed skilful enough to graduate from basic instruction and to concentrate on perfecting their technique in practice missions. Therefore on 6 April, 24 more crews were called in for training. Since this expansion required additional equipment, IX Troop Carrier Command decided to allot the pathfinders 52 aircraft, including the eleven equipped with SCR-717 which were then on hand and all of the same type subsequently received by the command. The rest of the 52 aircraft were to be equipped with 'Gee' and, after the successful installation of a 'Gee' set in a plane with SCR-717, all aircraft so equipped were also provided with 'Gee'.

As early as 18 March pathfinder aircraft had participated in exercises and dropped paratroops with 'Eureka' beacons and visual aids. However, in several early exercises the 'Rebecca's in the troop carrier aircraft were ineffective because they were badly tuned or even set for the wrong channel. The pathfinder school requested and was given the responsibility for designating channels and for the tuning of 'Rebecca-Eureka' equipment. With precise tuning this radar improved remarkably thereafter in reliability and in range. Some poor performances had occurred because the paratroop pathfinder teams dropped to operate the 'Eureka's had only limited knowledge of their instruments and were ignorant of troop carrier plans and procedure. Therefore 300 pathfinder personnel from the American airborne divisions were sent to North Witham to study and work with the troop carrier pathfinders. This also produced dividends in greater efficiency and better teamwork. By 10 May the second batch of crews had completed their basic training and fourteen fully trained crews were returned to the groups to lead serials in 'Eagle'. Lack of coordination in 'Eagle' between those fourteen crews and the serials they were supposed to lead resulted in a decision to keep at North Witham only 24 crews for further training and return the rest to the groups to get practice as leaders. The aircraft of the 28 crews which were returned had to fly to North Witham every three days for servicing and current radar data, but the move was probably a wise one. Reintegrated into their groups and usually with group commanders or executive officers as pilots pathfinders would do well in 'Neptune'. By 'D-Day' all navigators at the pathfinder school had operated 'Gee' for at least 25 hours and were considered qualified operators. Most had had from fifteen to 45 hours training with the SCR-717 to orientate oneself over inland areas was much more difficult and few if any were prepared to do this with assurance.

During the late evening hours of 5 June with faces blackened and weapons checked and rechecked, Wright and the other pathfinders laboriously loaded into their airborne C-47 troop carriers destined for Normandy in German-occupied France. When the paratroopers walked up, the jumpmaster had them stand and strap on all their extremely heavy equipment. By the time a trooper had on all his weapons, his two chutes and other equipment, he was so loaded down (with around 150lbs) that men had to help push some of them up the stairs into the plane. Before they boarded, a few paratroopers gave away their British money - something of no value to them, they thought, in France.

'This is it!'

In 'Chalk No.4' (temporary numbers chalked on the sides of each C-47 to aid paratroopers in boarding the correct plane) Wright and the rest of his stick would be one of the leading planes in the invasion of northern Europe. Drop time was scheduled for shortly after midnight on the 6th of June. At the controls of his plane were pilot Captain Clyde E. Taylor and co-pilot Harold H. Sperber of the IX Troop Carrier Command Pathfinder Group of the 9th Air Force. They departed England during the dark but moonlit hours over the Isle of Wight, flying at extremely low altitudes while maintaining complete radio silence. Below them were thousands of ships loaded with American and allied warriors who would shortly confront the Germans on the Normandy beaches. Wright was lost deep in his thoughts and praying to God that he would survive this time of great endeavour and uncertainty. As they encountered the Normandy coast, the German army was ready and waiting for them. 'Suddenly all hell broke loose with all sorts of antiaircraft fire with blue, green and red hot tracer bullets coming up to greet us,' said Wright. An explosion in the left engine caused Taylor to immediately feather the left propeller, which initiated a right turn in the plane's flight path.

'Hal' Sperber quickly pushed the aircraft's nose down to avoid a near collision with the other Pathfinder plane in their tight 'V' formation. With a full load of Pathfinders, the troopers with their heavy equipment and gear, the C-47 had quickly begun to lose altitude. Being much too low to jump and with no safe place to land, the men were forced to dump their equipment and gear out the door of the C-47 and head back out to open sea. The one remaining engine began to glow red from the excessive load required of it and as the props hit the surface of the waves, the men braced themselves for ditching in the dark, frigid waters of the English Channel. As a jolting wall of water enveloped the plane, the Pathfinders and aircrew went out the open door and into the waves of the Channel with many of the men desperately clinging to a single life raft. All of the men had miraculously survived the forced ditching as they swam, nervously waiting for rescue by the Royal Navy destroyer HMS *Tartar*. After rescue 'with a front row seat to the largest invasion in history' as Sperber said, the crew of the British destroyer gave the men a much-needed shot of hot buttered rum. Wright and his fellow Pathfinders were lucky to be alive, thanks to the heroic efforts of the troop carrier pilots. By noontime of 6th June, Wright and the rest of the men were transferred to Air Sea Rescue and quickly taken back to Southampton, England for questioning and debriefing. Their top-secret mission in the invasion of Normandy was over before it started, but all were grateful to be alive.

'D-Day', which would end with more than 12,000 Allied casualties and 4,414 dead, had begun.

At 2150 hours on 5 June under cover of darkness a small fleet of twenty C-47 transports started departing North Witham at five-minute intervals, their destinations: Sainte-Mère-Église and Sainte-Marie-du-Mont, more than two hours' flying time in Normandy for the massive Allied invasion set to begin that night and the following morning. The transports carried a total of about 200 paratroopers of the 101st Airborne Division's Pathfinders Group, all wearing their 'Screaming Eagle' with the distinctive 'white tongue' Pathfinder patch' with pride as befits an elite unit. It was a fitting emblem for a division that will crush its enemies 'by falling upon them like a thunderbolt from the skies'. The role of the Pathfinders was critical. That the Pathfinder Group (Provisional) was formed within the 52nd Troop Carrier Wing was the outcome of numerous meetings held in Comiso, Sicily between senior American and British commanders to critique the disappointing results of the airborne landings there. It was clearly established that the use of assigned drop zones, marked in advance of the arrival of the main body of airborne troops, was sound thinking. In addition, the idea was that even if the pathfinders missed the zones a bit and the zones were improperly marked, that at least the main body of the paratroopers would be dropped together. This would avoid the tragic scattering we experienced in Sicily.

Having trained at North Witham with the 82nd Airborne Division, the Pathfinders' task was to blaze a way for the airborne missions of IX Troop Carrier Command by marking drop zones behind the invasion beaches; placing lights and radar beacons so that more than 13,000 jumpers who would immediately follow in the all-out airborne assault could find their way to bridges and road crossings designated as strategic targets. In the planning for 'D-Day', Allied generals estimated that these airborne troops might take up to seventy percent casualties.

Flying the lead aircraft (42-93098) at the head of twenty C-47s from North Witham that night was Lieutenant Colonel Joel L. Crouch. As the first pilot in the vanguard fleet, he was, in the words of reporter Lorelle Hearst of the *New York Journal-American*, 'the spearhead of the spearhead of the high-stakes allied invasion'. Before the war, Crouch ('everybody calls him Joe or Colonel Joe,' wrote Hearst), had been a pilot for United Airlines, flying passengers between Los Angeles and Seattle. In the army, he became a specialist in pathfinder operations for aerial assaults and had been the lead pilot in the invasion of Sicily a year earlier and at Salerno, Italy in September 1943. During the planning for 'D-Day', Crouch had run the 'Pathfinder School' at North Witham to train both paratroopers and pilots for the job of setting up drop zones. Each pathfinder team had eighteen paratroopers, including twelve men to carry the lights and navigational beacons.

Crouch had his pilots make at least one jump themselves, just to experience what the paratroopers would be up against. It was logical then that Crouch should pilot the lead C-47 on the night of 5 June. His co-pilot was Captain Vito Pedone of Mount Vernon, New York ('a laughing, dark-haired boy, precisely 22 years old,' wrote Hearst) and their navigator was 25-year-old Captain William Culp of Denver, 'a square-jawed thoughtful sort of man.' In back, leading the paratroopers was Captain Frank Lillyman of the 502nd Parachute Infantry Regiment, 101st Airborne who dreamed of the day when he would sail into New York Harbour and greet his wife, Jane and three-year-old daughter Susan. Lillyman intended to be the first man out.

At 0950 on 5 June the small fleet of C-47s began departing North Witham at five-minute intervals, carrying a total of about 200 paratroopers from the 101st Airborne, the first pathfinders for the massive Allied invasion set to begin that night and the following morning. The Pathfinder force consisted of six three-aircraft serials, one for each of the six drop zones and another serial of two aircraft added in accordance with a late decision. The troops carried by this serial were to jump on Drop Zone 'C', move about a quarter-mile west and set up aids for the 101st Division's first glider mission. DZ 'C' was an oval 1½ miles long from west to east and over a mile wide. It was 2½ miles south of DZ 'A' and a mile east of the road from Carentan to Sainte-Mère-Église. Through it went a road running east from the hamlet of les Forges to the village of Sainte-Marie-du-Mont. A large flooded area just southwest of les Forges provided a landmark to guide the troop carriers' approach. Each aircraft carried panels, holophane lights, two 'Eureka' beacons and a team of pathfinder troops averaging thirteen in number. In addition the pathfinders brought the two BUP beacons.

The pathfinder drops in the 101st Division area were to begin at 0020 and those for the 82nd Division at 0121, Double British Summer Time, which was the time used throughout the operation. Mass drops by the respective divisions were to begin half an hour after their first pathfinders landed. It was estimated that at least one team from each serial would be in operation on its zone in time to guide them.

Colonel Crouch crossed Portland Bill slightly ahead of scheduled time of 2324 as he followed his preset itinerary without any further radio communication. Twilight still glimmered in the western sky as the aircraft crossed the English coast. The expert pathfinder pilots and navigators had no trouble reaching Normandy. They crossed the Channel in good formation 'on the deck,' risking collision with Allied shipping, in order to conceal them from German warning radar. A favouring wind brought them to a stationary marker boat code-named 'Hoboken' and carrying a Eureka beacon about five minutes ahead of schedule. There they made a left turn to the southeast and to their initial point on the Cotentin coast at Portbail ('Muleshoe'), relying on the outline of the coast and islands displayed on the scope of the SCR-717 to guide them safely between the anti-aircraft guns as they flew between the Channel Islands of Guernsey and Alderney and to show them the proper points at which to make landfall. In this they were successful, although radar maps prepared to help them interpret the SCR-717 had not arrived in time to be used. After reaching Normandy the fliers relied on 'Gee' and dead reckoning, supplemented to the limited extent feasible by visual recognition of the terrain and SCR-717 which were of limited value in airborne operations because although it produced a rough map of the terrain on a scope, only coastlines and large cities showed up well. 'Gee' was complex and time consuming to use. It required special training and many crews found it awkward in combat. Some crews used it successfully, however.

The pathfinders for the 101st Division had been given a special course in order to facilitate their use of 'Gee'. After passing Jersey they were to swing south of the main route, make a 90° turn to the left five miles offshore and fly east-northeast to points two or three miles south of Montebourg. There they would strike the 'Gee' Chart lattice lines which passed through their respective drop zones and make a 90° turn to the right to run down the lines to the zones. On approaching the Continent the pathfinders found their navigation impeded by a layer of clouds which extended from the western shores of the Cotentin almost to the drop area. The lead C-47 ran into a bank of low-lying coastal cloud and disappeared from the view of the pilots in the rest of the formation. The loss of visual contact completely destroyed the essential integrity and the discipline of the formation that had been drilled into the pilots during their training. Some pilots elected to climb above the clouds, while others tried to go below them and others tried to stay together. The disorder caused the formation to break up and the force scattered. Flying over the French coast just after midnight, sporadic German fire, mostly from small arms damaged eight aircraft slightly but had no serious effect. Planners had feared that the Germans might jam the 'Gee' sets, but interference was negligible.[23] The lead serial navigated by 'Gee' from landfall to destination, although it did get a visual check at the final turn.

At 0016 the jump signal was given. The troops came down about a mile northeast of the objective, Drop Zone 'A', northernmost zone of the 101st Division; a rough oval about a mile and a half long from west to east and about a mile wide, situated 2½ miles east of Sainte-Mère-Église and half a mile southwest of Sainte-Martin-de-Varreville. Only a mile east of the zone was the flooded areas behind 'Utah' Beach, a hazard to troops who were slow to jump or whose pilot overshot. Unable to reach DZ 'A' in time, the Pathfinders set up their portable 'Eureka' responder beacons on a drop zone or landing zone on the ground near the village of Sainte-Germain-de-Varreville

---

23 To prevent jamming, new bands had been chosen at the last moment and each 'Gee' set was put on a different frequency.

and after they were activated, it indicated it's approximate location on the 'Rebecca' receivers in the Troop Carrier C-47 cockpits.

In the first serial for DZ 'C', the 101st Division's centre drop zone, one aircraft was ditched with engine trouble before reaching Normandy. All aboard were rescued, the first of many to be picked up that day. The other two aircraft in the serial made their drop at 0025, having depended on 'Gee' entirely except for some visual checks at the turn and a glimpse of Sainte-Mère-Église by one crew. One stick of troops hit close to the zone and the other about half a mile southeast of it. The pathfinder equipment was put up on the zone, but about a quarter-mile southeast of its planned position. The second serial to DZ 'C' overshot the final turn but dropped its troops at 0027 between one and two miles south of the zone. However, the equipment brought by that serial was not to be used until dawn - for the glider missions - so the pathfinder troops had plenty of time to move into position.

The serial which was headed for DZ 'D', the third and southernmost of the 101st Division zones, misjudged its position because the 'Gee' in the lead aircraft had not been properly set; failed to recognize its final turning point and ran out over the east coast before discovering its mistake. It made a sweeping circle to the right and approached the DZ from the southeast over the Carentan estuary. The first of four drop zone teams arrived in the vicinity of Sainte-Germaine-de-Varreville about fifteen minutes after midnight. Lillyman's C-47 arrived over the DZ ten minutes early, but the pilot overshot and had to go round again. The delay led to the jumping order being changed. Lillyman hit the ground at fifteen minutes after midnight on the 6th, his habitual jump cigar clenched in his teeth. He would claim later to be first and is given as such in many published accounts but he was actually second or third. First man through the door was Pfc John G. McFarlen and as he said later, 'unless Captain Lillyman found a way to beat me to the ground, I was the first to land'.[24]

The drop, believed to be accurate, was made at 0045; the troops actually landed about a mile from the zone. Lillyman and his team were ordered by Lieutenant Colonel Patrick J. 'Hopalong' Cassidy, battalion commander of the 1st Battalion, 501st Parachute Infantry Regiment to set up a roadblock near Foucarville. Even though the men were scattered, they were still able to set up some of their lights within ten minutes. Cassidy's men secured

---

24 Lieutenant Colonel Frank Lillyman died of a stroke at Walter Reed Hospital on 8 March 1971. He was 55 years old.

Sainte-Martin-de-Varreville by 0630, sent a patrol under Staff Sergeant Harrison C. Summers to seize 'XYZ', a German barracks at Mésières and set up a thin line of defence from Foucarville to Beuzeville.

The three pathfinder serials scheduled for the drop zones of the 82nd Division were to go straight from the Initial Point ('Peoria') on the west coast of the Cotentin about six miles north of the towns of Carteret and Barnesville to their zones, just as the main paratroop serials of the division were to do. This course cut diagonally across the lattice lines of the 'Gee' charts, a satisfactory if not ideal arrangement. An approach down the lattice lines was not feasible for them, since it would have required passing close to German anti-aircraft concentrations.

The pathfinder serial bound for DZ 'O', an oval about a mile long from west to east and half a mile wide from north to south outside Sainte-Mère-Église, attempted to cross the Cotentin on 'Gee' but swerved north, passed close to Valognes and made its final run parallel to the lattice lines. It was fired on but surprise and the cloudy weather saved it from serious damage. At 1115, six minutes ahead of schedule, it dropped its teams on the basis of 'Gee' indications supplemented by a visual check. All troops landed on or close to the zone.

Of the two DZs on the west side of the Merderet, the northernmost was called DZ 'T', the southern one DZ 'N'. The three aircraft bound for DZ 'N' made their approach according to plan at 0138 and had a good look at the DZ area. Their navigators were sure the drop had been accurate, but the troops landed over a mile southeast of the zone.

The pathfinder serial for DZ 'T' made landfall appreciably north of 'Peoria', but made accurate use of 'Gee', sighted some landmarks near the zone and dropped its team with precision. Unlike the other serials it had come in considerably above the prescribed altitude of 600 feet.

Overall, the first pathfinder operation was a mixed success at best. Cloud cover made it hard for the pilots to navigate and some of the jumpers ended up far from their targets, while others came under heavy fire. The pathfinders soon learned they'd been miss-dropped so they made no effort to get the rest of the regiment lost with them and left their radios and beacons turned off. Coming in unguided, the formations of C-47s broke up in a combination of low clouds and heavy enemy anti-aircraft fire. Some planeloads, including two sticks of 'Able' Company, were dropped over the English Channel and drowned. Consequently, most of Colonel Moseley's troops landed way off their designated DZs, up to five miles away. Moseley badly broke his leg and had to relinquish command to his XO, Lieutenant Colonel John H. 'Iron Mike' Michaelis.

Most of the pathfinder pilots who supposed they had pinpointed their DZs with 'Gee' had actually missed them by over a mile. This was attributed by an AEAF radar expert to the navigators' relatively limited experience with 'Gee' and to the combat conditions under which they worked. He thought the normal margin of error in such cases would be about three times as great as under favourable conditions. However, other factors besides 'Gee' should be considered. Difficulty in allowing for the brisk northwest wind probably contributed to the deflection of some teams and slight delays in jumping might account for an apparent tendency to overshoot. At any rate, though only two serials achieved the degree of accuracy prescribed in the directives, all teams were put near enough their zones to perform their missions in spite of cloudy weather which might easily have caused the pilots to lose their way completely had they not had 'Gee' to help them.

On 29 June the 101st was relieved from the VIII Corps and sent to Cherbourg to relieve the 4th Infantry Division elements that had the German garrison pinned down in that seaport city. The 502nd PIR returned to England shortly thereafter for refitting, earning a Presidential Unit Citation for the campaign.

Upon his return to base in England, Hearst asked Colonel Joe Crouch, who was now a little freer to talk, 'what it had been like over in France.... He thought for a minute and then said very seriously and carefully: 'Well, there is some activity over there. We put a lot of our men down.' Her story continued: 'These fliers, being the first out, were also the first back and they said that the paratroopers whom they carried into France and dropped there were singing all the way. No, I couldn't find out what they were singing - the door between was closed and anyway 'Colonel Joe' and his crew were too busy to listen, I guess. They said if I want the name of that song I'll have to go to France and find Captain Lillyman, who was in charge of the men who jumped from Colonel Crouch's plane - and thus the first of the airborne infantry to set foot in France in this operation.'

The pathfinder troops on DZ 'O' had put their 'Eureka' in operation by 0125. The first serial received its responses clearly when fifteen miles away and the third did so at distances up to 21 miles. The pathfinders also had three 'T's of green lights gleaming on the zone, one for each battalion, but not until it was almost on top of the lights did the lead serial see them through a break in the clouds. In consequence it made a high drop from about 1,000 feet. Some pilots overshot and dropped troops east of the zone. Others who overshot or straggled off course made another pass. The second serial had begun a descent through the clouds on 'Rebecca' before reaching the DZ and dropped on the 'T'. The 315th Group's serial had to change its course and lose altitude rapidly after it sighted the 'T' but was able to drop over the zone from about the proper height. At least one of its pilots missed the zone in the overcast, turned back at the coast and dropped at what he believed to be the alternate zone, DZ 'D'. Although accounts differ, the first drops were probably made about 0145 and the last about 0204. As in so many other cases the arrival had been slightly ahead of schedule. Half an hour after the first American pathfinders jumped, the main paratroop drops began.

With all the preparations complete, at midnight, under a clear sky, 16,000 paratroopers in the 82nd and 101st divisions and half as many British paratroopers began taking off at roughly 3-5 second intervals - in a 300-mile long formation, nine planes wide. Mid-air collisions were their biggest fear. Most of the pilots lacked combat or instrument weather or night flying experience. They were flying almost incognito, only two small white lights on either side of the aircraft nose, along with a small red flashing light on the belly, signalling their presence; and were flying low to reduce detection and lessen time descending, when they would be subject to enemy fire.

The main task of both the 101st and 82nd Airborne Divisions was to backstop the seaborne invasion at 'Utah' Beach, preventing - during the early invasion hours when the seaborne soldiers were clawing for a foothold - massive counterattacks by German forces stationed to the east and south. During the five hours or so between about 0100, when they would jump and 'H-Hour' (0630), when the invaders hit the beaches, the paratroopers were ordered to capture certain bridges, destroy others, cut communication lines with interior Normandy, mop up pockets of German defenders and capture the town of Sainte-Mère-Église, a small but vital road centre. Above all, the paratroopers were to seize control over four of the 'exits' from the beaches, that is, roads headed west from 'Utah' that could take heavy traffic because they were built up on causeways over the sandy beach soil and the bogs and marshes behind them. It was at the western end of these causeways that the seaborne troops would join up with the airborne troops, once the Germans caught in the middle were overcome.

General Gavin called Operation 'Neptune' 'perhaps the most complex that had ever been attempted.' The whole operation could be thought of as a demonstration of 'Murphy's Law'- whatever can go wrong, will.

Chapter 5

'Albany' - 'Stand Up and Hook Up'

We went directly from the briefing theatre to our planes. The troopers, sitting on the runway near the plane door, looked sullen and resentful and made a couple of bitter cracks to crew chief 'Bob' Obermark and me. We didn't blame them...

Sergeant Boris 'Marty' Wolfe in the 81st TCS, 436th TCG, writing on 15 June.

'At Greenham Common, the large 428th Troop Carrier base near Newbury west of London the gentle English countryside was bathed in semi-darkness as reveille sounded' recalled Flight Officer John C. Hanscom, a 25-year old glider pilot assigned to the 89th Troop Carrier Squadron. 'It was the third of June and British Double Summertime was in effect. Nights were short. Days were long. Out of a number of identical GI sacks we tumbled at 0700. Out of a number of identical Nissen huts we staggered at 0715. Out of a number of identical barbed wire barricaded, heavily guarded troop carrier areas we stumbled into trucks which hauled us to the mess hall for a breakfast of powdered eggs, salt pork, dry cereal, powdered milk and coffee. After partially recovering from this sumptuous mess, we were herded back to the squadron area and into improvised briefing rooms set up in vacated Nissen huts. It was here that we shortly came to realize that this was to be a day of intense preparation for 'D-Day', a day that would usher in huge movements of mighty forces involving countless numbers of men and machines.

'Sleep would not come easily for me that night. I kept mulling over in my mind the events of the past few days. These had included lectures on air-sea rescue with demonstrations of life rafts and other equipment, sessions on first aid, the departure of ten of our glider pilots from the 89th Squadron on detached service to another group, the zeroing of our M-1 rifles on a thousand inch range, the observation and supervision of the loading of our Horsa gliders, lectures on mines and booby traps, the erecting of barbed wire barriers around that part of the hut area occupied by combat crews, our restriction to this enclosed space, the patrolling of it by armed guards and our being herded to and from the mess hall under guard. All this had taken place during the four days preceding that morning of June the third. A state of tension had come to exist over that big base at Greenham Common and morale was high. The weather turned bad late in the afternoon. We had at least a twenty-four hours' reprieve. Sunday, June the fourth found us in chapel listening to the glowing phrases of Chaplain Charles Lusher on our duty to mankind in the name of Christianity. He was obviously impressed with the occasion. He expatiated eloquently on patriotic and religious themes.'

Chaplain Charles Wendell Lusher had joined the 438th Troop Carrier Group following chaplaincy training at Harvard University. He was born on 1 December 1914 in Crown City, Ohio. He took a wife, Gladys Pauline Sheets who bore him four sons and in 1943 he had enlisted as an Army Chaplain to help young soldiers who were so desperately in need of spiritual counsel as they faced death. The week before when the men were confined in barbed wire enclosures and not even allowed to talk with other units of the group, Lusher was about the only one given a pass to these enclosures. 'We all knew, however, that the 'dry runs' were over and the next alert would be 'it' he wrote 'and the invasion of Europe would be on. We had known for some time that our 438th Troop Carrier Group had been chosen to lead the invasion, carrying the 101st Airborne paratroopers, but we didn't know when or where the operation would occur.'

For two days a NBC radio stringer, 38-year old six foot and skinny William Wright Bryan, had been living at Greenham Common with the 89th Troop Carrier Squadron. Bryan had graduated from Clemson College in 1926 and then spent a year at the University of Missouri, School of Journalism. 'All day Monday they watched the weather' he wrote. 'After an early supper they broke up into small groups for volleyball games in their small recreation area. The combat crews lived apart from the ground personnel, with barbed wire surrounding their quarters and guards protecting them from any contact with outside persons. In the early evening Major Clement G. Richardson of Salinas, California returned from a conference with Lieutenant Colonel Donalson commanding the lead group. As he came within the barbed wire enclosure of his own squadron, Richardson blew a long shrill blast on his whistle. The pilots, co-pilots, navigators and radio men clustered around him. 'Come into the briefing room,' he said to his combat crews. There he stood for a moment in front of the large scale map on which their course was plotted. As quickly as his men were all in the room, Major Richardson said, 'Do you know your stuff?' There was no word of dissent spoken. 'Get your stuff and report to the operations room immediately. I'm going down to the colonel's to get the weather report. I think this is it. Good luck.' Major Clement G. Richardson's combat crews had been fully briefed as to their initial mission, the course they would fly and all procedures they would follow.

'You want to get back don't you?' he asked. 'There was a quick murmur of assent.

'Then damn it, get in there and fight!

'The crews piled in their trucks to go first to the operations office and then to the line where their planes were drawn up and ready to go.'

'Around 1900 Monday, June the fifth we were summoned to the squadron briefing room by a shrill blast from the commanding officer's whistle' recalled Flight Officer John C. Hanscom, who was to make final preparations for the 'Elmira' mission the following day. 'We forgot whatever we doing and dashed. This was it! We learned that our planes loaded with paratroops would take off that evening at 2230.'

On 5 June the Medical Officers and nurses in the 818th (Medical Air Evacuation Squadron) at Cottesmore were alerted to help care for casualties, 'which may result from D-Day activities the 316th Troop Carrier Group was participating in'. Four days' earlier the 818th had moved to Cottesmore from Spanhoe by motor convoy because the latter was inadequate quarters for the two dozen or so nursing personnel. One of the nurses was 24-year old First Lieutenant Evelyn 'Chappy' Kowalchuk, the youngest of three sisters to parents born in Ukraine, who was from New Jersey. Her mother so strongly opposed her daughter's military service that she ripped up all of her applications to the various service branches. Sidestepping her mother and persevering, 'Chappy' was accepted by the Army Nurse Corps as a flight nurse. The flight nurses were to care for patients as they were ferried by C-47s from the Normandy beaches to ambulances stationed around the field and in the Station sick quarters. It would be a particularly difficult position to provide a personal touch to patients during the short flight to England and then never seeing them again after they reached the ground. The flight nurses were warned to expect that they would be often under fire from enemy forces. While she and her fellow flight nurses were 'bound together' by the horror of what they would observe, they were also scarred. Later 'Chappy' was haunted by post-war nightmares and more than one flight nurse she had known committed suicide after they returned home.

'At Membury the day before 'D-Day', wrote Sergeant 'Marty' Wolfe: 'we had fresh eggs, a wonderful change from the powdered variety and pancakes for breakfast; luscious roast chicken for lunch; and a big steak for supper. Favouring the combat crewmen this way could not help but draw an irritating and in many ways, unfair line between the aircrews and everybody else. However, the security precautions involved in this did work: most of the ground crew personnel had absolutely no idea of where 'Neptune' was headed until the planes were actually in the air. You moved from one building to another together, you ate together, all under the eye of the military police. I had a group of guys with me guarding one of the gates on the main highway running through our camp. Suddenly a British car just zipped right through the gate without stopping or answering a challenge. So we telephoned and got a motorcycle MP to overtake that car and bring it back to the gate. When the driver of that car came back, it turned out he was a member of British intelligence; and he had been ordered by Eisenhower to do just that, with the idea of testing out our base security! Another morale builder was the visit to the base by some high brass, particularly General Paul Williams, CG of the entire IX Troop Carrier Command (not related to our own Colonel Adriel Williams, head of our 436th Group).' Colonel Adriel Newton Williams, born in Shelby County, Kentucky in 1916, had gone directly into pilot training following his high school graduation, received his wings in 1939, became an officer and in 1942 assumed command of the 436th Troop Carrier Group, a position he held until the end of World War II.

'Two British Air Chief Marshals, Sir Arthur Tedder, Eisenhower's Deputy Supreme Commander and Sir Trafford Leigh-Mallory, also visited. Leigh-Mallory gave us a *veddy, veddy* British harangue. Finally, on June 5 Eisenhower himself came to visit. 'Ike' was there mainly to pump up the spirits of the 101st paratroopers we would haul; we nevertheless felt that some of the honour of his visit rightfully belonged to us.' At that visit, 'Ike' asked if there was anyone from Kansas. A young private raised his hand and Eisenhower replied, 'Go get 'em Kansas!'

First Sergeant David 'Buck' Rogers in HQ Company, 1st Battalion, 506th PIR, 101st Airborne Division, recalled: 'Upon arrival at Upottery airfield, on 31 May we were placed in a closely guarded area. After getting settled we spent most of our time in the large briefing tent. In this tent there were wall maps, sand tables and aerial photographs. We listened to lectures did an intense study of the maps, sand tables and aerial photographs. We learned that we would land on DZ 'C' just west of Sainte-Marie-du-Mont, Normandy. This would be inland from a beach labelled 'Utah'. The food served while at Upottery was better than any we had since leaving the States. We had ice cream, white bread, steaks and many other food items not usually served to us since arriving in England We joked that we were being fattened for the kill.'

'For several days the airborne troops had been moved onto our base and slept on cots in the hangars' wrote Second Lieutenant Roger Airgood, born on a farm near Manchester, Indiana on 1 March 1921 and now a C-47 pilot in the 436th at Membury. 'They were sweating out the mission also under severe restrictions. On 5 June we proceeded on schedule on British Double Summer Time. Typically we wore flight suits or fatigues. Everyone wore a Mae West. The pilots wore a chest pack harness over their Mae Wests. It was too cramped in the cockpit to wear seat pack parachutes. We used chest pack parachutes that were stored behind the cockpit. If necessary the chest packs were clipped onto the harness while en route to the door to exit the aircraft. Other crew members wore regular seat pack parachutes. We were issued British flak suits which consisted of two pieces, front and back, which were fastened at the shoulders and sides. Most used a third piece to sit on. Pilots wore goggles and a steel helmet in case the windshield was damaged or blown out. Basically the C-47 was unarmed, lacked armour and self-sealing fuel tanks - sometimes referred to as a 'sitting duck'.'

Airgood's Group had borrowed the 85th Troop Carrier Squadron from the 437th Group at Ramsbury. Altogether, five squadrons (ninety C-47s) stood ready for their part in 'Albany', a mission by 432 aircraft carrying troops of the 101st 'Screaming Eagles' Division. Together with 'Boston', a 369-aircraft mission for the 82nd 'All American' Division these two missions consisted of three regiment-sized air landings whose paratroopers were organized into 'sticks', a plane load of troops numbering fifteen to eighteen men. All twelve troop carrier groups, helped by beacon ships in the Channel and the pathfinder signals, were divided into serials, containing thirty-six, forty-five, or fifty-four aircraft. In 1943 it would have been all a group could do to contribute one such serial. Within the missions the interval between successive serials was to be six minutes from head to head. The C-47s; individually numbered within a serial by 'chalk numbers' were organized into flights in trail, in 'vee of vee's'. With two minor exceptions, each was made up entirely of nine aircraft 'Vee's of Vee's in trail with the leader of each nine-ship flight keeping 1,000 feet behind the rear of the preceding flight. The leaders of the wing elements in each flight were to fly 200 feet behind and 200 feet to the right and left respectively of the rear aircraft in the lead element. Within each three-plane element the wingmen were to hold positions 100 feet back and 100 feet to the left and right of their leader. This was a tight formation at night for aircraft approximately 65 feet long and 95 feet from wingtip to wingtip.

6,928 troops were carried aboard 432 C-47s of mission 'Albany' organized into ten serials. ('Boston' was also a lift of ten serials organized in three waves, totalling 6,420 paratroopers carried by 369 C-47s.) The first four serials, two from the 438th Group at Greenham Common and two from the 436th Group were tasked in bringing the first battalion of the 502nd Parachute Infantry Regiment and the 377th Parachute Field Artillery Battalion to DZ 'A'. The second serial's fifty-four transports - the 79th, 80th and 85th TCSs - would carry the Field Artillery Battalion, plus one C-47 with medics and five packed with ammunition. Much would depend on the twelve 75 mm howitzers disassembled in pararacks under the C-47s and in door bundles inside the cabin. Until the seaborne soldiers would be able to bring ashore their own artillery, the paratroopers' big guns would be the best protection available against counterattacking German tanks. The 438th TCG squadrons were to assemble into a formation over their base, join with the others in the 436th Troop Carrier Group and fly out over the English Channel. They were to fly southwest toward a turning point about sixty miles west of the Normandy coastline. From there they would turn southeast, toward the west coast of the peninsula and then directly eastward over the Cherbourg peninsula for about twenty-five miles to the drop zone.

Like all zones of the 101st DZ 'A' was on low, flat land broken into small fields and orchards. The fifth and sixth serials destined for DZ 'C' consisted of a total of 81 C-47s of the 439th Troop Carrier Group (45 of which carried the headquarters and 1st Battalion of the 506th Parachute Infantry Regiment and 36 which carried the 2nd Battalion) and 45 aircraft in the 435th Group at Welford, which carried the 3rd Battalion the 501st PIR plus divisional headquarters and artillery and signal personnel. Two serials of 45 aircraft each flown by the 441st Group and two of like size flown by the 440th Group were the last serials of 'Albany' and they had DZ 'D' as the objective. The six troop transport groups in 'Albany' had the shortest distance of all the groups to fly but would encounter the most severe weather conditions.

The main task of the 101st (and 82nd Airborne Division) was to backstop the seaborne invasion at 'Utah' Beach. Their task, during the early invasion hours while seaborne troops were clawing for a foothold, was to prevent massive counterattacks by German forces stationed to the east and south. During the approximately five hours between their jumps and dawn, the paratroopers were ordered to capture certain bridges, destroy others, cut lines of communication, mop up pockets of German defenders and capture the vital road centre town of Sainte-Mère Église. The 'Screaming Eagles' objectives were to secure the four causeway exits behind 'Utah' Beach, destroy a German coastal artillery battery at Sainte-Martin-de-Varreville, capture buildings nearby at Mésières believed used as barracks and a command post for the artillery battery, capture the Douve River lock at la Barquette (opposite Carentan), capture two footbridges spanning the Douve at la Porte opposite Brévands, destroy the road bridges over the Douve at Sainte-Côme-du-Mont and secure the Douve River Valley. In the process units would also disrupt German communications, establish roadblocks to hamper the movement of German reinforcements, establish a defensive line between the beachhead and Volognes, clear the area of the drop zones to the unit boundary at les Forges and link up with the 82nd Airborne Division. The 'Deuce's (502nd PIR) mission, was to secure two northern causeways leading inland from 'Utah' Beach and destroy a German battery of 122 mm howitzers near Sainte-Martin-de-Varreville.

'Our final briefing was at 2000 hours, just a few hours before we were to take off' wrote Sergeant 'Marty' Wolfe. 'There were guards all around the Group briefing theatre and you had to show your credentials to get in. I saw how flushed and bright-eyed everybody looked tense but not jittery. The bulletin board on the stage seemed covered with maps and photos. First to speak: Operations, with the essentials about mission objectives. Then Navigation: courses, beacons, turning points, our DZ. Then Communications: what frequencies to monitor, the recall message that would abort the mission and turn us around back to England. Absolute and unquestioned radio silence to be maintained; radar and radio aids; what to do if forced to ditch in the Channel. Then Weather: clearing, full moon, scattered clouds. Finally Intelligence, at the maps: 'You can expect this sort of antiaircraft fire here and there but don't worry about German fighters; there are concentrations of Krauts here and there; use this road for a check point as you come in to the DZ; before you leave this hall you must turn in every scrap of identification you have on you except your dog tags; if forced down, retain your status as a soldier and fight your way to the Allied lines.'

A preliminary warning would be given to the paratroops when their aircraft was twenty minutes from its zone and the door cover would then be removed. At four minutes from the DZ, the lead pilot of each serial was to flash a red warning light by the door to alert the troops. They would then line up for the jump and would hitch their parachutes to the static line. An order to flash the red light would be transmitted to the rest of the serial with a red Aldis lamp displayed by the radio operator from the astrodome and would be passed on by the other flight leaders to the pilots behind them.

Approaching the zone the formations would descend to 700 feet and slow down from the cruising speed of 140 mph prescribed for the outward route to 110 mph to give the paratroops the best possible drop. When in position over the drop zone the serial leader would give the green light which was the signal for an immediate jump. The signal would be passed back as before by a green Aldis lamp, with the flight leaders repeating the signal when they found themselves at their jump point. Before the men jumped the crew chief and the paratroops nearest the door were to shove out bundles of supplies and equipment.[25] References in unit histories indicate that these procedures were generally followed.

'All crews and airborne reported to their aircraft at 2200 hours' wrote Second Lieutenant Roger Airgood in the 436th Group formation. 'This provided about forty minutes to help load the heavily burdened paratroopers and check out the aircraft. The paratroopers all had leg packs tethered to their waists. These packs would be lowered after the jump so the sacks weighing 40 to 80lbs would hit the ground first. We had worked with the airborne before and they were cocky, unruly characters but this time they were very serious. A couple of them had us lace the strap from their backpacks so they would have to cut the strap to get out of the chute. We started the engines at 2240 and taxied into take-off position so we could get the planes up and in 'V' formation very quickly. Take off was at 2300. We had a very precise route to follow over the Channel and across Normandy. The return route brought us back over the out-bound route. Although we experienced many night formations with paratroopers in the States and in England, the plan for getting the troops to the Drop Zones in Normandy was the most complex and ambitious mission we had ever faced. There were several changes in altitude and direction over the course. There were no check points from the IP to the DZ to aid in maintaining the desired course. The Pathfinders who were supposed to be on the DZ did not reach the area and no signals were emitted. Our serial of six waves of nine planes each was led by Lieutenant Colonel John D. Kreyssler of the 79th Troop Carrier Squadron followed by the 80th Squadron. Len Hayes and I were in the left flight lead position of the first wave. Len was in the pilot's seat and I was in the co-pilot's seat.'

Pfc Joseph G. Clowry in the 319th Glider Field Artillery waiting for takeoff from Membury recalled: 'Outside the engines of the tow planes were warming up and the noise was such that any verbal communications had to be shouted. At last this was it, this was what we had been training for

---

25 The usual number of bundles was two.

and we were ready to go. Sitting there, there was a feeling of anticipation. How would the flight go, the landing and after? There weren't any external or internal signs of fear - this was a great adventure and, after all, what could happen to a twenty-two year old. It could happen to the guy across the way, or the one next to you - but never you. Soon the roar of the lead C-47 was heard as it inched forward slowly on the runway at Membury airfield. The tow line began to uncurl like a serpent from its preset configuration and the lead plane was off at 2037 hours. Then it was our turn, the tow-rope unravelled, tightened and with a slight jerk our Horsa glider began to roll forward. We gathered speed and soon the rumble of the wheels on the runway was silenced and we were airborne. The glider lifted off first and the taut tow-rope lifted the tail of the tow plane. We were veering off and climbing to the preset altitude for assembly. 'Our serial was completely airborne with 418 airborne troops, thirty-one jeeps, twelve 75mm pack howitzers, twenty-six tons of ammunition and twenty-five tons of other equipment.'[26]

BBC war correspondent Robert Barr, born December 22, 1909 in Glasgow, Scotland; one of four correspondents who trailed General Eisenhower from 'D-Day' until the end of World War II, recorded the anticipation as paratroopers prepared to board a C-47 destined for France. Barr broadcast his first report for the BBC using the new midget recorder as the 101st Airborne Division prepared for takeoff. 'Men were blacking up their faces and tearing up pictures and letters from their wives so that there would be no identification. Their faces were darkened with cocoa; sheathed knives were strapped to their ankles; Tommy guns strapped to their waists; bandoliers and hand grenades, coils of rope, pick handles, spades, rubber dinghies hung around them and a few personal oddments, like the lad who was taking a newspaper to read on the plane. US paratroopers, heavily armed, sit inside a military plane as they soar over the English Channel en route to the Normandy French coast for the Allied D-Day invasion I watched them march in a long, snaking, double line, almost a mile long to draw their parachutes. Later I saw them gathered around their C-47s and making final adjustments to their kit, before they started. There was an easy familiar touch about the way they were getting ready, as though they had done it often before. Well, yes, they had kitted up and climbed aboard often just like this - twenty, thirty, forty times some of them, but it had never been quite like this before. This was the first combat jump for every one of them.'

---

26 *Put On Your Boots and Parachutes!; The United States 82nd Airborne Division* written and edited by Deryk Wills (self-published, March 1992).

Next day Barr was on 'Juno' Beach, having crossed the Channel, again reporting for the BBC's new nightly *War Report* programme.

The loading, take-off and assembly of the troop carrier serials in 'Albany' was accomplished as the 101st Division later reported with 'notable efficiency.' This was the well-earned result of the many months spent in planning, training and preparation of equipment. It is true that both troops and aircraft were loaded to the limit. Some paratroops were loaded to the limit. Some paratroops when fully laden weighed as much as 325lbs and had to be boosted aboard their aircraft much as 14th century knights were hoisted onto their horses. Partly as a result of this individual overloading some aircraft contained more than the 5,850lbs prescribed in the field orders as the maximum. Also, several carried more than eighteen paratroopers, although this was considered the maximum for a good drop from a C-47. These overloads, generally slight, did not hinder the flight of the aircraft but may have created some delay and confusion in the drops.

The last of the 81 C-47s which would fly the lead serials from Greenham Common to Normandy were warming up their engines as Chaplain Lusher finished his rounds. 'On my way around, I met General 'Ike' Eisenhower, who visited during the afternoon, quietly passing among the men and chatting with them, asking their names and their homes and their jobs.'

Lieutenant Marvin Litke, one of a number of pilots in the 71st Squadron in the 434th Troop Carrier Group sent to Greenham Common to fly with the 438th on 'D-Day' recalled that 'General Eisenhower drove onto the field just before the loading process started. He walked among the troopers and crews with a greeting or a question. I at last felt that we must be doing something important for him to show up. After the troops were loaded a printed message from Eisenhower was read to the troopers on board. I always remembered the starting sentence: 'Soldiers, Sailors and Airmen, you are about to embark on a great crusade...'[27]

Chaplain Lusher was visiting the 88th crews in their enclosure area when news of the big event came. 'Major Gates, the CO came by and shook the hand of each man that was to fly and told them to get ready. Within five minutes they were out the door and heading toward the planes. My heart went with them for I knew the heart of each man and the confusion of courage and fears that had accumulated since we first landed in England. I spoke to them singly and in groups. There weren't many words, just a clasp of hands and a deep look into each other's eyes. I could only promise

---

27 *Flying With The 71st Troop Carrier Squadron, 434th Troop Carrier Group*, an autobiography by Marvin Litke.

to pray. The 89th Squadron was only a few yards away, but the pilots were already gone by the time I reached their area. Most of the crews were still about the barracks so I had a word with them. I found the men of the 90th Squadron still putting on their impregnated clothing and making final preparations. I shook every man's hand as they left their 'Concentration camp' and felt the extra grip that gave me a better understanding of my men than I had before. Captain Pawloski, the CO, gave me a jeep lift to the line for most everyone was there by now. He tried to sing *My Wild Irish Rose* but soon apologized saying, 'It isn't good, but it is loud.'

'I had not yet spoken to the crews of the 87th Squadron so I set out for their area. Paratroopers were about each plane inspecting their chutes or resting on the ground because of their heavy equipment. One said, 'Chaplain, here is the latest version of an army mule.' A few paratroopers were veterans of the earlier Mediterranean battles, but most of these men had never before made a combat jump. Here they were now with faces painted with chocolate, helmets camouflaged and a mountain of equipment. Here they stood ready to do the things for which they had trained for months. Most of these boys had never killed a man and I shuddered to think of the thoughts that must be in their minds. Frankly, I didn't know what to say for my gospel is of Jesus, Prince of Peace. I wondered what I could do here and still wonder, but I kept on. Most of the fellows were resting under the wings of the planes, smoking a cigarette and trying to be as comfortable as possible.

'I made my way from plane to plane. Inside the planes, I went down the long line of paratroopers as they sat inside the ship. I tried to touch their hand and often a pat on the head. I missed one lad and he seriously said, 'Chaplain, lay your hand on my head.' I did it too and no one laughed. The grip of my crews and pilots were especially long and hard. To them I said, 'I can't run your ship, but I will pray.' Their response was an emotional, 'Thanks, chaplain' or 'Thanks for coming.'

'Around 2130 air crews began warming up the planes down on the line' wrote John Hanscom. 'A tremendous racket and effusion of dust ensued.'

'As they moved toward the airfield proper' wrote Chaplain Lusher 'they passed long columns of airborne troops, trudging slowly under their full loads of battle equipment from the bivouac area where they had been camped awaiting this day, toward the planes which would carry them into battle. It was 12:10pm when Lieutenant Colonel Donalson commanding officer of the 438th Troop Carrier Group and Lieutenant Colonel David E. Daniel; commander of the 87th Squadron pulled the lead ship out of the parking area. Soon they would be pushing the jump button on their plane and the invasion of Europe would be on. In that ship was Chaplain Hall and the leaders of the 101st. After the lead ship came then others and soon all were in take-off position.'

Lieutenant Colonel John Munnerlyn 'Snake' Donalson was a Georgia Institute of Technology graduate and engineer with Tennessee Coal and Iron in Birmingham, Alabama. He joined the National Guard in Alabama as an observation pilot trainee and graduated in Flight School in Texas with Charles Lindberg in 1925. After he became Commander of a National Guard unit in 1939 he was activated for regular service and became a Base Commander of several USAAF bases before going to England. Ordinarily, Donalson would have flown the *Belle of Birmingham* in which to lead his Group but he had not wanted holes cut in the underside of the aircraft required for equipment that would follow the pathfinder's signals, so he had been assigned a new C-47, 42-92847, now better known as *That's All Brother,* which was his message to Hitler that with the invasion, his plans were done. In other words; 'That's all, brother.' Daniel had his little Scottie dog sitting on a flak suit beside him when at 2230 sharp *That's All Brother*, towing a glider carrying men of the 82nd Airborne Division, began to ease down the runway.

'One by one eighty C-47s laden with their precious cargoes of human destroyers followed Donalson's ship' wrote John Hanscom. 'They were all pulling well over forty inches of mercury on that long take-off and the resulting din was terrific. In that shadowy rather overcast sky, which was not yet entirely steeped in night, the long caravan of planes began to circle widely about the field, continuing thus until the formation was complete. At last it headed south and disappeared into the gloom.'

The 438th Group got their aircraft in the air between 2232 and 2256; an average of eighteen seconds per aircraft. When the last ship was airborne, Chaplain Lusher knelt there on the runway asking God for their safety. 'Sergeant Long, Colonel Daniel's driver, waited for me and drove me back to the chapel where a number of us had decided to meet for prayer. Before going into the chapel door, I stood watching the mass of red and green lights form in perfect formation and then head toward the southwest for the 53rd Wing rendezvous point. When the lights had faded into the distance, we went into the chapel together. We prayed for God's help and protection for the men in those 81 planes and also for millions of men in air, land and sea combat units that were at the crisis of life in this very hour. We prayed for our enemies, too and asked that God might cause wars to cease unto the ends of the earth. Oh, that mercy and forgiveness might be granted unto ALL his children.'

Five days' earlier Lieutenant Orlando H. 'Bill' Allin, pilot of *Drag-em-Oot* in the 87th Troop Carrier Squadron had celebrated his 22nd birthday. His C-47A (42-100882) was the third of a three-plane flight and he was carrying a stick of eighteen paratroopers. The C-47A had acquired its nickname from an expression Allin's maternal grandmother used to say. She was from Winnipeg and the Sault St. Marie areas of Canada before moving to the United States. On the first of two missions *Drag-em-Oot* would drop eighteen paratroops of the 82nd Airborne Division near Sainte-Mère-Église and would then be used in re-supply missions as well as bringing out the wounded troops. Allin delivered five gallon cans of gasoline top France for Patton's tanks and one time Patton thanked him with a case of champagne and cognac.

William Bryan, the NBC radio stringer would fly in *Snooty* in the 87th TCS, piloted by Lieutenant John E. Peters of Chicago and co-pilot, Lieutenant Bertrum Clare Maxwell of Clare, Michigan. Bryan wrote: 'In the navigator's dome and on the flight deck of a C-47 I would ride across the English Channel with the first group of planes from the Troop Carrier Command to take our fighting men into Europe.

'Outside the door of each C-47 the soldiers assembled and checked their equipment, while ground crews gave their planes a final tuning up.

'As the first squadron [87th] commanded by Lieutenant Colonel David Daniel of Birmingham, Alabama began to take off, the planes rushing in swift succession down the runway, Lieutenant General Lewis H. Brereton, Ninth Air Force commander, moved up and down the line of planes, giving the thumbs-up sign to his crews.

'Meantime the paratroopers had adjusted their packs, donned their Mae Wests and chutes and climbed into the plane. Each was so heavily loaded that he had to be pushed from behind and pulled from above to get up the steps into the plane.

'In our plane Lieutenant Colonel Robert Cole of San Antonio, Texas was the senior officer aboard.' The 39-year old commanding the 3rd Battalion of the 502nd Parachute Infantry Regiment was born at Fort Sam Houston, in San Antonio, Texas, to Colonel Clarence F. Cole, an Army doctor and Clara H. Cole on 18 March 1915. He graduated from Thomas Jefferson High School in San Antonio in 1933 and joined the United States Army on 1 July 1934. On 26 June 1935, he was honourably discharged to accept an appointment to the United States Military Academy at West Point. He earned his jump wings in 1941 and rapidly advancing through the ranks at Fort Benning as the parachute infantry battalions were expanded to regiments he was a lieutenant colonel commanding the 3rd Battalion of the 502nd Parachute Infantry Regiment on 6 June, the date of his unit's first combat jump. 'He moved quietly up and down the passenger compartment' wrote William Bryan 'speaking to each man and asking if he had everything he needed. As the men settled in their bucket seats, Colonel Cole said: 'This doc is going to give you some pills to guard against airsickness. Make yourselves as comfortable as you can. Better try to sleep a little.'

The eighteen men in Cole's stick included his radio operator Joseph L. 'Lofty' Lofthouse and his aide, Captain Cleveland R. Fitzgerald, who wrapped Cole's Colt with tape so he would not lose it during the jump. Fitzgerald was WIA on 'D-Day' and went missing for about two weeks and Cole thought he was dead. Fitzgerald ended up fighting with members of the 82nd for the first week in Normandy when he rejoined the 'Deuce' and the XO, Major John Stopka quite unfairly greeted him by asking 'What barn have you been hiding in?'

'The soldier sitting farthest forward on the port side, Private Robert C. Hillman of Manchester, Connecticut said, 'I know my chute's OK because my mother checked it. She works in the Pioneer Parachute Company in our town and her job is giving the final once-over to all the chutes they manufacture.'

'On the flight deck of our plane, the '*Snooty*', Lieutenant John Peters and Lieutenant Maxwell muttered soft curses as their motors were slow to start after a long pause on the taxi strip. But when the engines did turn over, they droned steadily and powerfully. Almost before we knew it, we were trundling along past the operations building and the control tower where all the ground personnel of the base were standing, some held thumbs up. Some made the V-sign. Some waved. It was like the take-off of a big mission from a bomber station - only more so. This was the first combat mission for this outfit and everyone on the base now knew this was the day.

'Our ship was leading the second section of the second squadron in the first group. As we picked up speed down the long runway, I stood between the pilot and co-pilot and watched the formation lights of the ships ahead of us, almost imperceptibly climbing and then gradually swinging into wide circles.'

To achieve surprise, the parachute drops were routed to approach Normandy at low altitude from the west. The serials took off beginning at 2230 on 5 June, assembled into formations and flew southwest over the English Channel at 500 feet MSL to remain below German radar coverage. Once over water all lights except formation lights were turned off and these were reduced to their lowest practical intensity. German forces opposing the missions included the 3rd Battalion 1058th Grenadier Regiment (91st Air Landing Division) in the vicinity of Sainte-Côme-du-Mont, the 919th Grenadier Regiment (709th Infantry Division) behind 'Utah' Beach, the 191st Artillery Regiment (105mm mountain howitzer, 91st Air Landing Division) and the 6th Parachute Regiment, sent to Carentan during 'D-Day'.

Aircraft take offs averaged intervals of ten seconds apiece. Such speed was made possible by high proficiency and the excellence of the RAF airfields. Assembly, never an easy matter at night, was handled with equal success. All serials spiralled into formation over their home fields and swung onto course over the Command Assembly Point 'Elko' at approximately the prescribed six-minute intervals. The weather over England was then in process of changing and varied from hour to hour and from base to base. The wind ranged from ten to 30 mph from the north and west. Cloudiness ran the gamut from none to 10/10, the overcast, fortunately, being above 4,000 feet. However, over the Channel the sky was generally clear and visibility excellent. As one pilot put it 'It was a beautiful night. You could fly formation by moonlight. Under these conditions navigation was easy as far as 'Hoboken'. Apparently all the serials in 'Albany' approached Normandy on course and in good formation. Almost all were four or five minutes ahead of schedule, probably because of the wind, but the condition was so general that they kept their relative positions and did not overrun each other.

The coastline at the IP was visible, but immediately beyond it the mission ran into an unforeseen obstacle which disrupted its formations and very nearly caused it to fail. This was the cloudbank already encountered by the pathfinders. It extended solidly for ten or twelve miles inland, becoming progressively thinner and more broken between the centre of the peninsula and the east coast. Near the IP the base of this layer was at an altitude of 1,100 feet and its top at about 2,000 feet. With any sort of warning the troop carriers could have flown over or under it, but no provision for such a warning had been made and radio silence was in effect. Thus the pilots, flying at 1,500 feet as prescribed, did not know of the overcast until it loomed up close ahead and most of the formations plunged into the heart of it.

The four lead serials had the easiest approach of any. They reported light, scattered clouds over Normandy but apparently had little trouble keeping clear of them. They had greater difficulty with a ground fog which limited visibility in the drop area to about three miles. Moreover, they achieved a degree of surprise which gave them substantial protection from the enemy. The lead flight reached the drop area without being under fire; the second was near Sainte-Mère-Église when first shot at; and all the rest of the 438th was several miles inland before the enemy went into action. The serials of the 436th came under fire soon after landfall, but it was inaccurate, sporadic and mostly from small arms. So feeble was the opposition that the two groups lost no aircraft, suffered no serious damage and had no casualties. In the 438th Group five or six aircraft received slight damage, mostly bullet holes and eleven in the 436th had similar damage.

Of 1,430 troops carried in the first two serials all jumped but one man who had been stunned by a fall, as William Bryan on *Sooty* confirmed in his report. 'Are you all set?' asked the colonel. 'Get this thing hooked for me' he said as he took his own place closest the door. The jump lights, as small bank of signal lamps, were gleaming beside the door. They blinked as the pilot threw his switch and before I could look up they began jumping. I wanted to know how long it would take the eighteen men to jump. I tried to count; 'one hundred and one-one hundred and two-one hundred and three' to estimate the number of seconds. Before I had counted to ten seconds - it may have been eleven or twelve but no more - our passengers had left us, all but one of them.

'I watched from the rear door of the *Sooty* - as seventeen American paratroopers, led by Lieutenant Colonel Cole, jumped with their arms, ammunition and equipment into the night of German-occupied France. Our Group, at the head of the leading wing from US Ninth Air Force's Troop Carrier Command, was met with only scattering small-arms fire from the fields which were dark and quiet as we entered enemy territory. The paratroopers shoved each other so swiftly and heavily toward the open door that they jolted against the door frame. One man among the last half-dozen hit the rear side of the door so heavily that he was thrown into the back cabin and dazed. The men behind shoved him aside and sent on jumping. Before the unhappy soldier could get to his feet, our place was well past the drop zone and in a matter of minutes it was back over the water and setting course for home. It was not too late and that soldier had to return with us. He was inconsolable. He thought his comrades might think him yellow. The plane crew assured him that they would think no such thing, but he sat moody and glum all the way back.

'As soon as I had watched the jumps, I ran back to the front of the ship and looked straight from the glass dome. The streams of tracer bullets were curving upward from the ground but they were well behind us. One of the pilots in our squadron had unwittingly left on his formation lights and the tracers came closest to his wing tips. But we saw nothing that looked like heavy ack-ack except in the far distance. Our course had been well plotted and navigated to avoid the known German batteries.

'We were over France only eleven minutes. With our ships lightened by unloading their cargo we picked up speed and streaked for home. Behind us we could still see the tracers and an occasional flare, below as few more ships but we couldn't tell just what they were.

'As we headed back toward the English coast we saw tracers arching through the air behind us and a steady parade of Allied planes moving out, over the course we had just navigated, to strengthen the ground forces we had left below. In the Channel under us we could see a few ships but could not be certain whether they were part of the armada carrying Allied soldiers to the beaches for attacks which were quickly following the first landings of airborne troops I had witnessed.

'The Battle of Europe had begun and our squadron had delivered the first Allied foot soldiers to their scene of action.'

William Bryan became the first newsman to give a report on the 'D-Day' invasion. He went on the air in London and made his broadcast immediately after a one-sentence announcement by the Allied command and tape-recorded statements by King George VI and President Franklin D. Roosevelt. Later that same day Bryan returned over Normandy with the C-47s that carried the gliders. While covering the Allies' further advance across Europe on 12 September, Bryan was wounded and captured by the Germans and spent six months in hospitals and spent the rest of the war in Oflag 64 in Szubin, Poland. He was freed by Soviet troops in January 1945.

Lieutenant Marvin Litke's takeoff had been routine. 'The aircraft were carrying max loads and were a bit more sluggish than usual but we had plenty of runway and there were no problems. As far as the 71st was concerned there were no aborts. Although we had done this a hundred times and where pretty relaxed the flight was one of the smoothest night formations that I had ever flown. The fact that this one was for real seemed to make every one extra sharp. Although we were the tail in element there was practically no stacking and, therefore, little or no prop wash to fight. The weather was clear with little wind and no natural conditions to worry about. As we passed the Channel Islands we could see flak coming up at something that was much closer then we were.

'The moon was bright and I could see the coastline from a good distance out. This caused a big problem when we hit the shoreline. There was a huge thermal cumulus cloud bank that started just below our altitude and extended much higher than I could see. The fact that, at a distance, we could see under the cloud bank made the sudden entry into the clouds something that we could not prepare for. One moment we saw the lead aircraft against the background of the clouds and then he disappeared and we were in the soup. We had an SOP for taking a formation through a cloud formation but this was unexpected and unplanned for. The cloud was not very extensive and we broke through in about 45 seconds: But, the natural reflex to turn away from the flight direction to prevent mid air collision caused the formation to break up.

'Later, Troop Carrier was later accused of not having the experience to carry out such a mission the fact was that it was only through superior flying on the part of all of those involved that resulted in zero collisions and the dropping of all of the paratroopers, even if some were a great distance from their drop zones. When we broke out of the clouds I could see the moon reflected from a large area of water. This was further confusing as there was no such body of water on our briefing maps. It was later found that recon of the area was done during daylight hours and the water could not be seen through the thick growth that covered the area. Tragically, many troopers drowned when dropped into this area. The water was not very deep but the equipment that each trooper carried made it almost impossible to get to his feet after landing in the water. I am sure that I got beyond the flooded fields before giving the green light but I can never be sure exactly where I did drop.

'The anti aircraft fire was pretty heavy after breaking into the clear. At night every tracer round looked like it was coming directly at you. We got back to the coast without being hit. I saw no other aircraft going back to Aldermaston. I did see large amounts of flak being fired from the Channel Islands at the serials coming in. We landed safely at our regular base and reported for briefing. The rest of the 434th Group was then in route with the group's first glider tow. We had not lost any aircraft from the element at Greenham Common. The aircraft that I usually flew was equipped with a glider 'snatch' system. This required a large housing for the winch just in front of the jump door so it could not carry troopers. For this reason I switched aircraft with another crew for the paratroop. This crew were shot down on the first glider tow mission and all were killed. It seemed that all or most of the crew had bailed out and captured. It was reported later that they were killed by allied fighter bombers as they were marched off to a prison camp.'[28]

---

28 *Flying With The 71st Troop Carrier Squadron, 434th Troop Carrier Group*, an autobiography by Marvin Litke.

Second Lieutenant Roger Airgood in the 436th TCG formation recalled: 'The pilot flying on Kreyssler's left wing turned off the formation lights so low they were not visible. At that time Hayes could see nothing of Kreyssler's wing man from the left seat, so I flew from the right seat since I could see the exhaust stack glow and the phantom outline of the plane. We maintained our position flying as tight a formation as possible.

'When entering an unexpected cloud bank we continued on without any appreciable differences in visibility. We maintained the course and when coming out of the cloud bank we could see tracers coming up from many angles. The lines of tracers arched over us as we flew under them. There was a tremendous racket such as experienced when flying through hail.

'I had very few glimpses of the ground since I had to keep the outline of the plane in sight. It was standard procedure for the serial leader to show red or green lights from the astrodome so that all pilots would signal the jump masters. It was done this way so that all the troopers would jump in unison. Shortly after getting the four minute red warning light (stand up and hook up) I got a glimpse of a steeple of a church about half a mile ahead and off to the right about a quarter of a mile. Assuming this to be Sainte-Mère-Église, I felt we were on course and that DZ 'A' lay straight ahead. (Much later, I learned there are at least seven steeples in the eastern part of Normandy). There seemed to be a delay in slowing down to the jump speed at 110 mph. When Kreyssler did slow down it was too fast. Wingmen had to cut power and hold the nose up to keep from over-running the lead planes, which in turn was followed by a blast of power to keep the plane from stalling out. The net result was that when we got the green light, we were flying about 105 mph and pulling a lot of power. The paratroopers went out in a terrific prop blast, which was the last thing we wanted to happen. We dropped our troopers at 0102 on 6 June. As soon as the paratroopers were out, Kreyssler dived down to get down to 100 feet. Before I could follow in the dive the lead flight was out of sight.'

C-47 pilot Don Skrdla in the 81st TCS, 436th TCG recalled: 'After we were in those clouds a few minutes some bright searchlights came on; the way they lighted up the clouds almost blinded me. Flak and tracers were everywhere. One of our squadron's planes was taking such wild evasive action that he almost drove me into the ground. And that so-and-so wasn't even part of my flight - which shows how big a piece of sky he was using up! It took every bit of my strength and know-how, plus that of our co-pilot, Doug Mauldin, to prevent a collision.'

Sergeant 'Marty' Wolfe in the 81st TCS wrote: 'Our first troop carrier planes, undetected even by radar until they arrived, were able to follow the moving band of partially clearing weather right across from southern England into Normandy. As we turned southwest from our corridor over the Channel and toward Normandy, the feeling grew that this monstrously complicated operation was clicking along perfectly. This feeling was strengthened when we saw that the anti-aircraft fire from the German-held Channel Islands (Guernsey and Jersey) was short, as we had been told it would be. A few minutes later, as we reached the western coastline, disaster loomed up at us; we slammed headlong into a dense cloudbank. Nothing had prepared us for this. The weather briefing had not foreseen it; our flight over the English Channel had encountered only scattered clouds. The cloudbank was thicker in some spots than others. For some of us it was so thick that it was as if we had stopped flying through the air and were now flying through a greyish soup. The pathfinders had also flown through these clouds, but because of the orders for strict radio silence, they had not warned anyone of this terrible danger.

'Flying in almost zero visibility, wing tip to wing tip, at the assigned altitude of 700 feet and level at 110 mph, the pilots suddenly had to decide how to save their crews, the paratroopers and the planes. Immediately, pilots flying in the number two and three positions in each V pulled away, back, right or left to minimize the imminent danger of colliding with their leader. Some pilots climbed, getting out of the cloudbank at about 2000 feet and some pushed their planes' noses down and broke out of the clouds at around 500 feet. A few bulled their way through at 700 feet, the altitude they had been flying before hitting the clouds. All miraculously escaped smashing into other planes. In a few tragic moments, without the discipline and control of the formation, the prospects for a concentrated paratrooper drop had been demolished. Meanwhile, our drop zones were coming up in ten or twelve minutes.

'A terrible responsibility now fell upon the shoulders of every pilot and every navigator (in planes that had them). The murderous cloudbank thinned out as we flew east over the Cotentin peninsula - and soon we could begin to see some features on the ground. Each pilot knew that in the preceding formation breakup he could have strayed many miles off course. The Cotentin peninsula is only 23 miles wide and we had about six or seven minutes left before our Drop Zone was to come up. Decisions had to be made quickly. Each pilot - now essentially on his own - had to climb (or descend) to 700 feet, the best height for the paratroopers to jump from;

and he had to slow down to 100/110 mph to avoid too much stress on the parachutes.

'Looking down you could begin to spot a few landmarks - a town, a railroad and a river - that might or might not correspond to the checkpoints we were briefed to look for around our Drop Zone 'A'. As if things were not bad enough we now saw that the 'Eureka-Rebecca' radar beacon system was not fully in place to guide our flight leader to the correct DZ. Crews of the few planes that had the more sophisticated 'Gee' radar location device didn't find them useful under these conditions. The pathfinders had also been hampered by the fog and had been unable to find the right locations to set up their holophane 'T' lights and radar beacons. All that remained for most of the pilots and navigators was to try to recognize some landmarks in the darkness and give troopers the green light when there was a reasonable chance of their jumping close to our Drop Zone.

'Arriving in Normandy, roughly 24,000 paratroopers began parachuting into the darkness - taking incredibly high-risk jumps. Upon reaching the coastline, it was zero visibility. Suddenly they were under attack. The C-47 transports hit were heading down - men anxious to jump to evade the crossfire, even if the enemy waited below. Watching the tracers come up at them made the hairs on the back of Crew Chief 'Bob' Obermark's neck feel as though they were standing up and it's still hard to laugh about things like that. These things are stamped indelibly in my mind: the rattle of flak fragments against our plane; the sight of flak and tracers above us, some seeming right on the mark for planes in front of us; the stark terror in some paratroopers' eyes, their vomiting into their helmets and forgetting to empty these helmets when it came time to make possibly their final jump. The red light at the door was on - four minutes to go! The paratrooper jumpmaster yelled out 'Stand up! Hook up! Sound off for equipment check!' The troopers yelled back in sequence from the rear; 'Sixteen, OK! Fifteen OK! Fourteen, OK'. Then the jumpmaster screamed out, 'Stand in the Door'! And the troopers squeezed forward against each other, their right hands on the shoulders of the man in front. One last jump master yell: 'Are we ready? Are we fucking-a ready!'? There was no answering yell; everybody was waiting for the door light to change from red to green.

'When the pilots finally snapped on the green light it must have been a kind of momentary relief to the paratroopers, as they went out the jump door, heading for uncertain but presumably solid ground beneath. American paratroopers were some of the most Gung-Ho soldiers we had. They were convinced they could lick any bunch of 'Lousy Krauts' with one hand tied behind their backs. No one thought much about this at the time, but the troopers were left literally and figuratively in the dark during the flights. There was very little information to go on from that time on. Many of the airborne troops were purposely kept in a supercharged state of physical and emotional awareness. They were a tough bunch - not to be messed with. All they wanted to do was to jump and fight Germans.

'Mercifully, up to this point the paratroopers had no way of knowing we were in big trouble. But now pilots in some planes, already badly rattled by the loss of formation control, began to see flak and small arms fire coming up at them. They dived and twisted under the upcoming arcs of tracer bullets while the heavily laden troopers struggled to stay on their feet. Some planes whipped around badly, forcing troopers down on their knees. Barf buckets were knocked over and vomit spilled out, causing a dangerously slippery floor. Crew chiefs and radio operators in the rear screamed at the pilots to keep the planes steady.'

The instant before the lead trooper jumped, the heavy door bundles had to be pushed out. In the C-47 piloted by Don Skrdla the awkward bundles jammed the door space with fiendish perversity, thwarting every effort of the crew and the troopers to push them out. There would have been no time for Skrdla to have dropped his troopers short of the English Channel. He flew out over the water, turned right, came back over land again and made another pass at his DZ - but the door bundles were still malevolently stuck. Skrdla had to make yet a third pass before the bundles could be un-jammed and his troopers could get out. For this exhibition of skill and cool judgment he was awarded the DFC; the only one granted to his Squadron. Asked what was going through his mind at that time, Skrdla said, 'Nothing much, apart from how scared I was' and he claimed much of the credit should go to the crew chief, 'Dick' Nice, the one who managed to un-jam that door. Pressed further, Skrdla added, 'It just wasn't in the book for me to go back with paratroopers in my plane.' After his plane was headed home over the Channel, Skrdla got a shock when he looked back and saw one of his passengers still sitting there, but it turned out he was not a paratrooper but a newspaper reporter who had no intention of jumping.

The pathfinder troops allotted to DZ 'A' had been unable to get their beacons in operation in time for the arrival of the first serial of the 438th Group, so Colonel Donalson made his approach and dropped on 'Gee'. His passengers jumped at 0048, two minutes ahead of time, from the prescribed altitude. By 0058 the Group had completed its drop, although several aircraft had had to circle back for a second pass. The 2nd Battalion, 502nd PIR was dropped as a compact unit but most of the seventy of eighty groups dropped in a disorganized pattern around the impromptu drop zone set up by the pathfinders near the beach. The commander, the taciturn Lieutenant Colonel 'Silent Steve' A. Chappuis, came down virtually alone on the correct drop zone. He and his stick captured the coastal battery soon after assembling and found that it had already been dismantled after an air raid.[29] The second serial of the 438th carrying the 3rd Battalion of the 502nd PIR commanded by Lieutenant Colonel Patrick J. 'Hopalong' Cassidy was more accurate than its predecessor, but seems to have flown a rather loose formation. Its leader dropped members of the 3rd Battalion near the south side of DZ 'A', but none of his flight dropped with him. He may have relied on 'Gee', while the others homed on the 'Eureka' near Sainte-Germain. Thirty-six of the pilots put their sticks in an area about four miles long from west to east and about two miles wide, with the pathfinder aids at its centre. Three others, including the leader, dropped within two miles of the zone; five impatient pilots dumped their men three or four miles short of the DZ and one stick went unaccounted for.

Cassidy's Battalion was the only one in the 101st to come down on target, landing near the pathfinder beacons outside Sainte-Germain and that through blind luck. He and Lieutenant Colonel Cole, undaunted by the confusion, gradually collected whatever men they could find and set off on their missions. Cole and his men secured the two causeways coming inland from 'Utah' Beach. Five days later, moving the 3rd Battalion down the causeway under heavy German fire, Cole ordered a bayonet charge and eventually achieved his objective in time to secure the beach landing of the 4th Infantry Division whose parachute artillery did not fare well, its drop, one of the worst of the operation, had lost all but one howitzer and all but two of 54 loads were dropped four to twenty miles to the north. The assault, which came to be known as 'Cole's Charge,' proved costly; 130 of Cole's 265 men became casualties. At the end of the day Cole's battalion was ordered into regimental reserve. It had accomplished its mission. The brave colonel was nominated for the Medal of Honor[30] but did not live to receive it. On 18 September during Operation 'Market Garden' he was commanding the 3rd Battalion

29 Chappuis was awarded the DSC.
30 His XO, Major John Stopka, was nominated for the DSC.

of the 502nd PIR in the Dutch town of Best. Colonel Cole got on the radio. A pilot asked him to put some orange identification panels in front of his position. Cole decided to do it himself. For a moment, he raised his head, shielding his eyes to see the plane. Suddenly a shot was fired by a German sniper in a farmhouse only 300 yards away, killing Cole instantly. Two weeks later he was awarded the Medal of Honor for his bayonet charge near Carentan on 11 June.[31]

About the time the second serial of the 438th TCG had reached the drop area the pathfinders got a 'Eureka' beacon and amber 'T' into operation near Sainte-Germaine-de-Varreville, a mile north of the zone. The 436th Group carrying 1,084 men and twelve guns obtained responses from the 'Eureka' at a point ten miles away, probably at the moment the set was switched on. Some pilots also sighted the amber 'T'. Several pilots had to make extra passes and one made three to get all his troops out; a bundle had stuck in the door on his first run. 'Everything was working fine as scheduled' wrote Second Lieutenant Roger Airgood 'until we got to the last light boat at which time we were to turn off the amber down light and reduce the formation lights to half power. The formation lights (shielded blue lights on top of the fuselage and wings) were controlled by a rheostat - there was no half power position.

The 436th dropped all but two or three injured men and one who refused to jump. Being busy Roger Airgood had not seen the beach after leaving the DZ. 'Navigator Norbert Milczewski told Hayes when three minutes were up to turn again. We checked frequently to see if our wingmen were still in position. 'Hank' and Butz were on our right wing and Camp and Shurman on the left. They stayed with us all the way to Membury. We had another ticklish problem also. When the troopers had jumped we had a strong stench of gasoline in the cockpit and cabin. When I lost sight of the lead flight, Len Hayes took control, descended and turned to the new heading. I checked the gas tanks and found the main tank we were using for the right engine indicated empty. I switched to the auxiliary tank even though the engine was still running.

'The trip home was uneventful even though no one dared smoke in this potentially dangerous situation. Coming back across the Channel at 3,000 feet, planes and gliders at 500 feet lit up a continuous column going into Normandy. I didn't envy those glider pilots having to fly and land in the

---

31 Major John Stopka succeeded Lieutenant Colonel Robert G. Cole as Battalion commander after Cole's death in Holland. Stopka was killed on 14 January 1945 west of Bourcy, Belgium by a misplaced 500lb bomb dropped by a P-47.

dark. When we landed at Membury, Hayes turned off into the first available hardstand and very cautiously shut down the engines. When Hayes and I alighted, 'Norb' Milczewski, Hoyt Rose and 'Tom' Anderson were already standing about 100 feet away in the grass. Gasoline was running out of the tail and the moisture drain holes along the leading edge of the wing. Later it was found that a 30-calibre slug had punctured the tank and lodged in the float. The hole in the tank was the only hit we had.'[32]

William M. 'Rip' Collins was co-pilot in an 81st TCS, 436th TCG C-47 piloted by Jack Wallen. Collins, born 11 August 1925 in Youngstown and a 1942 graduate of South High School, recalled: 'After the drop, we had some bad moments. Of course by then we were all alone. Out over the Channel, I called 'Hello Darky' to get a steer home. The fix they gave me didn't seem right but I figured they knew what they were doing. I made about a 180-degree turn; but pretty soon I saw all those lights and gun flashes and I saw that I was damned near over Cherbourg again! So then I turned around and headed back home. By the time I got in, they'd given us up for lost.' We began to yell and thump each other on the back as soon as the wheels touched the runway at Membury. The release from that frightful tension made us all a little giddy. Crews walked in a glow across the field toward the Operations room. One plane after another came in; most with little damage. When the last plane's wheels touched down, about 0400 June 6, the crews all broke out in crazy yells and whistles. For this, our first combat mission and a terribly dangerous one - we had sent out eighteen planes and returned eighteen planes. The contrast between what we had been led to expect in the way of 'expendability' and what actually happened for this mission was stupefying.

'We got boisterous, almost hysterical, congratulations from the men who had been waiting for our return. While we were being debriefed we were given a medicinal double shot of rye by Jesse Coleman, our Flight Surgeon, plus the usual post-flight coffee and sandwiches. Later we all trooped over to the Group theatre for a critique by Colonel Williams. He told us that none of the Group's ninety planes had been shot down, though three planes had been hard hit by bullets or flak. Colonel Williams told us he was proud of us. Who could blame us for thinking that the first D-Day mission had been a great success?'

---

32 Roger Airgood missed the 'Market-Garden' operation because of an attack of Malaria. In 'Varsity', the crossing of the Rhine in March 1945 he completed a double glider-tow in the C-47.

At Greenham Common at 0130 hours Chaplain Lusher returned to the line. 'The fellows were quite sober about everything for our buddies were giving their lives at this very hour. The pilots who were extras on the mission and were scheduled to fly later in the day were especially nervous. I wanted to be alone, so Sergeant Long drove me to the medical tents - my official station in battle. One of the ground officers and I talked about God, faith and home. We never mentioned hate or killing for God seemed the only thing - Person, I should say - that seemed worth talking about.

'Long strings of planes were constantly flying toward the East. I was praying for those men, too, but our eyes were glued to the southwest straining to see a formation of lights coming our way. Finally, at about 0215 - even before they were due - formation lights appeared in the right place. Over the field they came and the leader 'peeled off' for a landing. Major Harrity and I counted them - the first element of nine was there, the second, etc. In fact 82 ships came back and not one fired a red flare on the final approach to signal wounded were aboard. When I counted the extra ship, I thought God had performed a sure 'nuff miracle'. He answered our prayers beyond our request.'

'If our previous nights had been sleepless, they were as nothing compared with this' wrote Flight Officer John Hanscom, one of many anxiously awaiting the return of the power pilots both for their safety and for their reports of action.'

'Never have I seen such a jubilant bunch of men!' wrote Chaplain Lusher. 'Now they had completed their first combat mission. Most could not hold back tears as they said, 'God was with us tonight, Chaplain.' Others said; 'God was my co-pilot, He was our Command Pilot.' 'I never prayed more seriously in my life' and 'God was good with us tonight.' It was a rowdy gang in the mess hall afterward for we all acted like a bunch of kids and I was the worst of the bunch.

'Then to the chapel to thank God for the completion of a perfect mission and ask His care for our paratrooper friends and the boys who were to follow. I prayed for the folks at home also for I knew how the invasion news would affect them. Every parent and wife would feel their loved one was facing death - and many were dying! O that the God of all comfort would be near each one of them.

'It was now 0440 and so to bed.'

About four in the morning several of the power pilots piled into John Hanscom's hut 'brimming with excitement and eagerness to relate their adventures.' 'We were overjoyed to see them' says Hanscom. 'According to their witness the flak had been light, no enemy aircraft had been encountered, all sticks of paratroopers had been discharged successfully and not a plane or a man had been lost. It had been a milk run! Excitement and joy unbounded reigned throughout our camp that night.'

The 436th and the 438th Groups reported their drops as 'ranging from good to excellent' and unit histories, written three weeks later, reiterate assertions that the drops were both accurate and compact.' The diarist of the 82nd TCS wrote. 'The mission was successful - all planes dropped on or near the 'T' and there was very little opposition - some small arms fire and almost no flak.' The diarist for the 79th TCS stated, 'On this mission all planes discharged their troopers over or at least very near the appointed 'DZ' and returned without loss of either personnel or aircraft. It wasn't until much later, when we heard rumours of complaints from paratroopers dropped far from their assigned DZ that we began to question our performance.'

Actually, none of the four serials had done very well and one had done very badly. Colonel Donalson's lead serial which carried the 1st Battalion of the 502nd PIR to DZ 'A' had dropped them compactly but inaccurately. Through some maladjustment or misinterpretation of his 'Gee' set, Donalson gave his troops the green light on the far edge of DZ 'C' and 26 of his pilots in tight formation followed his example. Six others dropped within a mile of this concentration. One straggler in the serial put his load within a mile of DZ 'A'; one dropped five miles northwest of that zone; and one stick was missing. In contrast to this respectable performance was that of the second serial of the 436th, which was supposed to deliver the 377th Parachute Field Artillery and twelve of its guns, a planeload of medics and five aircraft of supplies. All the flights in this formation missed the DZ by a wide margin and all but the first two flights had become badly dispersed before they made their drops. The three or four mile deviation of the lead elements might possibly have resulted from radar misuse or malfunction, but how a majority of the serial, could have dropped north of Montebourg is an enigma. Those two flights followed a line of approach which passed about three miles north of the DZ. The first did drop its troops about three miles away near Sainte-Marcouf, a village near the coastal marshes which might have been mistaken for Sainte-Martin-de-Varreville. The second flight dropped prematurely from five to seven miles northwest of the zone. The last four flights in the serial got thoroughly lost and badly dispersed. Most made a pronounced deviation to the north, with the result that five sticks were dropped beyond Valognes at points between ten and twenty miles northwest of the zone; and 21 loads came down between five and ten miles north of it; and two sticks went unaccounted for. Of the eight sticks which landed within a five-mile radius of the zone, only one was within a mile of it and one other within two miles. If the two pilots delivering them knew approximately where they were, they were the only ones in the serial who did. As a result, only a handful of the men of the 377th Field Artillery Battalion played a significant part in the fighting on 'D-Day' and only one of its twelve guns supported the operations of the 101st Division. Scattered many miles north and west of the drop area, the artillerymen engaged the enemy in innumerable little fights and showed great resourcefulness in regaining the Allied lines, but their actions had at best a nuisance value.

'Between 0400 on 'D-Day' says 'Rip' Collins 'when we in the 81st TCS returned from Operation 'Albany' and 1800 that same day, our aircrews were able to relax'. 'Air Chief Marshal Sir Trafford Leigh-Mallory had ruled that glider missions must never be risked in broad daylight. Therefore our Squadron's second Normandy mission, part of Operation 'Elmira', had to wait until dusk began to settle over 'the longest day'.'

Chapter 6

'Albany' - The Fifth and Sixth Serials

We're fortunate in being Americans. At least we don't step on the underdog. I wonder if that's because there are no 'Americans' - only a stew of immigrants - or if it's because the earth from which we exist has been so kind to us and our forefathers, or if it's because the 'American' is the offspring of the logical European who hated oppression and loved freedom beyond life? Those great mountains and the tall timber; the cool deep lakes and broad rivers; the green valleys and white farmhouses; the air, the sea and wind; the plains and great cities, the smell of living - all must be the cause of it. And yet, with all that, we can't get away from the rest. For every one of our millions who has that treasure in his hand there's another million crying for that victory of life. And for each of us who wants to live in happiness and give happiness, there's another different sort of person wanting to take it away... those people always manage to have their say and Mars is always close at hand. We know how to win wars. We must learn now to win peace... if I ever have a son I don't want him to go through this again, but... I want him powerful enough that no one will be fool enough to touch him. He and America should be strong as hell and kind as Christ.

From a long letter written on 26 May by 22-year old Lieutenant Thomas Meehan III, 'Easy' Company, HQ Section, 506th PIR to his wife Anne in which he described why he and all his men were sitting in the planes, waiting to go into France to liberate it and conquer Nazi Germany.

Upottery in East Devon is a few miles from the little market town of Honiton close to the River Otter, which flows through the Otter valley until it reaches the sea at Budleigh Salterton. In a Nissen hut on the base 1st Lieutenant Gerald 'Bud' Berry, a pilot in the 91st Squadron of the 439th Troop Carrier Group occupied the bed next to his friend, 26-year old 1st Lieutenant Harold Andrew

Capelluto who was from Nassau, New York. 'I flew with him on a number of occasions as he was approved in the technique of the glider snatch as was I. He wanted to enlist in the Army Air Corps but was too young and they would not take him so he went to Canada and enlisted in the RCAF. When the US entered the war after Pearl Harbor, he transferred to the Army Air Corps and was assigned to Troop Carrier. Another pilot, 2nd Lieutenant Cliff Savercool and I were acquaintances only. He was in the squadron when I arrived in March of 1944 and by chance I never had the opportunity to fly with him. Paul Wachter, who flew overseas with me as my co-pilot, flew as co-pilot with Savercool in Normandy and for sometime thereafter. Savercool was affectionately known in the squadron as 'The Cool'. We spent many hours in the air practicing what we would be doing on 'D-Day'. Just as the troopers were required to make practice jumps, we practiced night formation flying and navigation. Some of these practices were made with the same outfits that we were assigned to carry to Normandy. As a result it became ingrained within each one of us that the big night would be no different from all the practices.

1st Lieutenant Harry Capelluto and 2nd Lieutenant John J. Fanelli would pilot 'Chalk 66' *The Cool,* one of the thirty-six C-47s forming 'Serial 12'; and take seventeen troopers in HQ Section's 'Easy' Company in the 506th PIR to DZ 'C'. The stick's commander was 22-year old Lieutenant Thomas Meehan III who had recently replaced Captain Herbert Sobel, having been transferred to command a parachute training school for non-combat officers. Meehan enjoyed drawing and painting as a hobby and after graduating from Germantown High School in 1939 he completed two years at the Philadelphia Museum School of Industrial Art to become a commercial artist, but the war intervened before graduation. He enlisted in his hometown of Philadelphia, Pennsylvania on 16 March 1941, but when the United States entered World War II, he joined the Cavalry while it was still mounted, but found himself in a tank, not so much to his liking and managed to get transferred to the infantry, as a paratrooper. Before takeoff at Upottery on 5 June, Meehan only had time for a short letter, which he handed out the door of Harry Capelluto's C-47, to be sent to his wife:

> *Dearest Anne:*
> *In a few hours I'm going to take the best company of men in the world into France. We'll give the bastards hell. Strangely, I'm not particularly scared. But in my heart is a terrific longing to hold you in my arms.*
>
> > *I love you Sweetheart - forever.*
> > *Your Tom*

Raymond Geddes in the 501st PIR recalled: 'About a week before 'D-Day' they moved us from the town of Lamborne to Welford airdrome, where we would remain until the start of the invasion. Once again hooked up with the 435th Troop Carrier Group; an outfit that we had worked with before, both in England and back in North Carolina in 1943. On 5 June we marched out to the tarmac to board the planes. One thing stands out in my memory - our Regimental Commander, Colonel Howard R. 'Jumpy' Johnson formed us up and made his famous 'knife in the back of the blackest German' speech that you can read about in the history books. Then he did something else that I will never forget. We walked past him and he shook the hand of every man in the battalion!'

Howard Ravenscroft Johnson was born on 18 June 1903 in Maryland, the son of a shipbuilder. Graduating from Central High School in Washington DC, Johnson (who was alternatively nicknamed 'Skeets') attended the Naval Academy in Annapolis. Before he was scheduled to graduate, Johnson went to Texas, where he tried to become a pilot in the Army Air Corps. The instructors sent him away because of poor 'side vision.'

'After the Colonel's speech we put all of our equipment on and were helped into the C-47s by Air Corps guys. My platoon had been assigned to the 77th Squadron and one of my friends on the plane, Staff Sergeant Jack Urbank, actually knew the pilot, a Lieutenant Harrison, from previous jumps he had made with the 77th. Like the others, I had a hell of a time getting into the plane as I was loaded down with my two parachutes, four or five grenades, a full cartridge belt of ammo, a SCR536 radio, an M-1 Garand rifle in a Griswold bag, musette bag,[33] canteen, gas mask, first aid pouch, entrenching tool, bayonet and heaven knows what else. They also made us wear, in addition to GI shorts, long underwear and ODs under the impregnated jump suit. Needless to say it was very difficult to move!'

The lead aircraft of the 435th Group containing General Maxwell Davenport Taylor the Commanding General of the 101st Airborne Division and several of his staff was flown by the group commander, Colonel Frank J. MacNees, one of the most experienced pilots of the Troop Carrier Command and one General Taylor had every confidence that, if anyone could, he would get their plane to the drop-zone. The second aircraft of that group

---

33 Griswold bags where designed to carry an M1 Garand rifle stripped into two pieces, Thompson and M3 Machine guns would also fit. The bag was then attached to the T-5 Parachute harness using the karabiner sewn onto the bag. The musette bag could be carried as a shoulder bag via the GP strap, or attached to the combat suspenders and worn as a backpack.

carried the 'Screaming Eagles' artillery commander, Brigadier General Anthony C. McAuliffe. General Maxwell Taylor recalled, 'The parachutists in a plane, about a dozen in number, constituted a 'stick' which was under the supervision of the jumpmaster, always a picked man and an experienced parachutist. For the moment, he was an autocrat with unchallenged authority somewhat like that of the skipper of a ship. Regardless of the rank of the members of his stick, he was responsible for them for the duration of the flight and could give whatever orders were necessary to carry out his duties. Major Larry Legere, four years out of West Point, performed that role for our stick, checking our equipment, reminding us of exit procedures and getting us into the proper bucket seat. My fellow passengers included my aide, Captain Thomas White, personal bodyguards, several communications personnel and British journalist, Robert Ervin Reuben of the Reuters news agency.'[34]

Major Barney Oldfield of the 505th Parachute Infantry Regiment had offered to train correspondents willing to jump or glide into Normandy; promising them a spot with the Airborne. As Oldfield braced for the crush of journalists only Reuben, the 101st Airborne's lone volunteer; and one other - signed up.

War correspondents carried the 'honorary' rank of captain for Geneva Convention purposes in case they were captured. If they were to drop with the Airborne they had to complete a full five jumps to get qualified. Some never even made the first. John H. 'Jack' Thompson, who had already parachuted into Sicily in the course of covering World War II, was banned from jumping on 'D-Day' by his publisher, Robert McCormick of the *Chicago Tribune* with a four-word telegram: 'Jump no more. McCormick'. (Thompson instead went into action in an assault boat with the 1st Infantry Division on 'Beach Easy Red' on 'Omaha' Beach). Robert Capa (real name Endre Erno Friedman) the famous war photographer and several others became jump qualified but decided to go by boat instead - famously so in the case of Capa, who had joined the 82nd for their Sicily jump. (He took photographs in the C-47, but he did not jump and flew back to North Africa).

'Fifty-eight correspondents were selected to be on the first wave for the invasion of Normandy' Oldfield recalled. 'In May I was told to secure some apartments in an obscure section of London. The correspondents were

---

34 After landing, when a German patrol mistook Major Larry Legere and a companion for French farmers and were challenged by the Germans, Legere explained in French that they were returning from a visit to his cousin. As he spoke, he pulled the pin of a grenade, which exploded among the unsuspecting Germans.

instructed to come to this address alone. I was there in one of the apartments - no furniture - with a typewriter and asked them their telephone numbers so that they can be told when to go and I also told them the items they could take with them. I told them they had to understand if they leaked information they could die. They weren't above the fray; they were part of it. Then I had to ask them to sit down at the typewriter and write their own obituaries.'

Before the invasion there was speculation that it was imminent. Many news stories talked about how 'sorrow will come to a million homes.' Oldfield did the advance work for a visit from Eisenhower, Winston Churchill, General Bernard Montgomery and General Omar Bradley to the troops waiting in England for the order to invade. Oldfield remembers how Eisenhower told the soldiers they would be given the best chance to get on shore and not to be dismayed by the rumours. There were smaller moments at this visit too. 'The 101st Airborne had a display of weapons. Churchill asked Eisenhower how many yards the 81 mm mortar would reach and Eisenhower said 3,000. One of the soldiers piped up and said '3,250'. Eisenhower turned to him and said, 'Son, you're not going to make a liar out of me in front of the prime minister for a lousy 250 yards'.

'Churchill had a cold. There were 9,000 troops standing at attention in front of him. He told them to break ranks and he got up on the hood of a jeep. He took off his bowler hat and out of his mouth came the words I will never forget: 'I stand before you with no unrealized ambitions except to see Adolf Hitler wiped off the face of the earth.' The troops went crazy.'

Once the invasion was on Oldfield used his ingenuity to ensure words and pictures made it out. To get the film back from the many photographers who risked their lives on the beaches, Oldfield had courier boats and special canvas bags with red stripes on them. The order was if you saw the bag, throw it on the boat. He also distributed condoms to press and Army Signal Corps photographers, but not for what you might think. 'History will always owe a debt to these contraceptives, at least the ones used according to our directions. Each cameraman was advised to drop his completed film pack into one of these rubber receptacles and close it tight with a knot. This would provide the negatives with a raincoat of sorts to ward off seepage or splashing salt water.[35]

---

35 The 165th Signal Photo Company of the Signal Corps covered the landings for the Army and their company commander had his right leg shot off on 'D-Day'. One reason that photo coverage of the landings is so sparse is that the 165th's film and negatives were given to a colonel to take back to England and he dropped the sack in the English Channel while transferring boats.

'One of the many problems was the question (of) which reporter had the right to the Normandy dateline. That was settled when Robert Reuben took two carrier pigeons with leg capsules, one in each hand holding the wings down and parachuted with the 101st 'Screaming Eagles' Airborne onto Carentan at 0330 on 6 June. Reuben had decided to gamble on carrier pigeons as part of his personal communications equipment. At impact he let the pigeons go. A call was directed to me and the voice on the other end said 'We got some pigeons here with leg capsules; can we open them? Well, when they did they saw the words 'Landed Normandy Reuben Reuters (sic)' written on cigarette rolling papers.'

'Promptly at 2300 our plane placed itself at the head of the squadron departing from the field' continues General Maxwell D. Taylor. 'MacNees gunned the engines, we hurtled down the runway and we were off on what was to be, for most of us, our greatest adventure. To me, it was a moment of relief to be off after so many months of laborious preparation. I was content in the feeling that I could think of nothing which we had left undone to assure success. Now it only remained to go into action in the spirit of the verse of Montrose which Montgomery had quoted to the Allied commanders at their last conference:

> He either fears his fate too much
> Or his deserts are small,
> That dares not put it to the touch
> To gain or lose it all.

'Our parachute planes circled in the dusk over England for more than an hour as the successive squadrons rose from the airfields to join the airborne caravan which now included not only the planes of the 101st but also those of the 82nd arriving from their fields in central England. In all, there were over 800 transport planes in the formation as it turned toward France, carrying about 13,000 parachutists of the two divisions. By the time my plane reached the Channel, it was dark with a faint moon showing. We were flying very low in a tight 'V of V's formation to keep below the vision of the German radars on the French coast. As I stood in the open door of the plane, I felt that I could touch the sparkling waves of the Channel so close below. The men were strangely quiet, some seeming to doze on their hard metal seats in spite of the load of their equipment. They too seemed to have left their cares behind.'

Technical Sergeant John J. Ginter Jr. was the flight engineer on 'Chalk 49' (41-00825) in the 92nd Troop Carrier Squadron piloted by Lieutenant

Imschweiler, in 'Serial 12' which would carry one of the sticks in the 2nd Battalion, 506th PIR. At pre-flight Ginter checked the para racks. 'The paratroopers were sitting, standing, constantly relieving themselves - nervous, very nervous. As I'm under the aircraft checking the para racks which I found later on contained mines I knew the reason.'

On the afternoon of 4 June Ginter and two of his ground crew had painted alternate white, black, white, black recognition stripes on the aircraft to hopefully prevent their being shot down as had happened to some of the crews in the Sicily invasion by the US Navy. 'Overlord' planners were less worried about the Germans shooting down the transports as they were about the itchy-fingered gunners on Allied ships. In early May IX Troop Carrier Command was still thinking of camouflaging its aircraft, but since the decision not to use IFF made visual identification almost essential, it was ruled that certain types of aircraft including the troop carriers would be marked with three white and two black stripes, each two feet wide, around the fuselage back of the door and from front to back on the wings. On 17 May Leigh-Mallory had decreed that the gliders too, would be painted. At air bases throughout Britain, everyone became a painter, putting the famous 'D-Day' stripes around the fuselages and wings of every plane and glider. Ten thousand aircraft were striped like zebras in a single evening. To familiarize the naval forces with these markings an exercise was held on 1 June in which marked aircraft were flown over the invasion fleets. However, for security's sake, general marking of aircraft and gliders was not ordered until 3 June ('D-2'). It proved an arduous task which in many groups occupied all available troop carrier personnel far into the night.

The fuselage was marked and each wing was marked and the way Ginter did it was to put a piece of string around and mark with crayon and fill it in with a flat white and flat black paint. 'We boarded up and set up, took off - an extremely heavy load. We took every inch of the runway and we did get airborne and we formed up and we came out over the Channel. I'm up in the cockpit with the pilot and the co-pilot, checking the instruments, making sure that everything is OK and from there we found the pilot marker and made a turn going in towards the Islands - Guernsey and Jersey and of course, the Cherbourg Cotentin Peninsula. As we were going in I see tracer bullets, but they looked just like Roman candles for sure and as we approached them they were more intensive. We seemed to have been out of range. But the second island, as we turned, all hell started to break loose...' After dropping their stick 'Chalk 49' returned safely to Upottery.

Twenty-one-year old Joseph R. Beyrle in 'Item' Company, 506th Parachute Infantry Regiment waited to take his place in a C-47 of the 439th Troop Carrier Group at Upottery for Normandy. Born in 1923 in the small town of Muskegon on the eastern shores of Lake Michigan, he was a child of the Depression years and during this period his parents, William and Elizabeth, were evicted from their home following financial difficulties. Despite these setbacks 'Joe's parents were determined that at least one of their children should graduate from High School and the burden of responsibility fell upon him. Joe was not a great academic but he excelled in sport and in September 1942 was offered a scholarship at the university of Notre Dame. Joe saw army life as a way of escaping from ignominy and an opening for new opportunities. Attracted by its higher rates of pay he volunteered to become a paratrooper. Initial training took place at Camp Toccoa, Georgia before the regiment moved to Fort Benning where 'Joe' made his first parachute decent from an aircraft. By August 1943 the 506th was ready for action and following a hazardous crossing of the north Atlantic the regiment arrived, on 17 September, at the small Wilshire village of Ramsbury. Here Joe's regiment underwent an intensive nine month period of training in preparation for 'D-Day'. During this time Joe volunteered to take gold to resistance units in occupied France and was dropped twice by parachute behind enemy lines. Following each mission Joe was picked up in a RAF Westland Lysander and returned to England.

Shortly before midnight the 50th Troop Carrier Wing's 200-odd C-47s [in the 439th; 440th; 441st and 442nd] waited close-packed on the longest runways of their south England bases, engines idling impatiently. At last, zero hour. The first Skytrains, marked like the others with alternate white and black invasion stripes, loaded to capacity with smudge-faced Airborne troops bent with equipment, struggled off the runway and circled slowly as others joined the formation.

In the 439th TCG the final briefing began at 2030, just prior to take-off, at which there were many photographers, movie cameramen and war correspondents; Colonel Harlan Miller and a crew of six and Bruce W. Munn of United Press among others. 'Bud' Berry, who fly co-pilot to his squadron CO, Major Harry Tower, in the lead ship recalled: 'Colonel Charles H. Young said to us: 'It's going to be about the same tonight as it was on the last big practice mission, except we'll fly a little different course. But it won't be so monotonous because we'll get to fly over some territory we haven't seen before. There may even be some little yellow lights flashing at us from the ground - just ignore them - they're not occults.'

'We were confident that with proper conditions, we could put those troopers on the ground where they were supposed to be. We knew we would be flying 500-700 feet above the ground with no armour plating and no self-sealing gas tanks but we were not alone, we had those troopers in the back that would be with us most of the way. This was both their lot and ours for this great operation which would be the beginning of the end for Hitler...'

'The 439th Troop Carrier Group carried the 506th PIR (Headquarters Company and 'Able'-'Fox' Companies). There were two Serials in the flight. The first serial led by Colonel Young was comprised of 45 planes (sticks 1 to 45). Major Harry Tower led the second serial of 36 planes (sticks 46 to 81). Each flight included nine planes made up of three three-ship elements. We carried the tail end of 'Dog' Company in stick 64 in my plane. We were leading the third flight of the second serial. *The Cool* was flying left wing in our No.2 (right hand) element. My friend Harry Capelluto was flying stick 66 on our left wing. Sitting in the right seat I could not see him.'

C-47 *The Argonia,* the lead aircraft of the 439th Troop Carrier Group flown by Colonel Charles Young had on board jumpmaster Colonel Robert Frederick Sink, commander of the 506th PIR. The spirit and dedication of all was exemplified by the briefing Colonel Young gave his pilots on 5 June. 'The main thing we're interested in tonight, even above our own safety - repeat, even above our own safety - is to put a closed-up, intact formation over our assigned drop zone at the proper time, so these paratroopers of ours can get on the ground in the best possible fighting condition. Each pilot among you is charged with the direct responsibility of delivering his troops to the assigned DZ. Their work is only beginning when you push down that switch for the green light. Remember that.'

19-year old Pfc Donald R. Burgett, a rifleman and a machine-gunner in 'A' Company, 1st Battalion, 506th PIR, in the 101st 'Screaming Eagles' Division flew in 'Chalk 58' piloted by 24-year old 1st Lieutenant Marvin M. Muir of Elkhart, Indiana. Burgett wrote: 'Once in the plane... it was beginning to get dark... I can hear the pilots cranking the engines - the cough and firing as they caught and revved up. The pilots pushed the throttles to proper RPMs, checked their maps and gauges. The C-47 shook and vibrated as though eager and we were silent to the man. The ship farthest to our left added throttle, moved forward toward the runway, did a right ninety and paraded left to right before us as vanguard, moving between us and the runway [as it headed] to the right end of the runway and takeoff point. We watched the flames of exhaust in the growing dark, as the ship filled with 101st Eagle men loaded with tools of war, shadowed past.

'It became our turn; the ship shuddered and moved, turned right and followed the ships in line before us. Our pilot fire-walled the throttles and we went as over a bumpy country road, heading toward the skies and Normandy. When the gear cleared the ground, we were airborne, we cheered as one, breaking the silence.

'We were going to war.'[36]

Colonel Young describes the take-off and assembly of his 439th Troop Carrier Group:[37] 'Stations time at 2200, take off with 81 ships started at 2313. We left England at Portland Bill on a course of 213 degrees magnetic for 55 miles, then on 132 degrees for 57 miles, then east on 93° across the Cotentin peninsula in Normandy.

'The Skytrains upon take-off, turned in a closely held well-practiced formation, passing back over the airfield as the last airplanes were taking off. As the last crews formed up on their flight leader, the formation flew toward Portland Bill, a checkpoint on the English coast, headed southwest and turned off the red and green navigation lights. Then, 47 miles later, at the point where the formation turned southeast toward Normandy, downward recognition lights were turned off and the blue formation lights on top of the wings and fuselage were dimmed until they could just barely be seen. Serials of aircraft, made up almost entirely of 36 or 45 C-47s, flew as nine-ship 'Vees on Vees' in trail. The leader of each nine-airplane flight kept 1,000 feet behind the rear of the preceding flight. Leaders of the Wing elements in each flight were 200 feet back and 200 feet to the right or left. Within each three-plane 'Vee', wingmen were to fly 100 feet back and 100 feet to the right or left of their leader. This was a tight formation at night for aircraft approximately 75 feet long and 95 feet from wing tip to wing tip.'

'The horseman guiding his steed sideways to get him squared away for his jump over a high bar and broad pit, then turning, loosens the reins and feels the surge of power ripple through his spirited mount. That is how I felt on the night of 5 June as I turned our formation of 81 C-47s at the last check point in the English Channel, leading in the first group of the 50th Troop Carrier Wing and started on the final straight run in to German held Normandy. Not that I'm kidding myself about the lumbering old C-47 Skytrains being powerful or spirited, but the potent fighting cargo we

---

36 *Currahee! A Screaming Eagle at Normandy* by Donald Burgett, first published in 1967. *Currahee* is the battle cry and motto of his regiment.

37 *Into The Valley* by Charles H. Young.

carried, the eager tough young paratroopers of Colonel Sink of the 101st Airborne Division, gave us that sense of power and spirit.

'Crossing the coast at 1,500 feet, I saw a cloud bank too late to get under, so started over and the group was on instruments temporarily. I had formed the habit of leading a formation with the auto-pilot engaged, as it made it possible to lead more smoothly. When we hit the clouds, I disconnected only the altitude control and started climbing, hoping to break out on top so we could keep our formation together. We shortly broke out on top and a few miles inland some breaks began to appear, until we were able to start a gradual descent down to about 700 feet.'

The flight turned, outlined against the full moon and disappeared into the cloudless night as 2nd Lieutenant Vincent J. Paterno of Lyndhurst, New Jersey, radio/radar and 2nd Lieutenant Paul Foynes, pilotage;[38] took over, computing ground speeds and drift, looking eagerly ahead for check-points.

'Since we had not changed our heading', continues Colonel Young 'we were still on course and shortly I began to recognize some of the features of the landscape and knew where we were. Our navigators confirmed that we were on course and soon I could see the pattern of the flooded areas in the reflected moonlight which was filtering through the clouds somewhat. By the time we were halfway across the peninsula, I picked out the road that ran through the north part of our assigned drop zone, DZ 'C'. I made a slight course correction to the right and we went directly over the DZ, which was located about three miles southeast of Sainte-Mère-Église, three miles west of the east coastline and close to Sainte-Marie-du-Mont and north of Hiesville.

'We had been receiving some fire, evidently from machine guns and some heavier flak from the time we had crossed the west coast. As we were approaching the DZ machine gun fire and flak began increasing and a ship in our 45-ship serial, flown by 2nd Lieutenant Marsten Sargent, was shot down. The intense flames from the gasoline fire lit up the lower cloud layer above us and gave an eerie orange yellow cast to the formation and to the scene below us.'

'Inside the other planes' wrote Donald Burgett on Lieutenant Muir's C-47, 'I could see the glowing red tips of cigarettes as men puffed away. It was weirdly beautiful, lots of sparks and tracer shells. But I knew that between every tracer shell are four armour-piercing bullets.'

'Machine gun fire with yellow tracers came from the right rear where we crossed the railroad that ran from Cherbourg to Carentan' said Colonel Young.

---

38 The other crew members were 1st Lieutenant Adam Parsons, pilot (flying right seat); Staff Sergeant John A. Dougherty, radio operator and Staff Sergeant Charles E. Patterson, crew chief.

'The tracers went by the nose of my ship so thick at this point that they lit up the inside of the cockpit. Later I found out that much of my No.2 element had been shot up, though none were shot down by this fire. Tracers of various colours - red, green, blue and orange - came from guns two to three miles from the north in a head converging on our column and by now tracers were crossing in front of us and around us and large explosions were occurring along the coastline ahead of us. The combination of these several guns shot down two more ships of our second serial of 36 ships, led by Major Tower. The two that crashed were flown by Lieutenant Marvin Muir and Lieutenant Harold Capelluto.'

The C-47 being flown by 1st Lieutenant Harold King was following 'Chalk 66' commanded by Capelluto and Lieutenant Meehan's stick. King's co pilot, 1st Lieutenant Frank Deflita, remembers: 'As we flew over Normandy, DCA's started shooting at us and Harold's plane got it several times. I could see shrapnel going straight through his plane. After maintaining its course and speed for a while, the plane left the formation and slowly initiated a right turn. I followed it with my eyes and noticed its landing lights coming on. I thought it was going to be all right. Then, suddenly, it came crashing down and instantly exploded.

'Meehan never should have been in that plane' said Paratrooper Ed Mauser in Easy Company's 2nd Platoon regretfully. His plane, 'Chalk 69', was flying the rear of a diamond formation with '66' in front, '67' to the left and '68' to the right. On 3 June Mauser and his comrades had learned at briefing, by way of rumour that the hedgerows in France were going to be tough. It turned out eerily prophetic. Mauser thought Capelluto's plane was going to make a landing but it hit the hedgerow and exploded. 'I knew all the fellows on it' said Mauser.

Henry Margerie, Mayor of Beuzeville-au-Plain, witnessed the loss of Meehan's aircraft: 'As we awakened to flak shooting and planes flying over the area, I saw a plane close to the village which seemed to be trouble and attempted to land. I lost sight of it for a brief moment and then heard a loud explosion. The plane had crashed on a hedgerow bordering a field near the village. It burnt for three days and the heat created by the fire made it impossible for us to approach.'

'Chalk 66' crashed behind the church of Beuzeville-au-Plain approximately two miles northeast of Sainte-Mère-Église, killing Thomas Meehan, 'Easy' Company's entire company headquarters group and all five crew.[39] 'Easy' Company got a new commander in Lieutenant Dick Winters.

---

39 Capelluto; 2nd Lieutenant John Fanelli; navigator, 2nd Lieutenant Bernard Friedman; engineer, Sergeant Albert R. Tillotson Jr. and radio operator Sergeant Norman E. Thompson.

Flak began hitting Mauser's plane, but fortunately no rounds penetrated the fuselage. The fire had an electric effect on the paratroopers. Men began shouting, 'Let's get the hell out of here!' Everyone stood up and hooked up while the pilot tried to manoeuvre away from the tracers. 'We went from 1,500 feet to 400 at high speed,' Mauser said. The men had been issued with motion sickness pills, but Mauser refused to take his. He had packed his M1 Garand rifle diagonally across his chest and stuffed his leg bag with a box of ammunition and grenades. Included in his equipment was a toy 'cricket' that had been issued to signal other airborne troopers upon landing in the dark. His parachute, reserve chute and all his equipment weighed about 80lbs. It had taken two or three troopers to help get him on the C-47, 'pushing his rear end the whole way.' Once seated in the plane, he took off his reserve chute to lighten his load. When the green jump light went on Mauser jumped out. The prop blast from the propellers snapped his neck back. Because of the rough exit, he faced backward as he floated to the ground, witnessing the crash of 'Chalk 66'. Mauser had little time to think about what he had seen. After his parachute deployed, the strap of his leg bag yanked down to his ankle. 'I thought I was going to break my legs,' he recalled. He reached down to adjust the strap, but the bag fell off. Within seconds he hit French soil. 'It was one of my better landings.'[40]

'Inside the other planes' wrote Donald Burgett on Lieutenant Muir's C-47, 'I could see the glowing red tips of cigarettes as men puffed away. It was weirdly beautiful, lots of sparks and tracer shells. But I knew that between every tracer shell are four armour-piercing bullets. 'Let's go', shouted Lieutenant Muir and we began moving in what seemed slow motion towards the open doorway as the green 'go' light spread a glow across our faces.'

Burgett was dropped at less than 300 feet instead of the specified 600-700 and was bitter about it[41] but 1st Lieutenant Marvin Muir saved seventeen of his eighteen paratroopers at the cost of his own life and those of his four crew by holding his burning aircraft steady while they jumped. All but one of the 506th Parachute Infantry Regiment paratroopers, Sergeant Simmie

---

40 *Ed Mauser: Easy Company's Silent Brother* by Kevin M. Hymel, *WWII History magazine.*

41 Burgett's book, *Currahee! A Screaming Eagle at Normandy* was the only World War 2 book to be endorsed by General Eisenhower, who called it a 'fascinating tale of personal combat'. Burgett was one of only eleven men out of the original 200 in his company to survive from D-Day in Normandy to the war's end.

C. Ervin, was able to bail out. In a vain effort, Muir tried to crash-land the flaming C-47 hoping to save his trapped crew.[42] 'Chalk 58' crashed at L'isle Marie, between Chef du Pont and Picauville. Muir was posthumously awarded the DSC.

'Bud' Berry wrote: 'After the 'D-Day' mission, there was a great feeling of sadness yet optimism as no one in the squadron had seen Capelluto's plane go down and the hope was that he was at an alternate airbase. But no reports were received and after a few days, Group Leadership appointed someone to come and pack up his personal possessions. We were then fully aware that he probably was lost. His grave was later found at a US Cemetery in Normandy and the tragic loss was confirmed.'

Three aircraft in the 439th Group were shot down (with seven others damaged) and crashed with their crews and a total of 27 aircraft were damaged, but only three severely enough to need the attentions of a service unit later.

The formations of the 439th and 435th reached Normandy in good shape; only to run squarely and unexpectedly into the cloudbank that covered the western Cotentin. Colonel Young climbed through the overcast on instruments, descended through a hole in the clouds eleven miles inland and headed for the drop zone using the 'Gee' and 'Rebecca' navigational aids. The pathfinders responsible for DZ 'C' had managed to get a 'Eureka' beacon in operation a few moments earlier but a loss of lights and the presence of enemy troops had prevented them from setting up a 'T'. All they could do was to flash a single green Aldis lamp. Colonel Young apparently did not see this, but he did recognize the principal landmarks around the DZ. He flipped the switch to give the green light to the 50th Wing's first paratrooper over the target north of Carentan and dropped accurately at a bend in the road to Sainte-Marie-du-Mont on the northeast side of the zone at or slightly before his scheduled time of 0114. Colonel Young's serial managed to give its troops a fairly good drop, landing two-thirds of its sticks and Colonel Robert F. Sink on or within a mile of the drop zone. Only two or three serials in 'Neptune' did better.

Besides Young, fourteen pilots put their loads on or almost on DZ 'C'. Another thirteen bunched their sticks within a mile and a half east and southeast of the zone. The rest straggled, dropping troops from three to seven miles from DZ 'C' and one pilot who ended up seventeen miles away and a three-aircraft element which dropped its unfortunate troops 21 miles to the northwest.

---

42 2nd Lieutenants' Kenneth C. Bell, co-pilot and John A. Martsay, navigator; Staff Sergeant Clifford L. Burgess, crew chief and Sergeant Philip A. Synder, radio operator.

All but a few of Colonel Young's serial had lost contact with him in the clouds and their formation had loosened and broken. The other two serials disintegrated. This was natural, since in the overcast pilots generally lost sight of the dimmed lights of aircraft in other flights and were often unable to see even the aircraft in their own element. In addition, they had reacted to the situation in different ways, some going stubbornly ahead, others climbing to get above the clouds or diving to get under them.

Colonel Young again: 'After our troopers were dropped and the area cleared, we turned north-eastward to cross the Sainte-Marcouf Islands. North of the islands I got up and looked back through the astrodome to check on the formation. Tracers were coming from a point about six miles behind us, up through and among us in a huge, snake-like arc, so I climbed back into my seat with some speed where I had a little protection from some armour plate I'd had installed there.

'Passing Cherbourg, well off-shore, shells started lobbing out at a point ahead and getting nearer our course with each shot. I veered slightly to the far side of the course to make it more sporting.

'As we intercepted the course that we had taken from Portland Bill, on the way in, other formations could still be seen going in, as the airborne train was several hundred miles long. I called those formations - breaking radio silence for what I was certain now to be an emergency - and told them to hit the coast at 700 feet instead of 1,500 feet. These were some of the serials bringing in the 82nd Airborne Division.'

After 'Joe' Beyrle in the 506th PIR jumped from his C-47 he landed on the church roof in Sainte-Côme-du-Mont before sliding down into the churchyard. 'Joe' tried desperately to reach his objective (two wooden bridges crossing the river Douve) but after twenty hours or so of dodging German patrols was eventually captured. 'Joe' did not like the idea of being taken prisoner and quickly escaped only to be recaptured the following day. A German soldier took his dog tags and uniform but was killed later in Normandy. When the German's body was found it was believed to be that of Joe Beyrle and was buried in a US cemetery. Joe's parents received a telegram informing them that their son had been killed in action! Meanwhile Joe had been transported east and spent time at several prison camps in Germany before ending up at Stalag IIIC in Poland. Joe's desire to escape was as strong as ever and he broke out on two occasions. The first ended in Berlin where he was interrogated and tortured by the Gestapo before being sent back to IIIC. The second escape took him to the Eastern Front. Here he joined forces with a Russian tank regiment commanded by a woman major!

Joe, who the Russians called 'Yo', fought alongside his new 'friends' for a number of weeks, thus becoming the only American paratrooper to fight for both the USA and Soviet Union during WWII.

On emerging from the overcast the 435th Group at Welford were harassed by light flak and small arms fire which was moderately severe over the last eight miles of the route. Its effect was intensified by the fact that many stragglers passed over danger spots such as Pont l'Abbe (Etienville) a mile or two off the proper course. Three aircraft in the serial from the 435th Group blew up or went down in flames before reaching the drop zone; the only survivors were a few troops who were lining up at the door of one aircraft when it was hit. Seven other aircraft in the group were hit, but not seriously damaged. 'Chalk No.28' (43-15618) piloted by Captain Lewis A. Curtis in the 435th TCG arrived over the DZ at 0132 hours. The other flights did not arrive in formation as when they approached landfall and going from west to east over the peninsula they ran through overcast which seperated some of the C-47s from the formation although, all of the transports dropped their men. However, 'Chalk No.37' (43-30735) piloted by Captain Seymour M. Malakoff from New York State, crashed two fields east of 'Dead Man's Corner' after dropping a stick from the 3rd Platoon of H/501. It was probably hit shortly after crossing the French coast and fell back in the formation. Losing altitude and unable to reach the drop zone, Malakoff switched on the green light allowing the eighteen paratroopers to jump to safety before the plane crashed.[43] Two other C-47s shot down from that 3/501st and Division HQ Welford serial were carrying members of G/501.

'Chalk 17' The *Urgin' Virgin* (43-30720) in the 77th TCS, 435th TCG, was piloted by 24-year old Jess Harrison, carrying 'George' Company of the 501st PIR to Normandy. 'The 77th Squadron under Colonel Osmer had received lots of blind flying training (instrument only) before 'D-Day'. I cannot speak for the other two squadrons in the 435th Troop Carrier Group but the 77th stayed in formation when entering the cloudbanks at approximately 650 feet altitude over Normandy. Jess was one of those pilots who missed the DZ on the first pass, but who courageously turned around 180° to drop his passengers. After emerging from the infamous cloudbanks on the west side of the Cotentin peninsula, Jess and the other planes in

---

43 Captain Malakoff; co-pilot 2nd Lieutenant Thomas A. Tucker; navigator 1st Lieutenant Eugene E. Gaul; crew chief Sergeant Paul Jacoway and radio operator Staff Sergeant Robert Walsh were killed. See *Tonight We Die As Men* by Ian Gardner & Roger Day (Osprey 2009).

his 'V' encountered heavy flak near Picauville. Two planes near the *Urgin' Virgin* were hard hit. One exploded in mid-air with all aboard killed. The other caught fire, drifted down and crashed with all but three of the original occupants still aboard. Seeing this, Harrison dropped down to treetop level to foil the German gunners, but he soon arrived at the east coast and realized he had overshot the DZ. Conferring with Lieutenant Norman Barker, the jumpmaster, they decided to turn around and make another pass. Jess asked the lieutenant how high he had to be for the parachutes to deploy. Barker guesstimated about 350 feet. When Harrison was re-approaching DZ 'C' he climbed to about 400 feet, turned on the Green Light right over the DZ and checked his airspeed indicator. He says he was flying at 135-140 mph when he gave the Green Light. The drop was right on target. One paratrooper was struck by ground fire and killed as he exited the door. Another trooper, Don Castona, had a bullet cut the heel of his boot, travel up through the calf of his trouser leg and exit without wounding him, as he floated down. Jess made another 180° turn and headed east again, dropping back down to treetop level. As the *Urgin' Virgin* went out over the Channel, a large dark shape suddenly loomed up directly in its path. Harrison stood the plane on its tail just in time to avoid a collision with the battleship *Texas*. The Navy had reluctantly agreed to withhold fire on all aircraft flying during the time of the troop carrier drops 'because of the importance attached to the Airborne missions'. He resumed deck flying the rest of the way across to England. After landing, he counted 67 flak and small arms' holes in his plane.[44]

On another C-47, Crew Chief John J. O'Conner of Mosinee, Wisconsin heard the bail-out bell and dived after the last trooper, only to watch his aircraft fly on, unharmed. After two weeks' fighting with the Airborne and being captured at an advanced aid station, the Sergeant returned to his squadron to learn the 'abandon ship' order was just a case of the wrong switch.

The 435th Troop Carrier Group made its first drops about 0120, six minutes ahead of schedule. Its serial had scattered so widely that at least 25 stragglers felt justified in using 'Rebecca'. This action was probably decisive in enabling most of them to make a good drop. The 'Eureka' signals came through strong and only slightly cluttered despite the heavy use. With their aid about twenty pilots came close enough to the pathfinders to see their green light blinking. However, several overshot the zone and had to circle for a second try. None of the group hit DZ 'C', but 25 dropped troops or

---

44 On 17 September, 1944 the *Urgin Virgin* in the 435th TCG flew a stick of 101st paratroopers to DZ 'C' near Son, Holland, with Jess Harrison again at the controls and on 18 September, this plane towed a glider to Holland without incident.

supplies within 1½ miles of it. Of these, sixteen bunched their loads close to the east end of the zone near the pathfinder aids. All but one of the bunch were from the first 21 aircraft in the serial and among them were the first two sticks with Generals Taylor and McAuliffe. Another six sticks came down between 1½ and three miles from the DZ. For some strange reason eight pilots of various flights concentrated their loads near Sainte-Jores about eight miles southwest of DZ 'C' on the south side of the Douve. Since it is unlikely that they would make the same gross mistake independently, the presumption is that these pilots had formed an improvised flight after emerging from the overcast and made their erroneous approach in formation behind a pilot who either did not use radar or could not use it properly. Three other loads were dropped between five and ten miles from the zone and one bewildered pilot of the 435th returned to base with his troops.[45]

Las Vegas Kid, one of the C-47s that flew in the 439th TCG's second serial was piloted by 1st Lieutenant Russell Carl Hennicke in the 98th TCS, 440th TCG. Born 14 October 1919 in Buffalo, New York, he grew up in Cleveland Hills, Ohio before moving to Las Vegas where he acquired the nickname, 'the Las Vegas Kid'. His parent Group's roster was full for Operation 'Neptune' but the 439th had an opening for one more plane and crew as they required another C-47 and crew to transport a stick from 'Fox' Company in the 2nd Battalion, 506th PIR. As a result Hennicke was privileged to fly his own plane and his crew on this mission. Hennicke made his run-in and dropped his stick from 'Fox' Company in the 2nd Battalion 506th PIR. 'My position was 'Stick 81' right at the back of the second serial on the extreme left' Hennicke recalled. 'As the formation approached France a mass of aluminium strips was dropped intended to blank out German radar. We then went into a left turn towards the Cotentin Peninsula and encountered clouds. Our rate of turn became sharper and as I was on the inside of the turn, I had to keep throttling back to stay behind the wing of the lead aircraft of the '3 plane V'. Consequently I lost my flying speed and had to put my nose down and then give the engines full power to regain my flying speed. I then found myself in cloud on instruments while trying to retain my altitude and rate of turn. I was unaware of what rate of turn we had been doing because in close formation flying, you never take your eyes off the plane whose wing you are on.

'I tried holding a 5° rate of turn but it did not feel as steep as it did, so I increased to 7°. About then my co-pilot, 2nd Lieutenant Wilbur Leonard informed me we had reached our compass heading for the drop

---

45   He tried again next night with the 435th's glider serial and made a successful drop.

zone approach. As soon as I picked up that heading I came out of the clouds, a searchlight in front of us lit up a parachute ahead, so I gave the paratroopers the red signal to stand and hook up and as I switched on the green jump light, the searchlight picked us up. Tracer bullets began coming up ahead of us and fortunately the searchlight then went out. I am leaning forward closer to the windshield to see upward and to determine if any more chutes are coming down. However, as I leaned forward my flak jacket pushed my helmet and tilted it over my eyes. So I threw the helmet on the floor!

'Then the tracers began arcing back towards us and one hit us somewhere behind the cockpit. We immediately spotted a parachute which was falling into our path and it was not going to miss us! So we had to do a violent turn. For sure the paratroopers did not appreciate what was happening for they were trying to stand up with their heavy loads and hook up to the cable. I throttled the left engine back for their exit so as they do not drop into the normal prop blast. Suddenly Leonard said 'our right engine is dead.'

'Feather the prop!' I replied.

'The crew chief, Sergeant Bernard Perry tells us all paratroopers had exited.

'I reinstated power to the left engine. Now Leonard yells 'That's water right down there!'

'I see that we are just a few feet above it. Wow, do I pour it into that left engine and yell for the crew chief to throw out anything he can with the first thing to go being the bicycle that was always stored in the rear of the cabin followed by cutting the static lines that were trailing behind. These would normally be pulled back into the cabin.

'Leonard suggests we head for the Isle of Wight, the closest place for us to make a forced landing.'

Meanwhile the situation at DZ 'C' was difficult and dangerous. Despite the relatively good drop by the 439th TCG the 1st Battalion the 506th PIR was unable to assemble quickly. One reason for this was lack of communications. Most of the signal equipment and all the operators had come down many miles outside the drop area. Two hours after the drop only about 45 men from headquarters and fifty from the 1st Battalion had gathered under Colonel Sink at Culoville on the south side of the zone. The 2nd Battalion, much of which had jumped too far west near Sainte-Mère-Église, eventually assembled near Foucarville at the northern edge of the 101st Airborne's objective area. It fought its way to the hamlet of le Chemin near the Houdienville causeway by mid-afternoon, but found that the 4th Division had already seized the exit hours before.

The 3rd Battalion of the 501st PIR carried by the 435th TCG at Welford, assigned to jump onto DZ 'C' was more scattered than the 1st Battalion the 506th PIR, (carried by the 439th TCG) but took over the mission of securing the exits. An ad hoc company-sized team that included Major General Maxwell D. Taylor reached the Pouppeville exit at 0600. After a six-hour house-clearing battle with elements of the German 1058th Grenadier Regiment, the group secured the exit shortly before 4th Division troops arrived to link up. About 150 paratroops gathered during the morning at a divisional headquarters set up at Hiesville by a few men Taylor had left behind. At noon they were reinforced by over 100 troops who had landed at dawn in the 'Chicago' glider mission.

Colonel Sink's CP at Culoville was also reinforced by more than seventy additional men of the 1st Battalion of the 506th Parachute Infantry Regiment who had found their way to the DZ. These, however, seemed all too few. The enemy were swarming around like hornets and twice pushed attacks close enough to threaten the Culoville position. Unknown to the Allies, the Germans had installed an entire battalion of the 191st Artillery Regiment in and around Sainte-Marie-du-Mont. Many paratroops that landed near their positions had been shot before they could get free of their chutes. The rest gave a good account and even took one of the German batteries, but it was not until after 1420 when elements of the 8th Infantry Regiment pushed into the town that the issue was decided and German resistance in Sainte-Marie was broken. At the end of the afternoon the portions of the 1st and 2nd Battalions of the 506th PIR which had been at the causeways returned to DZ 'C', giving Colonel Sink a total of 650 men, including a few from other units. Their initial task had been accomplished and the 2nd and 3rd Battalions of the 8th Infantry Regiment had moved into positions around les Forges thus shielding the 506th from the west. However, efforts to seal off and occupy the area between them and the Douve had not succeeded and the situation there was so chaotic that General Taylor, returning from Pouppeville, ordered the 506th to make a reconnaissance in force into this no-man's land next morning.

Nursing *Las Vegas Kid* back across the Channel to England, Russell Hennicke picked up the compass heading and adjusted the left engine to enable them to climb a little but not so much as to overload it to the point of failure. 'We regained about 100 feet altitude and could then see the Isle of Wight. Leonard is calling on the radio requesting clearance for a forced landing. Their response required a few more exchanges than he cared for, however clearance was finally given.

'I am following instructions as we were taught for a one engine landing. Stay high enough to reach the runway without having to gun the engine, for this would produce too much torque all on one side and flip the plane over. I successfully drop the undercarriage, then call flaps and nothing happens. I could see that we would be halfway down the runway before we touched down. Expecting to burn up the brakes to stop, I discovered we had no brakes!! We had lost hydraulics. The question now was; what is at the end of the runway? It was about 2am in the morning so I ignored orders not to use landing lights and flicked them on for a second which revealed no obstacles in our path so we kept going. My other option was to do a ground loop at the end of the runway which would have probably collapsed the undercarriage and do all kinds of damage.

'So we landed using the entire runway and then rolled down a grass embankment almost hitting a gun emplacement with two gunners ducking under our left wing. Then we went through a barbed wire fence and eventually came to a halt a few feet from a creek. The tower said, 'OK '775' turn right and taxi back to the tower area.' My reply was 'I'd love to but we are down here by the creek. Can you send down a jeep or something to get the four of us back?'

'Before we left we noticed that some of the para packs were still hung in place on the belly of the plane. They sure would have messed us up if we had ground looped.

'The airfield was in the hands of the Royal Canadian Air Force. Talking to one of their pilots later, he said it was he who had shot out the searchlight over Normandy that I referred to earlier. It sure was some experience!

'He never could get more than three feet over the Channel all the way back,' reported Sergeant John Brown, Ajo, Arizona crew chief of another C-47 in the Group. 'His crew threw out everything and anything to keep the ship in the air.' After his own aircraft, *Ain't It Awful* wobbled in on one wheel, Brown commented, 'Yeah, but it could have been a lot worse.'

At Upottery Bruce W. Munn of United Press was waiting to interview the returning C-47 pilots. 'Most amazing thing I saw,' said Flight Officer Norman J. Thompson, San Antonio, Texas, on his return from Normandy, 'was a good-looking girl nonchalantly riding a bicycle down the middle of the road as I came coasting in with my CG-4. Maybe that was Hitler's secret weapon.'

There were plenty of stories for the newsmen to devour. Captain Woodrow Meck of Lancaster, Ohio a group operations commander whose 28th birthday fell on 'D-Day' gave his description: 'The beach where we crossed resembled Coney Island on Monday morning after the crowd had left. There was debris everywhere and plenty of obstructions left. Some of the defences had been cleared as if torn up by some powerful force to make a lane. On one part of the beach a hospital unit had been set up. The red crosses on the tents were prominent from the air. I was disappointed by the lack of action.'

The plane of crew chief Tech Sergeant Mario V. Pissaro, White Plains, New York caught fire on the take-off and crash-landed at the field's edge. With a leg broken, the sergeant opened the cargo door to free paratroopers and crew from certain death. The aircraft also was carrying a heavy load of ammunition and land mines.

One glider and tow-plane from the 440th Group made a solo trip into the southern France LZ. When the tow-rope broke, Lieutenant Marion L. Clem Barnsdall, Oklahoma made a forced landing a few miles after take-off; a truck from the field immediately retrieved both personnel and equipment, returned them to the airstrip shortly after the tow-plane landed. With frantic effort, a spare glider was wheeled into position, loaded, hooked up with a new cable.

Although the formation already was over the LZ, the glider, towed by Lieutenant Arthur Douglass, New Orleans, took off for France alone. When he returned hours behind the others, the Lieutenant reported the glider safely landed in the proper location.

Most appreciated expression was heard in a London pub several weeks later. A stocky Airborne sergeant wearing a new Purple Heart stopped one of the troop carrier pilots to say, 'Lemme shake your hand. You guys got guts.'[46]

---

46 *Invaders: The Story of the 50th Troop Carrier Wing* a small booklet covering the history of the 50th Troop Carrier Wing, one of the series of GI Stories published by the Stars & Stripes in Paris in 1944-1945.

Chapter 7

'Albany' - The Last Serials

Every colour of the rainbow was flashing through the sky. Equipment bundles attached to chutes that did not fully open came hurtling past me, helmets that had been ripped off by the opening shock, troopers floated past. Below me, figures were running in all directions...My chute floated into the branches of an apple tree and dumped me to the ground with a thud. My ears were very sharp and I would hear a faraway drone, like myriad bees flocking, away over to the north-east, but not from any particular point of the sky.

Private John Fitzgerald, 502nd Parachute Infantry Regiment, who after he jumped, looked up to check his parachute and watched as enemy bullets ripped through it.

At Exeter airfield on the outskirts of the cathedral city on the River Exe on a dreary, overcast June afternoon Corporal William Wildes, a special vehicle operator in the 96th Troop Carrier Squadron, 440th TCG attached nozzles to the wings of the green and white C-47 Skytrain aircraft formerly known as the *Pride of Minnesota*. Pouring approximately 100 gallons of fuel into each wing, he did it exactly like he had done several times before in the previous months for the training missions to prepare for the Normandy invasion. Nothing seemed out of the ordinary, except the white invasion stripes and the large '6Z' that was painted onto the fuselage earlier in the day. 'The planes were fuelled in the afternoon of 5 June' says Wildes. 'We didn't know where they were going. We just fuelled them like normal' said Wildes. 'One pilot had *Pride of Minnesota* inside an arrowhead painted on the nose, but they made him take it off when they put the invasion stripes on for 'D-Day'. But not everything went without a hitch. 'I heard that somebody ran into the de-icer boot and tore it up. They replaced this one plane and put another plane in its place. The crew chief was a guy named 'Ed' Bluestone. I remember him well and I fuelled his plane.'

The task of the 440th TCG was to transport the 3rd Battalion, 506th PIR and 'Charlie' Company in the 326th Engineering Battalion in the 101st Airborne to DZ 'D'. On 27 May the paratroopers of the two battalions had waited at the railway station in Hungerford for the trains that would take them to their 'D-Day' marshalling area. The weather was unusually hot for May and the men sweated as they waited in their steel helmets and jumpsuits. 'Everyone was trying to figure out exactly where we were going,' remembers Sergeant Amos 'Buck' Taylor. 'We knew it was probably going to be Normandy, but exactly where nobody knew.' Though the location of the invasion had not yet been revealed, the men had some idea of what General 'Bill' Lee, former commander of the 101st, had called 'the responsibility ahead of us.' The past nine months had been a blur of gruelling training exercises that had tested the mettle even of these men, elite volunteers trained to jump directly into the turbulence of combat. Their training had culminated in Exercise 'Tiger', a full-scale rehearsal of 'D-Day' that had involved all units of the 101st Airborne.

In a few short hours the men of 3rd Battalion would discover their objective: to lead the way on 'D-Day' by seizing and defending two bridges spanning the Canal de Carentan - vital links between the German bases in and around Carentan, a small port city just south of the Cotentin Peninsula and the American invasion beaches. One of the thirty men at the initial briefing on 27 May was Staff Sergeant 'Ed' Shames, Company HQ who built the sand tables the 101st Airborne used in planning the airdrop into Normandy. Born in Virginia Beach, Virginia Shames had joined the army in September 1942, volunteering for paratroopers. He was sent to Toccoa, Georgia for training and started as a private for 'Item' Company. He would make his first combat jump into Normandy on 'D-Day' from a C-47 in the 440th. He recalled: 'The briefing tent fell silent as the SHAEF officer stood up in front of a flip chart mounted on a stand. The guy did the big showbiz thing, like a magician pulling a rabbit from a hat. He flipped open the cover of the chart to reveal a large heading that read, 'Operation Overlord - the invasion of Normandy June 4.' Third Battalion's commanding officer, 29-year old Lieutenant Colonel Robert Lee 'Bull' Wolverton jumped out of his seat and said, 'I had a hunch it was going to be there, boys, I knew it, I knew it!' Born 5 October 1914 in Elkins, West Virginia, 'Bull' was just nine years old when he began to talk of going to West Point, which remained uppermost in his mind during the next eleven years. It was largely through his own efforts that he secured his appointment in 1934. He graduated from West Point in 1938 and on 17 August he married Kathleen Goodwin, a home town girl, in a military wedding with several of his classmates forming the guard of honour. On 24 August 1941 their son, Robert Lachlan was born.

On 5 June Ward Smith, *News of the World* Special War Correspondent with the American Forces who was embedded with the 440th TCG at Exeter had flown to London and back on urgent business. Immediately on his return to Exeter he was summoned to a squadron headquarters in the 440th Troop Carrier Group. But they didn't show him his room. Instead they led him right out to the airfield, to the first of a line of waiting planes. 'This is It!' they remarked. 'It had come at last - just like that....'

At Merryfield airfield north of the village of Ilton near Ilminster in southwest Somerset the task of the 441st Troop Carrier Group was to transport the 1st and 2nd Battalions of the 501st PIR to DZ 'D'. C-47 pilot Clifford D. Kantz in the 100th TCS waiting to fly the first of the sixteen combat missions he would fly in World War Two, recalled: 'We had trained long and hard. There was ground school and flight training on all the operations concerned with formation flying, day and night. We also practiced how to fly the airplane in a manner that would let the paratroopers exit the plane at the proper airspeed, configuration and time over the drop zone. Now the training days were over. It was time to 'separate the men from the boys' as was said before all major operations during the war. All airplanes - C-47s - crews and paratroopers were assembled on an airfield in England to fly over Normandy on 5 June but the weather put everything on hold. We were quarantined to the base. No one was allowed on or off.

'It must be added here that before leaving the United States for England, my grandfather gave me a verse of Scripture. It was written in pencil, on a small bit of paper. It was Psalm 91:7 *A thousand shall fall at thy side and ten thousand at thy right hand; but it shall not come nigh thee.* After reading it, I smiled, thanked him, folded it and put it in my left shirt pocket. I thought about it many times and wondered about it. But it was true. I went all through the war without even a scratch, even though our airplane had been riddled with anti-aircraft shrapnel many times. I carried that verse every day of the war.

'We were briefed again in great detail about the part of our squadron was to play in the vertical envelopment of the German forces in Normandy. 'The paratroopers were heavy with all the equipment they were going to jump with shortly after midnight the next day. We had to help them up the two steps to get into the plane because they were so heavily loaded. The fifteen men we carried that night where called a 'stick'. 'At the proper time engines were started and we taxied very slowly in the dark to await our turn to take off. The night was very dark and cool for a morning in early June in England. There was radio silence. No one was to transmit any voice or Morse code signals at any time during the operation. There were eighteen airplanes in the 99th Troop Carrier Squadron, 27 in our squadron, eighteen in the 301st and 27 in the 302nd Troop Carrier Squadron.'

The first serial of 45 aircraft in the 441st carried the 1st Battalion, part of the 2nd Battalion and Regimental Headquarters of the 501st Parachute Infantry Regiment. In its lead aircraft were Lieutenant Colonel Theodore Kershaw, the group commander and 40-year old Colonel Howard R. Johnson, the regimental commander. The second serial contained most of the 2nd Battalion, half the 326th Engineer Company and some medical personnel.

Father Francis L. Sampson, the 39-year old chaplain to the 501st PIR who would drop with his unit had found Colonel 'Skeets' Johnson's penchant for profanity offensive. When he instructed his men to carry condoms while on leave in London, 'Father Sam' expressed opposition. Johnson, whose nickname was quite appropriate for someone 'who wanted to knock the shit out of someone', in this case, the enemy) had retorted, 'You take care of their souls and I'll take care of their asses!' 'Frankly, I did not know when I signed up for the airborne that chaplains would be expected to jump from an airplane in flight' wrote Sampson.

Lieutenant Sumpter Blackmon leader of First Platoon, 'Able' Company in the First Battalion recalls: 'It was 10 o'clock in the evening of 5 June and it was nearly time to go. The officers and men of our First Platoon joined hands and prayed that God guide us. I took my 'stick' of eighteen men on to the aircraft. Our equipment was so abundant and binding that we could scarcely move. We took off just after 10.30 that night and all the planes circled above the airfield and waited, then began forming up in 'V's. It took us an hour to get into formation. The 'V' was so perfect that I could have pitched a grenade at the plane just outside the open cargo door of the C-47.'

The first 440th Group serial carried the 3rd Battalion of the 506th PIR and the second, the rest of the engineer company. The destination of these serials was DZ 'D'. Ten days before the invasion this zone had been located about three quarters of a mile southwest of DZ 'C' and only the 3rd Battalion, 506th PIR, was scheduled to drop on it, the battalion's mission being to secure the southern perimeter of the 101st Division along the Douve. At that time the 501st PIR (less the 3rd Battalion) was supposed to jump on DZ 'B', 1½ miles south of Sainte-Mère-Église for the purpose of taking that town and the bridges over the Merderet at la Fière and Chef-du-Pont.

On 27 May when those tasks were transferred to the 82nd Division, the 501st was shifted to DZ 'D' to help hold the Douve line. Since new objectives of the 501st were about 2½ miles south of DZ 'D', the zone was relocated about a mile further south at the request of the regimental commander. Its new position was between Angoville-au-Plain and Basse Addeville, a hamlet 1,200 yards east of Sainte-Côme-du-Mont. Somewhat smaller than the other DZs; it was less than 1½ miles long from east to west and slightly under a mile across. In making their final approach to the zone, the pilots would have four landmarks to guide them: the junction of the Douve and Merderet, 4½ miles from the zone; the railway, 2½ miles from the zone, the flooded area which lay east of the railway north of the line of flight; and the north-south road to Carentan, which they would cross less than a mile before reaching the DZ. A secondary road to Sainte-Marie-du-Mont skirted the west end of the zone.

All pilots were adjured to drop all their troops. Evasive action prior to dropping was prohibited lest it disrupt formations or throw the paratroops into confusion. Aircraft missing a drop zone on the first pass were to drop near it if possible. If they overshot so far as to fine themselves over the east coast, they were to circle to the right and drop their loads on DZ 'D'. Stragglers would be responsible for finding their own way to their zones, using 'Rebecca' if necessary. After completing the drop, the pilots were to dive down onto the deck and fly put over the coast to the Sainte-Marcouf Islands at an altitude of 100 feet as a precaution against anti-aircraft and other ground fire in the coastal area. They would proceed home at a cruising speed of 150 mph by way of 'Gallup' and Portland Bill to 3,000 feet at 'Gallup' in accordance with agreements with the naval commander. Over England they would retrace the routes taken on the way out, except that the 50th Wing was authorized to take a twenty-mile short cut from the coast to its wing assembly point.

Around 2000 hours on 5 June in an orchard on either side of a low earthen mound which fenced the fields Lieutenant Colonel 'Bull' Wolverton called his 750 men in his battalion in prayer. 'Men' he said, 'I am not a religious man and I don't know your feelings in this matter, but I am going to ask you to pray with me for the success of the mission before us. And while we pray, let us get on our knees and not look down but up with faces raised to the sky so that we can see God and ask his blessing in what we are about to do.' All were silent for two minutes as the men were left, each with his individual thoughts. His parting words were that he would meet them the next year at the Muehlebach Hotel in Kansas City. Then the colonel ordered, 'Move out.'

Most of 'Ed' Shames' team had gone out to the airfield. Captain Charles Shettle, S3 operations officer came in and set his prismatic compass with a bearing for the road bridge. Before the battalion departed Shames took down the maps and aerial photographs from the sides of the tent, crammed as much stuff as he could into his musette bag, grabbed his M1 and went out to his aircraft. 'I didn't even have time to blacken my face' he recalled. Captain Barney Ryan, Medical Detachment, recalled 'I realized I'd left the airsickness tablets in my tent and rushed back to get them. I scooped some pills off the table and when I reached the aircraft gave them to the men. After putting them in their mouths they spluttered, 'What the hell are you trying to do to us - these are salt pills!' Luckily nobody got airsick.'

Tech Fifth Grade John Gibson, Medical Detachment who flew in one of the 440th TCG C-47s carrying the HQ Company's 81mm Mortar Platoon, recalled: 'When you are preparing for a very dangerous mission you think of family and good friends. You don't know if you'll ever see them again - life becomes precious and you appreciate everything. The medical detachment seemed to do a lot of waiting and sitting around. I remember, just to take my mind off things, playing blackjack for hours with Sergeant Tom Newell - Tom cleaned me out real good. The amounts betted were small and I didn't see any big money gambled in the marshalling area.'

By the evening of 'D-Day' each of the 45 C-47s in the 440th Troop Carrier Group at Exeter was laden down with paratroopers from the 3rd Battalion, 506th Parachute Infantry Regiment for the flight across the English Channel. Among the notables flown by the 96th TCS was the famed 'Filthy 13', the name given to the 1st Demolition Section of the 3rd Battalion, Regimental Headquarters Company who washed and shaved once a week and never cleaned their uniforms because they used their water ration to cook illegally poached deer, rabbits and fish. The number '13' referred to the thirteen enlisted men of the demolitions section, two six-man squads and the section sergeant. They were best known for the famous photo that appeared in *Stars and Stripes* showing two members sporting Indian-style 'Mohawks' and applying war paint to one another, inspired by 24-year old Sergeant James Elbert 'Jake' McNiece, born on 24 May 1919 in Maysville, Oklahoma, the ninth of ten children and who was part Choctaw. The family moved to Ponca City, Oklahoma in 1931. In 1939, 'Jake' graduated from Ponca City High School and went to work in road construction and then at the Pine Bluff Arsenal, where he gained experience in the use of explosives. Of the activities of the 'Filthy Thirteen', another member, Jack Agnew, once said, 'We weren't murderers or anything, we just didn't do everything we were supposed to do in some ways and did a whole lot more than they wanted us to do in other ways. We were always in trouble.' The Demolition Section was led by Lieutenant Charles Mellen whose men were ordered to secure or demolish the bridges over the Douve.

It was all an unknown for us,' said Major George Johnson, Operations Officer of the 98th Troop Carrier Squadron at Exeter. 'It was agreed that Lieutenant Colonel Frank X. Krebs, the 440th TCG commander, would lead.'

Captain Don Orcutt, of Poulsbo, Washington, one of the pilots in the 95th Troop Carrier Squadron, wrote: 'All the planes for the mission were numbered with large white chalk figures on the left side just in front of the main cabin exit door.' Orcutt had enlisted with the 104th Engineers of the National Guard in 1940. He was promoted to 1st Lieutenant and joined the Army Air Corps in 1943 and married Marion Dorothy Wille on 15 September in Seattle that same year. Lieutenant Colonel Krebs and his co-pilot, Major Howard Cannon the Group Operations Officer led in 'Chalk 1' carrying Lieutenant Colonel 'Bull' Wolverton and his stick of seventeen paratroopers in the 3rd Battalion, 506th Parachute Infantry and war correspondent Ward Smith. On the right side of the nose on 'Chalk 1' were the words *Stoy Hora,* the contraction of a Spanish expression meaning, 'here and now' with artwork of a plump man in top hat and tails, a ringmaster, pointing to the name of the plane. Bill Quick, Colonel Krebs' radio operator, believed the nose art was painted by 98th Squadron member Gil Mantalvo who was Mexican born.

Take-off at Exeter and Merryfield went rapidly and smoothly despite the ban on the use of radios. 'Blinker' lights were used to control taxiing and take-offs. Not one aircraft had an accident and none had to turn back. The 441st reported that its aircraft took off from Merryfield at average intervals of ten seconds apiece.

Clifford Kantz piloting 'Chalk 36' in Serial 14 wrote: 'After takeoff we climbed out, rendezvoused in formation and headed for Normandy. The only lights we could see to stay in formation were the blue formation lights on the top side of the airplane in front of us. All procedures as to heading, altitude and airspeed were followed exactly so as to keep all airplanes in the proper position for the paratrooper drop which was soon to follow. As we approached the coast of Normandy we climbed to 700 feet, the altitude for combat jumps. Then things began to happen fast and furious. The land beneath us and the sky around us lit up like a gigantic Fourth of July. There were searchlights everywhere. We had heard that there were seven bullets between every tracer, which was not a comforting thought. The searchlights

During summer 1944 two separate combat missions were planned that took troops as far as the airfields before being scrubbed. General Maxwell Taylor addressed the mass of troops shown assembled here and apologised that the latest mission had been cancelled. When he promised troops he would get them another combat mission as soon s possible, someone booed. (Signal Corps)

A pre-Day air power demonstration at Welford for the benefit of Winston Churchill.

Practice drop by the 1st Canadian Division on Salisbury Plain on 6 February 1944.

1st Sergeant Jake McNiece poses for the camera at Exeter during a pre-invasion press call.

On the eve of D-Day Clarence Ware and Chuck Plauda of the 506th Regimental Demolitions Saboteurs who were members of Jake McNiece's 'Filthy Thirteen', US 101st Airborne Division, apply their war paint, using the same black and white paint that appeared as invasion stripes on the C-47, at Exeter airfield. Plauda is carrying a .45 calibre Thompson submachine gun, the M1 version used in WWII.

Final crew consultation in Charles H. Young's C-47 (43-15159) *The Argonia* for the last practice mission before Normandy. R-L: Lieutenant Colonel Young, Lieutenant Vincent Paterno, navigator; Lieutenant Adam Parsons, co-pilot; Staff Sergeant John Dougherty, radio operator. Troop Carrier crews were the only Air Force crew members for whom infantry helmets were required flight gear. (Young).

In September 1944 *The Argonia* (a city in Summer County, Kansas) took part in Operation 'Market-Garden'. On 28 March 1982 *The Argonia* flew its last flight during which Robert Murphy a 'D-Day' veteran of the 82nd Airborne and Yves Tarel jumped out of it over Sainte-Mère-Église putting an end to its career. On 13 February 1983 it was heliported by the US Army from the Cherbourg-Maupertus airport to its final resting place in the Airborne Museum at Sainte-Mère-Église.

Two members of the 502nd PIR help each other to adjust their T5 parachutes prior to boarding their C-47 in the 438th TCG on 'D-Day'.

General Dwight D. Eisenhower talking with Lieutenant Colonel Robert Cole commanding the 3rd Battalion of the 502nd Parachute Infantry Regiment in the afternoon of 5 June.

Lieutenant General Lewis H. Brereton, Ninth Air Force commander talks to Lieutenant Colonel Whitacre CO, 434th Troop Carrier Group at Aldermaston.

Captain Frank Lillyman's stick of 377th PFA, in the 502nd Parachute Infantry Regiment which flew in C-47 42-93098 on the night of 5 June piloted by Lieutenant Colonel Joel L. Crouch commanding IX TCC Pathfinder. As the first pilot in the vanguard fleet, he was, in the words of reporter Lorelle Hearst of the *New York Journal-American*, 'the spearhead of the spearhead of the high-stakes allied invasion'.

C-47 42-93098 and crew. Standing L to R: Navigator, Captain William Culp, pilot Lieutenant Colonel Joel L. Crouch, Unknown crew chief; co-pilot Captain Vito S. Pedone. Kneeling L to R: Surgeon Captain Edward E. Cannon; radio, Corporal Harold E. Coonrod.

508th PIR paratroopers, commanded by Captain N. L. McRoberts of the 505th PIR and the flight crew in front of 'Chalk 18' at North Witham. The pathfinder sticks were made up of a group of eight to twelve pathfinders and a group of six bodyguards whose job was to defend the pathfinders while they set up their equipment. The pathfinder teams dropped approximately thirty minutes before the main body in order to locate designated drop zones and provide radio and visual guides for the main force in order to improve the accuracy of the jump.

British paratroopers in their C-47 before take off for Normandy.

British paratroopers in their Horsa glider before take off for Normandy.

Technician 4th Class Joseph F. Gorenc from Sheboygen, Wisconsin the assistant S3 of HQ Company, 3rd Battalion, 506th PIR, 101st Airborne Division climbing aboard the lead C-47 42-92717 *Stoy Hora* (note the cross-hatched number '1' chalk number to his right) in the 98th TCS, 440th TCG at Upottery on 5 June 1944. Gorenc was taken prisoner on 8 June at St. Côme-du-Mont and reported as MIA but later escaped from a Prison train and he was in action again at 'Operation Market Garden'. He returned home after the war, married and had two daughters and at the age of 34 was an officer in a new startup manufacturing firm. While he, the owner and another man were working late in the shop one night, an oil tank exploded. All were injured but Joe's injuries were life threatening and he died two weeks later.

C-47 42-92717 *Stoy Hora* in the 98th TCS, 440th TCG and members of the 3rd Battalion, 506th PIR, 101st Airborne and HQ stick commanded by Colonel Robert L. Wolverton ready to load at Upottery in the last hours of 5 June. The aircraft was the command ship of Colonel Frank X. Krebs, CO of the 440th whose job was to lead a 45 ship formation to Drop Zone 'D' in Normandy. *Stoy Hora* is a slang form of 'estoy ahora', meaning, 'I am here for you right now.

Left to right: Howard Cannon, co-pilot; Lieutenant Colonel Wolverton, CO, 3rd Battalion, 506th PIR and Colonel Frank Krebs, pilot and CO, 440th TCG.

Lieutenant Colonel Robert L. Wolverton in prayer before takeoff. Wolverton was killed seconds after landing in Normandy.

Crew of *That's All Brother* (42-92847) in the 87th Troop Carrier Squadron, 439th Group at Upottery that was the lead ship of Mission 'Albany' flown by Lieutenant Colonel John Munnerlyn 'Snake' Donalson commanding officer of the 438th Troop Carrier Group and Lieutenant Colonel David E. Daniel; commander of the 87th Squadron. 1st Lieutenant Barney Blankenship, navigator is kneeling bottom left; John M. Donalson is stood behind his left shoulder. The other members of the crew are 2nd Lieutenant John N. Shallcross, navigator, Staff Sergeant Harry A. Chalfant; crew chief, 2nd Lieutenant Robert G. Groswird, 2nd navigator, Staff Sergeant. Woodrow S. Wilson, radio operator (wounded by flak on the D-Day mission).

No.1 stick, HQ Company, 3rd Battalion, 506th PIR, 101st Airborne Division on *Stoy Hora:* Sergeant Joseph F. Gorenc (2nd left); 30-year old Technician 5th Class William H. Atlee (cigarette in mouth), an accountant from Iowa and Private Ray Calandrella (wearing goggles) who was captured during the fighting but escaped in August. Just after the drop, Atlee and 'Joe' Gorenc ambushed several German soldiers on a horse and cart. In the firefight, the two troopers managed to kill the enemy unit. The two paratroopers eventually met up with a group from the 501st led by an officer who ordered Atlee and Gorenc to scout ahead. As they left the field and started to cross a sunken road in Chemins de Campagne, they were hit by crossfire from a group of German paratroopers. Atlee was killed instantly.

C-47 (42-92847) *That's All Brother* which was Donalson's message to Hitler that with the invasion, his plans were done. In other words; 'That's all, brother.'

The crew of C-47 42-100849 ('Chalk 76', Serial 12) 94th TCS 439th TCG just before takeoff from Upottery Airfield on the night of 5th June 1944. From left: 1st Lieutenant Frank De Felitta, co-pilot (wearing flak suit); 2nd Lieutenant Thomas Waldman, navigator; 1st Lieutenant Harold King, pilot; Sergeant Jerome Sterling, radio operator; Tech Sergeant Victor Zielinski, crew chief.

A smiling, smut-darkened John H. Taylor of Lufkin, standing far right, a paratrooper with the 101st Airborne Division Screaming Eagles, waits with Stick #77 just before take off at 1107 hours on 5 June.

'F' Company, 2nd Battalion, 506th PIR, 101st Airborne Division in their C-47 'Chalk 76' in the 436th Troop Carrier Group in Serial 12.

Waiting to take off on 5 June in C-47 'Chalk 76' in the 436th Troop Carrier Group in Serial 12 are, from left: William G. Olanie, Frank D. Griffin, Robert J. Noody, bazookaman and Lester T. Hegland of Fox Company, 2nd Battalion, 506th PIR, 101st Airborne Division.

Paratroopers of the 82nd Airborne.

C-47 42-24022 in the 71st TCS, 434th TCG at Aldermaston.

C-47 42-92847 *Sugar Puss* in the 438th TCG at Greenham Common. (Estelle; centre).

C-47 42-100637 in the 436th TCG at Membury.

C-47 42-108991 79th TCS, 436th TCG at Membury.

1st Lieutenant Edgar H. Albers, pilot of *Iron Ass* in the 435th TCG at Welford.

C-47 42-92099 *Iron Ass* in the 75th Troop Carrier Squadron, 435th TCG at Welford which dropped paratroopers on DZ-C. This was as part of Serial 13 that dropped the 3/501 PIR and elements of Div HQ, Div Signal and Div Arty HQ. That same afternoon when the 435th was involved in towing fifty gliders to Normandy in Serial 33 *Iron Ass* was flown by the same crew.

lit up the cockpit when we were caught in them, causing our eyes to adjust to the brilliant light. When they continued past our plane, our eyes tried to adjust to the darkness, causing us to experience brief periods of vertigo; a highly dangerous situation.'

When the C-47 carrying Sumpter Blackmon turned inland he was in for a shock. 'The sky erupted in fireworks - flak. All around my plane the others were jinking and diving, but my pilot - I never did learn his name - flew the course without a tremor. He flew directly into a fogbank and all the other planes disappeared. When we came out of the fog, we were all alone. I stood at the cargo door with the equipment bundle of machine gun and ammunition, ready to kick it out when the jump light came on. I saw the proper landmarks come up, but felt no tap from the No 2 jumper, Private Thurman Day, or from Sergeant Adams. Then I saw the ground disappear and then whitecaps - we were back over the sea. Private Day pulled me back from the door and shouted that the pilot wanted to see me. He looked worried. 'Lieutenant' he said, 'we missed the drop zone and are over the Channel, headed back to England. What shall we do? I told him to take us to land and we'd get out. The pilot dived, came around and headed for the French shore again. He took us down just above the waves to evade the flak and as the plane reached the shoreline, he put it into a climb so steep that it threw several men off their feet. I decided it was now or never. I pushed out the equipment bundle, hooked up my chute ring and followed. I was jerked by the ring and my parachute opened automatically just before I hit the ground.

'After I landed hard, I cut myself loose from the parachute. I found the equipment chute in a low tree, a part of one of the Normandy hedgerows - thick, nearly impenetrable lines of trees and bushes. I pulled the red light attached to the pack, which was showing clearly and pulled it down and turned it off. Then I pulled out my carbine. I crawled into a hedgerow and waited and listened. Finally Private Day came up. We had no idea where we were. I pulled out my flashlight and map. I studied the map but could not find any points of terrain that matched - we'd obviously jumped off the map. We waited some time, but no-one else showed up and we decided we'd better take the machine gun and two boxes of ammunition out of the bundle and head south. After about half a mile, we were exhausted and had to stash the gun and ammo. Finally we met up with some other troopers and I really felt as if I had an army, with the 34 men I collected.'

At Exeter Ward Smith had walked out to 'Chalk 1'. As he climbed aboard the aircraft, paratroops, steel-helmeted, black-faced, festooned from head to foot, were in their planes in the bucket-seats lining each side of the fuselage. 'Major Cannon was reading a historic message from General Eisenhower. It spoke of the 'Great Crusade' and ended: 'Let us beseech the blessing of Almighty God on this noble undertaking.'

'As the door slanged to on us, sitting there in the dusk, we realized that we had suddenly passed from one world to another. Perhaps that was partly the effect of the all-red lights on the plane. They made our faces look slightly blue. They turned white the red tips of our cigarettes. I think that perhaps all of us had rather a sinking feeling in the pit of the stomach. But that didn't last long. Somehow we seemed to leave it behind on the ground. Almost before we realized it we were off. Here and there lights, friendly lights, winked at us. Other planes, their red and green wing lights twinkling cheerfully, fell into close formation behind to left and right. As everyone adjusted parachute harness, flak suits and Mae Wests, our mood brightened to a spate of banter.

'Say,' someone sang out suddenly, 'what's the date? I'll feel kinda dumb down there if some guy asks me and I get it wrong.'

'We laughed uproariously at things like that - the littlest things, the silliest things. We exchanged cigarettes and we talked on - but somehow never about things that mattered.'

At 2353 Cannon and Krebs, call sign 'Ada,' took off and were followed by 44 other aircraft in the 95th, 96th, 98th and 98th troop carrier squadrons that comprised the group. Captain Don Orcutt continues: 'Krebs taxied around the perimeter displaying his chalk number for all to see and we fell numerically into line behind him. At 2350 45 aircraft were lined up ready for takeoff. We had a signalman who flashed a green light at the end of the runway. If my memory serves me correctly, we took off at ten-second intervals and the entire group was airborne in roughly eight minutes. The colonel flew at a speed of 130 mph and as each aircraft took off it went 'balls out' playing catch the leader before eventually falling into position. Every plane had a series of dim blue lights, three on each upper wing surface and three on top of the cabin. After staring at those for a while your eyes began to cross. Krebs kept his landing lights on so that outbound planes could spot the head of the formation. This was always a little bit hairy because there was little room for error, particularly at night.'

Once airborne, the only navigational aids used were blue lights on the tops of the wingtips and fuselage, as the aircraft rendezvoused with other Skytrains from the IX Troop Carrier Command. It was dusk as our air fleet, advance guard of the invasion, left England - left twinkling lights for dark hazards' wrote Ward Smith. 'So closely had the secret of 'D-Day' been preserved that not all the flying crews themselves knew the signal had been given 'till they took off. The paratroops had been in barbed-wire enclosures for some days. No one had any chance to talk.'

With only the moonlight to navigate them in complete radio silence, the American and British forces joined together to make the big jump across the English Channel as the lighthouses of England slowly slipped away beneath them. Krebs honed into the radio signal from the Pathfinders who jumped in an hour before to mark the drop zone. Captain Don Orcutt remembered: 'A layer of clouds became visible that looked like they rose to a height of at least 3,000 feet. Continuing at our present altitude would have meant flying into the cloudbank. The colonel chose to descend and fly under the overcast - a wise move as it turned out. He must have studied terrain maps of the peninsula and knew how low he could go without danger, as our new height of about 900 feet above sea level was just right.'

'Down below a beacon flashed out a code letter' wrote Ward Smith. 'We made a sharp turn over to the coast. Then our roof lights, our wing lights and the lights of all the fleet behind abruptly flicked out. We were heading out to sea.

'We fell silent, just sat and watched the darkened ghosts sailing along behind us in the twilight.

'I noticed a red sign on the jump door, just one word: 'Think.'

'I tried to remember what the jump master had told me: 'If you have to bail out, don't forget to pull this tag to strip off the flak suit'; 'when you jump remember to count to two before you pull the rip cord'; 'if you hit the sea you MUST unbuckle this 'chute clip here before you pull the tassel to inflate the Mae West or it'll choke you.'

'While I was reflecting that I was certain to forget something, shore lights flashed in the distance. We could just make out land on the horizon under a glimmer of moon.

This was it - the 'Great Adventure' everyone had lived for and worked for so long and so hard. I hated to see it; and yet it thrilled me. Hitler's Europe.

'Those lights went out. A flare went up. Had they seen us? Had they heard us? The moon silvered the fleet behind.

'A pity someone said we were going in here,' one of the paratroopers remarked suddenly. We knew what he meant. He was talking of that extraordinary report that reached America some hours before that the Allies were already landing in France. Well, as it turned out, it was right. We were going into Northern France. Up here, now that lives were at stake, someone's idiocy didn't seem amusing.

'We took a sharp turn towards the land. And here I must pay tribute to the planning. So cunning was our routing, so many our twists and turns, that at no time till we reached our objective could the enemy have gained an inkling as to just where we were bound.

'The land slid by, silent and grey. And still nothing happened. Some of the paratroopers chorused, *Put that pistol down, Momma* and *For Me and My Girl*.

'Someone called out: 'Ten minutes to go'. The paratroop battalion commander talked quietly to his men. A final briefing. I shall never forget the scene up there in those last fateful minutes, those long lines of motionless, grim-faced young men burdened like pack-horses so that they could hardly stand unaided. Just waiting....

'So young they looked, on the edge of the unknown. And somehow, so sad. Most sat with eyes closed as the seconds ticked by. They seemed to be asleep, but I could see lips moving wordlessly. I wasn't consciously thinking of anything in particular, but suddenly I found the phrase *Thy rod and Thy staff* moving through my mind again and again. Just that and no more. It was all very odd. Then things began to happen. Below we saw fires on all sides. Our bombers had done their work well.'

'Among the paratroops [on Krebs' plane] were a doctor and two medical orderlies. They were going to drop with the rest to set up first-aid posts wherever opportunity offered. There was a chaplain, too. They all wrote their names and addresses and some messages in my notebook.' The doctor, Captain Stanley E. Morgan, the 3rd Battalion Chief Surgeon (and Sergeant Thomas E. Newell, a medic) were both captured and held prisoner from 'D-Day to 8 June.

Private Ray Calandrella, sitting opposite Ward Smith chatted briefly during the flight and Smith asked, 'Where are you from and how long have you been in the army?' Calandrella replied, 'Nearly two years. I'm from Hamden; you've probably never heard of it, but its near New Haven, Connecticut.' Nodding politely, Smith handed his notebook over to Calandrella and asked him to write down his name and address. He then passed the book around the remainder of the stick.[47]

'Corporal Jack Harrison of Phoenix, Arizona leaned over and thrust a packet of cigarettes in my hand. 'You might need them on the way back,' he said.

'I said 'What about you?' He just shrugged. Then he lined up with the others.'[48]

---

47 *Tonight We Die As Men* by Ian Gardner & Roger Day (Osprey 2009). Ray Calandrella was captured during the first day's fighting but he escaped in August.

48 R/5 Jack W. Harrison was killed during the first day's fighting.

At 0136 the paratroopers received the command, 'stand up and hook up.' Four minutes later, the green light came on giving the okay to jump.

'At 0140 we were over Carentan, in the Cherbourg Peninsula' wrote Ward Smith. 'A moment later the plane was empty. The paratroops were making one of the initial descents of the Second Front and the enemy from the ground was firing the first shots of this most momentous of all campaigns. All around the plane, rocketing less than 100 feet from the ground, a Brock's benefit of flak rainbowed us for something like eight minutes on end by my watch, though I could have sworn it was at least half an hour.

'The jump door opened, letting in a dull red glare from the fires below. The time had come. We were over the drop zone. I wish I could play up that moment, but there was nothing to indicate that this was the supreme climax. Just a whistling that lasted for a few seconds - and those men, so young, so brave, had gone to their destiny. I'd expected them to whoop battle-cries, to raise the roof in that last fateful moment. But not one of them did. They just stepped silently out into the red night, leaving behind only the echo of the songs they had been singing.'

In a matter of seconds, the sky was filled with the billowing white parachutes of the 101st Airborne Division heading for Drop Zone 'D' near Sainte-Mère-Église, 400 feet below.

'Then we got it' wrote Ward Smith. 'The flak and tracer came up, from all sides. Through the still-open door in the side of the plane I could see it forming a blazing arch over us - an arch that lasted for minutes on end, so close it seemed that we could not escape. It felt very lonely up there then in that empty C-47. I think I sat on the floor. About the only thing I can be sure of is that I was bathed in perspiration. I knew we were a sitting pigeon. We didn't have a gun or any armour-plate. Our only safeguard was our racing engines and the cool-headedness and skill of the pilot, Colonel Krebs, as he twisted and dived. I thought their fighters would be after us. But, fortunately, not a single one showed up from start to finish. Well, we came back. Three of Colonel Krebs' fleet didn't. 'We had luck,' said the colonel as we streaked for home. Standing behind him in the cockpit, you could see fleets of planes passing in each direction, guided by beacons on the water in a perfectly organized system of traffic control. The sea seemed full of ships. Soon the first seaborne forces would be going in....'

Tech Fifth Grade John Gibson, Medical Detachment recalled: 'Talking over the roar of the engines was almost impossible but I yelled at my buddy, 'How do you feel, Lee?' After two attempts at making him hear, Lee replied, 'Better than expected, how about you?' I yelled back the same answer he gave me. Inside I was nervous, had butterflies in my stomach and my hands were damp and cold with sweat. The plane rocked and fell a few feet, only to quickly regain its position. As we approached the peninsula I could see our formation of aircraft stretching for what seemed like miles behind us.'

Pfc 'Teddy' Dziepak of 'Item' Company recalled: 'Some of the guys were praying, smoking cigarettes, or being sick. As we crossed the coast the red light went on. The enemy fire coming up at us was heavy. You could hear shrapnel ripping through the fuselage and we wanted out!'

Sergeant Ralph Bennett in the 3rd Platoon, 'H' Company who flew on 'Chalk 36', remembered: 'When the red light flicked to green nobody moved. I could hear people shouting, 'For Christ's sake let's go, let's get out, what's happening up there and why aren't we moving?' I was the 'push out man' and it was my role to clear the plane. I started pushing and shoving furiously from the back and suddenly the stick began to move. I think this delay may have actually saved our lives.'

Private 'Bill' Galbraith in 'Item' Company adds: 'The plane didn't slow down for the jump and most of us lost our leg packs because of the exit speed. We were completely unaccustomed to parachuting with those things, as we'd never jumped with them before. The gun, ammunition and everything my crew needed was lost when our leg bags broke free.'

After cutting himself out of the risers Private Ray Calandrella set about chopping a small piece of nylon from his reserve chute as a souvenir. 'I pulled the D-ring and the brilliant white canopy burst out announcing for all to see that I had arrived! In a panic I gathered up the billowing chute and wrapped it inside my camouflaged main canopy. I then lay quietly on the ground trying to calm down. I saw the hunched shape of a man creeping toward me through a gap in the hedge. As he got closer I began to run a couple of scenarios through my head - should I use the bayonet or squeeze the trigger? I didn't want to do either but time was running out, so I nervously used my cricket. Click-clack - no response. I repeated the process. Click-clack - there was still no response and I raised my rifle to shoot. Suddenly I noticed a jump rope hanging from the guy's belt - it was 1st Lieutenant Howard Littell, our 81mm platoon leader. After introducing myself I whispered, 'Why the hell didn't you use your cricket?' In a hushed voice Littell replied, 'I'm sorry, I just couldn't find it.' 'Couldn't find it!' I said in disbelief. 'I came that close to pulling the trigger.' Littell just shrugged his shoulders and told me he'd got separated from the rest of his stick and that I should join him.' Calandrella was taken prisoner on 7 June.

The 441st and 440th Groups, like their predecessors, had little trouble reaching Normandy, but over the French coast the first serial of the 441st ran into the clouds and broke up. The two lead flights of the second serial ducked under the overcast and kept formation, but its other flights hit the cloud-bank and dispersed. The serial from the 440th appears to have avoided the clouds and held together.

'Father Sam' in Kershaw's C-47 studied the deadpan faces. 'These men were generally quiet. Some tried to sleep; others smoked steadily and a few tried to be nonchalant by humming modern songs.' He wondered how many would survive to see daylight again.

Colonel Kershaw took the 441st straight through the grey soup and the formation gradually nosed down to 700 feet, the jump altitude. Little fire was encountered over the western part of the Cotentin. The 441st reported considerable shooting near Sainte-Sauveur de Pierre Pont and at other points between there and the DZ. One C-47 in the 441st blew up before reaching the drop area. Captain Don Orcutt had seen in his peripheral vision, a tremendous blast of light when the C-47s took the hit. 'There were no survivors from that one' he recalled. 1st Lieutenant Charles J. 'Sandy' Santarsiero in Company 'I' in the 506th PIR saw it too. 'The explosion shook our plane. Someone asked: 'What the hell was that?' I said that one of our fighter pilots had just shot down a Kraut. They cheered! For their morale, I thought it best that way. How does one tell their men that their buddies were just blown to Hell?'[49]

Now, at the DZ, with the last man gone Donald Orcutt stopped his watch. It showed 36 seconds had elapsed (more than twice as long as normal). 'Someone must have stumbled and held the stick up' he reasoned. 'I applied the power as needed to maintain position in formation. I had no way of knowing at the time what was going on behind me.'[50]

A second C-47 in the formation occurred when it crashed soon after dropping its load. A third, hit by anti-aircraft fire as it left the DZ made a forced landing near Cherbourg, its crew later reaching the Allied lines in safety. Fourteen others in the 441st were damaged. At 0126, five minutes ahead of schedule, the first serial of the 441st started its drop. The next began at 0134. Between them they carried 1,475 troops, of which they dropped at least 1,429. Returned were one soldier who had fainted and twelve who had slipped in vomit and had become entangled. A 'Eureka' which

49   Santarsiero was awarded the DSC for his heroism on 7 June.
50   Excerpted from *Tonight We Die As Men* by Ian Gardner and Roger Day (Osprey, 2009).

the pathfinders had set up west of the zone was received up to seventeen miles away. Signals from the beacon on DZ 'A' were also received, but were readily distinguished from the correct ones by their coding and by their position on the 'Rebecca' scope. The lighted 'T' supposed to mark the zone was not observed. The enemy thereabout were so numerous and active that the pathfinder troops had been unable to operate the lights. Except that the lead pilot of the 441st made some use of 'Gee' to check his position, the three serials relied on 'Rebecca'-Eureka' or on visual recognition to locate the zone. The 'Rebecca' was a poor guide at close range and the cloud-swept landscape proved hard to identify. Many stragglers from the first serial of the 441st and some from other serials had to make two or three passes to orientate themselves. Some of them grew completely confused and ended up by making drops many miles from the drop area. However, most pilots believed that they had achieved accuracy and only one, a member of the 441st Group, gave up after three attempts and went home with his load.

On Kershaw's C-47 Father Sampson watched the jumpmaster, 1st Lieutenant Ted Fuller, pull himself to his feet and yell, 'Get ready!' The C-47 flew through a hail of flak and small arms fire. One projectile hit Technician 5th Grade Stanley E. Butkovich and penetrated his left thigh. Waylon Lamb, a medic, clambered to the wounded trooper who insisted on jumping. Fuller consented and unhooked Butkovich from the anchor cable and moved him to a seated position in the doorway, his legs dangling overboard. Fuller re-attached Butkovich to the cable. Over the DZ Fuller gave Butkovich a shove out the doorway. Equipment bundles followed him and then his fellow troopers in rapid succession. 'Father Sam' followed, 'It will always remain a mystery to me how any of us lived' he wrote later. 'I collapsed part of my chute to come down faster. From there I placed myself in the hands of my guardian angel.'

He plunged into a flooded drainage ditch but his canopy stayed open and wind gust pulled him into shallow water. As bullets zipped over the swamp he dived into the water five or six times to get his musette bag containing his ciborium and its sacred contents. He spotted another man from his stick, his assistant, 'Buck' France, who had lost his rifle after nearly drowning. Soaked to the skin, the two men scrambled to a hedgerow for cover. They looked up to see a C-47 heading their way, flames gushing from its left wing. The aircraft approached low, its pilot fighting to gain control. The C-47 pitched into a field and exploded in an orange fireball that billowed high into the sky. The two men prayed for the dead crewmen now cooking in the funeral pyre. They also prayed for the souls aboard two other flaming aircraft that blazed across the distant sky 'like bottle rockets'. 'Father Sam's heroic efforts on behalf of his wounded men would later earn him the DSC.[51]

Major Lloyd G. Neblett of Texarkana, Texas in the 301st TCS, 441st TCG had almost missed the big show when mechanical difficulty forced him to drop out at the start, but his crew chief, Sergeant Willie Brown of Asheville, North Carolina did a rush job. Neblett took off again, cut corners at full speed and caught the formation just short of the objective. But a heavy supply bundle from another C-47 landed squarely on his right wing. Struggling with the controls, he and co-pilot Lieutenant Thomas O'Brien of St. Paul, Minnesota kept the transport from stalling while paratroopers were discharged. Hearing the bail-out bell, Crew Chief John J. O'Conner, Mosinee, Wisconsin dived after the last trooper, only to watch his plane fly on, unharmed. After two weeks' fighting with the Airborne and being captured at an advanced aid station, the Sergeant returned to his squadron to learn the 'abandon ship' order was just a case of the wrong switch! From 600 feet the aircraft fell out of control through a flak barrage that sheared eight feet off the wing and a third of the aileron. The C-47's fall finally was checked at roof-top level and flying alone, returned safely to Merryfield where the aircraft was no good for anything but salvage.

The 440th had scant opposition until it was within six miles of the zone. Then it received intense light flak and automatic fire which caused many pilots to take evasive action and drop out of formation. In the final miles to the DZ the 440th lost three C-47s to enemy fire. 'Chalk 15' *Donna Mae* in the 95th TCS piloted by 1st Lieutenant Ray 'Ben' Pullen crashed at Magneville en route into the DZ with the loss of all four crew and 18 paratroopers in 1st Lieutenant Gerald V. Howard Jr's stick. 2nd Lieutenant Alan R. Keller in the 96th Squadron piloting 'Chalk 24' was able to drop the nineteen men of 1st Platoon, 'Item' Company accurately on the DZ before his C-47 was hit as it left the zone and plunged into the sea. Only four men in the stick, which included Corporal 'Bobbie' Rommel from Modesto, California who incredibly, was related to General Field Marshal Erwin Rommel, survived. 'Bobbie' was nineteen years old when he joined the 3rd Battalion at Camp Mackall, North Carolina as a machine gunner.[52] Another pilot, Arthur

---

51 See *Drama At The Klondike Aid Station* by Bill Warwick. 'Father Sam' was in fact put forward for the MoH, a citation supported by General Eisenhower. 'Father Sam' was captured later during the Battle of the Bulge and was taken prisoner.

52 See *Tonight We Die As Men* by Ian Gardner & Roger Day (Osprey 2009). Bobbie Rommel was wounded at Bastogne on 9 January 1945. After nineteen weeks in hospital, he became a driver for the USO shows. He finally received his campaign medals 62 years later.

Douglass, watched helplessly as the ill-fated transport lost altitude with one engine dead and the other on fire. Though he saw some parachutes, he later learned that Keller and his crew including the crew chief, T/4 Ed Bluestone perished in the crash into the Bay of the Seine. C-47 (42-100733) piloted by 25-year old 2nd Lieutenant William H. Zeuner of Philadelphia, Pennsylvania, which was carrying nineteen troopers, was shot down by flak. The only survivors on the aircraft were four troopers who could only jump from the aircraft before the crash.

A dozen other aircraft of the 440th suffered damage but they would be quickly repaired. Searchlights and magnesium flares further loosened the formations by dazzling pilots and forcing them to dodge. Some searchlights were quickly attacked and extinguished by Allied night-fighters but others survived long enough to cause trouble. Very intense flak and automatic weapons fire countered on DZ 'D' and immediately east of it.[53] The Germans had spotted the area as a likely one for airborne use and were present in force. Fortunately their fire was not accurate and the actual number of anti-aircraft guns was probably small. The rate of aircraft losses for the three serials was less than five percent.

The headquarters and first battalion of the 501st PIR had received only a partially satisfactory drop by the C-47s in the 441st. Nineteen aircraft, including the three in the lead element of the serial put their sticks on DZ 'D' or close to its southern edge. Two others came within a couple of miles of it. On the other hand, the whole last flight veered north of course onto a line passing close to DZ 'C'. Eight of its nine loads landed between two and four miles northwest of DZ 'D' between Chef-du-Pont and DZ 'C' and the other was about three miles further east on the same line of flight. One stick came down about seven miles north of the proper zone. These sticks at least landed within the 101st's prescribed perimeter, but another nine had been scattered from four to ten miles south of DZ 'D' in the Carentan area on the far side of the Douve.

Private Ellsworth Helmer Onger had left a quiet farming community in Strandquist, Minnesota to join 'Dog' Company in the 2nd Battalion. Onger's mother had died while giving birth to twins when Ellsworth was four years old; this left his father to raise seven small children, the oldest just eight years old. Ellsworth's platoon was commanded by 1st Lieutenant Ian D. Nicholson who was also the jumpmaster in the 17-strong stick on 'Chalk 54' (42-101025) piloted by 2nd Lieutenant Eugene Frederick 'Sack' Hennig. As Serial 15 approached the drop-zone Nicholson's stick never had

---

53   One account states that some aircraft had not turned off all their lights and so attracted fire.

a chance to use their parachutes. 'Chalk 54' was shot down by anti-aircraft fire near Varenguebec on the Cotentin Peninsular. The four crew and all eighteen troopers including Ellsworth Onger went down with the aircraft.[54] Four other sticks carried by the serial are unaccounted for. Those troops who did come down near the zone were involved in fighting from the start.

Clifford Kantz in the 441st wrote: 'We were approaching Sainte-Mère-Église. All fifteen paratroopers were drifting rapidly downward. Even at this speed I could see their eyes and they were terrified for a few brief moments as much as I was. Suppose they hit the wing and their shroud lines snagged. Or worse yet, suppose they hit the engines! All would be lost, airplane, crew members and possibly all the paratroopers who would be on board. 'I screamed at the top of my voice, 'Green light, green light, get 'em out!' As they exited the plane I could hear the 'whoosh-whoosh' of each paratrooper. At the same time power was added to the engines and I pulled back on the controls to gain altitude so as not to be underneath any other planes and paratroopers who might be above us. We continued across the Normandy peninsula dropping down to sea level to avoid any more searchlights or anti-aircraft fire.'

After receiving one of the best drops in either 'Albany' or 'Boston' the 2nd Battalion of the 501st Parachute Infantry Regiment had a hard and seemingly fruitless day. At least forty of its 45 sticks had come down on or within a mile of the drop zone, mainly near its southern edge. (One was 1½ distant and another 2½ miles away). Twenty-four-year old Captain Sam Gibbons from Tampa, Florida was the third man to step out of 'Chalk 42' and dropping 800 feet. 'My equipment was typical for the jump that night. Two parachutes - one main on my back and a reserve on my chest in case the main malfunctioned - both camouflaged green and brown and made of nylon. We had used some silk ones in our early training. We all wore a Mae West inflatable-type life jacket because we crossed 150 miles of sea and jumped near a river. Many were used that night. We also wore an equipment harness and ammunition belt with thirty rounds of .45 calibre pistol ammo and about one hundred rounds of .30 calibre rifle ammo, two hand grenades, a .45 calibre pistol [M1911], loaded and cocked, a .30 calibre folding stock rifle [M1A1 carbine], loaded and cocked, a ten-inch-blade knife strapped to the calf for hand-to-hand combat, a canteen with one quart of water, one spoon and canteen cup used as a cooking utensil, some water purification tablets, a combat first aid kit tied to the camouflage material that covered our steel helmets helmet (special helmet liner required so wouldn't be blown

---

54 *Little Minnesota in World War II: The stories behind 140 fallen heroes from Minnesota's littlest towns* by Jill A. Johnson and Deane L. Johnson (Adventure Publications, 2017).

off in jump), special first aid kit containing two shots of morphine, sulpha drugs and compress bandages to stop bleeding. In a leg pocket we carried a British-made anti-tank mine because there were plenty of tanks nearby; an equipment bag containing a raincoat, a blanket, toothbrush, toilet paper and six meals of emergency 'K rations' - a combination shovel and pick for digging in; maps, flashlight, compass; also an 'escape kit' containing a very small compass, small hacksaw blade, a map of France printed on silk and $300 worth of well-used French currency. This kit was enclosed in a waterproof container measuring four inches by six inches by one-quarter inch - everyone was encouraged to hide it in a different place on the body. I carried mine inside my sock, just above boot top on my right leg'

'We wore our identification dog tags on a light metal chain around our necks, taped together so they didn't click or rattle. And at noontime before the invasion we had received our last surprise: A 'cricket.' This was a metal device made partially of brass and partially of steel. When you depressed the steel it made a snapping sound or a 'crick.' And when you released the steel part, it would crick again. This was something we had not counted on and had never heard about, but it was to be our primary means of identification between friend and foe during the night assault. One click of the cricket was to be answered by two clicks. We cricked them a few times and rehearsed (we were to crick once and wait for a response of two cricks) - laughing all the time.'

Kapitän Ernst During who commanded a German machine gun company at Brevands near where the Vire River empties into the Channel had been asleep for a couple of hours when, shortly after midnight he was awakened by the sound of explosions: 'There was the noise of many planes coming from the direction of Sainte-Mère-Église. I thought to myself, this is it! I got dressed as quickly as I could...When I got to my command post I telephoned battalion headquarters two miles to the rear and said, 'paratroops have landed here'. The answer came back. 'Here too'. Then the line went dead...Then I heard strange sounds - a kind of click, click, click at regular intervals. It sounded like the castanets of Spanish dancers. I couldn't explain it...I felt very uneasy and isolated.' The 101st Division used the metal snappers for recognition and assembly. In the Bocage these proved helpful even by daylight. The 82nd Division relied on lights and patrol for assembly and did not have the crickets.

Like the thousands of other paratroopers of the 101st, 82nd Airborne 'All Americans' and British 6th Airborne thumping to the ground that night, Gibbons checked himself for all his component parts, got out of his parachute harness and began to search for other paratroopers from his unit.

After 45 minutes of crawling over and through hedgerows and ditches, with the sound of gunfire rattling through the night, Gibbons saw the distinctive outline of an American helmet silhouetted against the sky and after taking cover and raising his carbine, cricked his cricket.

'Instantly the response came back with two cricks. I felt a thousand years younger and both of us moved forward so we could touch each other. I whispered my name and he whispered his. To my surprise, he was not from my plane. In fact, he was not even from my Headquarters group. He was a sergeant and lost, too.'

In the 501st PIR Master Sergeant Charlie Vess, born in 1922 in Rutherford County, North Carolina jumped from his C-47, landing in water. Cutting himself free, he vividly remembers 'the legs of drowned paratroopers sticking up in the air because of the gas mask bags'. He found four others from his stick and by daylight 'the scrimmage got pretty hot'.[55]

Raymond Geddes in the 501th PIR recalled: 'The flight over to France was uneventful. It was dark and it took about two hours. I looked out the window once and saw a red light down there somewhere. Then someone said, 'We are over land!' I looked out the door. It was sort of moonlit haze. Shortly thereafter the red light came on and the drill started - 'Stand up! Hook up!' etc. Then the plane started to bounce around in a manner which I had never experienced before. We also began to hear explosions and what sounded like hail hitting the plane. We heard a loud explosion at the same time as a large flash of light. One of the planes in our group had gone up in a giant explosion. Someone called out, 'Look, those guys are on fire!' I leaned over and looked out the left windows and could see bits of flaming wreckage as the plane next to us also began to go down. I saw tracers from anti-aircraft fire all over the sky and I realized that the 'hail' hitting the plane was flak. Along with others I began to yell to our jump master, 'Let's get the hell out of here!' - or words to that effect. Then our plane went into a dive and we tried to keep from falling down. The plane levelled out just above the ground. I don't remember what happened next, but I learned later from Sergeant Don Castona that the pilot had passed on the message for our jumpmaster, Lieutenant Barker to come up to the front of the plane. During the time Barker was in the cockpit Castona noticed that the plane had changed course. We began climbing and suddenly, the green light came on.

'Immediately the line started out the door and we jumped. We were going fast and the opening shock was terrific! I remember seeing a farmhouse

---

55   In September he jumped into Holland and was a veteran of the Battle of the Bulge receiving a Bronze Star and Purple Heart.

below and then I was on the ground. My harness was so tight I couldn't get myself free. Cows were all around me as I reached for the knife attached to my boot. It was gone, pulled loose when the chute opened. I finally got hold of my jump knife, which I had stored in a pocket in my jacket and destroyed government property by cutting myself out of the harness. I stood up and checked my radio operator's watch, which I noticed had stopped from the opening shock at exactly 0125 hours.

'I was very glad to see that I had not lost my M-1 rifle stored in its Griswold bag. I assembled the rifle and moved off, trying to find someone. There was noise coming from every direction, planes overhead and shooting on the ground, but I was totally alone. Finally, in the moonlight, I saw some helmets. I gave one click on the 101st recognition signal (a toy cricket) and waited for the reply of two clicks. There was no reply. I tried again. Still no answer. I was reaching for a grenade when thank God I saw the shape of the helmets. I called out and found that the soldiers were men from my company. They told me they never heard the cricket. I found out later that we had landed in the centre of Drop Zone 'C', exactly where we were supposed to be (near Hiesville), one of the few units in the whole US Airborne to make that statement.

'Fifty five years later I learned that our pilot, Lieutenant Harrison, had saved our lives by diving away from the anti-aircraft fire that shot down the other two planes in our flight. He flew past the DZ and then, after talking to Lieutenant Barker, he turned 180° and dropped us in the middle of the DZ going the wrong way. He deserved a medal and he got it, but it took sixty years and that's another story.

'I have only a few memories of events between the time I joined up with 'George' Company and sunrise. I remember how beautiful the German tracers looked as they flew into the sky looking for targets. I watched a plane explode. I also remember that I fell into a ditch and found it was full of dead soldiers - I still don't know if they were Germans or Americans. One thing I do remember is that at dawn, when I could see, I took my trusty jump knife and dropped my trousers so I could cut off those damn hot GI long johns.'[56]

56 June 8th turned out to be my last day in combat in WWII and my last day with G/501. Our battalion had been released from our assignment with 101st HQ and was part of an attack towards Sainte-Côme-du-Mont. The attack started at dawn. Later in the morning I received my first wound of the day, in the leg, from an artillery shell. I also picked up a replacement for my ruined watch. When I got to England they operated on my eye. Several weeks later I was on my way back to the US by airplane, in one of the first groups of 'D-Day' wounded to be sent home. When I arrived at Mitchell Field on Long Island I was told that I could take the weekend off and return to the hospital on Monday morning. I used that ten dollar bill from the butt of my rifle to buy a train ticket to Baltimore and be with my family.

Most of the 101st had been dropped miles from their objectives. Some groups of paratroopers managed to reach and attack their objectives that night; many more were too far away, but decided to move toward the nearest objective and start their war there. The drop zones were so scattered that it caused the Germans more confusion than it would have had the jumps gone off without a hitch. The Germans could not make any sense of where the main concentrations of paratroopers were or what their objectives were.

Gibbons and the sergeant moved off, collecting more paratroopers throughout the night, including two more officers, as they moved toward Sainte-Côme-du-Mont, which was at least one of the regiment's objectives, finally halting at dawn to hold a war council on the best method of attacking the town. There were two non-issue items Gibbons jumped with that night. In his gas mask case, instead of the gas mask, he had placed two cans of Schlitz beer. 'At the end of this council I brought out my two cans of beer, which we shared,' Gibbons wrote. 'When the cans were empty we decided to leave them in the middle of the road as a monument to the first cans of Schlitz consumed in France and moved on.'

In the following hours and days Gibbons and other paratroopers would fight a series of small unit actions as well as a major battle at Carentan. He and the 101st would go on to seize four of five bridge objectives during Operation 'Market Garden', hold Bastogne during the Battle of the Bulge and capture Hitler's 'Eagles Nest'.[57]

The drop by the 440th Group had begun at 0140. The 3rd Battalion, 506th PIR had been given a good drop by the 440th Group. Out of 723 troops carried 719 jumped. Flak had wounded one man and he had blocked the exit of the other three. About eight of its sticks landed on the zone and 26 more within a mile of it, the principal concentration being near the eastern end. Only two sticks, dropped thirteen miles to the south are known to have landed far from their goal. In the No.2 ship carrying part of Major Grant's stick the men landed along a line between the southern edge of the hamlet of Sainte-Côme-du-Mont and the flooded fields below L'Amont. The

---

57 When the war in Europe ended, Gibbons returned home, went to law school and served in the US House of Representatives for 16 consecutive terms. At a White House dinner, Gibbons was brought two cans of Schlitz beer on a silver platter. When the dinner was over, Gibbons took the two cans with him, unopened. Sometime later that year, Gibbons returned with his family to Normandy, where they drank those two cans of beer and left them sitting on the road as a monument of a different sort, in the same place where five decades earlier, a 24-year-old captain and a few American paratroopers finished their shared beer, got back to their feet, checked their weapons and moved toward their objective.

stick suffered many fatal casualties, including Major Grant and the three naval observers in the stick. Captain Barney Ryan recalled: The antiaircraft and small arms fire was horrendous and our plane began taking violent evasive action. As we stood up on the red light we were thrown about and the plane didn't seem to slow down when we jumped. I felt a terrific shock as the 'chute opened. The ground was ablaze with enemy fire. Tracer bullets seemed to be coming in all directions and I instinctively pulled y legs up to make a smaller target. I must have been in the air for about thirty seconds, which would have made our jump height around 400 feet.'[58]

Of the 575 men from 3rd Battalion who jumped that night, 75 were taken prisoner and 93 were killed during the Normandy campaign. Eight members of 'Bull' Wolverton's stick were taken prisoner shortly after they landed on French soil. Within thirty seconds of leaving the C-47 six men including 'Bull' Wolverton and Sergeant Nagy the US Naval Artillery observer were killed. Tragically Wolverton and Nagy got entangled in apple trees in an orchard just north of Sainte-Côme-du-Mont and were shot before their feet could touch the ground. 'Bull' Wolverton died after being hit repeatedly by German machine gun fire. According to 'Ed' Shames, Wolverton sustained '162 bullet holes and bayonet wounds' due to German troops using him as target practice. The planned reunion at the Muehlebach Hotel in Kansas City in 1946 went ahead without him.

Sergeant Edward D. Shames, who had built the sand tables the 101st Airborne used in planning the airdrop, recalled: 'A C-47 fell out of the sky right in front of the door. They completely scattered us. I jumped in ten kilometres from the place that was planned and ended in the barn of a factory with milk, with cows. I did not know where I was while I was supposed to know everything. I had to find my group of eighteen men and go towards our objective, which were two bridges. We had the mission to hold these bridges to prevent the Germans from bringing reinforcements on the beaches of landings.' The 22-year old Jew was affected deeply later by seeing Nazi Germany's concentration camps.

Despite their early losses, 140 paratroopers in Wolverton's 3rd Battalion managed to seize the bridges in the early hours of 6 June and they held them for three days. But because their radio equipment had been lost during the drop, they were unable to report their success to the division. Having heard nothing, the air force assumed that the mission had failed and that 3rd

58 *Tonight We Die As Men* by Ian Gardner & Roger Day (Osprey 2009).

Battalion had been wiped out. On 7 June they sent a pack of fighter-bombers that strafed and destroyed both bridges. Incredibly, only one American was killed by the friendly fire.

Sergeant Louis E. Traux of the 1ˢᵗ Battalion, 506ᵗʰ PIR flying in a 439th TCG C-47 at Upottery recalled: 'The front men were jumping. The first twelve men got out pretty close together. I was running down the aisle. Suddenly the plane was hit in the left wing by flak. The wing went straight up. My left shoulder crashed into a window. With ammo, a 1903 Springfield rifle, twelve grenade-launcher rounds, two cans of blood plasma, two cans of distilled water, gas mask, helmet, 'K rations'... I must have weighed 225-250lbs. Stripped, I weighed 130. I was surprised the window didn't break. The pilot was fighting to right the plane. When he succeeded, I was appalled at the view which greeted me - I was the only one standing. Four men lay on a tangled heap on the floor. I realized it was almost impossible for them to stand up with their equipment loads. Also that an absolute sequence had to be maintained or we'd have a glob of human hamburger dangling outside the door at 150 mph. I grabbed the ammo belt in the centre of the man I thought next and gave him a heave out nose first. The next man made it crawling on his own power. I reached up and pulled the salvo switch which released the machine gun and mortars attached to the bomb racks under the plane. Then I dived out.'

When First Sergeant David 'Buck' Rogers' parachute opened he was directly above the church steeple of the church in Sainte-Marie-du-Mont. 'The moon was full and there were scattered clouds which made everything on the ground easy to see. When I looked down I saw Sainte-Marie-du-Mont. It looked just like the picture I had studied so intensely at Upottery. I knew without a doubt that I was over the church steeple in that small French village.'

Of the 231 soldiers of the 506th PIR who lost their lives at Normandy, 103 were from the 3rd Battalion, including those who died in three of the 440th TCG aircraft that perished in the operation on 5/6 June. Half the 'Filthy 13' were either killed or wounded or captured, but they accomplished their mission. Lieutenant Charles Mellen was among the dead. Following Mellen's death, Sergeant 'Jake' McNiece who had inspired the unit's Indian-style 'Mohawks' and war paint led the unit. They also participated in the capture of Carentan.

The return of the 'Albany' serials was generally uneventful after they left Normandy. Over the Channel the sky was becoming overcast, but the clouds were above 4,000 feet and visibility was good. In southern England there were scattered squalls, one of which caused returning aircraft to stack up for a time over Membury. Except in the 438th and 440th Groups most of the pilots returned singly or in small formations. Some must have wandered far and wide, for the flow of returnees lasted from 0210 when the first aircraft reached Greenham Common until about 0430.

As Clifford Kantz in the 441st TCG approached Merryfield the Group had to circle to let damaged planes or those carrying wounded land first. 'When all planes that had fired red flares, indicating an emergency landed, we also landed. We went immediately to the operations building and gave an account of what happened during the flight. 'The invasion of Europe had begun. The flight from England to Normandy to England had lasted only three hours, 45 minutes. Strangely, it seemed much longer and much shorter, but my first combat mission was over. Dawn was breaking over the white cliffs of Dover. We didn't realize how tired we were from our first day of combat. Many of my friends never returned that day.[59] It was time to get some rest for the days and months that were yet to come. I shall never forget the small part that I played in the greatest military operation of any war in history. There are many good memories, many bad memories. But we were young and tomorrow was another day.'[60]

The size of the American build-up had already been such that it would have taken two regiments of Germans rather than two battalions to create a threat to the 'Utah' operation. Nevertheless, by resolute action these thrusts could have caused enough trouble to delay VII Corps for many days. Actually they accomplished little. During the night the German regimental commander, gradually realizing the odds against his men, ordered them back. The second battalion got the order and returned safely to Sainte-Côme. The first battalion, which did not acknowledge the order and may not have received it, retired southward next morning. Unable to make contact with its comrades, it marched without reconnoitring toward the crossings at la Barquette and le Port in apparent ignorance that the Americans held those points. About 1600 the battalion approached the river.

The 101st Airborne Division had accomplished its most important mission of securing the beach exits, but had a tenuous hold on positions near the Douve River, over which the Germans could still move armoured units. The three groups clustered there had tenuous contact with each

---

59 Two C-47s in Kantz' serial - 42-101019 and 42-101006 - were lost with their crews. 15 paratroopers were killed also on 42-101019..

60 Clifford published his story previously in *The Daily News*, Lebanon, PA.

other but none with the rest of the division. A shortage of radio equipment caused by losses during the drops exacerbated his control problems. The accomplishments, against the opposition of two battalions had required two and a half days and the help of tanks and artillery brought in by sea. On the 9th the 101st Division paused to reorganize for its drive toward Carentan. This pause may be taken as the end of the airborne stage of its operations. The subsequent attack by the 101st which made contact with V Corps on 10 June and took Carentan on 12 June was made as a ground unit striking out of an organized beachhead.

In the week following 7 June, six small parachute and glider resupply-missions were flown on call by the 441st and 436th Troop carrier Groups, with ten C-47s making parachute drop and 24 towing gliders. All of these went smoothly without enemy opposition and without appreciable hindrance from weather. This brought the final total of IX Troop Carrier Command sorties during Operation 'Neptune' to 2,166, with 533 of those being glider sorties.

These glider missions were not the end of glider landings in Normandy. Some days after these missions, the 436th Troop Carrier Group executed resupply missions to Normandy with gliders landing on an airstrip. Among the glider pilots who flew this resupply mission were also pilots who had landed in Normandy a few days earlier. This was their second trip to Normandy. These later missions were without casualties.

On the 8th a single aircraft of the 441st Group, staging from Greenham Common, took off at 0700 hours with 150lbs of medical supplies for the 101st Division. Escorted by four P-38s, it flew over the route used in 'Hackensack', made its drop, probably on LZ 'E' and returned unmolested. Next day two gliders with badly needed signal equipment landed successfully near Sainte-Mère-Église about 1845. The recipient in this and the four following missions was the 82nd Division. On the 10th the 436th Group dispatched six aircraft from Membury with Wacos. The gliders held two jeeps, two soldiers and six and a half tons of combat equipment. Released at 1740 near Sainte-Mère-Église, they made excellent landings in the area designated. On 12 June nine aircraft of the 436th Group flew a paradrop re-supply mission, carrying two tons of 60 mm and 81 mm mortars and five tons of ammunition stowed in 54 parapacks and 25 bundles. At 0802 they made an accurate drop of all but one parapack from an altitude of 300 feet on a zone just east of Sainte-Mère-Église. Five aircraft of that Group towed Waco gliders to the same zone that evening. Aboard the gliders were two jeeps and 42 airborne troops and one of the aircraft carried fifteen paratroops. Such a dual role was unusual because paratroops preferred to jump from a tight formation rather than a long glider column and because of the restriction of gliders to follow-up operations.

The gliders were released and the paratroops then jumped about 2021, all landing safely on the zone. The Germans, who still held positions within four miles of Sainte-Mère-Église, responded to the landing by shelling the area. The last of these missions was flown on the 13th by eleven aircraft of the 436th Group. Escorted by twelve P-38s they towed eleven Wacos to Sainte-Mère-Église. The gliders contained 1½ tons of ammunition and thirteen tons of equipment. Release was made at 1913 from a height of 600 feet and the landings were thoroughly successful.

At Exeter, war reporter Ward Smith who had accompanied the 501st Parachute Infantry in the lead C-47 in the 440th TCG wrote: 'We came back. Our paratroopers hadn't - yet. At the moment, they're too busy to tell their story.

'Just in case Corporal Harrison happens to read this, I'd like him to know that I'm keeping his cigarettes for him. Perhaps he might like a smoke on the way home. But if he can spare them I'd like to keep them always.'

Harrison died from wounds received on 'D-Day' morning and never read Smith's article.[61]

'Back at the base, as we ate, two young officers walked in to breakfast and flipped over the morning papers. 'So the Allies have taken Rome' they remarked. 'Well, it shouldn't be long now before the invasion starts.'

They didn't know, yet....'[62]

61   *Tonight We Die As Men* by Ian Gardner & Roger Day (Osprey 2009).
62   *I Saw Them Jump To Destiny* by Mark Durivage, 440th TCG historian.

Chapter 8

'Boston' Begins

'No one was surprised when the sand tables and the maps appeared again and they were briefed on 'Operation Neptune' and no one was surprised to learn that they would be the first men there. There was a moon, that night. The planes mounted and circled, with their wing lights close and slowly the long sky train straightened out and headed for France. Those who were part of it said it was beautiful: in daylight, the sea, solid with ships, was beautiful too. That giant departure of men for the invasion of Normandy was a terrible and handsome sight.
Martha Gellhorn. *Saga of the All American.* **The 82nd Airborne Division divided itself into three forces: Force 'A' (parachute): the three parachute infantry regiments and support detachments commanded by Assistant Division Commander Brigadier General James Gavin; Force 'B', the glider infantry regiment and artillery battalions and airborne support elements commanded by Division Commander Major General Matthew Bunker Ridgway; and Force 'C' (seaborne): remaining combat elements, division support troops and attached units including tanks, landing at 'Utah' Beach. Force 'A' and 'B' were carried by 369 aircraft in Mission 'Boston' by the following Groups, moving into the stream of traffic in this order: the 316th at Cottesmore: the 315th at Spanhoe; the 314th at Saltby; the 313th at Folkingham; the 61st at Barkston Heath and the 442nd at Balderton.**

Early in the first week of June at the end of a weeklong stay at an Army Air Forces rest home in southern England, 1st Lieutenant David E. Mondt, a C-47 pilot in the 62nd Troop Carrier Squadron and two pilots from the 32nd Troop Carrier Squadron and one from the 50th Troop Carrier Squadron, were waiting for transportation back to the 314th Troop Carrier Group at Saltby in Leicestershire about eight miles northeast of Melton Mowbray. They talked about the upcoming invasion. They had not been moved from the Mediterranean to England for nothing; and even the newest pilots had eleven hundred hours of flying time, 700 of them overseas. They also had two invasions for experience and the never-ending night training formations since March. They were ready and able - willing too - although no one looks forward to being shot at. It was their duty and they would have missed it with mixed emotions had 'D-Day' occurred while they were in the rest area. The same weather that could prevent the occasion of 'D-Day' was keeping the C-47 that would come for them on the ground at Saltby. The long train ride back was boring, but David Mondt was going home to his friends and the only family he had known in the three years with the Army Air Forces. He thought about making a run to town, but that would have to wait until the next day. No flying was scheduled; the guys out on the flight line were busy putting on the pararacks and men like Master Sergeant Jessie 'Jiggs' Russell was checking with the crew chiefs to make certain that all aircraft were ready and that the wings and fuselages were well covered with black and white invasion stripes. Communications Chief 'Bill' Watson was also on the job, making sure the radios worked. Even if the C-47 crews had 'radio silence' they had to be in working order. Most important was the navigation system.

June 2nd was not a day to go down in history, unless you count the promotion of David Mondt to 1st lieutenant. He was invited to attend the promotion party for Major Wilson at the Senior Officers Mess. No one noticed that Mondt was wearing borrowed silver bars but he enjoyed the meal and they did have a better supply of Scotch at Group. Great evening, but he really had planned on going to town. 'Oh well, the girls could wait another day' Mondt wrote. Then, 'Damn! June 3rd arrived and so did the MPs; they're all over the place'.

'Everyone is restricted and will attend the briefing. They must be getting serious, checking the roster and IDs when going into the briefing, lines on the map going south and then east to that little peninsula. Time, course, altitude, 62nd will lead the Group; Colonel Clayton Stiles will fly lead ship to Drop Zone 'N' and the 314th will be followed by the 313th Group. It's called the Cotentin Peninsula, a part of Normandy and it's all laid out on a sand table.'

Mondt never saw one of these before, but he had heard about them. 'Here's the route past the Channel Islands, Guernsey and Jersey. Germans there. Remember that Granddad had cows by that name. Must be where his cows came from. Ah Ha! The Initial Point is on the shoreline and there's our Drop Zone. Nearest town is Sainte-Mère-Église.' Mondt had never heard of it.

The crews returned to squadron operations and in checking the aircraft assignments David Mondt was just a little miffed to see that Ray Roush, Operations Officer had him in the right seat of 'Chalk 11' with Glenn 'Bolivar' Grimes as pilot, Vic Palumbo, navigator, 'Billy' Hensley, crew chief and Emanuel Wodinsky, radio operator. Mondt was wondering why Roush assigned him to fly right seat considering he was a brand new first lieutenant. Two second lieutenants were assigned as pilots. Three others had not made first pilot until after he had, way back in Kairoun. 'Must have done something that teed off my good friend Ray Roush' said Mondt. 'It was true that he arrived at operations a little late some days. He did take advantage of their friendship - not a few times but on a regular basis he tested the friendship to the limit. He knew it would do no good to complain.'

Roush would not change the assignment. Major Arthur E. Tappan the squadron commander would back him all the way and Mondt and Grimes were flying 'Tap's right wing. 'Tap' or Roush had decided that there should be four experienced people in the two aircraft flying formation with Major Tappan. Some of the others had newly assigned pilots with less time and no combat experience. 'Maybe Roush was looking after me as well and wanted to make sure that he had good people together at critical positions' wrote Mondt. 'Sure, that's why 'P. J.' Warren is flying with 'Tap'. One of the best, that 'P. J.' Same thinking went into the assignments on the lead element. Colonel Stiles has Downhill and Poling. Suppose flight leaders are expendable; they have one experienced pilot per wing while leading an element. What the hell, if the co-pilot has to fly with someone, it might as well be Glenn 'Boliver' Grimes.'

Major Tappan had already earned undying fame in his squadron. Code names had been introduced throughout the groups so that tasking might be given over unsecured telephone lines. The 62nd TCS was at one time assigned 'Yacht Club' as their code name. At a group level meeting, a fellow squadron commander had chastised Major Tappan with the comment, 'You're running your squadron like a country club. Better still, a Yacht Club!' As news of this conversation made it's way around, these words became a source of pride among the troops and the name stuck. A glider pilot, Armand Prosperi designed the original squadron logo featuring a sailboat superimposed on the centre of a playing card symbol, the black club. The squadron motto, *Primus in Toto* ('First in Everything') was scribed below the hull of the boat. Carrying the nautical theme a step further, Tappan was often referred to as 'Commodore'.

'Nothing to do now but wait' wrote David Mondt. 'The airborne forces have yet to arrive; we have the 82nd again. Dropped 505th and the 504th in Sicily and Italy; wonder who we will have on this trip. Kind of funny, the Air Force gets paid extra for flying, paratroops get paid extra for jumping. They don't like airplanes but have to use them to do their job. The crewmembers want no part of jumping out of airplanes if there is any chance of a safe landing. Takes all kinds of people and everyone thinks he has the best deal. The word is that the mission is on for tomorrow night - take off late on June 4th. That will make 'D-Day' on 5th. Might as well hit the sack, long day tomorrow and a longer night.'

'June 4th is dragging on' wrote David Mondt. 'The weather is not the best. Possible postponement of the invasion. Eighteen 62nd Glider pilots have been sent to the 53rd Troop Carrier Wing based in the group of fields west of London; Ramsbury, Membury, Welford, Greenham Common and Aldermaston. Flight Officer Louis H. Zeidenschneider, about 5' 6", 120lbs when wet was in this group. No one called him Louis or Lou. Few or any knew what the 'H' stood for; he was just Zeidenschneider; a friendly little guy looking for a poker game or a crap game.'

Mondt was relieved, but only for a moment when word was passed that the invasion was postponed 24 hours. 'Another long day and evening. I would just as soon get it over with and if all went well, the restriction would be lifted and I could enjoy the social life in Nottingham.

'For the first part, 5 June was much the same as the day before, except that the sun was shining. The hours slipped by and I found myself again at Operations hoping someone might have been removed from flying for any reason and I would find an empty left seat. No such luck. Glenn Grimes and all the crewmembers were checking the aircraft and watching the 508th Parachute Infantry Regiment get their equipment on. Must be a hundred or more pounds on each. Some had a spare chute, some didn't.'

At Saltby on 5 June *Time* correspondent William 'Bill' Walton (34) and paratroopers in the 50th PIR wiled away the hours playing poker as Allied aircraft of every type, black and white insignia painted on wings and fuselage, waited expectantly outside. Walton was born in Jacksonville, Illinois and followed his father into journalism, working for the *Jacksonville Journal*, where his father was editor and became a seasoned reporter. After leaving Jacksonville, Walton was an Associated Press reporter in Chicago and received his first national recognition when he covered the FBI's slaying of John Dillinger, 'Public Enemy No. 1,' in 1934. Working out of the London bureau as 'Operation Overlord' kicked into high-gear, Walton, who had already been on several bombing raids over Germany, knew he would have difficulty getting credentials. A mere fraction of 550 journalists covering the war would get them, i.e. three per news organization division, plus three photographers. Ships filled to the gills with troops going ashore would have little room so Walton vowed to find another way to get the story. He soon learned that Major Barney Oldfield of the 505th Parachute Infantry Regiment had offered to train correspondents willing to jump or glide into Normandy. In January 1944, waving off the concerns of his boss, 'Bill' Walton entered Jump School in England - a three-week training programme, including jumps with paratroopers. 'Four hours of exhaustion are rounded off by a three-to-five-mile run,' wrote Philip Bucknell, *Stars and Stripes'* staff writer of the experience. 'Bill' Walton's attempts to do Oldfield's exercises - walking and quacking like a duck going uphill and walking and roaring like a bear - elicited gales of laughter. But no one knew how badly he had injured his right ankle on his first jump; he was mum, lest he be disqualified. Bandaging it up, he made four more jumps in excruciating pain - completing the requisite five. A nearby scenic village overlooking Bristol Channel provided some respite from the rigours. At night, under the 'blackout's' total darkness, social life was restricted to two pubs - having plentiful beer, no whiskey, darts and conversation. Nor, he wrote his mother on 30 January could he read in his 'barren room (with) two canvas cots and nothing else.' By the end of February he was both a qualified parachutist and inspiration to the younger men. 'If a 34-year-old correspondent could endure the regimen, so could they.

'For his efforts, 'Bill' Walton could now strut around with wings on his chest... But, like all young men, he was naive about what lay ahead...Some events he would never discuss.'[63]

With Robert Reuben of Reuters having been assigned to the 10st, it was decided that Walton would jump with the 82nd, on the same C-47 as General James Gavin, now the Assistant Division Commander. Often referred to as 'The Jumping General' because of his practice of taking part in combat jumps with the paratroopers under his command 'Jim' Gavin was the only American general officer to make four combat jumps in the war. As usual Gavin wanted the 82nd Airborne's death-defying feats reported and he had suggested that reporters cover the action.

---

63 *William 'Bill' Walton: A Charmed Life* by Mary Hackett.

The 'Boston' briefings began in the War Rooms in the 52nd Wing and the attached 442nd Troop Carrier Group at their bases around Grantham in the north of England at 1000 hours with officers from the 82nd Airborne. Crews were briefed on the route of flight, formation and radio procedures, ditching and dingy procedures and the current enemy situation; then they were served a hearty lunch and released to get some sleep. The men reconvened at 2100 hours for a final brief. Combat crewmembers were dressed in gas-impregnated khakis, to protect the crews from chemical attack, were issued side arms, searched for security and were given their escape and evasion kits. Navigators and flight leaders studied courses and plans and each aircraft was given a flimsy with the route of flight, navigation aid and notes that was mimeographed on edible rice paper.

1st Lieutenant 'Bud' Rice in the 316th Troop Carrier Group at Cottesmore was down to fly 'Chalk 41' (42-24328). 'My group was to carry the 2nd and 3rd Battalions, 505th Parachute Infantry Regiment of the 82nd Airborne from Cottesmore to DZ 'O'. 'My assignment was clear and simple - fly the plane, keep strict radio silence, stay in tight formation and deliver 21 paratroop passengers on time to our designated drop zone northwest of Sainte-Mère-Église. The briefing in the Operations Room was thorough: All the compass headings en route to the various checkpoints and the final heading to the drop zone after crossing the Cherbourg coastline were carefully noted. My DZ was half a mile northwest of the town. The Pathfinders ahead of us would locate the designated DZ's and setup lighted 'T' markers on the ground to help incoming pilots find our targets. Aerial photos were screened on the briefing room wall to point out the location of anti-aircraft defences. All paratroops were to be dropped on or as near as possible to the designated drop zones. Captain's warnings were clear: 'Caution he warned - watch your airspeed at the DZ. As you know an airspeed below 110 mph could cause a fatal stall - especially since your planes are hauling additional overload weights up to 1,000 extra pounds.. NO paratrooper is to be returned to England that night unless disabled or killed by anti-aircraft fire. Any paratrooper refusing to jump will be court-martialled. Only lead planes will have navigators on board. It is imperative that all planes without navigators stay in tight formation throughout the mission. You'll arrive about midnight and maintain strict radio silence. One more thing: only the lead planes will have navigators on board. For those of you without navigators it is imperative that you stay in tight 'V'-formation so you don't lose sight of the lead plane ahead of you.'

'I thought; 'just stay tight and follow the lead ships all the way in'.

'Concluding the briefing, the 316th Group Exec, Lieutenant Colonel Walter R. Washburn looked around at the roomful of pilots and said, 'Gentlemen, you will be taking part in the largest airborne armada ever assembled. The 316th will be putting 72 planes in the air from here. There are thirteen more identical groups just like ours and they will join us en route to complete the two-hour 51-minute flight to our drop zone in Normandy. By the time you reach your last checkpoint, 800 C-47s will meet mid-air and blend into a long train of airplanes in the sky all the way to Normandy. You will fly in tight 'V'-formations. Let's do the job you have been trained for. Keep the formation tight; give your troops a good trip to the DZ. Good luck. Let's go!'

Units of the 82nd Airborne would disrupt German communications, establish roadblocks to hamper the movement of German reinforcements, establish a defensive line between Neuville and Baudienville to the north, clear the area of the drop zones to the unit boundary at les Forges and link up with the 101st. The intended objective was to secure an area of roughly ten square miles on either side of the Merderet River. They were to capture the town of Sainte-Mère-Église, a crucial communications crossroad behind 'Utah' Beach and to block the approaches into the area from the west and southwest. They were to seize causeways and bridges over the Merderet at La Fière and Chef-du-Pont, destroy the road bridge over the Douve River at Pont l'Abbé and secure the area west of Sainte-Mère-Église to establish a defensive line between Gourbesville and Renouf. Gavin was to describe the operation as having two interrelated challenges - it had to be 'planned and staged with one eye on deception and one on the assault'.

The 82nd Division's total lift was ten serials organized in three waves, totalling 6,420 paratroopers carried by 369 C-47s to Drop Zones 'T' and 'N' west of the Merderet River from north to south and DZ 'O' east of it, just northwest of Sainte-Mère-Église. The serials were to assemble over their bases according to group SOPs, pass over the wing assembly point at six-minute intervals and fly the course already taken by the pathfinders from there to 'Hoboken', 'Peoria' and the drop zones. Between the command assembly point and the IP the lead aircraft in 'Boston' would fly ten minutes behind the leader of the last serial in 'Albany'.

In the first wave the 316th and 315th Troop Carrier Groups were to drop the 505th Parachute Regiment on DZ 'O' between 0151 and 0208, ten minutes after the last serial of the 101st Airborne's drop. DZ 'O' was to be marked by 'Eureka' beacons and green 'T's. From a pilot's viewpoint it was conveniently boxed in on the west by the Merderet, on the south by a road running west from Sainte-Mère-Église and on the east by the north-south road. The 316th had dropped the 82nd on 'Husky 2' in Sicily, losing twelve aircraft destroyed by 'friendly fire'. In the second wave a serial of sixty C-47s in the 314th Troop Carrier Group at Saltby and two serials of 36 aircraft each from the 313th Group at Folkingham were to carry the 508th Parachute Infantry Regiment and a detachment of divisional headquarters to DZ 'N' near Ranville. DZ 'N' was a relatively small zone, about a mile long on the axis of approach and half a mile wide from north to south. It lay 1½ miles west of the Merderet and almost two miles north of the Douve in flat country chequered with hedgerows. Touching its southern edge was a road running southwest from la Fière to Pont l'Abbe, a town on the Douve about 1½ miles southwest of the zone. About a mile south of DZ 'N' was the hamlet of Picauville. Unknown to the Allies, the German 91st Division had recently established its headquarters a little way north of Picauville and had stationed considerable forces in that area. In the third and final wave, the 507th Parachute Regiment would be carried by two serials of 36 aircraft each from the 61st Troop Carrier Group and one of 45 aircraft from the 442nd Group to DZ 'T', an oval about 114 miles long on the axis of approach and half a mile wide, lying on flat alluvial ground one and a half miles north of DZ 'N' and about the same distance northwest of the la Fière bridge. A thousand yards northeast of the DZ loomed the embankment of the Valognes-Carentan railway slanting south-eastward across the Merderet to la Fière.

In the first wave the lead serial (Serial 17), 36 C-47s in the 44th and 45th Troop Carrier Squadrons of the 316th TCG carried the 2nd Battalion, 505th PIR. In Serial 18 another 36 C-47s in the 37th TCS and 36th TCS took the 3rd Battalion, two 75 mm howitzers and twenty artillerymen of the 456th Parachute Field Artillery Battalion. Chalk 37' (43-30652) flown by Lieutenant Colonel Leonard C. Fletcher and Captain Warren D. Rayburn in the 37th TCS carried Lieutenant Colonel Edward C. 'Cannonball' Krause, Commanding officer of the paratroopers. The radio operator, Staff Sergeant Maurice E. 'Speedy' Smith, had been impatient and wanted to go after their early morning breakfast followed by 'hurry up and wait.' Navigator, Captain Frank B. Waters and crew chief, Tech Sergeant Wilbur E. Evans made up the rest of the crew.

1st Lieutenant 'Bud' Rice recalled: 'By 2130 hours the various 'sticks' of paratroops had marched out to their respective planes, which had been identified with large chalk numbers next to the left side door. They clambered aboard with their heavy equipment load, assisting each other up the portable metal steps and sat down to wait on the long cold aluminium side benches inside. The jumpmaster, a big man with black smudges covering his face was an impressive sight. He must have weighed well over 300 lbs loaded down with equipment. He looked to me like he could win the war single-handed. He was anxious to get started and reminded me to do everything possible to jump his stick at 700 feet altitude and at 115 mph. I assured him that I didn't anticipate any problem doing that. (Little did we know what lie ahead)? We climbed aboard.

'A few minutes later Cottesmore airfield shook with the loud rumble of 288 Pratt Whitney engines coming to life. We taxied in turn to our position on the perimeter leading to takeoff Runway 50. While we sat and waited for the green 'go-light' from the tower, I went through pre-flight cockpit check (for the 3rd or 4th time). I also threw in a prayer or two. At precisely 2300 hours, the green flare signal illuminated the control tower. The Invasion was ON! The Group leader in first position on the runway began his takeoff roll. One by one the following flights climbed into the night sky.'

When finally it was time to board the C-47s at Saltby to begin takeoff General Gavin told them: 'When you land in Normandy, you will have only one friend: God.' Boarding Gavin's C-47 an officer noticed that 'Bill' Walton did not have a hunting knife, so he strapped one to Walton's boot.[64]

Pfc Leslie Palmer Cruise Jr. of 'H' Company in Colonel Krause's battalion recalled: 'We reached our aircraft and unloaded our chutes for the final adjustment of all our gear. We all had trouble getting our chutes tightened over everything else and the Mae West that we were required to wear got in the way of all the other stuff. I wondered how the hell I was going to get out of my chute and assemble my rifle and other equipment before I was shot by the enemy. Even the heavy duty suspenders seemed to sag under the load. Being right handed I had earlier strapped my trench knife around my right ankle and before I could secure my chutes I had to place the 9-inch Hawkins mine into my bag which would ride under my emergency chute across. The cardboard between the detonator and outer ring really concerned me I would be glad to place that on our roadblocks as soon as possible

'The C-47 was really vibrating as its motor turned over chugging and coughing as the pilot was endeavouring to get it running smoothly. The crescendo increased as the planes began moving into line for the takeoff I wondered if they would get off the ground with their heavy loaded

---

64 *William 'Bill' Walton: A Charmed Life* by Mary Hackett.

cargoes. Trying to talk was useless over the increasing noise. This was the time in the jump process that I became the most nervous, just before the takeoff. I believe that the uncertain sound of the motors contributed to my intensity. Tremendous excitement filled the air and much more on the way I was chewing gum with a passion unknown before. The planes were all lined up and stopped at the runway waiting their turn to lift off as the crews checked their instruments. One by one the planes filed onto the runway revving their motors in anticipation of the impending acceleration for takeoff. We could hear the louder roar as each plane following the leader accelerated down the run-way and lifted into the air. Our turn came and the quivering craft gathered momentum along the path right behind the plane in front. Stubbornly it clung to the ground as if uncertain of its role, but finally it reached the proper speed. Rising slowly over Cottesmore it gently lifted its load as those before it had done. We kissed old England goodbye. We knew we were in for real trouble now and parting wasn't easy. All the little chickens had assembled into formation at the assigned altitudes and we were on course for Normandy and all those other names we had learned in the past week.'

Second Lieutenant James J. Coyle, a platoon Leader in Company 'E' in the 3rd Battalion, recalled: 'We took off from Cottesmore airfield where we had been isolated under strict security for several days. I was the jumpmaster on our C-47 which carried eighteen paratroopers. Our machine guns and mortars were in bundles slung beneath the airplane and could be released and dropped by parachute when we jumped. I had a beautiful view of the English Channel as we crossed. The door of the plane had been removed and as I sat by the open door I watched the moonlight shine on the waves. It was a peaceful prelude to the violent invasion.

'Shortly after we crossed the western coast of the Cherbourg Peninsula the anti-aircraft fire filled the sky. This continued at intervals in the distance until we reached Sainte-Mère-Église. My primary concern was that the pilot would locate our proper Drop Zone and that we would be able to assemble all our men and equipment. The red warning light finally came on and I gave the order to 'Stand up and hook up'. This order was relayed from man to man over the roar of the engines and each man checked the parachute of the man in front of him. Beginning with the last man '18-OK', the count was relayed from man to man until the man behind me shouted 'Two - OK' then I knew we were ready.

'The plane's engines slowed down and I knew we would receive the green light to go soon, but I still could not see the lights which were to be set up by the Pathfinders who had jumped earlier to mark the D-Z. Suddenly we made a sharp left turn and I picked out the blue lights in a 'T' formation directly in front of us. Just at that moment the green light beside the door flashed on and giving the order 'GO', I jumped. I had no trouble on landing despite all the equipment we carried. As soon as I got out of my parachute harness and stood up I saw the green light which was our Battalion's assembly signal, a short distance away.'

'The first man Coyle encountered after landing by parachute was his Battalion Commander, Lieutenant Colonel Benjamin H. 'Vandy' Vandervoort. 'He asked if I had found my medical aid man but I told him I was alone. At the time he did not mention that he was injured, but he had broken his leg on the jump (and fought for weeks with his leg in a cast).[65] He ordered me to continue to locate my men. This I did for the next hour.'[66]

Lieutenant Colonel Vandervoort recalled: 'We reached France intact and in formation. As we came in across the coast we saw a little ack-ack from the ground and I thought that there were some planes from the 101st Division shot down. As we approached our DZ the pilot informed me that he could see our 'T'. The pathfinder group had been dropped essentially where they should have been, a little further inland and they only displayed two 'T's. One was lighted when we dropped. The pilot I had was extremely reluctant to come down to the correct jumping altitude. We came in at 1,400 feet and our speed was excessive. I talked to the crew chief and asked him to slow down. We went through a bit of scud as we came in and it caused the formation to break slightly. At the time I thought the Germans had smoked the area. I lost two platoons from Company 'E'. The green light was turned on about 45 seconds before we reached the Douve River. I told them to turn it off. We dropped pretty well on our DZ. I was a quarter of a mile from the DZ and I had a little hard luck on the landing and banged up my foot. I watched the battalion come in and they were all spread out, the ships being too high and too fast. Within fifteen minutes after I got on the ground I started putting up some green flares that worked out well. We encountered no resistance from the enemy at night, only some fire from ack-ack around

---

65 Vandervoort had broken his left tibia about one inch above the ankle on the jump into Sainte-Mere-Église but carried on with his jump boot tightly laced and a rifle as a crutch. He later 'persuaded' two 101st Airborne sergeants to pull him rickshaw fashion on a collapsible ammunition cart until he transferred to a glider-borne jeep and managed to borrow crutches from a crippled French housewife in Sainte-Mere-Église!

66 *Put On Your Boots and Parachutes!; The United States 82nd Airborne Division* written and edited by Deryk Wills (self-published, March 1992).

our DZ. Some members of the battalion were dropped in Sainte-Mère-Église and were engaged in a fire fight at once. There was movement of vehicles on the road, one of the first things I heard being vehicles moving on a road to the South. I went north to the nearest hedgerow. I think it was about 0410 in the morning when I felt I completed the assembly sufficiently so that I could move out on our mission and take the town of Neuville au Plain. Later my mission was changed to Sainte-Mère-Église and from there on it was essentially a ground operation. The 2nd Battalion met no resistance as we went into the town. A small group of Germans attacked our left flank, but one platoon from 'D' Company was enough to drive them off and it was a ground operation thereafter. It was 0141 when I landed.'

After the first two serials came Serial 19 consisting of 47 C-47s of the 315th Troop Carrier Group at Spanhoe bearing the Headquarters and 1st Battalion of the 505th Parachute Infantry Regiment and a platoon of engineers. On 3 June 864 paratroopers had arrived at Spanhoe about 80 miles north-northwest of London and slept in one of the hangars while they waited for 'D-Day'. On 5 June the troopers began boarding their aircraft. By 0002 all the C-47s in the 'Neptune Boston' formation were in the air except the C-47 of Flight Officer Harper in the 43rd Squadron, 315th Group, which did not go because a Gammon grenade carried by one of the men of the 1st Battalion, HQ Company exploded before take-off. Four men were killed and fifteen were wounded, one being the aircraft's radio operator. The only man unharmed was Corporal Melvin Fryer, who, not wanting to be left behind elbowed his way on to another C-47. He was killed twelve days later in Normandy.[67] The 315th Group Commander, 40-year old Colonel Hamish McLelland, led his C-47s off from Spanhoe just before midnight on 5 June, headed for DZ 'O'.

Radio operator Sergeant Michael N. Ingrisano Jr., on 'Chalk 50' in the 37th TCS at Cottesmore, carrying elements of the 505th PIR, recalled: 'The airborne troops were already at the planes doing their pre-flight readiness when we arrived at approximately 2130 hours. We were met by public relations types (from our Intelligence Office) who handed us a copy of Eisenhower's 'Great Crusade' leaflet. I folded my copy, unread and put it into my flight suit. I boarded my aircraft with my gear which I put into the flight deck compartment which was right behind the co-pilot's position and just in front of my position. This gear consisted mainly of our clumsy seat-pack parachutes and arms which for the enlisted men were M-1 carbines.

---

67 *Put On Your Boots and Parachutes!: The United States 82nd Airborne Division* written and edited by Deryk Wills (self published, March 1992).

We also carried gas masks and escape kits and a water-filled canteen on our ammunition belts. All personal identification, save for our 'dog tags' were left in our quarters. We were also clothed in leggings and steel helmets and were provided with flak jackets, which I chose to place on my seat rather than to wear on my body. My reasoning was to protect myself from any incoming fire from underneath the plane. Once those chores were done, the crew chief and I went back out of the plane to boost those overloaded paratroopers up the three steps into the cabin. The rear door had previously been taken off and the hinged areas on both sides had been taped to prevent any trooper snagging his chute as he left the plane. The crew chief remained in the back of the plane to work with the jumpmaster, while I assumed my position on the flight deck. Lift off by the 44th Squadron was at 2300 hours. The last plane in the 36th Squadron was off by 2320. My plane was in the fifth flight, where we flew on the right wing of the leader. Our target was DZ [drop zone] 'O' just slightly northwest of Sainte-Mère-Église.'[68]

Major Benjamin F. Kendig commanding the 44th Troop Carrier Squadron in the 316th Troop Carrier Group recalled. 'I can't explain the feeling but on every mission I was relieved when we started the engines and were ready to go. Then the anxiety left me and it was all down to business. We formed up on the perimeter strip with our loads of paratroopers and para-bundles. The 44th Squadron was in the lead with the Deputy Group Commander Colonel Washburn in our lead plane. I was number ten, leading the second element of nine planes of the 44th Squadron. The group had four squadrons. Each of the squadrons put up eighteen aircraft. In spite of the large number of aircraft, the take off and form up were uneventful. We then proceeded, on course, to our point of departure from the coast of England. We crossed the Channel with no problems; flying at about 2,000 feet above the water.'

'Ted' Weatherhead, a 21-year-old green 2nd lieutenant was the co-pilot of a C-47 carrying nineteen fully-equipped paratroopers in the 316th Troop Carrier Group. 'We took off for France and flew south from Cottesmore to Land's End at the southern tip of the country and crossed the English Channel. We came across the north side of Normandy and dropped our paratroopers. The weather was terrible and I was scared to death of hitting another plane flying in formation with us. Our sixteen-plane squadron was flying in groups of four planes each. There were twenty or thirty of these squadrons each filled with paratroopers headed for Normandy. We flew in a 'V'-formation following our leader until he gave us the green light on the

---

68 *Valor Without Arms: A History of the 316th Troop Carrier Group 1942 – 1945* by Mike Ingrisano.

top of his airplane. That was the signal to drop our paratroopers. As we did we turned on the three black lights atop our fuselage and on both wings of our transport plane. We were flying 500 feet off the ground when they jumped. The paratroopers didn't like it because we were flying too fast and too low when they bailed out. We were going about 120 mph. when they jumped which was awfully fast for them. They would have much rather jumped at 2,000 feet, not 500. Because we were flying so low and fast the Germans didn't have much chance to shoot at us. Even so, the enemy's .50 calibre machine-guns were effective. We counted thirty bullet holes in our C-47 after the first flight.'

When 'Bud' Rice's turn had arrived he taxied off the end of the perimeter strip to the runway. 'I locked the tail wheel in position, called for 15 degrees flaps and shoved the twin throttles 'to the firewall'. A moment later the heavily laden ship staggered into the air. I could really feel the ship drag. Basically a large truck with wings the C-47 was rugged and dependable, but clumsy when over-loaded. Co-pilot Lieutenant LaRue Wells pulled up the landing gear into flight position while I fought the sudden impact of the twisting vortex of prop wash from the planes ahead. Reaching 500 feet LaRue closed the flaps and I began a 180-degree climbing turn left where I slid into the right wing position in 'B' Flight. As we reached 1,000 feet, the 316th Group had gathered into a tight 72-ship formation and headed for precise checkpoints where we would collect and blend into our position line with thirteen other groups arriving from different airfields. Try and imagine if you will - multiple groups of 72 aircraft taking off from scattered airfields in England and flying through the dark night to various check points - arriving at the same altitude - no radar - no radio communication - just dead reckoning navigation and straining eyesight by lead pilots and navigators looking for the dim amber wing lights of the other groups. Imagine if you will this huge armada of over 800 planes merging successfully that night, wing-inside-wing, without one collision.

'Reaching southern England, we were now assembled into one long sky-train carrying over 10,000 paratroops of the 82nd and 101st Airborne headed for Normandy. I recall our last warning: 'Remember - only 10% of the planes have navigators on board. The Group and Squadron Leaders and some secondary backup Flight Leaders fly these planes Therefore, the rest of you orphans better hang in close and tight so you don't lose your way!

'We left the southern English coastline at Portland Bill. The night sky was still dark despite occasional streaks of moonlight coming through the receding clouds. The air was reasonably smooth. Strict radio silence was maintained. For a while the amber wing lights on each plane helped keep the pilots in good position. Crossing the Channel, the lead ships flew at 500 feet; squadrons and flights following were stair-cased upward to avoid the twisting prop wash. A short distance after departing the English coast, all normal amber wing lights were turned off according to plan Guiding us now were four small-cupped blue lights installed along the top fuselage spine and mid-upper wing surface of each plane. Keeping these four small lights in view required the flight leaders and wingmen to keep their Vee formation tightly in position. This was critical. Losing sight of the blue lights left only the hazy moonlit silhouette of the adjacent plane. Sweat time.

'So far so good. Right on schedule we passed the check-points: 'Flatbush', 'Gallup' and Hoboken etc and then met up and blended with the other groups. With all 800 of us flying in formation, we looked like a huge grey chain link fence sailing through the black sky toward Normandy.

'The cockpit was dark except for the fluorescent reflections from the instrument panel. The left seat felt different because of the flak cushion pad under my butt. In addition, I wore a parachute harness, which seemed to me to be a meaningless gesture. The small sausage shaped parachute bundle was tucked under my seat. If my plane became disabled and it was necessary to bail out, I'd have to grab the chute, find and attach its metal connectors to my harness, climb out of the cockpit, run back through the fuselage to the side door, (assuming none of it is on fire) and jump. Good luck, I thought!

'Crossing the Channel, we passed the various checkpoints on time: 'Flatbush'... 'Gallup' and 'Hoboken' etc. Shortly before reaching the island of Guernsey, the lead planes led us to a 135 degree heading toward the Cherbourg Peninsula. The 101st PIR split off slightly to an approach heading of 140 degrees. As we passed just east of Guernsey, some enemy anti-aircraft fire was seen, but caused no damage to our formation that I could see. Below us the English Channel was striped with the wake of thousands of ships heading for the landing beaches of 'Omaha' and 'Utah'. Eventually we will see the Germans heavily defending these beach areas with gun emplacements in the famous concrete pillboxes atop the cliffs. The troops we carried were to be dropped inland to seal off the bridges and roadways around Sainte-Mère-Église. This was needed to prevent German reinforcements from reaching the German soldiers defending these beaches. The plan made perfect sense.

'At this point, 2½ hours into the flight, everything had gone smoothly. Nevertheless, I was perspiring from the strain of keeping the cupped blue lights in good sight. In the background of my mindset, I'm not ashamed to say, I could hear some quiet praying going on - 'Lord keep us safe; keep us safe.'

'Finally, through the murky gloom ahead, the darker outline of the Normandy coastline began to appear. Our group's lead pilots were going in low at 500 feet levels, whereas the following squadrons and flights were stacking up to 1,000 feet. Our airspeed had slowed to 120 mph in preparation for the upcoming drop zones, 18 to twenty miles ahead where we would slow to 115 mph for the planned jump. Captain's warning repeated over and over in my head. *Remember - when approaching your drop zone, watch your airspeed. Anything under 110 will lead to a fatal stall without enough altitude for recovery.*

Since weather patterns in this part of Europe generally flow from the northwest to the southeast, the weather was clearing over southern England and the Channel. The moon shone brightly through high, scattered clouds and visibility was generally excellent. Under these conditions the 'Eureka' beacons and flashing aerial lighthouses at thirty-mile intervals made it easy to stay on course and the bright lights on the aircraft made it easy to keep formation during the trip to the south coast. One pilot said it seemed as though they were following a lighted road. The marker ships proved equally efficacious and, as in 'Albany', all serials appear to have approached Normandy on course and in formation. Only in Normandy and most of northern France, the weather the night of 5/6 June was terrible. In fact, the weather was so bad that most German garrisons relaxed in their barracks, confident that no invading planes or ships could be expected any time soon.

Sergeant 'Mike' Ingrisano again: 'After forming into three ship vees and three vees to a flight, we headed for France. The flight was rather uneventful but as we approached the coast of France, by craning my neck to the left, I was able to see out of the front windscreen. I saw a solid wall of light in which were embedded puffs of black smoke. (Flak and small arms fire, I guessed, never having before seen such a sight). Because of radio silence, my chores were quite limited so I moved across the aisle to the navigator's usual position because there was no opening where I could look out from my position. Since only the lead plane in each flight had a navigator on board, that area of our plane was vacant. There was a small opening approximately eighteen inches long and four to six inches high, which the navigator used for dead reckoning; that is, viewing the ground for known site locations, rail tracks, roads etc. When I looked down and out I could see the vast armada sitting off the coast. Then I was astonished to see a woman, dressed in a white gown, sitting on our left wing tip. I immediately recognized her as my fiancée. She turned toward me, smiled and said, 'Mike', don't worry; you'll be OK.' With that she disappeared. We continued on our flight toward Sainte-Mère-Église. My pilots estimated that we dropped our stick of troopers just slightly off to the northwest of the DZ. After dropping our troops I helped the crew chief push out a 75 mm piece that we were carrying and then helped him to pull the shroud lines into the plane to minimise drag. I recall little about the flight home.'[69]

Major Benjamin F. Kendig in the 316th Troop Carrier Group adds. 'As we approached the coast of Normandy, we found a cloud formation had formed just below our altitude. My first thought was that the Germans had spread poison gas in the area. The cloud formation appeared to lay in rows and looked to me as though it might have been spread by airplanes. I quickly realized that my imagination was working overtime! The clouds were a natural formation and could have resulted from the planes that were ahead of us flying through nearly saturated air, causing it to condense into clouds.

'Suddenly, without warning' says 'Bud' Rice, 'the shit hit the fan! A heavy barrage of enemy anti-aircraft shells burst right; then left. Black and grey flak clouds burst all around us. Machine gun tracers search us out. I hear bullets beat a tattoo across my tail assembly, upsetting the elevator controls, which loses our balance. I quickly pull back on the yoke and re-adjust the elevator trim wheel. With no self-sealing gas tanks, everybody in the plane is pretty much a nervous wreck. With no protective armour, a tracer would be fatal to a C-47. The sky is now a smoky yellow haze from fires. Shells explode mid-air that violently jerk our plane up and down like a basketball.

'A fireball exploded off to our front right. Tragically, a trail of fire followed the speeding plane downward. Then another to the left. Now we passed over my drop zone where the Germans were putting up an intense barrage of ground fire. Amid this pandemonium I spotted a huge fire in the middle of my drop zone - looked like a plane crash - no doubt some of our guys. So I adjusted my target a bit away from the fire. I flipped the red warning light on to ready the troops for the jump, but now I had to get down to 700 feet - no faster or slower than 115 mph - and still manage to steer the men clear of that big ground fire. With so much extra weight on board my unbalanced C-47 was kicking like a wild horse. Slowing down this lumbering air truck needed some fast thinking.

69 Mike Ingrisano is the author of *Valor Without Arms – A History of the 316th Troop Carrier Group 1942-1945.*

'OK, Now What? Just hit the brakes? What brakes? With no brakes to reduce speed and with only a minute or two left, you get resourceful. To produce drag, LaRue extended the flaps and lowered the landing gear while I kicked the rudder and man-handled the elevator and aileron controls to slow our descent. The resulting ride down was rough, but there was no other way to slow down in time and descend low enough for a safe drop. Then we saw parachutes billowing out from planes ahead. Some paratroopers caught enemy bullets before they hit the ground and I said another prayer for my troops in back.

'We finally made it to the target zone. With flaps down and landing gear extended we managed to slow down to 118 mph at 750 feet... slightly fast and slightly high, but the best recovery possible against the odds. A few seconds later we turned on the Green jump light. Thirty seconds later the troops were out the door.

'By the time we reached Normandy that night, last second adjustments seemed nonstop. Some pilots had to modify their target to find a safe place to drop their troops. Some pilots never found their targets because the T-Marker ground lights failed to work. We were blinded by the vortex wash from the lead planes. Flak pillows bounced us up, down and sideways and nearly threw us into each other. The surprises on 'D-Day' were countless. At least in training we could see. But worst of all was the fog. The Wall of Fog was something I will never forget. I do not know how all 800 airplanes avoided collision in that wall of fog covering the Normandy coast. With no lights, no radio, no radar, no visibility, those blind minutes in the soup felt like eternity.

'At the end of that long and horrible night, the mission objective was accomplished. Those of us lucky enough to survive headed our C-47s back to England to be patched up and sent back with supplies the next day. This would be our daily job for the rest of the war: Deliver the troops, bring them supplies; carry back their wounded.'[70]

As Lieutenant Colonel Leonard C. Fletcher's C-47 neared the Normandy shores they flew over hundreds of ships that lit up the night firing their guns at the enemy on shore. 'Overhead you could see tracer bullets from machine guns firing at the planes going in ahead of us' wrote Staff Sergeant 'Speedy' Smith. 'Then all at once it looked like all the tracers were coming up right at you and you thought, 'those poor paratroopers have to jump through all that machine gun fire. Then they were all gone and we were pulling in the static lines and getting out of there.'

---

70 The other two crewmembers on Rice's crew were crew chief Tech Sergeant Thaddeus J. Urbaniak and radio operator Staff Sergeant Harold C. Gondolfe.

Lieutenant Colonel Krause had found trip very uneventful on the way over. 'As we crossed the coast of France, I talked to my pilot on the interphone; and said, 'It looks like a good deal'. I looked back and saw my ships behind me. Just about that time we hit the soup (fog or cloud) and we started to see fires on the ground, a little ack-ack and we had some fighters come in on us and fire at us. An element of three ships was directly under us and not more than thirty feet below. One came up from under and passed miraculously between my ship and the left wing ship. I would say that in the next three minutes I came as close to being crashed in the air as I ever hope to. We tried to keep our formation, but ships constantly over ran each other. The pilot called for evasive action and we split up. Some went high; some went lower, others right and left. This split our formation and we were well spread. Just about two or three minutes before drop time we saw this green 'T'. It was a Godsend and I felt that I had found the Holy Grail.'

Pfc Leslie Cruise had heard the command 'Stand up and hook up!' shouted by Colonel Krause who was in the number one position. 'Almost as one the troopers arose and hooked up to the static line in the centre of the plane ceiling. 'Check equipment!' was the next command. Over the noise inside and outside the craft we could barely distinguish the replies of '21 OK, 20 OK, 19 OK, 18 OK' and up to me. 'Nine OK', I yelled and belted Taylor in the rear in case he didn't hear me. The last trooper yelled 'OK'! And the command to close it up and stand in the door came as we neared the drop zone. The green light flashed. 'Let's go', yelled the Colonel as he leaped into the dark Norman night. Quickly we followed and number nine wheeled out the door leaping in perfect jump school form into the flak ridden sky. The day of the Normandy invasion was now official! No turning back, no siree! The past is indeed prologue, the present, the reality. The chute tightened in my crotch, as the planes droned over head and I knew that my chute had opened though I could hardly look up to see it.'

'I would say that I dropped from over 2,000 feet' recalled Colonel Krause. 'It was the longest ride I have had in over fifty jumps and while descending, four ships passed under me and I really sweated that out. Just after I landed, a mine bundle hit about 80 yards away from me without a parachute and exploded. We tried to orient ourselves very quickly and ran upon a conical shaped field, which I remembered as the conical shaped field that we had studied during our pre-invasion briefing. Northeast of this should be the Battalion DZ Command Post which was to be in a wooded area on the Southeast end of the DZ. Further investigation proved this to be true and then I knew exactly where we were, or thought I knew where we were and I told the people all around me.'

The 3rd Battalion had received a good drop. They had received more than three quarters of the troops in the 505th PIR. They were needed, for casualties had heavy and no relief was in sight. For artillery the 505th had only one of the two howitzers dropped in 'Boston'[71] and six out of sixteen anti-tank guns brought in 'Detroit', the pre-dawn glider mission. Ammunition of all types was running very low. However, the rank and file of the 505th, battle-hardened in Mediterranean campaigns, felt themselves equal to the situation. 'We're staying right here,' they told the French that night. (The 3rd Battalion, 508th PIR captured Sainte-Mère-Église by 0430 against 'negligible opposition' from German artillerymen but the overall cost of the assault had been high).

German anti-aircraft fire over an area three to four times larger than planned ironically gave the enemy the impression of a much larger force. The C-47s carrying the 505th did not experience the difficulties that had plagued the 101st's drops. Pathfinders on DZ 'O' turned on their 'Eureka' beacons as the first 82nd serial crossed the initial point and lighted holophane markers on all three battalion assembly areas. The 2nd Battalion, 505th PIR, first to jump, was accurate but jumped from above the planned altitude. Sergeant Spencer Wurst, a 19-year-old veteran who had been with the 2nd Battalion since North Africa and had made his first jump at Salerno, wrote: 'The jump on 'D-Day' was the start of a bad day. We were flying much too fast and much too high and I had a terrible opening shock and lost my musette bag. I was under fire from the second that my chute opened until I hit the ground. Tracers were going through the chute. We jumped at 2,200 feet instead of the planned 600 to 800 feet, so I was under fire for a lot longer than I should have been. When I hit the ground, the landing was really bad. I crawled over to a hedgerow, pulled my pistol out and laid it beside me, then started to get out of my chute. When I looked around there where planes going every which way. That's when I knew things were all fouled up.'

Half the regiment dropped on or within a mile of DZ 'O' and 75% within two miles. The other regiments were more significantly dispersed and eight aircraft were shot down, several with paratroopers still inside.

All three serials carrying the 505th PIR apparently sighted the cloudbank over the western Cotentin soon enough for most of the aircraft to climb over it without losing formation. The clouds shielded them from observation and by following a different route from 'Albany' they achieved a degree of

---

71 The breechblock of the other landed on ground swept by enemy fire and was not recovered.

surprise. All three crossed the coast without opposition and even the last was four miles inland before it was fired upon. Such fire as was encountered was sporadic and ineffectual and was mostly from rifles and machine guns. No aircraft were lost. The 316th had a dozen slightly damaged and eleven in the 315th required minor repairs. One flak burst which wounded seven paratroops aboard an aircraft of the 315th prevented that stick from jumping. However, the clouds above the zone were more of a hindrance than the enemy.

C-47s carrying the 3rd and 1st Battalions were off course but adjusted in time to jump. Most flights were able to fly in formation above the clouds and none encountered serious anti-aircraft opposition. However most of the troops in two regiments of the division given the mission of blocking approaches west of the Merderet River missed their drop zones entirely. The other regiments were more significantly dispersed. Chester 'Chet' Harrington, in the 1st Battalion, 505th PIR stood at the back of his C-47 with his back to the pilot and co-pilot when they started to take on enemy anti-aircraft fire, damaging the transport. Harrington was one of the few men to make four combat jumps (Sicily, Salerno, Normandy and Holland).

Working as a nurse practitioner before Pearl Harbor, he had signed up to 'get into the fight, do some good and the airborne were just getting started and it seemed like a good place to start.' After jump school, he was set for medical training because of his nurse practitioner's experience, joining 'Able' Company. His first two jumps were into tough fights; the second campaign is where the Germans first used the term 'Devils in Baggy Pants' because of how tenaciously the 82nd fought. Soon after the green light came on Harrington exited the aircraft into the flak-filled night air, landing at the edge of Sainte-Mère-Église. 'We were scattered all over the place, but I got busy because there was a lot going on already.' Treating wounded Americans as he found them and later both US soldiers and German prisoners at the aid station set up near Sainte-Mère-Église, he worked with a couple of German medics. 'Chet' came close to losing his life when a German sniper shot one of the medics near him, despite the Red Cross painted on his helmet. 'Chet' was wounded later by an artillery burst, treating his own shrapnel wound 'because everyone else was worse off than I was.'

Of 1,276 troops aboard aircraft of the 316th Group, all but two jumped and all but 28 out of 844 carried by the 315th did so. Of those brought back, seven paratroopers had been wounded by a flak burst on one aircraft of the 315th and four had refused to jump. The last drop on DZ 'O'; that of Headquarters and the 1st Battalion of the 505th PIR by the 315th

Group was on a par with those by the first two serials. Major General Matthew Ridgway had originally intended to land by glider in Normandy but as D-Day approached, he made a sudden decision to jump with his paratroopers. He had made only four training jumps in the past. In the Sicily invasion he came ashore in a landing craft and it is generally believed that he later regretted that he did not jump with his men. Ridgway would fly at the rear of the 315th Troop Carrier Group formation at Spanhoe in 'Serial 19' on 'Chalk 49' (42-108912) which would be piloted by Captain Chester A. Baucke from the 52nd Troop Carrier Wing at Cottesmore.

'We flew in a V of Vs' wrote Ridgway, 'like a gigantic spearhead without a shaft. England was on double daylight saving time and it was still full light, but eastward, over the Channel, the skies were darkening. Two hours later, night had fallen and below us we could see glints of yellow flame from the German anti-aircraft guns on the Channel Islands. We watched them curiously and without fear, as a high-flying duck may watch a hunter, knowing that we were too high and far away for their fire to reach us. In the plane, the men sat quietly, deep in their own thoughts. They joked a little and broke, now and then, into ribald laughter. Nervousness and tension and the cold that blasted through the open door, had its effect upon us all. Now and then, a paratrooper would rise, lumber heavily to the little bathroom in the tail of the plane, find he could not push through the narrow doorway in his bulky gear and come back, mumbling his profane opinion of the designers of the C-47 airplane. Soon, the crew chief passed a bucket around, but this did not entirely solve our problem. A man strapped and buckled into full combat gear finds it extremely difficult to reach certain essential portions of his anatomy and his efforts are not made easier by the fact that his comrades are watching him, jeering derisively and offering gratuitous advice.

'Wing to wing, the big planes snuggled close in their tight formation, we crossed to the coast of France. I was sitting straight across the aisle from the door-less exit. Even at 1,500 feet, I could tell the Channel was rough, for we passed over a small patrol craft - one of the check-points for our navigators - and the light it displayed for us was bobbing like a cork in a mill-race. No lights showed on the land, but, in the pale glow of a rising moon, I could clearly see each farm and field below. And I remember thinking how peaceful the land looked, each house and hedgerow, path and little stream bathed in the silver of the moonlight. And I felt that if it were not for the noise of the engines we could hear the farm dogs baying and the sound of the barnyard roosters crowing for midnight.

'A few minutes inland, we suddenly went into cloud, thick and turbulent. I had been looking out the doorway, watching with a profound sense of satisfaction the close- ordered flight of that great sky caravan that stretched as far as the eye could see. All at once, they were blotted out. Not a wing light showed. The plane began to yaw and plunge and in my mind's eye I could see the other pilots, fighting to hold course, knowing how great was the danger of a collision in the air.

'You could read concern on the grim, set faces of the men in my plane as they turned to peer out of the windows, looking for the wink of the little lavender lights on the wing- tips of the adjoining planes. Not even our own wing lights showed in that thick murk. It was all up to the pilots now. There was nothing I could do and I did it. I pulled my seat belt tighter and sat back and closed my eyes, taking comfort from the words of 'Hal' Clark, Commanding General of the 52nd Troop Carrier Wing, whose planes transported us.

'Matt,' he had told me before the take-off, 'come hell or high wind, my boys will put you there, right on the button.'

'The cloud and rough air lasted only a few minutes, though it seemed far longer. As suddenly as we had entered the storm, we broke free. All at once, there was the moon again and clear skies and the sharp outlines of the land below, the little fields and hedgerows. But nowhere in the sky, in my field of vision, could I see another plane.

'It was too late now to worry about that. Beside the door, a red light glowed. Four minutes left. Down the line of bucket seats, the No. 4 man in the stick stood up. It was Captain Peter Schouvaloff, brother-in-law of Fedor Chalipin, the opera singer. He was a get-rich-quick paratrooper, as I was, a man who had no formal jump training. I was taking him along as a language officer for he spoke both German and Russian and we knew that in the Cotentin peninsular which we were to seize, the Germans were using captured Russians as combat troops.

'A brilliant linguist, he was also something of a clown. Standing up, bewilderment on his face, he held up the hook on his static line - the life-line of the parachutist which jerks his canopy from its pack as he dives clear of the plane.

'Pray tell me,' said Schouvaloff, in his thick accent, 'what does one do with this strange device?'

That broke the tension. A great roar of laughter rose from the silent men who were standing now, hooked up and ready to go.

'Are we downhearted', somebody yelled.

'HELL NO!' came back the answering roar.

'A bell rang loudly, a green light glowed. The jumpmaster, crouched in the door, went out with a yell - 'Let's go!' With a paratrooper still laughing, breathing hard on my neck, I leapt out after him.

'The shock of the opening was no worse than usual. I glanced up to see the most comforting of all sights, the spread of my canopy round and bulging, full of air. Below me, off to the left, for a split second I could see the canopy of the jumpmaster hanging, seemingly motionless, in the dark. Then I was alone in the sky. I saw neither man nor parachute, though I knew that all around me troopers and bundles of heavy battle gear were floating swiftly down. In the stillness of the fall, I could hear far above me the roar of the engines as the following planes sped on to their drop-zones.

'All at once, the ground was very near and I flexed my knees for the shock of the landing. Weighted with his heavy battle gear, a combat paratrooper lands hard. He may strike swinging forward, or sideways, or backward and he absorbs the shock by doing a tumbler's roll, loose-jointed, with springy knees.

'I was lucky. There was no wind and I came down straight, into a nice, soft, grassy field. I rolled, spilled the air from my chute, slid out of my harness and looked around. As I hit, I grabbed for my pistol, for on the advice of the men who had jumped in Sicily, I had got nearly all the division equipped with .45 automatics. In your first moments on the ground, trussed in your tight harness, you are almost helpless. You can't possibly get to a rifle or a carbine and if somebody is after your scalp in these first seconds, you are in bad shape. But in the tussle to free myself from the harness, I had dropped the pistol and as I stooped to grope for it in the grass, fussing and fuming inwardly, but trying to be as quiet as possible, out of the corner of my eye I saw something moving. I challenged 'Flash', straining to hear the countersign, 'Thunder'...'

By 0930 the 1st Battalion of the 505th PIR had assembled 22 officers and 338 men and by then or a little later division headquarters had mustered twelve officers and 61 men which Ridgway set up in an apple orchard, on almost the exact spot he had planned to be before leaving England. As Ridgway said, 'Hal' Clark's boys had not failed us. They had put us down on the button.'

The drops at DZ 'O' were, taken together, the best at any zone by IX TCC in 'Neptune'. Half the troops dropped were assembled and ready for action within eight hours. Among the factors contributing to this were the success of the 316th and 315th Groups in climbing over the cloudbank and descending to the DZ without losing formation, the absence of intense enemy fire during the approach and over the zone and the lighted 'T'. This last was an aid not available on the other zones, except at DZ 'A' where the lights went on too late for the first serials. Its presence at 'O' appears to have been important, since after seeing it two of the serials had to make hasty changes in course and altitude in order to drop correctly. Of 118 sticks delivered in Normandy and intended for DZ 'O', 31 landed on or barely outside the zone, approximately 29 more came within a mile and at least an additional twenty were within two miles of it. Seventeen were scattered within or just outside a five-mile radius. Only three sticks, dropped fourteen miles north of the zone, were certainly outside the objective area, but several were missing or unreported.

As Major Ben Kendig in the 316th Troop Carrier Group neared the drop zone he was faced with an important decision. 'Was it better to drop down and fly through the clouds and risk having the formation break up with the possibility of mid air collisions or to stay above and drop the paratroopers at an altitude that would cause them to become widely separated? We soon picked up the radar signal from the pathfinders! At about five miles distance from the drop zone, the cloud layer ended and I could clearly see the lights set up by the pathfinders. I immediately closed the throttles and started to descend. I quickly realized that I had better use some power, for my formation was overtaking my plane. By the time we reached the drop zone we were a little above the 500 feet altitude and a little faster than the desired speed for dropping the troops. However, it was, in my judgment, best to drop at this time rather than to circle and take the chance of colliding with the following formation.

'After dropping the troops we flew as low as possible and soon crossed the coast. I don't know if I dreamed this or not, but as we crossed the coast I thought that I could see trenches and soldiers. I don't remember seeing much ground fire. Compared to the second night over Sicily this was a 'milk run'. The remainder of the trip back to our base was uneventful. We all felt quite relieved to learn that there were few casualties. I believe that our group lost no airplanes that night.

'Several explanations are in order. The pathfinders were a group of troop carrier crews and paratroopers highly trained in navigation with the latest radar equipment. Prior to our drops they located the drop zones and set up lights and radar for our guidance to the drop zones. Our lead planes were equipped with 'Rebecca-Eureka' radar that had a scope in the instrument panel giving direction and distance to the pathfinder's signal. Another explanation concerns our night formation flying. Each plane had three purple hooded lights on each wing and three on top of the fuselage. They were only visible from the rear quarter and were adequate so long as the formation was fairly tight. The exhaust pipes had flame arresters to avoid being seen from the ground and presenting a target.'

Lieutenant Russell Chandler Jr. in the 44th Troop Carrier Squadron remembered one paratrooper, a sergeant, who had taken some shrapnel in the leg. 'By rights, he should have stayed on board and flown back with us. Instead, he told my crew chief, 'I'm jumping; it's too dangerous in this thing!' And he did. I guess we all have our own perspective of where the danger lies and I suppose he did get medical attention as soon as he hit the ground, instead of waiting two hours to go back to England with us.

'After exiting the drop zone we broke formation and it was basically a race home, with every man for himself. The safest location was down low, so we were screaming back across the Channel just above the deck and suddenly this large shape appears through my windscreen and starts firing its entire portsided armament toward us. I never identified the cruiser that we encountered. The encounter was reminiscent of a previous incident in which our Navy had shot down nearly fifty of our own C-47s returning from a drop zone in Sicily on 10 July 1943. Although I wasn't involved in the previous encounter, others in my unit were and they always reminded us of the fact that 30 percent of the aircraft used in the airdrop were shot down in such a manner. This only heightened our anxiety.[72]

All the C-47s in the 315th TCG landed back at Spanhoe at dawn and crews told the intelligence officers how it went, for which their reward was two ounces of Bourbon and fried egg sandwiches. Safely back Cottesmore, Sergeant 'Mike' Ingrisano recalled: 'At the debriefing by our intelligence officers, all I remember was the shot of scotch each of us was given to 'calm our nerves'. I also remember the fine breakfast which was prepared for us when we sat down to eat at approximately 0430 hours on 6 June.'[73]

Lieutenant Colonel Leonard C. Fletcher's C-47 flew across the peninsula and then headed back to Cottesmore just as the sun was coming up. 'It had been a long day already but our day was only half over' wrote Staff Sergeant 'Speedy' Smith. We flew back to base, landed and loaded the plane with bags of supplies. A parachute and static line were attached to a cable inside the plane so we could throw out the supplies. The parachute would open up and the bag would float down. Our whole squadron returned to where we

---

72 Interview originally published in the July 2004 issue of *Aviation History*.
73 Mike Ingrisano is the author of *Valor Without Arms – A History of the 316th Troop Carrier Group 1942-1945*.

had dropped the paratroopers and dropped the supplies to them. Only this time we did not have the element of surprise and it was not dark. We took a whole lot more flak and machine gun fire, but none of the planes from our squadron was shot down, some just had holes in them. Thus ended the 'D-Day' flights for the 37th Troop Carrier Squadron. Like all other Troop Carrier outfits, it became involved in evacuating wounded, bringing in supplies and new airborne operations in the future.'

Chapter 9

'Boston' - The Second and Last Serials

It was a grave-faced group that boarded the planes the night before D-Day. Gone was the habitual wise cracking and blonde talk. In its place was a sense of responsibility and a tense anticipation. After countless months of training, learning how to get the other fellow first, our men were ready.
Pfc Joe Stanger of Bridgeton, New Jersey, a veteran of the 508th PIR, 82nd Airborne Division which invaded Sicily.

At Saltby David Mondt in the 314th Troop Carrier Group could sleep in any day of the week. The best days were when the weather was bad and no flying. The other days started with Paul Cook opening the door, calling out names and announcing breakfast at six, flight line at seven. So what was Mondt doing awake at the crack of dawn with no place to go? Of all the days that he could use a little extra sack time, he was wide-awake. Might as well get dressed and go to the mess hall. The mess hall, which the 62nd Squadron shared with the 50th Squadron, was not only full and buzzing with conversation, but there was a long line. The line moved a bit slower today, fresh eggs any way you wanted them, sunny side up, over easy or burn 'em. David Mondt observed that rations improved when missions were scheduled. Was it the fresh eggs that brought everyone to the mess hall or was it the excitement of 'D-Day'?

'The 62nd Operations was full. The pilots were checking the board for changes in personnel or flight position. Same as yesterday. Some of the pilots were giving Captain Roush a hard time for not scheduling himself. They just wanted to make him explain again that when Major Tappan was on a mission, he had to remain behind - can't take a chance of losing all the good men at once. We understand that Ray, but how come you are not going on the mission? 1st Lieutenant Richard D. Stevens had been a flight leader since 1 June. He was not scheduled to fly while the other two newly appointed Flight Leaders, Don Broaddus and Ed Bohnsack were leading elements. 'How come you're not going Steve?'

'Because that damn Roush won't change the schedule. 'Doc' put me in the hospital for nothing and they set up the flights while I was gone. All I had was an ingrown hair in the wrong place.'[74]

Staff Sergeant Arthur Een, a radio operator in the same group strongly suspected that there was a touch of the heroic fantasy in all men. Long before D-Day and while he was still a civilian, he had dreams of being part of the avenging force that would put an end to the German march toward world domination. 'Now that the time had arrived I sat in my crew position aboard a plane, just as I had envisioned it so many years before. However, by this time it was a bit different; I no longer felt like a super patriot. In the dark of a low overcast night, with scores of engines revving up and a plane loaded with grim looking paratroopers, the sensation was more one of apprehension, if not downright fear. These missions did not always go 'just like in the movies.' Even the dry runs invariably resulted in some casualties. At this time of the war, all that mattered was getting it over with - and then my own speedy demobilization. In spite of all this, there was the feeling that this was one of the mightiest events in the annals of man. We were familiar enough with the ways of the news media to realize that in a matter of a few hours, the radio waves and newspapers all over the world would be blasting away with sensational banner headlines, which would never be equalled.'[75]

Harvey Cohen, the 25-year old pilot of 'Chalk 41' (43-30715) in the 32nd Troop Carrier Squadron at Saltby was a native of Manhasset, New York and the highest scorer in the state of Pennsylvania in 1939. He was selected to the All-Pennsylvania Team twice during his college career and served as team captain for three seasons. He was also a member of the football and soccer teams and was the golden gloves boxing champion in 1940. He recalled: 'The planning for 'D-Day', in retrospect, seems incredible. The airborne segment alone was awesome. All the thousands of men and machines had to be moved about, many from the USA and all of them had to be at assigned locations at specific times. In the case of Troop Carrier, with its function of dropping paratroops, this involved working backwards from the time of the planned paratroop drop, in our case at 0214 on 6 June. The route of each unit had to be plotted and the number of miles had to be accurately determined so that calculations at prescribed

---

74 *A Mid-Summer Night In Sicily* by David E. Mondt.
75 *The One Man Radio Show* Arthur Een's D-Day Communications Report.

air speeds (C-47s carrying paratroops at 140 mph) could be made. Still working backwards, each of the Groups, which came from three different Wing areas in England, had to be over checkpoints at specific times so that there would not be several Groups flying through an airspace at the same time. And, working still further back, the takeoff times and the assembly times had to be determined for each squadron of each group.

'Before all these events could take place, there had to be the fuelling and last minute maintenance of hundreds of airplanes. All the aircrews had to be briefed on the details (e.g. flying in 'V of V's, drop speed of 110 mph, return speed of 150 mph, no evasive action over the Drop Zone) and the scope of the entire mission. They also had to be fed. At the same time the paratroops had to leave their own barracks areas and had to be moved to various Troop Carrier bases. These men too had to be fed and provided with facilities for personal needs, so that they could assemble equipment and arrange the loading of the airplanes, including the parapacks on the underside of the plane.

'All of these matters and concerns were planned with great accuracy. The planning and logistics of the D-Day invasion were incredible - and good. The problems of the resupply mission on 7 June ('D+1'), were caused, not by the planning, but by the weather.

'As we walked into the briefing room, there was an undercurrent of nervous chatter throughout the room as the crews looked at the large map and observed the course. Could that be our Drop Zone? We had guessed wrong - thought it would be Calais! How long would we be over land? How much ack-ack did they have? Will we drop at night or during the day? How long would the flight be? A thousand questions were flying around the room. The briefing answered them all.'

'First we were introduced to the Commanding Officer of the American Airborne troops and he explained his Battalion's particular mission and then the general strategy for the invasion armies. Two great armies were to strike in France and the men we were to carry were to spearhead the attack. We were all amazed at the immensity of our own part in the invasion. Troop Carrier planes would be dropping airborne troops for five whole hours!'

'The briefing continued about how we were to form, the navigational aids along our course, the weather forecast for the route, the disposition of enemy troops and their anti-aircraft defences, the alternate airports for use in emergency, ditching procedure, methods of escape and evasion in case we were shot down and even the clothing and equipment we should carry. Nothing was left to chance as we filed out of the briefing room.

'We were ready to go, but because of weather conditions, the mission was postponed for 24 hours. All of us congregated at the Officers' Club to discuss this latest development. Generally we felt let down. The boys made wisecracks that 'Heinrich' had not had enough time to prepare for our coming and that was the reason for the postponement. Yet, despite the apparent jolly attitude of the men, we all felt worried because of the delay. What if the news leaked out? These thoughts pervaded the atmosphere all the next day until the time came when we reported to the planes. This time we were going!'

At Saltby the 62nd TCS would lead the sixty C-47s in the 314th Troop Carrier Group in Serials 20 and 21 with 36-year old Colonel Clayton Stiles flying lead with General James Gavin on board to Drop Zone 'N'. Stiles had begun his flying career in 1928, after passing the Flying Cadet examination and finished his flight training at Kelly Field, Texas, in 1930. From the summer of 1931 until May, 1942, he gained valuable flying experience; first with Delta Airlines, dusting cotton in Texas and then flying commuter flights in the east and Midwest for United Airlines. Upon taking command, the colonel's first order of business was to move the entire group including a headquarters unit, four flying squadrons, maintainers, mechanics, support personnel and an exhausting supply of aircraft and equipment from the United States to North Africa. The group arrived in late May 1943 and from this staging ground, began preparing for their first World War II mission. The young pilots in the 314th TCG, most of them 19-23 years old, looked to Colonel Stiles for leadership. The good colonel didn't let them down and flew the lead ship during every major campaign from Operation 'Husky' in 1943 to Operation 'Varsity' in 1945.

They would be followed by the two serials of 36 aircraft each in the 313th Group at Folkingham, which were also destined for DZ 'N'. The lead serial was scheduled to make its drop at 0208. The regimental mission was to hold the southern half of the bridgehead which the 508th and the 507th were supposed to establish beyond the Merderet. The sector assigned to the 508th was a rough quadrangle extending about three miles west of the Merderet and about two miles north from the Douve. The bridge over the Merderet at la Fière was just outside the northern edge of this area.

One thing Private Edward C. 'Bogie' Boccafogli in 3rd platoon, 'B' Company in the 508th PIR would never forget that morning was one of his buddies, 'standing outside his tent like a statue looking into space. His name was Private Johnny 'Bud' Daum, a blond, tow-headed kid.' Though Boccafogli thought Daum looked no more than seventeen, 'Bud' was born on 24 April 1924 in Marathon County, Wisconsin, the third child of four. He had three sisters; Helen, Marcella and Rosella.

Boccafogli, who was a few years older than Daum and thought of him as a little brother, went over to him and said, 'What's the matter, Johnny?'

'He said, 'I don't think I'll make it.'

Boccafogli tried to cheer him up: 'Nah, come on. Some of us will, some of us won't, but you ain't gonna be one; you'll be all right.' I sort of shook him because he was like in a daze. As it turned out, he was one of the first men killed in Normandy.'

In the 32nd Troop Carrier Squadron in the 314th Troop Carrier Group at Saltby the troopers in Harvey Cohen's plane ('Chalk 41', 43-30715), in Serial 21 were relaxing in the cabin when he and his crew boarded the transport. 'They asked me how high they would be dropped from, the speed the plane would be flying and how many planes would be behind us. I tried to reassure them by telling them I would slow the plane to 100 mph and that there were no planes directly behind us so they had no worries on that score. I went over the ditching procedures again and wished them 'Godspeed' and told them I'd treat for a drink in Paris.'

'I made a final check with my crew chief, Technical Sergeant Blake E. Craig of Elkton, Michigan and my radio operator, Sergeant Robert M. Freeman of Bellaire, Ohio. I put on my parachute harness and Mae West life preserver and took my place. We started our engines and followed our lead plane to the takeoff position. It is hard to describe the feelings I had as I taxied my plane past our operations and jerked my thumb up to the men standing there.

'Within a few minutes we were gathering speed as we moved down the runway and then we were airborne and moving into position on the right wing of our element. After circling while we formed, we started on our course - sixty airplanes in two serials, carrying 950 men to France.'

June 5 was 23 hours and twenty minutes old when Colonel Clayton Stiles released the brakes and started rolling. The two wingmen on either side rolled with him as the other element leaders followed with their three aircraft. Nine aircraft would be rolling or airborne by the time Colonel Stiles cleared the taxiway 6,000 feet on the other side of Saltby airfield. Without interrupting the timing or spacing, Major Arthur E. Tappan followed with the second nine aircraft of the 62nd. The co-pilot watched the airspeed, pulled the wheels up, adjusted the cowl flaps and milked the wing flaps up while keeping a lookout for other aircraft. Stiles flew formation; navigator, Lieutenant Victor Palumbo unfolded his charts; Hensley watched and listened to the engines and Wodinsky tuned in to the static. Colonel Stiles was checking with Lieutenant Colonel Thomas Shanley, 2nd Battalion, 508th Parachute Infantry Regiment, as 'Fred' Evans made a wide slow turn to allow the other elements of the 314th to catch the first nine. The pilots had done this so often that it took no more than ten minutes from takeoff till they were a tight group of sixty 'Gooney birds'. Easy with all the lights on - navigation, formation and the amber recognition. Evans fell in five minutes behind the 315th Group and maintained 133 mph ground speed and 1,500 feet altitude to the River Severn.

In the right seat of 'Chalk 11' piloted by Glenn 'Bolivar' Grimes, David Mondt watched the airspeed, pulled the wheels up, adjusted the cowl flaps and milked the wing flaps up while keeping a lookout for other aircraft. There was not much for him to do: keep his eye on the gauges; watch the formation ahead and an occasional light on the ground. He tightened the parachute straps and watched the English Channel approach as the formation descended to 500 feet. Mondt decided it was a good time to use the biffy and made his way to the tail. It was a nice smooth ride and the 508th troopers were relaxed, talking and for once, not airsick. On the way back to the cockpit Mondt climbed up and looked out the astrodome. What a view in the moonlight! C-47s as far as he could see to the front and rear. Hundreds of them and this is just from the 52nd Wing. Mondt strapped himself in again and reminded Grimes that it was time to turn off the navigation lights. Grimes nodded OK.

The next 56 miles from 'Flatbush', the Command Departure Point on the Isle of Portland, would take Mondt to two ships in the Channel marked with a green signal light. Somewhere in this area, Captain Clyde 'Pappy' Taylor was now on board a ship with crew and members of the Pathfinder troops that had departed North Witham with eight other aircraft. 'Pappy' was bumped by one of the other Pathfinders and required to ditch - the only 62nd crew that did not complete their mission. Made sense to 'Pappy' that if you had to put it in the water, land close to a ship. They never even got their feet wet. Fortunately, there were three C-47s assigned to each Drop Zone by the First Pathfinder Group to arrive thirty minutes ahead of the main body.

Colonel Stiles made the 90° left turn at 'Hoboken' and the co-pilot watched the amber recognition lights being turned off, as they started the run to the Initial Point. Just off the right wing the co-pilot could see the Channel Islands of Guernsey and Jersey in the bright moonlight. A little over two hours into the mission, a minimum of conversation had been exchanged between members of the crew. Lieutenant Victor Palumbo had been keeping his log on time and distance and was now standing between the pilots. His first combat flight, Vic had questions as he looked at the closest of the Channel Islands. 'Why don't they shoot?' The co-pilot had no answer but was content with the fact that they were out of range of the fifties and perhaps too low for the heavy anti-aircraft. The cloud bank at the Initial Point that would scatter later formations, draw the well-disciplined crews of the 62nd and other squadrons of the 314th together as they closed formation, the better to see the nine little blue formation lights. Grimes stayed close to Major Tappan as they descended and found clear visibility moments later in the moonlight.

Vic Palumbo's question was answered as the co pilot watched and became absorbed with how slow the tracers rose from the ground and then suddenly went by quickly out of sight. The view from the right seat is the best in the house; you can see it all, as Major Tappan would approach a line of fire and quickly rise over the tracers. When 'Tap' went up, Stiles would go under. So far so good, but the real problem is the five rounds in between each little red ball and those red balls are close together. Five hundred feet is not a good altitude when you are dodging hostile ground fire. Troop Carrier Command always referred to 'hostile fire' in the General Orders, or in the awarding of air medals and other decorations. They also used the terms, unarmed, unarmoured, unescorted. The co-pilot had time to think about a lot of things between the Initial Point and the Drop Zone.

Those serials intended for DZ 'N' ran headlong into the cloudbank a moment after crossing the coast at 'Peoria'. Most of the 314th Group apparently stayed in the clouds until within three miles of the zone. Near the DZ they met with some flak and much machine-gun fire. All eighteen C-47s in the 50th Squadron flying in Serial 21 returned to base but Lieutenant Sidney W. Dunagan from Idaho, piloting 'Chalk 49' (42-93088) was killed while making a second pass over the drop zone. Two paratroopers had fouled their rip cords as the plane passed over the drop zone and other troopers had jumped. These two were not able to exit the plane at that time. The problems quickly resolved; Dunagan circled to make a second pass over the drop zone to allow the two to jump. While making the circle, he was hit by a bullet in the left side of his chest, killing him instantly. Lieutenant Walter D. Nims, co-pilot, flew the aircraft on the return flight to home base. Sidney Dunagan was later buried at Madingley Cemetery, Cambridge. On this mission the 50th squadron delivered 319 paratroopers, 1,868 lbs of ammunition and 13,935 lbs of combat equipment into the drop zone.

The 508th PIR had been standing and ready since the Initial Point; they were more than willing to get out of that aircraft and on the ground where they could shoot back. David Mondt was relieved to see the lighted 'T' on the ground and the formation was slowing to a hundred and five. One problem - several guns were holding their fire steady over the Drop Zone and waiting for them to fly through. Mondt had his hand on the switch for the green light while watching the troops leave the first nine aircraft. If that 'T' was in the right place, the troopers would be on target. The pilot looked at his watch - 0208 - flipped the green light and counted the troops as he felt each step out the door. After number nine went out, the parapack loads were released.

Only seconds had elapsed when all the troops were out of the first nine planes except for 'Chalk 7' flown by Captain Charles S. Cartwright, who was leading the right element in the number seven position, leading the third element of the first squadron. 'Charlie' Cartwright's wingmen went for the deck and he made a right turn and had his navigation lights on. Cartwright reported later: 'Approaching the DZ, our airspeed was between 105 and 110 mph, our indicated altitude was 700 feet - the same as the leading element in our formation. In seeing the stick leave the lead ship, we gave the green light, but our stick did not jump. The jumpmaster, Captain Simmons, instructed the crew chief, Staff Sergeant Raymond H. Farris, to tell me that the plane was too low and that he would not jump his men at that height. The intercom was damaged and Farris could not reach me, so he passed the message to the navigator, 2nd Lieutenant Edward I. Osborne, who relayed it to me. As soon as the message was received, we went up to 800 feet indicated, made a right turn and began a second pass at the DZ. At this time the jumpmaster had come up to the cockpit to confer and I said to him, 'get the hell out: everyone except your stick has jumped!'

'During this second pass, we were hit by flak - probably 40mm - two rounds of which went through the plane. One round narrowly missed Farris, who was at that time in the door of the companionway and the other went through the rear of the fuselage. Paratrooper No.17 in the stick was hit by fragments, which detonated two of the hand grenades in his pouch, seriously injuring him. We went over the DZ again and once again the troops did not jump, although they received the signal. We turned for a third pass and this time Osborne told the jumpmaster that there was going to be a forced landing. The stick went out at once, a short distance south of the DZ, going in a westerly direction at 750 feet at 110-115 mph. The injured paratrooper, No.17, did not jump.

'Immediately after the jump, both engines quit, either at once or so close together that it made no difference. I turned the plane 180° to the right hoping to reach the ocean. He saw that he would be unable to do so and made a further 90° turn to the right, putting the aircraft on a south-westerly heading, hoping to reach the flooded area to the south of the DZ. The altitude was not sufficient to reach this area, so the crew took crash positions in the plane and I set it down in an open field. Going in it clipped a row of trees bordering the field. Both engines were on fire, but I made a relatively smooth belly-landing. The plane came to rest in the middle of the field and we evacuated it with all speed. The wounded paratrooper got out by himself. I, the crew chief and the radio operator, Staff Sergeant Frank A. DeLuca, carried the paratrooper, who had collapsed close to the plane, further away and then I went back into the plane for a first-aid kit and supplies. I recovered a kit, but was unable to reach anything else. Upon return to the paratrooper, I found that he had his own morphine and was asking to have it administered; the co-pilot, Flight Officer Alma M. Magleby and the navigator did this. We then began to carry the paratrooper toward the hedge bordering the field, which offered the only nearby cover and as we got a short distance away, the aircraft exploded. The paratrooper, now unconscious, was concealed in the hedge and about 0245 we began travelling south in a zigzag line, looking for a place to hide out. About 3/4 mile from the plane, probably in the vicinity of the village of Coquerie over a mile east of DZ 'N', we found a dry ditch covered with brambles and this became the hideout for all of us.'

Cartwright and his fellow officers eventually linked up with the 4th Division but when challenged, 2nd Lieutenant Edward Osborne was hit and fell to the ground, wounded in the fleshy part of the buttocks. They travelled back to England by sea, arriving off Portland at about 1400 Friday, staying on board until Saturday morning, 10th June. They then went through two straggler-survivor camps, the second at Weymouth, arriving simultaneously with 206 US glider pilots, who had just been brought back from the continent. They finally reached Saltby at about 2230 the same evening.[76]

David Mondt meanwhile, was still counting the last of the paratroops and watching 'Charlie' Cartwright make a 180 and the tracers were following him and not firing on the rest of the formation. 'Charlie' flew out of sight and Grimes hit the throttles and headed for the deck and the beach and the water. All of the eight planes in front were out of sight. All David Mondt wanted now was to cross that beach and get out over the water. One problem

76 *Troop Carrier D-Day Flights* by Lew Johnston.

suddenly appeared; a large dark dome, a pillbox on the coast. Grimes kicked rudder and flew around it. 'Got it made,' thought Mondt when a sudden bright flash filled the cockpit. Not knowing the condition of Grimes' night vision, Mondt grabbed the controls and pulled for altitude. As their vision returned, Grimes and Mondt looked at each other and asked if the other was all right. Satisfied that Grimes was not injured, Mondt relaxed his grip on the controls, placed his hands in his lap and found a small knob. He wondered what this was from and then realized that it was off the altimeter. Looked to his left at the hole in front of Grimes and discovered there was no altimeter. Checking the rest of the instruments, he found only that one tachometer was out and that all engine instruments were indicating normal operation. No problem, half the fuel remained and a shorter route to Saltby and lots of airfields in between.

During the 45-minute flight from 'Utah' Beach to checkpoint 'Gallup', where they would turn north to the coast of England, Mondt noticed that his left foot inside of the paratroop boots was warm and wet. He reached down and discovered that his pants leg was also damp, his thoughts turned to the fact that he was bleeding and yet he did not hurt, sniffed his fingers and wondered what blood smelled like, took another sample and tasted it. That's not blood, its hydraulic fluid. I looked at the gauges and found both on zero. Now we had a problem - landing gear, flaps and brakes would not operate. Flaps and brakes we can do without, but it would be nice to have a landing gear.

Mondt had not flown much with Glenn Grimes but they had been friends since early flight school days and now were about to work together on a small problem. Both knew that Captain Lennart Wuosmaa, Engineering Officer, had on occasions passed on information to pilots: 'On combat flights, don't use the cabin heater, might have a hole and you could be asphyxiated'. 'If you lose your hydraulics, get the gear down and the safety pin in any way you can. Three - point that bird and the gear will bind and hold.' As they approached Saltby at the return altitude of 3,000 feet, it was time to test 'Al' Wuosmaa's five second suggestion. Grimes cleared the area and went into a power dive and as he pulled out, Mondt dropped the gear and tried the lock pin. It went in. The rest was routine, fly the pattern and advise the tower, fire a few vary pistol shots and sit light in the seat while waiting for the gear to collapse. Five people aboard 074 held their breath as the tyres squeaked and the cockpit was a flurry of hands as throttles, mixture controls, gas selector valves and switches were turned off. 'Al' was right, the gear does hold and Grimes turned off the runway and rolled to a stop near Base Operations. Mission completed.

Three Lieutenants and two Staff Sergeants walked to the front of 'Chalk 11', fully expecting to see a large hole in the nose of the aircraft. They stood there and found no evidence of damage until someone said, 'There it is' and they found one small hole from a rifle bullet. If the German soldier had been a better marksman, he would have missed the altimeter and picked off Glenn Grimes. David Mondt thought there was a lot to be said for the right seat as they walked to Squadron Operations.

Harvey Cohen piloting 'Chalk 41' wrote: 'It was easy flying as we followed the course marked by plainly visible beacons - like a highway across the face of England. We left the land and started across the Channel to France. At this point I went back and put on my flak suit. Below us we saw the first ship and I felt once more the greatness of this combined operation. At this point we also saw the first planes coming back. They appeared scattered and I became apprehensive. They must have met a great deal of ack-ack.

'Soon we were turning towards land on the last leg before the run-in to the Drop Zone. I sent my crew chief to the rear of the plane to give a twenty-minute warning to the paratroopers. Then I adjusted my flak helmet. At this time we noticed the Island of Guernsey on our right - our first glimpse of enemy territory. I felt a hard knot in my stomach, similar to the feeling one has before the opening kickoff in a football game. I closed in tightly on my lead plane, observing that a bank of clouds lay over the Cherbourg Peninsula where we would cross the coast.

'Glancing at my instrument panel, I checked all my instruments carefully, remarking to my co-pilot that we would have to lose 1,200 feet before reaching the Drop Zone, to get down to the drop altitude of 700 feet. Soon we were over the coast heading toward the cloud layer and some scattered fire coming from the right. It was then our flight plunged into the clouds and I was pressed to follow my element leader who made a diving right turn.

'The next few minutes seemed to fly by. My element leader and I had become separated from the main formation and I was chasing him through the clouds. We had given our troopers the warning red light, when I sighted large amber 'T' identifying the Drop Zone about four miles to our left. The lead plane must have seen it because he turned toward it and within a few seconds was dropping his troops. I chopped the throttles and gave the troopers the 'GO' signal.

'Then I followed him as he dived to the 'deck' and headed toward the coast. He was turning wildly to evade machine-gun fire coming up from both sides. Following him, I was caught in the crossfire and although

I kicked and turned the plane violently. I was caught in it for what seemed like an hour. I felt the ship get hit and then smelled smoke and I yelled for the crew chief to check the damage and to the co-pilot to check the instruments. By this time we were over the water and headed for England. I stayed above the water for some time paralleling the land, especially when we watched the strong flak and machine-gun fire coming from what should have been Cherbourg.

'Within a few minutes we started climbing to 3,000 feet and I turned the plane over to the co-pilot in order to check the damage. We had received a 20 mm burst just behind the cargo door and the rear cargo section had approximately thirty bullet holes. This had been the crew chief's station at the time of the drop, but luckily, Craig had just moved forward. Returning to the cockpit, I noticed several other groups heading towards France and then passed two large glider trains. Again I was impressed with the large part the Troop Carrier Command was playing in the invasion.'

One trooper on Cohen's C-47 refused to jump. One trooper on Captain Warren S. Egbert's C-47 returned stating that he tripped on the floor mat of the C-47 or a Mae West and his gun struck him in the groin. He was second to last man in the stick and said that he was unable to jump on recovery due to the excessive speed of the aircraft.[77] On Captain Daubenberger's aircraft two troopers did not jump after fouled static lines jam caused a jam in the door way. One mile north of the DZ one C-47 had a jump light failure and the troops did not jump although the parapacks were released. Despite heavy, accurate and intense ack-ack and machine gun fire the pilot finally dropped two miles east of Montebourg.

Staff Sergeant Arthur Een was the radio operator in the lead plane of the first group (314th TCG) piloted by Captain Edwin Greer and Lieutenant Charles E. Johnson who later was to die in a crash near Liège, Belgium. 'Our course took us southward to a point slightly west of the Channel Islands - Jersey and Guernsey. Then we made a ninety-degree turn to the left; the desired objective being to pass equidistant between these two islands. At the radio briefing we were told that if this navigational feat were accomplished our flights should be out of the range of the German flak guns based there. There were eighteen planes from our squadron. We formed two 'V of V's of nine airplanes following each other 1,000 feet back. Other groups in front and back of us, flew in similar patterns. To visualize the enormity of this operation, besides being nine planes wide, it was strung out for something

---

77 Captain Warren S. Egbert was KIA on Operation 'Market-Garden' on 18 September 1944.

like five hours. The groups had to be coordinated from dozens of bases in England so that they would mesh into a solid train. The lead plane of each nine was equipped with a 'Rebecca' interrogator unit, which activated a 'Eureka' response unit set up on the drop zone.

'Visibility at times was zero-zero and other times it opened up a little. Captain Greer tried lower altitudes and then higher ones in an effort to find better visibility. As we approached the Cherbourg peninsula we were at fifteen hundred feet but had to let down to around seven hundred feet to drop our paratroopers and loads. We came out of the overcast just before reaching that lower altitude at about 0200. We were scheduled to be over Sainte-Mère Église at six minutes past the hour. Since our run over land was to take twelve minutes, we expected a fair amount of flak and small arms fire and it was certainly there. The first planes had dropped their troopers ahead of us and the hornet's nest had been nicely stirred up by that time. The sound of a flak burst hitting a plane can best be described as sounding like a hailstorm on a tin roof.

'Before take-off time, one of our paratroopers had asked me if I would stand back by the cargo door and give him a good solid push if he froze before jumping. A refusal to jump could result in a pretty stiff sentence. This didn't feel OK, so I didn't do it - and I don't know what he might have had in mind.

'In a matter of minutes, Captain Greer and co-pilot Lieutenant Charles Johnson spotted the lighted panel with the proper colour designation for our drop. The red light, or warning light, in the plane cabin had been on now for several minutes and then the green light was switched on to signal the paratroopers to jump. The planes had throttled back to slower speeds for minimal shock to the troopers as their chutes opened. And as usual, the landing gear warning horns were blaring away inside the planes. This provided some assurance of proper speed and altitude.

'This was a warning indication designed for quite another purpose - to prevent wheels-up landings, but in a paradrop situation, it provided some assurance of proper speed and altitude. It was triggered automatically when the aircraft was below 1,000 feet and the engine speed was below 1,000 rpm and the landing gear was still retracted.

'Many paratroopers told me later that they felt sorry for us since we could not get away from the flak, but had to fly back through it. I certainly appreciate hearing that kind of sympathy from the men I consider the cream of the fighting crop.

'After our stick of paratroopers had cleared the door, Captain Greer went into a rapid climb to get away from the flak, which was concentrated at the lower levels. At 6,000 feet he levelled off and we soon were over the Channel on our way back to England. I refused to relax however and thought up all sorts of possibilities like damaged gas tanks, wing bolts, hydraulic lines and perhaps tyres punctured by flak bursts. In those higher latitudes during the month of June, daylight comes quite early. When we touched down neatly back in the Midlands around five o'clock, the night had ended.

'After a calming jolt of Old Overholt rye whiskey, the crews went through an interrogation session before going to the mess halls. The usual questions concerned the amount of flak, whether the drop was on target, were any enemy aircraft spotted etc. I often wondered what was considered light flak. If I saw one burst or tracer bullet as far away as the horizon I rated the flak as heavy.

'A check of our aircraft by the ground crews found most of them still ready for flight. A supply drop was scheduled for the early morning hours of June 7th and since our plane was among those selected, the heat was on again.

'Chalk 40' (42-92055) that was reported missing on the 'Boston' mission, had ended well, as the pilot, 1st Lieutenant Richard Randolph confirmed: 'We were caught in a searchlight from about the door back and we were under heavy fire from both sides. This was after letting down through the overcast to about 500 feet. The oil line on the right engine was severed and I feathered the prop. The left engine was also acting up and the rudder cable was severed. The navigator had a sliver of wood from his desk pinning the lids of one eye together. I dropped on target and got out of there. We nursed the plane back across the Channel to a single strip airfield just over the coast called Tarrant Rushton. I landed straight in and while we were there contacting our base, the crew counted holes in the airplane. There were 326, some as close as six inches from the gas tanks. Part of the trailing edge of the left wing was turned up in a 90-degree angle. Someone flew down to get us and the airplane was later repaired and may have been the one we called *Patches*.

* * *

In the late-night darkness of 5 June, after receiving doughnuts and coffee from Red Cross Doughnut Dollies at Folkingham 'Bob' Nobles and the rest of the men in the 508th's 1st and 3rd Battalions had strapped on their gear and weapons. Nobles also packed four letters from his wife Bette. The men in Nobles' stick then loaded onto their C-47 and roared off the tarmac shortly before midnight, heading for Normandy along with hundreds of other planes. First Lieutenant Neal Beaver and his 81mm mortar platoon had gone to their C-47, which was piloted by 1st Lieutenant Robert Nelsen.

'Up to this time' wrote Beaver 'things had been bad enough, but from here on in they went downhill in a hurry. The paratroopers came out and we attached the parapacks. We loaded up and when the order to start engines was given, ours would not start. We tried hand cranking, but only succeeded in sticking the solenoids. Soon it was obvious that our bird was not going to fly that night. 'OK 'Joe' [co-pilot, 1st Lieutenant Joseph D. Denson], we've got to take the standby plane.' We alerted our paratroopers and they sprang into action and transferred all their gear (including parapacks) to ['Chalk 52', 42-32810] the reserve airplane. It didn't take fifteen minutes before we had made the transfers and had engines started. Nelsen's wingmen, 1st Lieutenants' Robert Kerr and Kreiser had waited for him.'

'When the port engine of Nelsen's plane wouldn't start we were in a panic; says Beaver. 'The worst feeling of being left behind I've ever experienced. We fell out of that plane like bloated frogs - pulled the bundle trip and waddled across the runway between trios of aircraft roaring by. One bundle chute carrying 81mm mortar ammunition burst open and we left it behind. When we were loading the spare plane we heard Lachmund having a rather violent 'discussion' with the crew of the spare about who was going to Normandy. Nelsen must have been the senior officer because he ended the discussion and boarded the plane.'

So, while most of the 313th Troop Carrier Group and its four squadrons departed from Folkingham, three C-47s in the 29th Troop Carrier Squadron delayed by mechanical problems got into the air. And these aircraft made it only after Nelsen, who was the flight leader, had to change planes. These aircraft flew the mission by themselves, without seeing any of the original formation.

Airborne over England and all the way to their drop, Beaver stood in the door with another of the battalion officers 'Bill' Gary and with Lachmund. 'We were alone - three planes - I never saw another aircraft. I recall critiquing Nelsen mentally as follows: 'Well, he is OK, he saw the blinking light on the submarine, he made the left turn, we're doing fine, etc. etc.' We saw the Channel Islands clearly and made landfall well south of our intended route. We were at 1,500/1,800 feet and I could see that the left plane was holding tight and of course found out the same was true of the plane on our right. We had very few cloud problems, if any, just some isolated ground haze. I could see the silver ribbons of the Merderet and the Douve rivers and could even see the large volume of fire rising from the flak train we had been told was parked at Sainte-Sauveur-le-Vicomte far to the north. I recall telling Lachmund to tell Nelsen to turn left. I had been drilled in the land features;

I could see the whole area just as the sand table had it. I don't know if the message got through or not because we started to take some machine gun fire and suddenly we were down to 600/700 feet and popped out over the opposite beach. In fact we were exactly between the targeted 'Utah' and 'Omaha' landing beaches.'

'Bob' Nelsen recalled: 'We led our individual flight out to the run-up position. All the other birds had gone south. We took off, got our flight together and headed for Bournemouth on the south coast of England. We didn't see any of the thousands of airplanes that were in the air that night. We flew southwest over the Channel and turned east ('Hoboken') and flew between the Channel Islands. What a greeting? Tracers were coming up from both sides. Fortunately, we were out of range of their guns. Soon the coast of France loomed up in front of us. I told Joe that we were going to make our own invasion with just our three-plane flight. We made landfall where we were supposed to and started looking for signs of the DZ. It wasn't there.

'Connors [navigator, 2nd Lieutenant Walter W.], where in hell is it?' It wasn't to be. I guess the pathfinders ran out of candles. Then all hell broke loose. Tracers were coming at us from all directions. We continued to look for some sign.

'Aldrich [radio operator, Staff Sergeant William F.], can't you get any radio signal from the Drop Zone?' That wasn't to be either. Soon another beach loomed up ahead.

'Joe', we've gone a beach too far. We've got to go around.'

'I set up a wide turn to the left. I set it up so we would pass over the site where we estimated the DZ to be. Tracers continued to light up the night. It looked ominous. We completed our 360° turn and slowed down to drop our stick of paratroopers. Finally the ground fire got us. What a racket! As far as I know our troops all got out per schedule.'

Beaver again: 'Clear sky - bright moonlight - the beach was a beautiful white strip and the water had some white caps. It was quiet and calm compared to the ride across the peninsula. Nelsen snapped that C-47 into a tight and wide open left turn. I recall thinking: 'he is turning the right way'. As soon as the direction stabilized on west, we came under machine gun fire. The first burst looked like it was coming straight for my forehead, but it swept by in a gentle curve to the east. The next burst caught us front to rear. The plane took a sudden lurch, lost some more altitude and roared back up to speed. Nelsen had evidently set up for the 'GO' light as soon as he completed the turn.

Lachmund again: 'We went around again and that is when we were hit. I cannot remember if paratroopers jumped when we were hit or if they had already jumped, but it was close. I grabbed the manual release for the parapacks because the box at the door had been hit and I did not know if they had been released. There was some yelling going on up front and, after I pulled in the static lines, I went toward the cockpit. The first person I met was 'Bill' Aldrich. The left side of his face looked as though it had been hit by a porcupine. One of the bullets had gone through the navigator's table and the splinters lodged in his face and some had pierced his eyelid. On getting to the cockpit, I found that Nelsen had taken one through his leg and that 'Joe' Denson was flying the plane from the right seat. The left control column was useless. The shot that wounded Nelsen took the skin off of Denson's flak jacket. An inch further back and this would not have been written.

'Connors and I got some morphine into Nelsen with Connors doing the honours. I got under Nelsen's shoulders and tried to lift him out of the seat while 'Joe' flew with one hand and tried to support his leg with the other. We finally got him out of the cockpit and onto a litter. Connors and Aldrich stayed with him while I went back to the cockpit.

'Joe' Denson recalled: 'We got shot up pretty bad. Nelsen took a hit in the leg; Aldrich took one in the face. Conners had one in the butt and Lachmund caught a piece of shrapnel in the hand. All crewmen except me sustained injuries, although flak did penetrate my flak suit. I looked over at Nelsen, he seemed to be nodding. The troops had jumped and I didn't know he was hit.'

Beaver found out later that Nelsen and some others of the crew had been wounded. 'That first burst nicked 'Bill' Gary (later killed in action in Holland) across the nose and I caught a 9mm round in the jaw. It knocked me back, but I bounced back into the door and as the green light snapped on, I kept right on going out of the plane. As it turned out, the full bore jump saved us because our chutes snapped open with such speed. I know I oscillated just once or twice and hit the ground hard.

'The troop carrier guys did a great job, considering the circumstances. Three planes, alone, out over the opposite shore and then directly into a flurry of flak and fire, yet the three planes stayed so tight. I had my entire platoon of 50+ troopers all together by 0600 that morning. (I hit the ground at 0130). As it turns out, the low altitude was a break also, not one man was fired at in the air. I had to leave seven men behind in a French home when I left at 0800. All had jump injuries: broken arms, two broken ankles, a wrenched back, etc. By 'D+3' or '4', all were on medical ships headed for

England. We left one broken mortar but found every single bundle. That's one hell of a tight jump, even by Fort Bragg training standards. I found my regiment on 'D+3' without losing another man. The medics dug the machine gun round out of my chin at that time and I still have it. Evidently it was a tracer with the phosphorus used up and light enough to just slide under my skin.'[78]

Nelsen had been hit but didn't know it for several minutes. 'The first indication I had was that my left foot wouldn't respond. I yelled at 'Joe' to take over and head for the Channel. Fortunately we were not able to detect any loss of oil or fuel. We were all excited. I instructed 'Joe' to get to 350° (direct course to Southampton) and high-tail it for England and the emergency strip. Good old 'Bob' Lachmund had put a tourniquet on my left leg to stop the bleeding and he gave me a morphine shot. I wasn't feeling a bit good. I began to sweat. I never sweated like that in my entire life. I never knew what trauma was before that time. After we settled down on a course to England 'Bob' pulled me out of the cockpit and got me stretched out on the bucket seats in the cabin. That's all I remember until we passed over the emergency landing strip and 'Bob' fired the red flare to alert the ground medical crew. The medics put me on a stretcher and into an ambulance that took me too a general hospital five miles away. It was about 0430 when at the emergency room they began debriding (wound cleaning) procedures. The doctor asked me where I had been. When I told him that we had dropped paratroopers in France and the invasion was on, he didn't believe me. Nothing was announced until 0600 that same day.'

Denson wrote: 'All the crewmembers of that plane went to the hospital except me. The medics at first sight thought I had also been hit. I was splattered with blood, mostly from 'Bob' Lachmund's hand as he performed cockpit duties. Nelsen's wounds were severe, while those of the other crewmen were considered slight. The British doctors gave me a few swigs of scotch - later a bottle of gin.'

---

78 Beaver's company commander, Captain Malcolm D. Brannen came down between Picauville and Etienville, south of the DZ, just a quarter of a mile from the German Beach commander's Headquarters. Near dawn, just after observing the landing of reinforcements by gliders in Mission 'Chicago', Brannen and the group of paratroopers he had assembled fired on a German staff car headed for Picauville at high speed. Generalleutnant Wilhelm Falley, division commander of the 91st Air Landing Division, who had just set out for 'Utah' Beach in his Volkswagen Kübelwagen staff car, ran into Brannan's ambush and in a brief fire fight, Brannen shot and killed him.

The 313th Group was harder hit than its predecessor, mostly by accurate small-arms fire. 'Chalk 16' (42-92868) crashed in flames near Surtainville shortly after the aircraft had dropped its stick of sixteen paratroopers. The bodies of 1st Lieutenant William P. Roycraft and his four crewmembers were found on a beach a few weeks later. 'Chalk 14' (42-68694) piloted by 1st Lieutenant Marlin L. Burelbach was hit by flak after dropping its stick of sixteen troopers near Picauville. With one engine on fire the aircraft was ditched in the English Channel. The crew was picked up by a Royal Navy destroyer after spending three hours in life rafts. 'Chalk 41' (41-38698) flown by 1st Lieutenant William S. Butler was shot down and destroyed by fire near Carentan after a para drop near Cherbourg. Two of the crew were rescued. Butler and his co-pilot, 2nd Lieutenant Thomas G. McCarthy were taken prisoner. The group brought back 21 aircraft with slight damage, eleven needing moderate repairs and one badly damaged.

Flying blind until almost at the DZ and harassed by enemy fire as they emerged from the clouds, the last four serials were peculiarly in need of pathfinder assistance. They got very little. The pathfinder troops had landed more than a mile southeast of DZ 'N' and found enemy forces blocking their way to the zone. In this dangerous situation all they could do was to operate a 'Eureka' and two amber lights. They reported later that the 'Eureka' was on in ample time and was 'triggered; by 'Rebecca' signals at 0156 when the first aircraft the 314th were still over twelve miles away. However, only the first serial of the 313th Group reported receiving usable signals from the 'Rebecca'. Some members of other formations picked it up but poor reception, possibly due to jamming. A few pilots did see the amber lights and used them as a guide. Although the pathfinders turned on the BUP beacon, there is no evidence that any of few navigators who had SCR-717 made use of it in selecting their drop point.

The leaders of both serials of the 314th and the rear serial of the 313th Group relied on 'Gee' to establish their position and obtained fairly good results. The most successful was Lieutenant Colonel Clayton Stiles, commander of the 314th Group, who placed his stick in good position on the south side of the zone. In the stick was Lieutenant Colonel Thomas J. Shanley, commander of the 508th's 2nd Battalion, an officer destined to play an important part the coming battle. The leader of the second stick made his drop about two miles north of DZ 'N'. The leader of the third, using 'Rebecca-Eureka' gave the jump signal in the vicinity of the pathfinders. The fourth leader made a fairly accurate drop on 'Gee'. Thus, if the serials had held together, about half the paratroops intended for DZ

'N' would have come down on or close to it and almost all would have been within two miles of it. In fact all four serials had disintegrated leaving only a small minority in formation behind the leaders.

The serials flown by the 313th and 314th Troop Carrier Groups had not seen the clouds and flew through, rather than over, them, with C-47s taking evasive action to avoid collisions. Minutes later they emerged into fierce anti-aircraft fire. In need of pathfinder aids, the pilots discovered that the sets near DZ 'N' were ineffective or not turned on. The flight leaders navigated accurately to the drop zone, but most of their flights were no longer in formation. The 508th experienced the worst drop of any of the PIRs, with only 25 per cent jumping within a mile of the DZ 'N' and another quarter within two miles. Another quarter was unable to perform its assigned mission because it had been flown past DZ 'N' and dropped on the wrong side of the Merderet and most of the remainder was ineffective because of dispersed drops in remote or dangerous places. Half of those who jumped more than ten miles away were missing. A platoon leader of the 508th, First Lieutenant Robert P. Mathias, who was struck by a blast of fire yet still managed to lead his team out of the C-47, was the first American officer killed by German fire on 'D-Day'.

Lieutenant Robert Clinton Moss Jr. of HQ Company, 508th Parachute Infantry Regiment recalled: 'We flew south and west out over the sea. It was dark and the formations had tiny blue lights around the wing edges and down the fuselages arranged to be seen only by the other aircraft. We turned south for a spell then east and hit the west coast of Normandy on an azimuth of 113 degrees. We supposedly had a few minutes to go to drop zone and the red ready light went on. All men stood up, hooked up and moved in position to jump. Flak at night is magnified similar to flying over the fairgrounds into the fireworks. The plane began jumping from the concussion but I don't think we took and hits. We flew and flew and flew and flew. We knew something was wrong. I could no longer see the formation light of other planes. The guys were getting edgy and that line was surging and pushing. And there was some profanity, I believe. Then the crew chief came up to me and said. 'Lieutenant, we can't find the drop zone. We are lost. Do you want to go back to England? Gawd amighry! Go back to England? Those guys would have thrown me out and jumped anyway or killed me when we got back to England.

'I said, 'Are we over France?'

'He said, 'Yes.'

'I said, 'Give us the green light; we're going.'

Major Warren Shield, Executive Officer, 508th Parachute Infantry Regiment, 1st Battalion recalled: 'The mission of the 508th was to go into Force 'A' reserve in the vicinity of Hill 30, west of the Merderet River. Our flight across the Channel was very uneventful, it was routine. As we hit the coast we got some flak. I checked and noted that all the planes were back there. But then we hit the clouds and it spread us a little. I could still see the leading 'Vee' even in the fog. We passed over Sainte-Sauveur-le-Vicomte and got a lot of flak which spread the formation. Then we went over Etienville and got a hell of a lot of flak there. Then I looked around and there were no ships around my plane. I jumped on the green light and just after coming out of the plane I turned around and looked over my shoulder and saw the Douve River behind me very close. I landed in an orchard about half way between Picauville and the Douve. After coming down I only saw one plane which was towing a glider and kept on going and another C-47 which was shot down in flames.'

For 'Bob' Nobles the flight over the English Channel was uneventful. 'We were all thinking,' Nobles said. 'A lieutenant walked the aisle, talking to everyone trying to both cheer the men up and calm them down, but Nobles did not appreciate it. 'I almost told him to sit down.' When the red light by the fuselage door lit up the cabin shortly after midnight, Nobles and his 16-man stick stood up and hooked their static lines to the anchor cable running the length of the cabin and checked the preceding man's equipment. Then the red light went off, replaced by a green one and the men charged out the door. Nobles could see tracers coming up and trees below him, but he did not have time to take it all in. 'By the time my chute opened up, I was on the ground' he said.[79]

Of 2,188 paratroops tasked for DZ 'N', 2,183 had been dropped. Two had refused to jump, two had fouled chutes and one was wounded. Over 95 percent of the 63 tons of supplies and equipment carried had been delivered, but a large part of the men and materiel landed far away from the drop zone. About seventeen out of 132 sticks did land on or very near to DZ 'N' and another sixteen were within a mile of it. Most of the latter were located beyond the zone, indicating that the pilots had been a little slow in recognizing their position. Perhaps they had seen parachutes beneath them or the Merderet ahead. Some thirty additional aircraft loads came down within a two-mile radius of the zone. Half of these were in the general vicinity of the pathfinders. The pathfinder beacons were near the Douve and

---

79 *Ed Mauser: Easy Company's Silent Brother* by Kevin M. Hymel, *WWII History magazine.*

several sticks fell into the river. No less than 34 pilots went past DZ 'N', crossed the Merderet and dropped their loads between DZ 'O' and the coast. At least three of these set their drops by the green 'T' on DZ 'O', nine put their sticks near Sainte-Mère-Église and ten dropped near Sainte-Martin-de-Varreville, which was six miles east of DZ 'N'. Most of the troops dropped east of the river fought on 'D-Day' with the 505th PIR or the 101st Division, then assembled on the 7th and reported to their regimental commander, on the east side of the Merderet near DZ 'O'. A number of jumps were made prematurely with the result that eight sticks descended between three and five miles short of DZ 'N'. Through gross errors two sticks were dropped near Valognes, nine miles north of DZ 'N' and five were dropped about fifteen miles north of the zone. The directional error in those cases is so great that it seems as though the pilots must either have gone off course before reaching 'Peoria' or circled for a second run and lost their bearings completely. Approximately twenty sticks went unaccounted for.

The regimental commander, Colonel Roy E. Lindquist and Brigadier General 'Jim' Gavin, standing in the open doorway of the C-47 and who remarked that he could not even see the wingtips of his C-47 from the cabin doorway, were dropped by the second serial of the 314th Group. They came down about two miles north of DZ 'N' within the territory of the 507th PIR and joined forces with elements of that regiment. Gavin later gave an excellent synopsis of the weather encountered. 'As we reached the western coastline, disaster loomed up. We slammed headlong into a dense cloudbank. Nothing had prepared us for this. The weather briefing had not foreseen it; our flight over the Channel had encountered only scattered clouds. The cloudbank was thicker in some spots than others. For some of us it was so thick that it was if we had suddenly stopped flying through the air and were now flying through greyish soup.' The Pathfinders had also flown through these clouds; but because of the strict radio silence imposed on all of us had not warned anybody of this terrible danger. Flying in almost zero visibility, practically wingtip to wingtip, pilots suddenly had to decide how to save their crews, paratroopers and planes.

'As the formations 'hit' the weather, the 'Vee of Vee's formations began to break up, miraculously avoiding midair collisions. The breakup essentially wiped away any prospect for a concentrated paratrooper drop, but the crew continued to press forward. It became the responsibility of every pilot and navigator to find the drop zone, climb or descend to 700 feet and slow to 120 mph to avoid too much opening shock on the chutes and men that they carried. In addition, the 'Eureka-Rebecca' radar beacons did not work as they were supposed to as the pathfinders had not been given enough time to get down on the ground, find their locations and set up the drop zone 'T' lights and beacons. Planes that included 'Gee' equipment could not make sense of their readings either. This was a visual drop in marginal conditions! Training, indoctrination and pride all kicked in and the crews were going to do everything within their power to deliver the troopers to the appointed drop zone.

'Mercifully, up to this point the paratroopers had no way of knowing we were in big trouble. But now pilots in some planes, already badly rattled, began to see flak and small arms fire coming up at them. They dived and twisted under the upcoming arcs of tracer bullets and while the heavily laden troopers struggled to stay on their feet. Some planes whipped around badly, forcing troopers down on their knees. 'Barf buckets were knocked over and vomit spilled out, causing a dangerous slippery floor. Crew chiefs and radio operators in the rear of the planes screamed up to the pilots to keep the planes steady.'[80]

Time reporter, 'Bill' Walton reports a fragmentary amazing conversation, in his C-47 in the 314th Troop Carrier Group, between men shuffling to the open door. 'Please don't shove me, I'll go quickly... Okay, don't shove me either...' 'Bill' Walton jumped, his Hermes typewriter strapped to his chest (in addition to other paraphernalia doubling his weight). Getting up he surveyed the 'fields among the daisies and Queen Anne's lace' now blighted by the signs of war: holes riddling homes and barns, trees cut down, equipment demolished cows and horses - stinking and mostly dead, as he sat at his Hermes typewriter on a makeshift table and recorded the events on 'D plus three'. He cabled: 'I plunged out of the plane door happy to be leaving a ship that was heading toward flak and more Germans. The jump was from such low altitude there was only a moment to look around in the moonlight after my chute opened. The fields looked so small that one couldn't miss a tree or hedge. Anyway I couldn't. I landed in a pear tree, a rather good shock absorber. But the trouble was I didn't filter on through to the ground; instead I dangled about three feet above ground unable to swing far enough to touch anything. My chute harness slipped up around my neck in a strangle hold, covering the knife in my breast pocket. I was helpless, a perfect target for snipers and I could hear some of them not far away. In a hoarse, frightened voice I kept whispering the password 'Flash', hoping someone would hear, call out 'Thunder' and help. From a nearby hedge

---

80 *Blackjacks At War 53rd TCS* by Major Steven C. Franklin.

I heard voices. I hung still a moment, breathless. Friends. Then I heard them more clearly. Never has a Middle Western accent sounded better. I called a little louder. Quietly Sergeant Auge, a fellow I knew, crept out of the hedge, tugged at the branches and with his pig-sticker cut my suspension cords. I dropped like an overripe pear. It took me two seconds flat to struggle out of my harness and drag my typewriter-laden frame into the hedge.

'There were three of us there, moving through the shadows one by one. We picked up five more men in the next hour and a half. It was four in the morning before we joined the brigadier general, who headed our jump. He did a wonderful job of assembling men, forming patrols to guard our perimeter and feel out German strength. Soon after dawn, he decided our position was not only untenable, it was tough. The only escape was across three-quarters of a mile of swamp to a railway track. At 0730 we plunged into the chest-deep swamp, holding our guns overhead and wading. Sometimes you'd step into a pothole up to your neck. When machine-gun bullets started pinging around us the sweat began to trickle. Water filled our pockets and every ounce became a pound. A few men were killed in that crossing, but most of us got across to the railway. By then our last ounce of energy seemed gone. But we went on two miles, panting and puffing up the track to dry land. Snipers were still taking a wham at us every now and then. Half our equipment was gone, but my typewriter was waterproofed and I have it still. Nobody has had his boots off yet. Until yesterday we were surrounded, under constant fire. There will be more of it. But the beachhead forces have joined up with us and now the shells are going in the other direction. In the first 72 hours we had only three hours of sleep, wrapped in parachutes out in the open.'[81]

Wrote Pfc 'Joe' Stanger: 'The plane ride lasted nearly two hours - two hours of physical as well as mental discomfort, for the cumbersome equipment, the flak, the chute opening and where and what you'll land in and on, can occupy even the calmest individual's mind in such circumstances. The wind was high and the plane bounced about plenty, but no one got sick. Finally, the crew chief yelled that we were twenty minutes out from the drop zone. 'OK guys, let's stand up and hook up' came the quiet voice of the jump-master. Everybody shuffled into line. Now was the time when all paratroopers get the old 'Butterflies' - the time spent between hooking up and waiting for the jump order. We must have checked our straps and equipment a hundred times. Then, suddenly, the jumpmaster's command: 'Let's go!'

---

81 Mary Claire Kendall, a Washington-based writer who edited *William 'Bill' Walton: A Charmed Life* published in fall 2013.

'The nervousness had lifted, just as it always does when the crucial moment comes. We all pushed towards the door - come what may. We were ready and wanted to get it over with. Out I went. Then with a jolting jerk that temporarily leaves you breathless, the old silkworm has blossomed again. Looking toward the ground, I am suddenly very clear headed and alert. Tracer bullets are coming up all around us. It seems almost as if you are walking down a fiery stairway. Coming to your senses, you see the ground right below you and get ready to land. With a dull thud, you hit the ground. Then, in a nervous jumble that seems like years, your thumby hands, clumsy with tension, unfasten your straps and you are free - for action.

'First, we must reorganize. At night, this is a real problem. Picking up men here and there from the widely scattered parachutes, you assemble as many as possible and then, when the flare goes up, you proceed to the Battalion assembly area.'[82]

Private M. G. Thomas reported: 'June 6th was the biggest day of my life. It was 'D-Day' for me and all of the Airborne. I was quite scared but not as much as I had thought I would be. Finally the time came. The jumpmaster said 'Let's go.' Well, everybody started to go when we were hit by ack-ack. Half the stick got out easily but the ninth man was hit as he reached the door. We were all knocked down. We got up except for the wounded man who couldn't move. When the last man had left, the wounded trooper got to the door somehow and followed him out... The night was beautiful. I didn't like to see our boys being shot in their chutes, while still in the air... I stayed in a ditch for a while until some troopers came along. We continued to move until daylight when we were boxed in by enemy fire. The Germans spotted us and began firing on the ditch where I was hiding. One of the boys carried a prayer book. He asked us to say a prayer but I told him I didn't know a prayer. All I could say was: 'God, if you could ever do anything for me, please do it now as I need it.'... We started out of there and kept moving until we met up with our General. We joined others who were ordered to take a town. We took the town and held out there until the troops reached us from the beach. We had lost some men but the Germans lost three to our one... I hope every general is as much of a man as General Gavin proved he was in combat when he led us in such a victory.'

'Corporal Jules Stollock writes of a friend: 'He was only eighteen. The men in his company used to call Private 'Tony' Vickery the 'Milk Bar Commando' - milk shakes being his strongest and favourite drink. As for

---

82 *Normandy By Parachute* by Joe Stanger, quoted in *Saga of the All American*.

women, he didn't have any. His mom, back in Georgia, was his only and best girl... The jump was uneventful except for flak and a few ambitious Jerries on the ground. Out of the entire planeload, he came across one man and together they started off in the direction of the Drop Zone. On the way they picked up eighteen more troopers and that night they chalked up three machine gun nests and about twenty-five or thirty Jerries. Daylight made it necessary for them to take cover and dig in but 'Tony' stayed on the alert. His vigil was not wasted for not more than six hundred yards away a skirmish line of German grenadiers broke out of a wooded area and advanced on the trooper's positions. He waited until the Jerries were about fifteen feet away before he squeezed the trigger of his Tommy gun. The fight lasted about twenty-five minutes and when the smoke cleared away he lay in a heap at the bottom of the ditch. Four slugs from a machine gun pistol got him in the throat. It was a rotten way to die, but if you looked on the other side of the hedgerow you would have seen the bodies of at least thirty-three dead Germans and the kid got every one of them.'

The dropping of the 507th Parachute Regiment on DZ 'T' beginning at 0232 was the last phase of the 'Boston' paratroop mission. The regiment was carried by Serials 24 and 25 of 36 aircraft each from the 61st Troop Carrier Group and one of 45 aircraft from the 442nd Group. The fastest departure appears to have been that of the 61st Group at Barkston Heath. Taking off in elements of three at seven-second intervals, it put its two 36-aircraft serials in the air in 2½ minutes apiece.

The 507th PIR's pathfinders had scored a bulls-eye on DZ 'T', but because of Germans nearby, marker lights could not be turned on. They did turn on their 'Eureka' at 0212 and received 'Rebecca' signals at 0217. The incoming serials received the responses very well and relied on 'Rebecca' in making their drop. The leader of the 442nd Group also picked up the responses of the 'Eureka' south of DZ 'N'. Checking it by 'Gee', he recognized that its location was wrong and also noted the difference in coding. The first aircraft of the 61st Group made its drop at 0226 and the last at 0245 or later. The main body of the 442nd dropped its troops between 0239 and 0242. Of 1,187 troops carried by the 61st Group all but one man, who refused to jump, were deposited in Normandy. Of 750 carried by the 442nd Group, all jumped with the possible exception of the one stick aboard a missing aircraft. Many of the C-47s straggled and only two or three sticks landed on the zone and about fifty more came within a mile of it. Unfortunately many pilots overshot, by between 1,000 and 1,500 yards and thirty to fifty sticks (450-750 troops) landed in the swampy backwaters of the Merderet. The water was shallow at most points and few men were drowned, but the rest, floundering in the water with most of their equipment at the bottom of the river were in sorry state to start a battle. Estimates of drowning casualties vary from 'a few' to 'scores' (against an overall 'D-Day' loss in the Division of 156 killed in action), but much equipment was lost and the troops had difficulty assembling.

Almost thirty sticks of the 507th PIR came down within approximately two miles of DZ 'T' in 101st Airborne areas and became temporarily attached to that division. The rest, with one odd exception, were scattered. About sixteen landed between two and five miles from the zone, eleven more within a ten-mile radius of it, one thirteen miles to the north and one 25 miles to the south. The only concentrated drop away from the zone was made by ten pilots in the second serial of the 61st Group who wandered to the vicinity of Montmartin-en-Graignes, eighteen miles southeast of DZ 'T' and dropped about 160 paratroops of the 3rd Battalion of the 507th Regiment there. This was the worst error by a formation of such size in either 'Albany' or 'Boston'. Once again the most plausible explanation is that after some mix-up in the clouds the pilots had fallen in behind a straggler who was not using radar. That they followed their false leader unquestioningly on such a wild-goose chase may be considered a triumph of discipline over common sense. The headquarters company of the 1st Battalion, carried by the last serial of the night, was dropped five miles beyond Carentan at Montmartin-en-Graignes. They rallied other stragglers and fought off attacks by the 17th SS Panzergrenadier Division for five days before 150 managed to infiltrate back to Carentan in small groups.

Raymond Wallace in the 507th PIR, jumped at 300 feet from a C-47 with one engine on fire. Drafted into the army in 1943 following induction in May of that year, he had volunteered for the Airborne after watching a movie about Airborne Ski troops. From such a low altitude his ankle was badly sprained upon landing. Despite the dark and confusion, he managed to find fifteen paratroopers from his stick far, far from their intended drop zone. For the next 21 days they fought the enemy but were finally captured after nearly exhausting their ammunition and food. At the holding facility outside Paris, he escaped and for two weeks fought with the French Resistance, harassing the enemy once again. After recapture, he was sent to Stalag 12A and later, to another prison camp near Leipzig where he spent the rest of the war. At the time of his liberation his weight had dropped from 165 to 95lbs.

The 61st Group had some trouble with the clouds, but most of its lead serial held together. The Group suffered little from ground fire. One pilot whose aircraft was hit within sight of the zone dropped his troops but crashed later. He and his crew bailed out safely. Only six other aircraft of those two serials were hit and none seriously. The 442nd Group had a harder time. Its formation ran into the overcast and dispersed. It was also the target of more fire, principally medium to intense light flak and small-arms fire near the drop zone. One aircraft was hit over western Normandy and had to crash-land after first dropping its troops many miles short of their goal. Another was missing with all aboard. One with both engines dead was ditched successfully on the way home. Among those returning were 28 with slight and three with medium damage.

Despite the confusion, the 61st Troop Carrier Group dropped its cargo of 1,167 paratroopers at 0232 hours amid a 'forest of enemy fire.' The intelligence brief prior to departure had informed the crews that their route of flight would take them within range of fourteen heavy AA guns and that 34 others were situated such that just a slight deviation to the north would bring them in range. On the same note, crews were instructed that 'evasive action prior to delivery of troops will not be tolerated. In the event a DZ is missed on the initial run-in, troops will be delivered within the combat area. In the event the coastline is reached and troops have not been delivered, aircraft will execute a right hand turn and deliver troops on DZ.'

A crew chief who flew with the 61st TCG, best described the chaos experienced by those approaching the drop zone that night: 'Watching the tracers come up at us made the hairs on the back of my neck feel as though they were standing straight up. These things are stamped indelibly in my mind: the rattle of flak fragments against our plane, the sight of flak and tracers above us, some seemingly right on the mark for the planes in front of us; the absolute stark terror in some paratroopers' eyes, their vomiting into their helmets and forgetting to empty these helmets when it came time to 'Stand Up! Hook Up!' as they prepared to make possibly their final jump'.[83]

The formation returned to Barkston Heath at 0415 hours. Remarkably, ten of the 53rd's eighteen aircraft reported dropping on the DZ, two reported dropping within half a mile and the other six reportedly dropped within one mile. The 53rd aircraft returned with no casualties, no damage and no paratroopers returning, but not all the squadrons in the Group were as fortunate.

Colonel Willis W. Mitchell, 61st TCG and flight lead was shot in the left hand while over the DZ. 1st Lieutenant William R. Hitztaler of Denver,

---

83   *Blackjacks At War 53rd TCS* by Major Steven C. Franklin.

Colorado in the 14th TCS piloting 'Chalk 31' recalled: 'Coming in low over the coast we received machine gun fire. Then we hit low clouds. Trying to follow Captain Harruff, leader of the first flight, we pulled up and then down, through the clouds, veering to the right slightly so as not to run into them. I could not find them upon re-emerging so I took up the proper course heading. In approaching the DZ our aircraft encountered flak, which hit toward the rear and the tail. One paratrooper was badly hurt and was believed dying.' Hitztaler's C-47 was shot down after its paratroopers jumped. All five crew bailed out, Hitztaler and his navigator, 2nd Lieutenant John Herbert Hendry of Jamaica, New York escaped and they were rescued by American troops on 19 June. The co-pilot, 2nd Lieutenant Stanley E. Edwards Jr. of Phoenix, Arizona and the crew chief, Tech Sergeant Alvin F. Vezina of Loadore, Idaho were taken prisoner. The radio operator, 2nd Lieutenant Orlo A. Montgomery of Denver, Colorado was killed. Twelve of the paratroopers were captured, five were killed and one escaped.

Directly over the DZ at 0226 Captain Gene Franscioni gave the troops in his aircraft the green jumping light. The gunfire from the ground kept streaking in and around the vicinity of the plane but no hits were received. Franscioni held 'Chalk 25' in the jump altitude for about fifteen seconds, levelled it off and still in formation, increased his speed to get out of enemy territory. 2nd Lieutenant W. Lyon the navigator then informed Franscioni that there were still some paratroops left in the plane. The 11th man in the stick had got jammed in the doorway causing the eight men behind him in line to fall so that all were rendered unable to jump on the target. Franscioni asked them whether they would jump if he were to take them all the way back to over the DZ. Their answers were all in the affirmative. Franscioni made a 180 degree turn to his right and flew in on the deck. He recognised the DZ by the hail of tracers coming up from around it. At 0234 hours, exactly nine minutes after he dropped the first batch, Franscioni gave the remaining eight troopers the green light.

Maintaining 'Vee of Vees' in thick cloud and with strict radio silence increased the risk of collision. Another 61st Group pilot, 1st Lieutenant Robert Ingram, recalled: 'Suddenly 'Chalk 2', Captain James Cargill's C-47 disappeared in the clouds even though I was holding position right up next to him. Lieutenant James Hurley's airplane was gone too. Just when I had about decided that I was invading France alone, their blue lights came back into sight and we were still in proper formation. I was relieved. Only the flight leaders carried navigators and radar receivers so that the rest of us depended on them to guide us to the DZ and home again. As our orders were to drop the paratroopers in France no matter what the situation, I was as intent on staying with Cargill as a Canada goose's gosling is when flying with its high-flying mother. My relief, however, didn't last long. He and Hurley went out of sight again when he went into a second, thicker layer of clouds. I was determined to stick with my mother goose because I had no desire to be on my own so close to the climax of our mission. So, hoping that Cargill was holding a constant rate of descent and airspeed, I began easing closer to where his C-47 should be. I believed I had a good chance to pick up his blue formation lights before my C-47 hit his. We came out of the clouds in a tighter formation than would be considered safe under the best of conditions. Hurley must have been thinking like me and had eased closer to our leader too. When we broke out his left wing must have been less than three feet away from my right wing tip and smack in between them was Cargill's rudder.'

Only minutes from DZ 'C' the other C-47s from Ingram's 45-ship serial were nowhere to be seen. ('Chalk 2' was hit by flak and ditched in the English Channel west of Grandcamp-Maisy. June 6 was Cargill's 25th birthday). All Ingram could do was search for the correct pathfinder T-lights and Eureka transmission and head for the DZ alone.

Mission interrogation, or debrief, was set up in the Officer's mess where the flight surgeon, 'Doc' Locker had broken out his hoard of 'medicinal' bourbon. Breakfast followed, the men retired to their sacks and the intelligence office switched to preparation for another mission supporting Operation 'Neptune-Freeport', a parachute resupply mission.[84] Less than 24 hours later, the Group put 52 more aircraft in the air and fought to find the flak-ridden DZ to deliver almost 1,000 lbs of ammunition, rations and equipment to the 82nd Airborne.

'Bill' Silberkleit, a 305th Troop Carrier Squadron, 442nd TCG navigator in the lead ship with Colonel Charles M. Smith at the controls, said of the paratroopers: 'They all had about 300lbs of equipment on them and they couldn't even get on board. We had to take two of us to sort of push them up piggy back to get them into the aircraft. They just had so much stuff on them. They were gung ho they were all really ready to go. I didn't see any of them that were reluctant; they weren't frightened, that's for damned sure. One thing interesting about Fulbeck is that there were three airfields within three miles of each other. Many times people would come in for final approach and find out they were coming in at the wrong air field. They were all that

---

84   Ibid.

close together. We flew from Fulbeck down towards southern England to a jumping-off point down there near Bournemouth. From there we flew down toward our destination flying right between the two Channel Islands coming in to the Cherbourg Peninsula. We came in over and between the Jersey and Guernsey Islands on to the west coast of the peninsula. As we approached the coast I was able to pinpoint myself along the coast line. As soon as we crossed the coastline, the sky was sort of lit up (with antiaircraft fire). There were tracers and everything coming up that you could think of. (To me) it was not a frightening thing, it was very fascinating. You don't think of those things that might happen or what is involved, you are intrigued with what you are doing at the time. We were flying at about 450 feet above the ground and we didn't see any fog. Everything looked perfect. I was astounded later to find out that our unit was stacked up (because of fog) and that there were a lot of aircraft in the clouds and above the clouds that could not see where we were. At 0244 the green jump light was switched on in Colonel Smith's aircraft and each ship, in turn, disgorged its heavily-laden paratroopers over Normandy. Years later Silberkleit was able to talk with one of the paratroopers who had jumped from his plane that night. 'He told me that we dropped him right on the area where he was supposed to go. It made me feel really good. I do know that we had some aircraft in our unit that dropped their paratroopers miles away. They were the ones that experienced the fog and the overcast. One of my navigator friends told me they had to come back around a second time to make their drop. They had missed it the first time in.'

Three of the 45 C-47s in the 442nd Troop Carrier Group failed to return from this mission. A 303rd TCS, C-47 pilot, 2nd Lieutenant John J. Prince of Cherokee, Iowa flying 'Chalk 18' (42-92415) in Serial 26, the very last paratroop serial to Normandy, had departed Fulbeck airfield heading for DZ 'T' to drop sixteen paratroopers of the 1st battalion, the 507th PIR and the HQ Company. They were over the DZ at 0244 hours. Prince said 'The closer we got the cloudier it got. There was just a layer of clouds right at the altitude that we wanted to fly, around 1,500 feet. So we dropped down a little ways and tried to get under it.' He did not have even one engine left on his C-47; he was forced to land 'deadstick' in the darkness of Normandy's tree-lined hedgerows. The Lieutenant's cool skill set the crew down safely and got three of them away with enough emergency supplies to last until their return to friendly lines. Crew Chief, Tech Sergeant Francis H. Schultz ended up as prisoner of war after wandering for days in Normandy, reaching friendly lines with help of a French lady and being captured the same day.

He spent the rest of the war at Stalag Luft III and Stalag Luft IV. Prince and co-pilot, Flight Officer Joseph K. Loeb and radio operator, Sergeant Ralph E. Charlton survived with the three canteens of water they had with them and food from the escape kits. After five days they started drinking water from a pool, which they strained through handkerchiefs and putting Horlicks tablets in it. On the eighth day of evading they got in touch with a farmer family who provided food and drinks every other day. After having to spend more than two weeks in hiding the Germans were finally driven from the area and on 21 June they were taken by a French guide to Saussemesnil where they contacted American soldiers of the 4th Division. From there they were taken to the Sainte-Mère-Église airstrip and found a ride back to England. Their arrival back at Fulbeck created quite a stir among those who had feared the worst for the missing airmen. 'Everyone in the squadron assumed they were held captive or they were dead until one day they showed up in the Mess Hall at Fulbeck with long scraggly beards,' Landon Cozad, a 24-year-old first lieutenant and a C-47 pilot said.

Major Kenneth L. Glassburn's ship *You Cawn't Miss It* in the 304th TCS, 442nd Troop Carrier Group had an engine knocked out and the plane was set on fire. Flames spread rapidly, but rather than risk capture by bailing out over enemy territory, the squadron commander from Turlock, California flew the blazing aircraft to the Normandy coast and ditched in the English Channel. When no report was received at the base, his first sergeant, Harold A. McGrath, Yonkers, New York picked him up the third day on the morning report as missing in action, remarking to the adjutant, 'I dreamed of the boss last night. He bawled the daylights out of me for doing this.' Ten minutes later a phone call disclosed the safe arrival in England of the Major and his crew.[85]

As 'D-Day' drew to a close, the feeling in IX TCC and 9th AF was that the delivery of the paratroops had been an outstanding success. Losses and aborts had been negligible and mission reports indicated that all serials had done well. (Forty-two C-47s were destroyed in two days of operations, although in many cases the crews survived and were returned to Allied control. Twenty-one of the losses were on D-Day during the parachute assault, another seven while towing gliders and the remaining fourteen during parachute resupply missions). On 10 June came the reaction. General Quesada returned from a visit to Normandy with news that the paratroops had been badly scattered and that General Bradley was much disappointed. The difficulties encountered in 'Neptune' once again raised the question of

---

85 *Invaders: The Story of the 50th Troop Carrier Wing.*

whether night paratroop operations were worthwhile. Never again in World War II did any considerable number of Allied paratroops make a night drop.

The troop carriers had undertaken to bring 13,348 paratroops to Normandy. Of these, about ninety were brought back for one reason or another and eighteen were in an aircraft ditched before reaching the Continent. About 100 in 'Albany' and perhaps thirty or forty in 'Boston' were killed when the aircraft carrying them were shot down. The rest jumped. Of the jumpers over ten percent landed on their drop zones, between 25 and thirty percent landed within a mile of their zone or pathfinder beacon and between fifteen and twenty percent were from one to two miles away. At least 55 percent of the pilots made drops within two miles of their goals. About 25 percent of the troops came down between two and five miles away from their zones or beacons. With few exceptions these landed east of Pont 1'Abbe and north of the Douve, seemingly within reach of the combat area. About ten percent were from five to ten miles off the mark and four percent were scattered between ten and 25 miles from their zones. The remaining six percent were unaccounted for.

The most impressive feature of the return from 'Boston' Mission was the splendid formation in which the first serial of the 316th Group reached Cottesmore at 0400. This achievement, unique in 'Neptune', indicates that the serial had at no time been badly scattered. On the other hand, the 313th and 314th Groups returned singly or in driblets. Also some elements of the 61st Group left their corridor and cut straight across from Normandy to Portland Bill. The last stragglers to reach British soil did so about 0540. Their arrival ended the troop carriers' role in the paratroop missions but there was still another mission to fly as 2nd lieutenant Ted Weatherhead in the 316th Troop Carrier Group recalled: 'When we reached Cottesmore we thought we were through for the day. After debriefing we immediately went to bed and slept until they woke us up later that morning for our second 'D-Day' flight. The second time we towed a glider that held a jeep and ten paratroopers over there. The Germans knew about our gliders. What they did was plant telephone pole-size posts in the ground standing three or four feet tall in many of the open fields along the Normandy coast to keep the gliders from landing. We tried to find a field that didn't have posts when we dropped our glider off. When we returned from our second flight over Normandy that day they gave each of us a shot of whiskey. We took it and slept like a baby all night long.'

'Bill' Walton was well aware he was lucky just to be alive. He did not know then that it would be the last large-scale night time paratrooper drop. 'The price was too high, the loss too great'; he wrote.

Chapter 10

'Tonga', 'Mallard' and 'Rob Roy'

'Then quite suddenly the sky above the horizon was filled with dots, like a huge widespread flock of homeward-bound crows on a summer's evening. It was a while before they came close enough to make out silhouettes - most of us were pretty skilled at aircraft recognition, when life might pivot on the knowing of a Messerschmitt 109 fighter from a Hurricane or a Spitfire. From the vantage point of the Woolwich Common we watched the hundreds of aeroplanes, some singly, some towing the Hamilcar troop- and equipment-transporting gliders. The aircraft were mainly American-built Douglas DC-3 Dakota transport planes, the air-workhorse of the war. The width of the flock was at least ten miles wide and it took at least a quarter of an hour to fly overhead. Even if the separation was 100 yards between aircraft there must have been close to two hundred aircraft abreast. Then they were somewhere above central London, with St. Paul's Cathedral's dome and towers shining, as if so proud that England was at last striking back at the grey-clad, half-million-strong German VII Army. A thrill of excitement ran through me as I stood alone, for a little while, watching approaching aircraft that surely and steadily carried the airborne troops that were to drop behind the Normandy beaches and have such a crucial bearing on the successes of that day: Tuesday 6th June 1944.

'One thousand bomber raids had become common by the Allies over Occupied Europe - but thirty thousand? No, it could not have been, although it certainly looked like it.

Alex Savidge, a boy living in London.

'We all felt that D-Day was looming' wrote Flight Lieutenant 'Jimmy' Edwards on 271 Squadron at Down Ampney 'and our suspicions were confirmed when the station intelligence officer issued an edict that all aircrew moustaches were to be shaved off. His reasoning was somewhat convoluted. We were all to carry passport-size photographs of ourselves which, if we were unlucky enough to be shot down, could be pasted into false identity cards to be supplied by the French underground movement. He thought that RAF-type handlebar moustaches looked far too British, so, before the photos were taken, off they had to come. And what a hirsute harvest it was. We appointed one of the senior WAAF officers as 'Official Shearer' and with great merriment and not a little beer she performed the solemn ceremony. So another Edwards' facial effulgence fell by the wayside.

From Down Ampney and Broadwell the target for the 9th Battalion The Parachute Regiment was the formidable Merville coastal battery whose casements were believed to contain four 150mm guns overlooking 'Sword' Beach. Destruction of these guns was vital. Dakotas at Blakehill Farm and some at Broadwell and Down Ampney were to drop the 8th Parachute Battalion on a Drop Zone five miles inland to give protection in depth to the other British airborne landings. On 25 May the 9th Battalion moved into a tented transit camp near RAF Broadwell where they and the 1st (Airborne) Battalion Royal Ulster Rifles, who were to land in gliders at LZ 'N' near Ranville on the evening of 'D-Day' were to complete their final preparations for 'D-Day', sealed off from the local townspeople and villagers to preserve security. The following days were spent in detailed briefings.

'The invasion was supposed to take place on 5 June' wrote 'Jimmy' Edwards 'and about a week before that we were given a detailed briefing on the various jobs we had to do. I was one of a group of 'Daks', which were to go over the night before and drop gliders on various special targets like bridges and gun-emplacements, so that these could be captured before the main onslaught took place. We did our best to memorize the lie of the land from maps and reconnaissance photographs. There were going to be so many machines in the air over the beachhead that, to simplify identification, all Allied aircraft were to be painted with wide black and white stripes on the wings and the tail end of the fuselage. This was such a well-kept secret that we didn't know about it ourselves until the day before 'D-Day' and it had to be done so speedily that our ground crew couldn't possibly cope with the task in the short time available. Accordingly, all the aircrew had to rally round and out we went to the dispersal points armed with large whitewash brushes and lent a hand with sloshing the stuff on to the wings. I was wearing my second-best peaked cap, which was already splitting open at the front of the peak and the addition of liberal amounts of white paint added to the rakish appearance. The CO eyed my get-up with a disapproving look, but said nothing. This was hardly the time for bullshit.'

On the morning of Saturday 3 June at all the bases for the airborne assault the battalions in the two parachute regiments paraded in full jumping order, complete with weapons and equipment containers and moved off in lorries to the airfield. Each lorry carried one 'stick' of paratroops and drove to the correct aircraft. There, parachutes were issued and fitted and containers were attached to the underside of the aircraft. Each man marked his parachute with his last two personal numbers and placed it on his seat in the aircraft. Take-off was planned for the evening of 4 June. Later that day Brigadier Stanley James Ledger 'Speedy' Hill, commanding 3rd Parachute Brigade, talked to all his officers. His final remark was: 'Gentlemen, in spite of your excellent training and orders, do not be daunted if chaos reigns - it undoubtedly will!' Shortly after, news was received that the invasion had been postponed for 24 hours because of bad weather in the English Channel. Tension was relieved and the teetotal rule relaxed - but only temporarily.

'When the whole operation was postponed for twenty-four hours' wrote Edwards 'this placed a great strain on all of us, but to save our mooching about with our morale sagging, we were all piled into a fleet of coaches and taken to Netheravon, where we filed into a very secret Ops room where we were allowed to gaze at a large-scale model of the actual piece of coastline we would encounter when we finally went over. Every house and farm building was there, as were all the Jerry emplacements.'

Flight Lieutenant P. M. Bristow, a Dakota pilot in 'C' Flight on 575 Squadron at Broadwell recalled: 'Once we had been given our first briefing and knew the DZ and the glider targets, a tight security clamp was imposed. No one was allowed off the camp; no letters were collected though we received incoming mail and no telephone calls were permitted. Even an ENSA concert party arriving by coach was turned away. On the other hand all our flight commanders went over to Netheravon for a special briefing. This was the operational centre for our part of the show and one of them told me later that he came out of the briefing room and put through a call to his girl friend in London. During these days we studied photographs, large-scale maps and then we got a sand table of the coastline with the River Orne running up to Caen. We were even shown a film of the run-in from the coast line to the DZ. I think much of the success of the final operation was due to these visual aids we were given in the last few days.'

The feeling of frustration caused by the delay due to weather was felt equally by the soldiers in 6th Airborne Division. 'We were supposed to take-off on the night of fourth June and were all geared for that' wrote Signalman Harry Read in the 3rd Parachute Brigade, who was living in one of the tents in a field at Tilshead before the Battalion moved to rest camp in Fairford Park near their departure airfield. 'During the afternoon when word came to the effect that the weather conditions were severe and the campaign was put off for another 24 hours it at least gave a lot of men another 24 hours of living.'

A final briefing for the whole 6th Airborne Division and the 1st Canadian Parachute Battalion took place on 30 May. Maps, air photographs and scale models gave every man a detailed and accurate picture of the battalion's objectives as a whole and his own section's in particular. Lieutenant Jack Sharples of 8 Platoon 'C' Company in the 13th Battalion, 5th Parachute Brigade was amazed at the amount of detail given at briefing. 'Such things as the tower was detached from the rest of the church and that we must expect to find cows on the DZ. When I came to brief the platoon and asked for questions, their only concerns were how to find the RV (turn to follow the line of fight and look for the church tower) and secondly the strength of the enemy in Ranville, but were reassured when I said 'There aren't enough Germans in the village to give 'C' Company any trouble.' The morning of the 5th was a slight improvement weather-wise and the whole procedure repeated. Divisional instructions stipulated that a fat free meal was to be served at least two hours before takeoff. I can't speak for the Battalion, but the machine gunners went to war on two slices of bully beef, mashed potatoes and lettuce; followed by boiled rice with raisins.'

'Whatever feelings of exultation any of us might have had were punctured when assembled to learn the strategy of the campaign and the precise parts we were to play. It was clear that very substantial casualties were expected on the landing itself. No wonder our section had such a generous supply of wireless operators! The casualty expectation looked to be in the region of 50%. If others thought as I thought, the prospect of a safe return home was diminishing by the minute but, having put our lives on the line there was no thought of backing out, we would sell our lives dearly. It was a very sobering experience [but] we were all in the same boat and we trusted each other to do our jobs well.

When the Dakota and glider squadrons gathered in Operations Rooms at 2000 hours on 5 June they learned the final details of their part in Operation 'Tonga', the British codename given to the 5-7 June airborne operation. Flight Lieutenant Alec Blythe on 48 Squadron at Down Ampney wrote: 'My DZ was one and a half minutes flying from crossing the French coast to dropping. The briefing therefore had to be tremendously detailed. Accurate models of the

Normandy coast and hinterland were constructed. From these models cine films were made of the tracks to each of the dropping zones. So we were prepared with a mental picture of what we could expect to see as we flew in. The films, however, were made in daylight, whereas we would be dropping at night.'

The Dakota crews that were to tow men of the 3rd Parachute Brigade in Horsa gliders to Normandy were addressed by the C-in-C of Transport Command Air Chief Marshal Sir Frederick Bowhill. 'He was an elderly man with a mass of ribbons on his rather ill-fitting battle-dress' wrote Jimmy Edwards, who would pilot one of seven glider tugs carrying twenty men and a variety of equipment and jeeps to their drop zone at Gonneville near Caen. 'Your task,' he said impressively, in a quite passable impression of Winston Churchill, 'is to support all the services in their various endeavours. You will nourish the Army. You will nourish the Navy. And you will nourish the Air Force.' I muttered to 'Tiger' [the observer, Flight Lieutenant Hunter, who had earned a DFC on Bomber Command], who stood beside me: 'There you are. We're nothing but a bunch of bleeding nourishers.'

Early on 5 June it was confirmed that the airborne assault would be mounted that night. After resting in the afternoon the men had tea, readied themselves and paraded at 2000 hours by sticks for the drive to the airfields. By 2245 everyone, including dispatchers of 48 Air Despatch Group, headquartered at Poulton near Cirencester and based on or near to the Dakota squadron airfields of 46 Group, were on their aircraft.

At Fairford Park a short service was held by Reverend Parry before moving off at 1900 hours to Fairford airfield. 'The RAF treated us very kindly' wrote Signalman Harry Read. 'They gave us a slap-up meal of bangers and mash after which we trooped out to the airfield where all the aircraft were lined up awaiting us; American Dakotas - C-47s. They looked very, very impressive. It was 2320 hours when we emplaned having been hanging about for a very long time. Getting a whole brigade into aircraft and airborne is a time consuming task but, eventually, we roared off the runway and were airborne. Getting a fleet like that into formation before heading for the battlefield was time consuming also and, after stooging round and round seemingly for hours, we set off for France. Our time of destiny had arrived. An interesting moment came when the pilot spoke on the intercom inviting us to look down to view the coastline informing us that we were passing over Poole Bay.'[86]

---

86   On the night of 5 June 45 aircraft were detailed to carry 887 paratroops and their equipment to the DZ. Three aircraft on 620 Squadron were lost.

Flight Lieutenant P. M. Bristow, on 575 Squadron at Broadwell recalled. 'By 1800 hours all our aircraft were marshalled on the perimeter track and taxi tracks so they could file out in the correct order for take-off. Not only was my Squadron the last to go, but as I was amongst the last of our squadron. It was a long wait and not without anxiety, for one had no sort of idea what reception we might meet. I do remember a strong sense of occasion and however small the part one felt one was taking part in an historic event.'

RAF Regiment Squadrons provided guards for the marshalled aircraft. 'The day before the 'off' wrote Jimmy Edwards 'all the Dakotas and Horsas were duly marshalled on the runway. There was a further complication when we did at last go down to the airfield to take off. 'During the delay, the wind had changed completely and was now blowing in the opposite direction from the day before. And there was no time to take all the 'Daks' and gliders to the other end of the runway. This meant a down-wind take-off with a heavily loaded glider in tow, but fortunately it was not a very strong wind, so as 'Wingco' Booth said, 'We'll just have to make the best of it.'

Alec Blythe had met the Royal Engineers, whom he was to drop on 'D-Day'. 'They seemed jolly nice chaps. However, when they came up to the Dakota on the night of the operation with blackened faces they looked a fearsome lot. One pulled out his dagger and said that it was going to find a German that night. I was rather glad they were on our side.'

Between them 38 and 46 Groups dispatched in the region of 270 aircraft as well as 256 Horsas and gigantic Hamilcar gliders (which with a capacity of 17,500lbs needed a four-engined aircraft to tow it); the glider tugs being Albemarles, Dakotas, Halifaxes and Stirlings. Not only must the 6th Airborne Division be taken to the right place, it had also to arrive at precisely the right moment, if surprise, essential to success, was to be achieved. All turned therefore on correct timing. The interval between take-offs was of paramount importance, as they were working with very little margin of range. The use of different types of aircraft and different types of combinations complicated matters because of the different speeds.

At 2230 the first of six Halifax aircraft, each towing a Horsa glider containing men of Major John Howard's coup de main force whose objectives were the Caen Canal and Orne River bridges, began to take-off from Tarrant Rushton. At 2300, from Harwell and Brize Norton, four squadrons of Albemarles took off carrying the pathfinders of the 22nd Independent Parachute Company and the advanced parties of the 3rd and 5th Parachute Brigades bound for drop zones behind Ouistreham and 'Sword' Beach.

Dusk had fallen over England when the first six Albemarles, who were to mark the three main drop zones ('K', 'N' and 'V') in the neighbourhood of the Orne to be used by the airborne troops took off at 2303 hours.

DZ 'V' which was allocated to the 1st Canadian Parachute Battalion and the 6th Airborne Division was situated in a valley with a wet and treacherous surface (for the River Dives, which ran through it had overflowed its banks) 1¼ miles east of the Merville battery. After 'Charlie' Company, 1st Canadian Parachute Battalion had captured and secured the DZ and the pathfinders had marked it an assault force in the 9th Parachute Battalion commanded by Lieutenant Colonel B. H. Terence Otway DSO were to capture the Battery. The 1st Canadian Parachute Battalion would then destroy the bridges over the Dives and its tributaries at Varreville and Robenhomme and protect the left (southern) flank of the 9th Parachute Battalion during that unit's attack on the Merville Battery, afterwards seizing a position astride the Le Mesnil crossroads, a vital position at the centre of the ridge. DZ 'K' between Cuverville and Touffréville, a few miles further inland from the Merville battery was assigned to the HQ, 3rd Parachute Brigade and 8th Parachute Battalion. The main body of the 5th Parachute Brigade bound for DZ 'N' north of Ranville, behind 'Utah' and east of the Orne left Fairford and Keevil. The Headquarters Company, Mortar and Anti Tank Platoons in the Brigade's 13th Battalion flew from Brize Norton in Albemarles, while Battalion Headquarters and 'A', 'B' and 'C' Companies were transported from Broadwell in Dakotas. Finally the Machine Gun Platoon travelled in two Stirlings out of Keevil. Aircraft in 38 Group also flew the coup de main and pathfinder sorties, contributing a total of 109 aircraft for this lift.

As the residents went to bed in the quiet little villages of Kencot and Filkins, Down Ampney and Marston Meysey, Cricklade and Chedworth the silence was ended as the 108 Dakotas of 46 Group started their engines on three airfields nearby and carried out their final pre-take-off checks. At 2310 Wing Commander Basil A. Coventry DFC commanding 512 Squadron, pushed forward the twin throttles of his Dakota to full power at the end of Broadwell's Runway 20 and took-off followed by 32 of the squadron's Dakotas. These and twenty-one of 575 Squadron's Dakotas deployed in tandem carried elements of the 1st Canadian Parachute Battalion and the 9th Parachute Battalion to DZ 'V'. Poor weather conditions, which had complicated navigation and the pathfinders who were to illuminate the drop zone with their beacons, landing them astray, the drop was badly scattered and only threadbare elements of both battalions were able to form up and go about their business. All went well until the areas were reached, when one of the aircraft mistook its own zone and dropped its passengers on the south-east corner of the neighbouring zone, where they erected lights and beacons. The result was that in the main drop fourteen 'sticks' of the 3rd Parachute Brigade arrived at the wrong zone and the situation was for a time confused. Of seventy-one Dakotas that conveyed the principal group to DZ 'V' only seventeen aircraft dropped their passengers on the correct spot, nine within one mile and eleven within 1½ miles. Two-thirds of the strength of the brigade was dissipated over an area fifty miles square although the advance elements of 9th Parachute Battalion, consisting of reconnaissance and rendezvous parties, had been dropped on the DZ with no problems and they had reached the battalion RV point without difficulty.[87] One party of men set out the lights marking the company locations whilst another set off towards the battery which was a mile away. Shortly afterwards RAF Lancaster bombers carried out a raid on the battery but missed it; most of their bombs fell to the south. The aircraft bringing the main body of the battalion were by now approaching the French coast. Unfortunately, most of the pathfinding equipment for DZ 'V had been damaged and there were only a few lights marking the DZ when the aircraft arrived. Consequently, few of the pilots saw them and visibility was further worsened by smoke from the bombing raid blowing across the zone. As a result, only a few sticks landed on DZ 'V whilst others dropped into the Dives marshes and some on the high ground between Cabourg and Dozule.

Lieutenant Colonel Otway, who, with the rest of his stick, had been flung untimely out of his Dakota as it was taking evasive action to avoid the flak, found himself heading straight for the roof of what he knew to be the headquarters of a German battalion. Anti-aircraft fire began as they crossed the coast of France; and not many seconds later, Otway had his first warning that the drop was going to go wrong. The pilot began to throw the aircraft about in violent evasive action. The effect on the drill of the parachutists was chaotic. When they tried to move down to the door to jump in the quick compact succession for which they were trained, the sudden lurches threw them off their balance. Some fell on the floor encumbered by their heavy equipment. Others tripped over them in struggling cursing heaps. Out of the melee, Otway shouted to the pilot: 'Hold your course, you bloody fool.'

'We've been hit in the tail,' one of the aircrew shouted back.

'You can still fly straight, can't you?' Otway asked angrily. But before he was given an answer, the signal came to jump. Otway's turn was early.

---

87 *Go To It! The Illustrated History of the 6th Airborne Division.*

He clambered along to the door and found he was still clutching the half-empty bottle of whisky. He thrust it at the RAF dispatcher. 'You're going to need this,' he said; and with that parting shot, he jumped. So accurately and clearly had the maps and models been prepared that, though he had never been there before, he knew exactly where he was. Missing the headquarters house by a few feet, he landed in the garden with one other man, who picked up a brick and flung it through a window through which the Germans were firing at them with revolvers. Presumably mistaking it for a bomb the enemy fled. Otway then made his way to the rendezvous, leaving behind him, unknown to himself, Wilson, his batman, who had fallen through the roof of the greenhouse, but who subsequently rejoined him. Otway learned later that only seven of the twenty men in his aircraft had managed to disentangle themselves in time to jump while it was over the dropping zone. It had to make three more runs to get them all out.[88]

By 0250 hours Otway had assembled 150 of the 550 men of his battalion. None of the eleven gliders, bringing in jeeps, anti-tank guns and trailers had appeared. Moreover, the battalion's 3-inch mortars, the sappers, the field ambulance section and the naval bombardment parties were all missing. However, the battery had to be destroyed by 0530 hours so Otway decided to press on regardless. In one of the greatest feat of arms on 'D-Day', he and his men overwhelmed the Germans defending the battery. Of 640 men who left England, only about seventy or eighty were on their feet and in one piece.[89]

It had originally been planned that the 6th Airlanding Brigade would land with the first wave of Airborne troops to secure the Ranville and Bénouville Bridges; however the discovery of considerable anti-glider defences on their dropping zone (DZ 'N') beside the River Orne at Ranville near Caen resulted in their arrival being delayed until the evening of 'D-Day'. Flight Lieutenant P. M. Bristow on 575 Squadron detailed to take paratroops from Broadwell to DZ 'N' wrote: 'the first [of the squadron aircraft] to get airborne in the last of the daylight were all towing gliders. Never shall I forget the first one of all, for he had just about used up the runway and was still on the ground. Around the periphery of the airfield stretched a low dry-stone Cotswold wall and a load of shingle had been tipped against this wall at either end of all the runways. It may have been imagination and the light was failing; it may have been a despairing heave back on the control

---

88 *Dawn of D-Day* by David Howarth.
89 See, *Go To It! The Illustrated History of the 6th Airborne Division* and *Air War D-Day: Winged Pegasus and the Rangers* by Martin W. Bowman (Pen & Sword, 2013).

column or it may have been a bit of both; but it always seemed to all of us who were watching that the Dakota ran its wheels up the shingle bank and was literally catapulted into the air. At zero feet it staggered along too low to make a turn but with a line of electricity grid poles not far in front. Next day the pilot said the trip had been uneventful apart from the take-off. To the best of my memory my take-off proceeded without a single hitch.

'Aircraft carrying paratroops started their take-off about an hour later and not until it was quite dark. There should have been a full moon that night but there was 10/10ths cloud cover so the night was dark. We had normal runway lighting for take-off but no navigation lights were used and we had to observe strict radio silence. Our signal to go was a green light from the control caravan at the end of the runway and we went off at pretty long intervals of one minute and thirty seconds. There was certainly no sign of the aircraft ahead of you by the time it was your turn to go. The whole flight was scheduled; So long after take-off and turn on to such and such a course; after another interval turn to a different heading, with times to leave our coast at Littlehampton, to make landfall at Normandy and a time to drop. Streams of aircraft were going off from several other fields, many destined for the same DZ, so they all had to be interlocked. So far as I could judge the staff work must have been good.

Ronald J. P. Warren, navigator of the lead aircraft of the third vic on 575 Squadron piloted by Flight Lieutenant Dixon recalled: 'Most of us had cause to be frightened at some time on 'D-Day' but I did not expect to get my biggest fright before we had hardly started. The first Vic of three Dakotas led by Wing Commander T. A. Jefferson AFC was due to drop at 0057.00. The second Vic led by Squadron Leader F. T. 'Tim' Cragg was due to drop at 00.57.20. Our dropping time was 00.57.40. We took off in loose formation and I was busy for some time making sure that we were on the right course at the right speed to arrive at Ranville at the right time. Twenty seconds between aircraft is not a big margin so, as soon as things were running smoothly, I looked through the astrodome to see how close were to the six aircraft in front. To my horror there was nothing there but empty black sky. What had I done wrong? Where had I boobed? I looked back and saw the lights of aircraft stretching back as far as the eye could see and probably beyond. For some reason the first two Vics had not formed up. I shot back to my position and for the next hour worked like never before making sure that we were on course to arrive at Ranville at the correct time.'

'We were supposed to be flying in Vee's of three' continues Flight Lieutenant Bristow 'and I was third in my 'Vee' so I kept my throttles well opened to catch up the others in front. Formation flying is not a normal part of a transport pilot's expertise, but we had done a little in the preceding months but not at night, yet here we were on a particularly dark night. I eventually caught up with the fellows in front and found that there were four of them. I decided I should be much more relaxed if I dropped back and flew on my own.

Ronald J. P. Warren continues: 'We crept very slightly ahead of our time so that our ETA became 00.57.00 I should perhaps have instructed the pilot to knock two three knots off our speed but I figured that with nobody in front and the whole invasion behind us, early was better than late and in any case 00.57.00 was the leader's dropping time. We arrived and 'Jock Young' our fourth crew member took over the map reading for the last few hundred yards. Then the fun started. Gerry Brown, the wireless operator went to the rear to see the boys out. The first four left in orderly fashion, they were Military Police, but the fifth man with a mortar barrel stuffed up his jumper fell in the doorway and blocked the way for the others. By the time they got him back on his feet we were past the DZ. Gerry passed the information on but, because he forgot to release his microphone button he didn't hear Dixon say that we would go round again so I had to nip back and tell him. They all went out in good order the second time round. With all the excitement only Jock noticed that we were being fired at but nothing hit and we made our uneventful way back to base. Because of the delay we were on the end of a very long queue for landing. It was a bit of an anticlimax and I didn't mind the mild telling off I got for being forty seconds early over the DZ.'

Flight Lieutenant Bristow continues: 'Bill' Dyson was giving me regular fixes from his 'Gee' box and confirmed we were on course and running on time. We had taken off at 2330 and were due to drop at 0110. Our stick went down within thirty seconds of the exact scheduled time.

'We were carrying twenty paratroopers and an Alsatian dog that had been trained to jump from the back of a lorry. On a temporary rack fitted below the belly off the aircraft we carried a number of small antipersonnel bombs. We had been briefed to drop these - as we crossed the Normandy beaches so that if there were any defenders they would be encouraged to keep their heads down. There were also a couple of folding motorcycles in cylindrical canisters. Shortly before we made landfall something exploded on the land right ahead. A vast sheet of yellow flame lit up the sky for a second or two and in that I saw a line of aeroplanes all going the same way, all at the same height I was part of this game of follow-my-leader. I made myself think I was all alone on a night course on Salisbury Plain, but kept keyed up to take smart evasive action if I got close enough to anyone else to see them. I felt the slipstream from other aeroplanes in front from time to time but once that rather shattering had died down never actually saw another.

'Bill' Dyson and the 'Gee' box brought us in for a perfect land-fall and 'Robbie' Burns and I found we could see enough to make our way visually to the DZ. 'Robbie' was a RAF navigator and was just ex-Ulster university he was a bright boy. There were not always enough pilots for every crew to have a second pilot, so I was given 'Robbie' as a map reader and that was a lucky day.

'We had been told we should be crossing heavy gun emplacements and that our bombers would be dealing with them before we arrived to prevent them bombarding the Navy. Whatever had happened to them had burnt them up to such effect that we passed over a number of glowing plates of ferro-concrete. The heat must have been generated inside but here was the topside of a concrete roof glowing like a red-hot plate of steel. I have always wanted to know more about those glowing gun-pits.

'Rebecca-Eureka' was working by now to help lead us in. This was a short-range homing device actuated from a portable ground station. Now the illuminated direction 'Tee' could also be seen and we were almost there. The paratroops had been standing lined up with the red light on - well back from the door opening - and at this point they got the amber and would go on the green. 'Doug' Strake, my Canadian wireless operator was acting jump-master and was able to speak to me down the intercom and he told me all was ready and well. I had started the drop at the right height, the right speed and all was as right as we could make it until I lost contact with 'Doug'. I should wait for him to tell me it was OK to open up, but he was silent and we were steadily losing height and advancing on the Germans who were clearly belligerent as witness the flames in the sky not long before. I was sure it was one of our lot had bought it, though I was later told that it was a Stirling. A moment later and 'Doug' came through again to say everything had gone and I opened throttles, made a climbing turn to port and disappeared into cloud were we all felt nice and snug.

'When he joined us in the cockpit 'Doug' told us that the dog, who with its handler was the last to go, had followed all the others to the door and as it came to its turn to follow its handler out decided this was not the same thing as jumping from the back of a lorry and backed away from the door and retired to the front of the fuselage. 'Doug' had had to unplug himself from the intercom, catch the dog and literally throw it out. Several weeks later he met one of our stick in Oxford who had been sent home wounded and he said they had eventually found the dog.'

At Blakehill Farm thirty Dakotas on 233 Squadron led by Wing Commander M. E. Morrison AFC began taking off for DZ 'K', the first six towing Horsas and the following 24 carrying paratroops of the 8th Parachute Battalion. All aircraft were airborne by 2336 into a moonless fine night sky with some medium level cloud. Their route took them north-east to a turning point between Chipping Norton and Banbury, where they joined up with 48 and 271 Squadrons at Down Ampney. 48 Squadron commanded by Wing Commander M. Hallam DFC dispatched 52 Dakota-Horsa glider combinations while 271 sent seven Dakotas towing Horsas at 2248 hours carrying bridging materials in case the strategic Caen Canal and Orne River Bridges could not be captured in the coup de main operation and these were followed by 39 Dakotas with paratroops of the Ist Canadian Parachute Battalion and the Headquarters troops of the 3rd Parachute Brigade. The entire formation then turned south-east towards London and flew along a beacon-marked route across the south coast. Meanwhile, at approximately 0140 on 6 June, having allowed enough time for the Engineers to clear the landing strips on LZ 'N', the remaining aircraft of 38 Group[90] took off with the main glider lift.

Dakota III KG424, one of the six on 233 Squadron which towed a glider with troops of the 8th Parachute Battalion on board, crashed at Giberville and was one of three 'Daks' the squadron lost on 'D-Day' The pilot, Squadron Leader C. Wright AFC, navigator Pilot Officer B. Cowie RNZAF and Driver Alexander (because of injuries), remained with the aircraft and were speedily captured by the Germans and taken prisoner. The Canadian 2nd pilot, Flying Officer E. Q. Semple and wireless operator, Flying Officer C. J. Williams and Corporal Owens RASC, Drivers Harold Ackley and Allen RASC, evaded capture by the Germans and remained as evaders until the night of 28/29 June when they attempted to return to British lines. On the night of 9/10 June they were joined by CSM Jones of the 8th Battalion The Parachute Regiment, who was the only survivor when three RAF, one RCAF and eighteen troopers were killed on KG429 on 233 Squadron, which was shot down the night previously. On the night of 28/29 June the party accompanied by three French guides attempted to cross over into British

---

90 Albemarles of 295 and 570 Squadrons carrying between them four loads of paratroopers to DZ 'K' and a further sixteen, accompanied by four towing Horsas, to DZ 'V'.

Lines but they bumped into a German position. Semple and Williams and Jean Roger the French guide became separated but the two RAF officers successfully reached British Lines. Ackley and Allen and their French guide were captured by the Germans and Jean Roger was later executed. Ackley, because of injuries sustained in the crash was admitted to a PoW hospital in Rennes. The hospital was captured by American Troops and Ackley was repatriated in August. On 14 July Corporal Owen and CSM Jones were caught by the Germans, but managed to escape and they joined up with the Maquis. Employed on weapon training and sabotage work in the Bordeaux area, they were repatriated to England on 13 September.

Flying Officer Harvey Edgar Jones RCAF had taken Dakota KG356 off from Blakehill Farm at 2317 hours. Flight Sergeant Jadaldorph the second pilot recalled: 'In the circuit, while climbing, we lost sight of the 'vic' leader and did not regain contact again, so the captain decided to proceed independently. Just after crossing the French coast we were hit by light flak, which must have caught one of our starboard petrol tanks alight. It could have been an underslung container holding petrol, although we did not realise that possibility at the time. At the correct point the order was given to drop the containers and Warrant Officer 'Cobby' Engleberg the Canadian wireless operator reported this had been done. With the aircraft now on fire the paratroops were also dropped. Just afterwards Flying Officer Jones gave the order to abandon aircraft, although the rest of the crew could not hear this command as the intercom was dead. The fact that the intercom was unserviceable made things rather confused. As far as I could make out Flying Officer Jones refused his own parachute when it was offered and wanted us to get out. Flying Officer L.N. Williams the navigator and I went back to the door at the rear of the aircraft and found the wireless operator pulling in the static lines. He then went to get his parachute. We waited at the door for a short while and as neither the captain nor the wireless operator came back, we abandoned the aircraft. A few seconds later the aircraft dived into the ground.

'During Tuesday morning we returned to the aircraft crash site on the outskirts of Bassenville, a village east of Caen and found that Flying Officer Jones was dead and that the wireless operator was unconscious but being attended by the villagers. Engleberg received severe internal injuries and was taken to the beach by stretcher bearers. He was still unconscious three days later, but was eventually evacuated to Britain and recovered from his injuries). We also found that the containers had not been dropped as previously thought, as apparently the electrical circuit must have been rendered unserviceable by the fire. In my opinion Flying Officer Williams and I were able to bail out safely due to the fact that Flying Officer Jones remained at the controls in spite of the fact that the aircraft was alight.'[91]

A recommendation dated 30 June for the award of the Victoria Cross to Flying Officer Harvey Jones said that Jones could himself have abandoned the aircraft through the pilot's escape hatch at the same time as the crew were ordered to jump. Although well aware of the danger of remaining in the aircraft, he refused his parachute pack when it was brought to him and stayed at the controls to keep the aircraft on an even keel and maintain sufficient height for his crew to jump safely. It further stated 'By his premeditated action in remaining at the controls until the mission was completed and the crew had left the aircraft, Flying Officer Jones deliberately sacrificed his life to carry out his orders and to ensure the safety of his crew. The dauntless courage and self-sacrifice displayed by this very gallant officer are a glorious example to all pilots in his Majesty's Service.' This VC recommendation was approved by the Blakehill Farm Station Commander, by 46 Group and by the AOC Transport Command. However, it was denied by the Air Ministry and Harvey Jones was simply awarded a Mention in Dispatches for his actions.

Dakota KG429 piloted by 22-year old Warrant Officer Munro Murdoch McCannell was approaching Drop Zone 'K' with a stick of paratroopers and was shot down by flak as they jumped. The plane crashed close by Sainte-Martin Church in Colombelles near the River Orne killing McCannell, Flight Sergeant Alexander Robert Porter the second pilot, Warrant Officer Albert Theodore Downing the 23-year old navigator and Warrant Officer Nathan Louis Berger the 22-year old Canadian wireless operator. Private Gerald Clarke, one of the troopers, recalled: 'We dropped at 0050 hours. It was on fire. There were three of us who got out. After three days two of us managed to get back to our lines travelling at night because there were Germans all over the place. The others didn't get out of the plane.'

After being dropped on DZ 'K' the 8th Parachute Battalion commanded by Lieutenant Colonel Alastair Pearson DSO** MC was to destroy three bridges, one at Troarn and two at Bures. William Holding's platoon (No.9) in 'B' Company was to drop close to the little bridge that spanned the River Orne near Troarn. 'Our job was to seize the bridge and hold it until glider-borne sappers, together with their explosives and a good number of infantrymen, landed close by. We were then to give the sappers a hand to

---

91   From an official report written on 17 June 1944.

blow the bridge, after which we'd settle down for twenty-four hours and wait for the seaborne troops to relieve us as they dashed like hares towards Paris. It was a simple plan; by denying the Wehrmacht use of the bridge, fewer of them would be able to get to the beaches to carve up our soldiers landing on them. It looked foolproof and to make us feel even better about it we were shown photographs of our bridge and then trained on a scale model of it. We grew so fond of it that in the end we didn't really want to blow it up. Our scepticism turned out to be well founded.'

'B' Company was 'squeezed' into a Dakota at an airfield near Burford. 'I use the word 'squeezed' wrote William Holding 'because we were encumbered by monstrously heavy loads. Besides a parachute and the usual battle gear, each of us carried either a two-inch mortar tube or its base plate, or two of its bombs. We also had bandoleers of extra ammo for the Vickers machine gun and extra rations, so in the end we had to be pushed up the landing steps by loaders as if we'd been cattle off to the slaughter. Some of the relief and the excitement we'd felt about at last going to war evaporated very quickly and it didn't help to be told that our Canadian pilot had never dropped parachutists before.

'Welcome aboard a one-way trip to nowhere! To add to our misgivings, once aloft we circled for what seemed like hours while history's largest air armada got into formation. Finally, buffeted by the slipstreams of hundreds of aircraft all around ours, we literally bounced our way across to France. I wasn't the only one to be airsick I hoped we'd be shot down and so have done with it. I was so happy when we got the order to stand up and get the green light on to go. I waddled like an overweight duck to the doorway and fell through it, turned left and like a ton of bricks dropped into the dark French sky. It was midnight and was an unusual mode of immigration, I suppose, but there I was, overseas at last. Knees locked together, I rolled over nicely to settle comfortably onto the French grass. I banged the 'box' on my chest to break the lock mechanism that closed my parachute around me and stood up to look for my mates and I hoped for road signs reading 'Troarn That Way ½ kilometre'. Above all I looked for a flashing purple light from a scout who had been dropped ahead of us and would beam a signal that we'd been told to aim for. Our platoon was to converge upon that light and, once formed up, be led by a French resistance fighter to our bridge. We'd also been told that there'd be no enemy soldiers about and that we'd be at our target within an hour of getting out of our parachute harnesses. What met my eyes instead was a dazzle of brightly coloured lights, several of which were purple, flashing from all directions. It was as if I'd landed on Blackpool promenade at illumination time. For another stomach-churning thing the only other living creature I could see was a white horse I'd nearly landed on. What's more, judging by the sound of gunfire blazing away on all sides, there were plenty of angry soldiers about; a good many of them appeared to be German, having been told that God was definitely on their side.

'When we'd put our stories together, it turned out that the Canadian pilots had cast us out of their aircraft while flying too high, meaning that few of us had come to earth where we'd supposed to and that we'd been scattered so far apart that, for instance, those carrying the 2-inch mortar tubes had dropped not metres but miles away from those carrying the base plates and so on. Nobody knew exactly where we were, where the seaborne soldiers were or what was best for us to do. Everybody was in the mood to lynch Montgomery, he of precise planning and overwhelming odds fame. What it boiled down to was that the airborne operation, which we'd been conned into believing would be flawless (and heavens knows the brass had long enough to make it so) had in practice been a right old balls-up.'[92]

The 8th Parachute Battalion's flight to Normandy was certainly eventful. Fourteen of the Battalion's thirty-seven Dakotas had released their parachutists some distance away, in the operational area of 5th Parachute Brigade.[93] Lieutenant Colonel Alistair Pearson recalled. 'When forming up over England, his rather senior Canadian pilots declared that they had lost the two aircraft that they were supposed to be flying in formation with; however they were not lost and proceeded to join the main body. Over the Channel the aircraft ran into a brief hail storm, which resulted in a 'fearful racket' along the length of the fuselage. Pearson's knees were still weak and he had not made a parachute jump since he landed in Sicily almost a year previously. Out of regard for sparing his knees a heavy landing, Major General 'Windy' Gale commanding 6th Airborne Division had sent him an extra large parachute, which he hoped would soften his descent. This served him well, however when he landed his knees were the least of his worries as one of his men accidentally fired his Sten gun, a weapon prone to such

---

92 The bridge was subsequently blown up by the 3rd Battalion RE. A full account of this action is quoted in *Paras: Voices of the British Airborne Forces in the Second World War* by Roger Payne OAM (Amberley, 2014).

93 The aircraft at Fairford and Keevil had found their dropping zone correctly marked and 123 out of the 129 aircraft dropped their loads accurately, though a high wind scattered the parachute troops far and wide. 2,026 out of 2,125 parachute troops of this brigade were dropped and 702 out of 755 containers.

malfunctions and a bullet hit Pearson in the hand. He was in great pain, but would not stop for a moment to have the wound dressed. Fully twenty-four hours passed before he even allowed a medic to remove the bullet. He wrote: 'We landed at ten minutes to one on 6 June. I had a good DZ 'K', about 3-4 kilometres from Troarn. The drop was a shambles. Instead of having 600-700 people within half an hour of landing, I had about 100.'

Captain Dennis Kelland adds: 'I was dressed in what was jocularly called 'Christmas Tree order' because one's parachute harness had to be sufficiently tight to stop it being jerked off one's shoulders when the chute opened. As a consequence, I could barely walk in an upright position. Strapped up in this way, I had a .45 Colt automatic, a Sten gun through my harness and a cartridge-pistol. On the run in to Normandy, the flak started to come up and when the pilot started to jink, I fell flat on my back in the doorway of the Dakota and it took two men to lift me to my feet again. This was despite the fact that we'd been briefed that we would go into Normandy on a flak-less route. In actual fact, the Germans were on an anti-invasion exercise in the very area in which we were to land. The man who said that he wasn't scared when he did a parachute jump was a liar, because every jump one did had its attendant nervous tension - but on this occasion we had the strain of going into battle for the first time.'

Flight Lieutenant Alec Blythe on 48 Squadron wrote: 'Pathfinders were supposed to set up 'Eureka' radar beacons, which would guide us to the dropping zones. Unfortunately very few Pathfinders were dropped accurately, so most of us found there was no 'Eureka' beacon to track to and we had to fall back on our own navigational equipment. As we crossed the coast, my navigator reported two large houses which we expected to see before a line of trees came out of the murk. I was getting ready to drop my troops south of the road to Caen. There was a fair amount of moonlight and I could see that the Germans had flooded the area south of the road where we were supposed to drop. I didn't have much time to think, but decided I had better drop to the north of the road rather than in the water. The red light was on and the engineers were standing ready. There was some flak but I hadn't had to take evasive action. I was intent on making as steady a run as possible when suddenly the aircraft banked almost 45°. In a flash of light from the ground I saw a Stirling bomber passing in front of us. Clearly we had been caught in his slip-stream which threw us off course. I had therefore to bring the wings level and regain heading as quickly as possible. The paratroops in the back no doubt were hurled about and were probably cursing me for taking violent evasive action. I never saw them again to explain the reason for their discomfort. Unfortunately the accuracy of the drops on 'D- Day' wasn't as high as one would have hoped. I would like to think that my engineers were accurately dropped, especially as the two bridges assigned to them were blown up. When I got back to Down Ampney and had been de-briefed, I quietly cycled home.'

The Dakotas on 233 Squadron carrying men of the 3rd Parachute Brigade proved to be a scattered drop, owing to the pathfinders being dispersed and unable to set up their beacons to accurately guide the aircraft to the drop zone although two of their aircraft were lost and a further two were brought down on the following day when the main glider lift of the 6th Airborne Division took place.

At DZ 'V' the advanced guard composed of part of the 3rd Parachute Brigade was dropped from fourteen Albemarles of 295 and 570 Squadrons. One, unable to find the dropping zone after seven unsuccessful runs was hit by anti-aircraft fire and returned to base with Major William Alexander Carlton Collingwood the Brigade Major jammed in the exit hole. There was a 60lb kit-bag attached to one of his legs, but despite this handicap his men heaved him on board and he arrived in Normandy later in the day by glider. Other aircraft loosed their cargo of parachute troops too soon. In the event, 106 out of 140 of the men of the advanced guard were dropped accurately. 1st Canadian Parachute Battalion landed between 0100 and 0130 hours; one hour in advance of the rest of the brigade in order to secure DZ 'V', becoming the first Canadian unit on the ground in France. In addition to their normal equipment the Canadians each carried a knife, toggle rope, escape kit with French currency and two 24-hour ration packs, in all totalling seventy pounds. For different reasons, including adverse weather conditions and poor visibility, the Canadian troopers were scattered, at times quite far from the planned drop zone. The Dakotas dropped the paratroopers over a very wide area; one stick falling several miles away, for some of the navigators had mistaken the River Dives for the River Orne, which was the pin-point. The first group were dropped accurately at 0020 but the Dakotas carrying the Canadians dropped over a wide area and only about thirty Canadians landed on the DZ. Pilots of the 32 Dakotas carrying the main body (around 540 paras) were hampered by a huge dust cloud caused by the RAF bombing raid and poor visibility caused by patchy cloud and a strong easterly wind. Almost all the Battalion and much of the 3rd Parachute Brigade were scattered over a wide area, many landing in the flooded fields. However, by mid-day and in spite of German resistance, they had achieved all their objectives. In the days following, the Canadians were involved in ground operations to strengthen the bridgehead and support the advance of Allied troops towards the Seine.[94]

'Quite how long it took us to reach the French Coast I do not know' wrote Signalman Harry Read in the 3rd Parachute Brigade, 'but we had the command to stand, hook up our parachutes and check the chute of the man in front. Our aircraft lurched drunkenly upwards and we wondered what had caused it. Over the intercom came the pilot's voice telling us that he had released two large anti-personnel bombs 'just to keep the enemy's heads down'. We were reassured but he might have forewarned us. The aircraft moved into a significantly slower, steady course, the red light came on, then the green and we were moving as quickly as possible to the exit. We were so cluttered with kit that we needed help to reach the door and get out and the dispatcher did not fail us. The roar of the engine increased as we left the plane and we were battered by the slipstream before our chutes opened - our war had truly begun.'

Harry jumped at 0120 hours on 6 June. 'The descent was interesting. There was no throat-swelling fear, just the awareness of what had to be done. The sky was alive and alight with shells, tracer bullets and noise from the explosions and yet we felt - I felt - an air of detachment. In the distance an aircraft plunged to the earth in a ball of fire and then I landed. If that is the right word to use because between me and the land was a couple of feet of water. It was an unexpectedly soft landing. I had landed in the area west of the River Dives that the Germans had flooded with water to discourage airborne troops. It was a successful ploy on their part. When daylight came we could see the silk circles on top of the water indicating that a parachutist had descending and drowned before he could free himself from his harness. It was a salutary sight.

'The plan outlined to us in the concentration area was that, on landing, we would look for a strong green light and rendezvous on it. Lights there were in plenty but not one that looked remotely like a rendezvous light. I thought I had better move through the water in the general direction of our flight. Picking up the heavy wooden-sided accumulator I had jumped with, I put it on my shoulder and fell straight into a trench full of flood-water. With much difficulty I extricated myself remembering that, before flooding, the Germans had dug trenches across the land to add further hazards to their

---

94 Of the 27 officers and 516 men of the 1st Canadian Parachute Battalion who took part in the Battle of Normandy, 24 officers and 343 men gave their lives. The unit had to be re-organized and retrained in order to regain its strength and combat-readiness.

defences. Another few paces and again, I virtually disappeared and had to scramble out. This was to happen frequently but, on the third occasion, I concluded that the accumulator had become a pointless burden so I tipped it back into the ditch and continued walking. We had landed fairly near to a village called Robhomme but we were further east than we should have been, hence the flooded area.'

'Jimmy' Edwards' Dakota had been the third to go and had just made it. 'This was the real thing at long last' he wrote. 'Although I was part of it I felt more like a spectator than anything else. 'For an eerie hour we droned across the Channel in the darkness. As we came to the French coast, I forced myself and my glider pilot to believe that we had made the correct landfall, but I was not really convinced. And then, in a few minutes, it all came unstuck. We had been warned that 'Bomber Command will be dealing thoroughly with gun-sites near your targets,' but we hadn't bargained for the massive clouds of smoke and dust they would leave behind. Suddenly the ground was completely obscured. I struggled on for a few minutes, with the conversation between myself and my Army friend behind me getting more strained and finally I said to him, 'I can't see a bloody thing. I'm turning back to get a pinpoint.' It was a foolish decision. No sooner had I made a rambling, lurching turn back towards the coast then we ran head-on into the formations of 'Daks' bringing in the paratroopers who were to follow us up. In the chaos I somehow managed to avoid a collision and turned yet again back towards our target.'

Crossing the coast of France, the 9th Parachute Battalion ran into a moderate concentration of anti-aircraft fire. This caused very little disorganization, but the strength of the wind was a more serious matter.

'Suddenly' continues Edwards, 'as we crept about at a ridiculously low altitude, there were gun-flashes beneath us and I heard one or two muffled explosions. 'Missed us' I thought and waffled on. By now we all knew that I had made a complete hash of it and on top of that there was simply not the petrol available for another search for our bridge, so with a shout of 'I'll have to let you go, goodbye and good luck,' I persuaded him to disconnect. I rammed the throttles open, dropped the rope and climbed away. In a few moments we were in unexpected cloud and I put 'George' in and set our prearranged course. Being empty, we gained altitude rapidly.

'I believe we got hit back there,' said 'Tiger' nervously.

'Nonsense,' I replied. 'We'd know all about it if we had.'

'My panel told me that we were OK but when we finally came out of the cloud into the moonlight above, we were at a very strange attitude, with the left wing down. I straightened her up and turned on to the course which would take us round Dieppe and back over the Channel. It was only when we were nearly back at DA that I realized that something was wrong. The wheels and the flaps refused to come down, which could only mean that we had lost all our hydraulic fluid. That explained our crazy emergence from the cloud back over France, for that same fluid activated the automatic pilot. As 'Tiger' frantically operated the emergency hand-pump to get the undercart down, I flashed my headlights on and off as a signal that I was in trouble. Soon I got an answering flash of green from the sound-controller and came straight in without flap to make a landing on the grass beside the runway. I knew that I would have no brakes, either, so as soon as we touched down I switched the engines right off and prayed. I kept old 'Treble Four' pretty straight with rudder for a while, but finally it was all in the lap of the gods. She swung round in a wild ground-loop, but the wheels stood up to it and eventually we came to a stop. I can't remember who was first out, but none of us took very long! As we gathered in the gloom under the wings, dim headlights came bumping towards us and a small van pulled up. Out leaped Flight Lieutenant Swann, one of our medical officers. 'Christ, it's you Jim. Everybody all right?'

'Yes, thanks, 'Doc'. There's nobody hurt,' I shouted, as another 'Dak' roared on to the runway beside us. Then he was off in his van in no time - we were of no further interest to him if nobody was hurt - but soon there were others all around us and with their torches we inspected the aircraft to try and see exactly what had happened. 'Hey, look at this,' shouted someone, 'you've been hit here.' He was standing underneath the port engine, pointing upwards. Sure enough, there was a small jagged hole in the exhaust pipe. But that wouldn't explain the complete loss of hydraulic power. I grabbed a torch and flashed it on to the wheel. 'Aha!'There was a tiny slit in the oil pipeline leading to the brakes. So it had been an explosive shell and all the fluid had drained out of that minute hole in that eighteen inches of pipe not covered by the engine cowling.

'Several more holes were discovered in the underside of the port wing and next day 'Jouby' was seen inspecting them with unusual interest. It seemed incredible, but he was actually jealous of them and expressed disappointment that no Jerry had had a go at him in the pre-invasion darkness.'

Only one of the seven gliders that were dropped by 271 Squadron landed on LZ 'V'. Very few of the ninety-eight gliders had landed undamaged on the correct LZs. Twenty-seven glider pilots (rising to 34 by the end of 'D-Day') were killed.

‘TONGA’, ‘MALLARD’ AND ‘ROB ROY’

Captain David Tibbs, Regimental Medical Officer, 13th Battalion recalled: 'the plane took off and one's pulse rate went up a little bit when you realised this was it. It was a Dakota with an open door on its side where we were going to jump so it was fairly noisy and there wasn't much opportunity for conversation. But most people were trying to rib each other a bit. Some chaps were a bit silent and looked a little bit green but really a general attitude of cheerfulness was kept up without any problems. I was tense and excited as I think anyone would be on this sort of occasion. It was my job as the officer in charge of the twenty men within the plane to keep up morale and not show any doubts but I think we all felt much the same.

'There was a blackout all over England so it was difficult to gauge where we were but we could judge when we were over the sea. I was sitting near the door of the plane so I could see down but really it was just blackness with the occasional burning embers of carbon from the engines coming back, which rather surprised me. At first I thought they were ack-ack shells coming up but they were little glowing embers off the aircraft engines.

'I was jumping No.1, standing at the door of the aircraft, when suddenly I saw to my horror another plane heading absolutely for us. The visibility was not very good so it must have been very close, it was a four-engined Stirling, which was one of the planes also involved in parachute dropping and glider tugging and what it was doing there I don't know, but we were clearly going to hit. At that point our pilot heeled right over to take evasive action and this plane did and by some miracle we did not hit each other. I glanced back at the men in the plane behind me and they had all been thrown to the floor, heavily laden men with parachutes all sprawling on the floor and one realised the difficulty they would have in getting out of the plane. The plane righted itself and immediately the green light came on warning us to jump. There was nothing I could do, I couldn't help the men behind me and so I jumped. But one didn't realise fully at the time the consequence of this. These men couldn't get upright with their heavy loads; they had to crawl to the door of the aircraft. And so, instead of jumping out one a second, because the aircraft was covering the ground at sixty yards a second they were spread out over a mile or two because they would be dropping every ten seconds, struggling to get out of the aircraft. So, as a consequence, many of these men we didn't see again. Only about five turned up on the dropping zone with me. Some were captured; others we didn't ever hear what had happened to them; others made their way back.

'I think 68 gliders landed in quick succession on the dropping zone. 'One or two crash-landed but the great majority landed safely. This was very

223

important because they were bringing a number of weapons we needed, such as anti-tank guns, both six-pounders and seventeen-pounders. The Germans didn't realise that we were able to bring down seventeen-pounder anti-tank guns, which were state of the art technology then and very much necessary for us. Also some light artillery came and a number of other heavy supplies of that sort. I went to one or two gliders where there had been crashes. One or two people had been killed. I retrieved some of the injured there. One of my chaps had been very resourceful and had got a gas-driven wagon belonging to the French and that was very helpful in lifting out these people and taking them back to Le Bas de Ranville, where the medical centre was being established.'

Understandably, to paratroopers young and old, the trip to Normandy was frightening, as Martin White recalls: 'As our Dakota neared the French coastline the dispatcher moved to the rear of the aircraft and looked out of the open door as we crossed the coast. At the same time the German anti-aircraft units began to switch on their searchlights and their anti-aircraft guns began to pour fire into the night sky. I was standing just behind the dispatcher and had something of an angled view outside the aircraft. At eighteen years of age I was overexcited at the momentous occasion I was about to become involved in and yelled into the dispatcher's ear, 'Jesus, all we need is that bloody thunder and lightning to jump into.' I was somewhat taken aback when the dispatcher yelled back at me: 'what the hell are you looking at, you idiot? That's not thunder and lightning - that's bloody flak!'

The 13th Parachute Battalion's drop, which began at 0500, was scattered over a large area and only around sixty percent of the battalion's men were at the forming up point when they headed off towards their objectives. The Dakotas from Broadwell which failed to locate the DZ were two carrying 'A' Company men. CSM McParland and his stick were deposited on the outskirts of Troarn and Sergeant Taylor's stick was even further away. In 'B' Company, Captain 'Mike' Kerr landed in the middle of the River Dives itself and only narrowly avoided drowning, while Lieutenant George Lee and his stick in 9 Platoon who changed aircraft at the last minute were dropped farthest away of all, thirty miles from the drop zone. Some aircraft had to make more than one run in before the complete stick had jumped, as Len Cox recalled: 'We emplaned with the rest of the sticks taking off from Broadwell, but then our Dakota wouldn't start, so we were switched to the reserve aircraft. The flight as far as the French coast was OK but then we ran into heavy flak and seemed to fly on and on. It wasn't until the third run in that we actually jumped; something or other went wrong on the first two.'

Sergeant 'Taffy' Lawley MM adds: 'When the green light came on, No. 1 jumped, followed by the remainder up to ten, a Bren No. 1 carrying a very heavy kit bag. He fell across the door, preventing anyone from jumping. The only one who could help him to his feet was the RAF aircrew dispatcher. This took some considerable time, during which the Dakota circled the DZ three times before I could jump. The first thing I knew, when I was airborne, was that my rifle, kit and shovel had fallen away from me. I landed in a cornfield and lay quite still for a moment listening. In the distance I could hear the sound of battle and guessed it must be the DZ. I got rid of my chute and with my fighting knife in one hand and a grenade in the other, I made for the RV. I had gone a considerable distance, when I suddenly saw three bent figures. I got up close and challenged them and heaved a sigh of relief to find they were our chaps. Guided by the Battalion call blown by Colonel Luard on his hunting horn we were soon at the RV.'

The Headquarters of the 6th Airborne Division landed by glider in the landing-zone cleared by the sappers and a company from 13th Parachute Battalion at 0335 hours, with only a few gliders missing the landing-zone due to the poor weather and errors in navigation. Once the headquarters staff and accompanying airborne troops had been gathered together, the headquarters was moved to the Le Bas de Ranville area and set up there. Contact was established with the headquarters of 5th Parachute Brigade at 0500 and with the headquarters of 3rd Parachute Brigade at 1235 and linked up with 1st Special Service Brigade as it advanced from the invasion beaches at 1353.

Altogether, 4,310 paratroops were dropped and gliders carrying 493 troops, seventeen guns, 44 jeeps and 55 motor cycles successfully released. Seven aircraft and 22 gliders were lost. Thus far 'D-Day' had cost the 6th Airborne Division 821 dead, 2,709 wounded and 927 missing and most of the parachute battalions, because of their scattered parachute drops, were well under strength.[95]

On returning to their Cotswold airfields at Down Ampney and Broadwell, the Dakota aircrews had been debriefed, fed and rested, while their aircraft were refuelled and prepared for Operation 'Mallard', a mass lift by 206 Dakota, Halifax and Stirling tugs of 38 and 46 Groups that towed 226 Horsa gliders transporting most of the 6th Air Landing Brigade to Normandy.

---

95 Between 5 June and 7 June the 6th Airborne Division suffered 800 casualties out of the 8,500 airborne troops who were deployed. By 27 August the Division had reached Berville sur Mer, where it halted and remained until the beginning of September when it was withdrawn to England.

At Down Ampney, 'Treble Four' being now unfit to fly, Jimmy Edwards on 271 Squadron had to use a spare aircraft to take another Horsa over. The glider towed by Edwards was flown by Captain Gordon Thomas Mills of the Glider Pilot Regiment, who had seen action in 'Husky'. 'Crossing the coast near Worthing at about 2,000 feet in the most glorious weather' recounted Edwards, 'we had a grandstand view of the whole impressive show. In front and behind, there streamed a steady flow of transport aeroplanes of all shapes and sizes. Above and all around, massed formations of [fifteen RAF fighter squadrons] formed a huge umbrella, which no enemy aircraft had the nerve to try to penetrate. And beneath us, as we approached the French coast, the assembled might of the British and Allied Fleets. I simply followed the man ahead and marvelled at the spectacle that he was so privileged to see. 'The Navy for once recognized us as friendly and forbore from pooping off at us as we trundled up to the coast and along the mouth of the River Orne. Our dropping-zone was already half-filled with gliders as we delivered Captain Mills and his men to their destination with all the panache of a postman delivering his mail.[96] We dropped the rope and losing height rapidly, turned for home as low as we could get. Halfway across the Channel we spotted a 'Dak' floating in the water with its tail up in the air and circled it twice to make sure that it was not one from Down Ampney and that the crew were OK. Sitting in their dingy, with two Air Sea Rescue launches already bearing down upon them, they gave us a merry two-finger salute, so we headed for home.'

Takeoff at Down Ampney and Broadwell began at 1840. The main lift crossed the English Channel unhindered; the weather was fine and the visibility ten to fifteen miles, allowing the aircrews and troops to see the escorting RAF fighters and, near the Normandy coast, the river and adjacent Caen Canal. Arriving in Normandy at 2100, as it was still daylight previous navigation problems that had affected the earlier operations were absent. Apart from an aborted takeoff of one of 575 Squadron's twenty-one Dakota-Horsa combinations, three gliders in the force broke their tows en route and three were forced to ditch in the Channel. The glider pilots - Staff Sergeant Harry Howard and Sergeant Holman of 15 Flight, 'F' Squadron released and landed safely. Their glider, which was carrying a stick of

---

96 On the evening of 27 September 1944 during Operation 'Market-Garden' surprised by the enemy, Captain Mills was shot near the bank of the Rhine. He and another glider pilot had been hiding out since the withdrawal over the Rhine on the night of 25 September. They had been unsuccessful in crossing and were awaiting another chance. Captain Mills died instantly. He was 27-years old and left a widow, Sybil. Put forward for a posthumous DFC he was instead awarded a MiD in April 1946.

1st Battalion Royal Ulster Rifles troops, was subsequently re-attached to a spare tug and they departed at the end of the stream.[97] As the remaining 249 gliders approached the two landing areas, LZ 'W' east of Sainte-Aubin-d'Arquenay and LZ 'N' east of the Orne they met with mortar barrages and small arms fire, but casualties were negligible.

Into LZ 'N' went the brigade headquarters and the 1st (Airborne) Battalion, The Royal Ulster Rifles who were greeted by German mortaring and a degree of small-arms fire. These, however, did very little to hinder the forming up of the Battalion and only one casualty was sustained. 'As we were on the final run into the LZ my DC-3 took a direct hit where the wing and the engine joined' wrote David Staines in the Ulsters. 'Luckily we were already standing up and hooked on and the dispatcher didn't hesitate and got us all out the door straight away. It wasn't a pretty sight, in fact it was a chaotic exit with no thought of proper drills, but we all got out. I never knew what eventually happened to the aircraft and crew. Although the wing was on fire, it turned and just headed straight for home. I eventually found myself on the ground and collected up all my equipment and tried to figure out where the hell I was. I knew I wasn't on the correct DZ, as the green light we had to look for hadn't come on. An hour later and after several near misses with German troops, I heard an English voice challenge me. I stopped and gave the correct password and found myself with my sister battalion, the 12th, miles from where I should be. They were digging in and preparing for yet another attack from the Germans. As luck would have it, my brother was in the 12th Battalion so I asked someone if they knew where he was. About an hour later, while I was helping the platoon I was with dig even deeper, my brother actually turned up. The first thing he said to me was, 'Don't tell me - Ma sent you to see if I was OK. Did she give you the cheese and chutney sandwiches she promised me last time I was 'ome?'[98]

Squadron Leader R. D. Daniell DFC AFC RNZAFR, born Hamilton, 29 October 1920, who flew a Dakota on 48 Squadron, afterwards related: 'The main glider force took off at 4 pm on 'D-Day' and we were glad of the opportunity to fly over the beachhead in daylight. We had our final briefing and the weather seemed more favourable. Out on the runway we checked our

---

97 During the following days, 575 Squadron participated in several resupply sorties in support of the 6th Airborne Division, During a resupply flight on 7 June one Dakota was lost, not through enemy action, rather a tragic case of misidentification on behalf of friendly naval forces below.

98 Quoted in *Paras: Voices of the British Airborne Forces in the Second World War* by Roger Payne OAM (Amberley, 2014).

aircraft, chatted with the glider pilots and the men who were going along to keep a field-gun company - eighteen of them were in my glider. Incidentally the total load carried in each of these Horsa gliders was nearly 3½ tons.

'We took off across a very stiff breeze which caused some anxious moments as the combination took the air. In taking off in these heavily loaded gliders the unusual feature is the slowness with which one gains flying speed. The runway flashes by under the wheels and its end, over a mile away, is almost reached before the whole contraption is in the air still clambering for more speed. From that moment onwards, both for the tug and the glider pilot, the actual control of their aircraft is a full time job of manual labour. Constantly buffeted by the slipstream of the aircraft in front the 'combinations' battle along in pairs which form a great stream. Ground speed in a head wind may fall to 80 mph and the usually accepted evasive tactics to A.A. fire are virtually impossible.

'However, as we jostled about on this evening of D-Day, we knew that many fighter squadrons would escort us and that others would be attacking enemy fighter airfields in France ahead of us. After nearly two hours over England we crossed the south coast in a great procession nearly eighty miles long; I think we were about half way down the 'stream'. Le Havre came in sight and I marvelled that it was possible to fly over the French coast without defensive armament at less than 100 mph. Soon the beaches of Normandy were in sight with the greatest array of ships I had ever seen; some unloading on to the beaches, some of them waiting off-shore and others still miles out to sea. The mouth of the River Orne where we were to cross the coast now came into sight below the battle haze and smoke. 'The sun was fairly low in the sky but it was not difficult to identify the landing zone which the gliders were to use. However, as aircraft jostled for position, the cumulative effect of slipstreams made things difficult since every pilot was letting down to the correct dropping height of 12,000 feet. A few miles inland towards Caen I called my glider pilot. 'Thirty seconds to go to release point 'matchbox' - Good luck.' He came back 'Thank you, tug - cheerio.' A few moments later I felt my aircraft surge forward as he cast off. In front we could see hundreds of gliders wheeling in free flight and preparing to land. Several crashed into each other as they ran along the ground like great beetles. Two spilled open and shot out their contents. Several caught fire and others struck mines. Little puffs of smoke mushroomed up as enemy mortar shells found their mark.

'Turning away we caught a glimpse of the great battle going on at the outskirts of Caen. Odd bursts of enemy anti-aircraft fire were now finding their mark. One of our flight just behind was set on fire. Two figures left by parachute and landed in the River Orne while the burning machine with the pilot still at the controls turned and eventually belly landed near the gliders.

'As I flew low out over the sea there was a Stirling and two gliders in the 'drink'. Back at base we learnt that the glider landing had been judged a great success.'

Generalmajor Edgar Feuchtinger of 21st Panzer Division watching the gliders casting off at a height of about 800 feet and then turning and come swooping down on the landing zones believed the arriving force would threaten his lines of communication ordered those elements of the division that had reached the beaches to withdraw to the north of Caen. The gliders' arrival had inadvertently stopped the only German armoured attack on 'D-Day'. Major General 'Windy' Gale wrote later: 'It is impossible to say with what relief we watched this reinforcement arrive.'

All units of the 6th Airborne Division however were scattered during the drop. The problem was acute for the 9th Battalion, mainly because the path finders who were to illuminate their zone were dropped too far from it to be able to set up their beacons. Due to a combination of bad weather and poor navigation on the part of the pilots of the transport aircraft carrying them, Glider-borne airborne troops also suffered from navigational errors, with ten of the eighty-five gliders assigned to the division landing more than two miles from their landing zone. Only a quarter of the battalion landed on target but an unintended but beneficial result of these scattered drops was that the German defenders were greatly confused as to area and extent of the airborne landings. By midnight 6th Airborne Division was the only Allied formation to have seized all of its 'D-Day' objectives.

Meanwhile, beginning at 2130 hours, thirty Dakotas on 233 Squadron at Blakehill Farm and ten Dakotas - five each of 512 and 575 Squadrons at Broadwell - took off carrying 116 tons of ammunition, food and equipment in Operation 'Rob Roy' for the troops in the area of the Orne bridges. As the Dakotas approached low from seawards they were mistaken for a further wave of German bombers that had just attacked Allied shipping. Once again, as in the invasion of Sicily, jittery naval gunners loosed a barrage on an airborne mission causing the formation to scatter and forcing some aircraft to return damaged, one ditching in the Channel and five others being reported missing. Less than a quarter of the supplies were delivered.[99]

---

99 Four small resupply missions flown in daylight by 38 Group were fairly successful, although in one of them seven out of twelve aircraft were recalled because of low clouds.

Total transport aircraft losses on 'D-Day' were nine Dakotas, two Albemarles, one Halifax and a Stirling shot down. [But] 'as far as 271 Squadron was concerned' wrote Jimmy Edwards, 'the invasion had been a piece of cake.'

'Back at base old 'Jouby' was jubilantly displaying three or four holes in his starboard wing with a smile on his monkey-like face that stretched from ear to ear. Ralph Fellows told me afterwards that the old maniac had deliberately held on to his course after dropping his glider, in the determined hope of attracting enemy fire. And when they did hit him, he had ordered Ralph into the astrodome to inspect the damage. 'You've got several holes in the starboard wing,' Ralph had reported over the intercom.

'Are they bigger than Jim's?' was all that 'Jouby' could say and chortled when Ralph had described them to him. He was the happiest man in the Mess that night.

'Having played our part in mounting the biggest ever land invasion in history one would have thought that we would now be plunged into a mad whirl of hectic 'nourishing'. But it was not so. Everything was going so well that there was no need for supply-dropping, but the army had not yet pushed far enough forward to be able to carve out landing-strips for us. Soon we were occupied once again with seemingly endless 'exercises', interspersed with pointless and frustrating hours in the 'Link Trainer'. There were also a great many 'Charley trips', as we called them, when, under the guise of a 'navigation exercise', you bogged off somewhere to collect some beer or take somebody on leave.'

'Four days after the invasion' recalled Leading Aircraftman Alan Hartley on 271 Squadron at Down Ampney 'our Dakotas made their first landings on French soil, taking vital supplies, ammunition, petrol, tyres, food, medical supplies and personnel. Once emptied, the Dakotas were then fitted with stretcher racks and we brought back our first casualties, one of which was a German prisoner of war with no boots. He had pretended to be dead whilst a Frenchman stole his boots because he claimed he had seen the Canadian paras lopping off heads with their meat cleavers. The casualties were cared for by a lone WAAF nursing orderly, who had no badges to show their trade and received 3p a day extra flying pay. They were the only WAAFs to fly operationally and were given parachutes. However, once casualties were loaded, so many on stretchers, so many walking wounded, they were forbidden to use their parachutes as their casualties did not have chutes. As our Dakotas were engaged on war duties they were not permitted to display a Red Cross so they were fair game for German fighters. Altogether these nursing orderlies on our Dakotas brought back over 100,000 casualties, many of whom would not have survived but for the rapid surgery they received in 'Blighty'. It was not unusual for a soldier to be wounded in France and on the operating tables at Down Ampney in less than three hours. This is a record that we are justly proud of but has now been forgotten in the mists of time.

'For the next few months we were busy taking urgent supplies to the forward airfields, to back up our advancing armies. Then a crisis arose because PLUTO (the pipeline under the ocean) developed a fault and our armour was running out of petrol. So at the beginning of September all of our five Squadrons of 46 Group Transport Command carried jerry cans of petrol twice a day to Evère and Melsbroek airfields near Brussels. How do you fancy flying a plane load of petrol and aviation fuel on an unarmed aircraft flying very slowly at 150 mph twice a day for a week?'[100]

---

100 *It's Only A Number.*

Chapter 11

'Chicago'

June 14 1944

My very dear adorable Jean:

Well sweetheart, here is the letter that I promised you. I'm in the Orderly room tonight so I can write and concentrate. This will be quite a letter so show it to the folks so they know what happened.

The Invasion really began for us several days before the first troops landed in France. We were restricted to our base and a schedule of briefings was published. At the first briefing, Col. Whitacre, our Group Commander, outlined the entire operation for us. As he told his story, we realized more and more that this operation was not a scheme that one or two men stat up an entire night over. This was an operation that had been decided on months before the newspapers and the people of the world started to even discuss the possibilities of such a move on the part of the Allied Nations. It was a wonderful plan from the choice of the places where the beachhead was to be established, down to the last and final part that each and every man was to execute.

The job for our group was glider towing. In the several briefings that followed the first, we learned all we could about our courses to and from the landing zones of the gliders. We memorized courses and distances; locations of the bodies of enemy units; studied photographs of France over which we would follow from the time we took off until we landed. We learned procedures in case we were forced down into the Channel.

Unfortunately, I didn't go on the first trip. Now don't worry. It wasn't because of anything I had done. I wouldn't have taken the risk of goofing up and missing the show we had trained so long for, for anything in the world. The first serial took off early in the morning of D-day. What a sight it was to see all the running lights in perfect formation as the group assembled over the field. It was beautiful. Needless to say I was excited that night and had a hard time going to sleep.

Everyone had quite a time when the ships returned that morning. They were telling their experiences and comparing theirs with the other fellows. I got quite a kick out of Stanley. He told about how, after they had been over France for some time and nothing had happened, he said to himself, 'H---! this is going to be a milk run.' He no sooner got the words out of his mouth when a stream of tracer bullets flashed by his cockpit windows.

Well, our turn came late in the afternoon of D-day. We had quite a rough time of it on the assembly because of propwash. Nothing flies well in propwash in any condition, so you can imagine what a time we had with a loaded glider in tow. The rest of the trip went well. It was carried out better than many of our training missions. The entire mission was flown in daylight. I might say that we weren't very careful about where we dropped our ropes. As soon as the glider cut loose, we dropped them. Later we found out that the ropes caused considerable damage to the German communication system.

Within a few hours after landing, we were in our ships again and ready to take off. We had coffee and sandwiches in between missions, so we felt pretty good.

The take-off and assembly was messed up because of bad weather. Practically all the ships lost the one ahead of him and all there was left for us to do in that case was to circle the field. We received instructions to go to our first check point where conditions where better and with day light coming on, the ships fell into formation by two's and three's. Even whole squadrons came along and dropped into their proper position. It was a wonderful piece of flying by everyone concerned.

We didn't run into any more trouble until we had crossed the coast of France and were approaching the landing zones. Somehow or other we started bunching up and our ship was flying closer to the glider ahead of us than at any time I had ever practiced in a glider tow. In addition we were flying with *propwash again which was so bad that several cases Paul had to use full power to keep our altitude and position in the formation. I have never seen a man push and pull so many controls and levers in such a short time as Paul did.*

Well the gliders cut, we dropped our ropes and headed for home. Now here comes the good part. What do you think was waiting for us when we walked into our interrogation room? Nothing less than a shot of good Scotch whiskey for each mission. I had my two put into one cup and sipped it, savoring each and every sip I took. By the time they had finished interrogating us and the critique was over, I was more than half gassed up. I guess being tired and hungry mad the liquor affect me more. Well anyway, we went to breakfast and now in addition to the Scotch we each got two FRESH EGGS. Well! By that time I was ready to fly to Berlin in a kiddy car just to get some more of all that.

Nothing happened the next two days. Then the glider pilots started to come back. All I can say about them is that this group knows what heroes look like and every one of the GP's is a hero. Two of my good friends who were GP's didn't come back. The last that was seen of them, was they landed and were running into a woods, chased by many German soldiers. Later the woods were searched but none of their bodies were found. We all are hoping that they evaded or are prisoners.

Well that's about all there is that can be told, my dear. We haven't done anything since then, but we have hopes.

As I look back, I shall never forget all that I saw. I saw hundreds of naval vessels of all kinds; some shelling the enemy, others sweeping for mines, many up on the beach being unloaded and their cargoes carried to definite assembly points. Men working their guns, or carrying supplies, or helping wounded. At one place I saw about 50 men standing in a shell hole watching the airplanes fly over them and looking as if there wasn't a thing in the world to worry about. This was at a place less than a mile from the German lines. I saw houses that looked like they hadn't been touched by anything and a few feet away were just four walls or less of houses that had been hit by shells or bombs. I saw cows in fields about a mine from enemy lines; grazing contentedly and once saw a

234

Frenchman out in his field herding his cows together to take them to a barn. I saw cows run in all directions when a shell struck in their pasture. At times it was hard to understand that there was a war being fought within a few thousand feet.

I can't think of any more to tell about, darling except that I love you and that I am looking forward to the day which isn't far off when I can hold you in my arms once more. Please take good care of yourself and remember, I love you, dearest.

Your loving and devoted husband,
Earl

Earl E. Johnson, 72nd TCS, 434th TCG. Earl joined the US Army Air Corps in 1942 and as a pilot he participated in the invasion of Normandy, Operation 'Market Garden', the resupply at Bastogne and Operation 'Varsity'. Lieutenant Colonel Earl E. Johnson was recalled to active duty for the Korean War and he also saw action during the Vietnam War. He retired from active service in 1974.

'There was a high level of nervous excitement and tension in the air' wrote Flight Officer George E. 'Pete' Buckley, a glider pilot in the 74th Troop Carrier Squadron in the 434th Troop Carrier Group at Aldermaston. 'Airborne troops in great numbers were moving onto the field with much more equipment than could be used in a training flight. Military police were stationed at all the gates and no one could get on or off the base. In the afternoon of 4 June all C-47 and glider pilots reported to the operations room for a briefing by the group intelligence officer. We all took our seats facing a small stage and when we had all settled down he unveiled a map of France, which showed exactly what and where our objective was. A low gasp and murmur went up, as we all realized that the time had finally come for us to put our skills as glider pilots and tow pilots to the real test. He also told us that, within the last 24 hours, the Germans had been studding the fields in the LZ area with poles and were digging large ditches across other fields to prevent glider landings. Evidently, the Germans were preparing a lively reception for us. His next announcement took us all by surprise. We, the 434th Group, had been chosen to lead the glider phase of the 'D-Day' invasion - with fifty-two CG-4A gliders carrying men and equipment of the 101st Airborne Division. The code name for this serial would be 'Chicago' and we would land on LZ 'E' near les Forges at Heisville on the Cotentin Peninsula.

'Five minutes behind us, taking off from Ramsbury, would be the 437th Group towing fifty-two CG-4As, carrying men of the 82nd Airborne Division. They would land five miles northwest of us in LZ 'E'. The code name for this serial would be 'Detroit.' We also learned to our dismay that we would be going in at night because the paratroopers who preceded us could not wait until dawn for the anti-tank guns, ammunition, medics, jeeps and medical supplies we would be carrying. This was a tough nut to swallow, since most of our training in the States and in England, had been for early dawn of daylight landings. The thought of a night landing in enemy territory, in strange fields, with a heavily loaded glider, sounded like sure disaster. The only good news was that 'Mike' Murphy, the senior Glider Officer in the ETO had convinced the top brass that the English Horsa gliders we were supposed to fly would not be as suitable for night landings as the American CG-4As and the switch was made at the last minute.'[101]

'Chicago' was originally designated to be the main assault for the 101st Airborne on 'D-Day' but in May, after both the troop carrier and airborne commanders' had protested to Leigh-Mallory that night landings on the small fields of the Cotentin might cost half the force in crashes alone the time had been changed to 0400 and that for 'Detroit' (which was to serve the 82nd Airborne to 0407), two hours before dawn.

About two days before 'D-Day' IX TCC was authorized to use Waco gliders exclusively in 'Chicago' and 'Detroit' in place of the heavier, less manoeuvrable and less familiar Horsas. The change entailed a hasty revision of loading plans and a substantial reduction in the amount carried. Since the two serials were to approach under cover of darkness they could safely follow the same routes as the paratroops. 'Chicago' therefore became the first artillery reinforcement mission after 'Albany' with Batteries 'A' and 'B' of the 81st Airborne Anti-aircraft Battalion aboard 44 gliders. Another eight gliders would carry small elements of the 326th Airborne Engineer Battalion, the 101st Signal Company; the anti-tank platoon of the 327th Glider Infantry Regiment and a surgical team of the 326th Airborne Medical Company. Forty-four of the gliders would carry personnel of the Airborne 81st Anti-aircraft and Anti-tank Battalion and sixteen 57 mm anti-tank guns. These field guns would be used to support the lightly armed parachute infantry regiments that had jumped into Normandy earlier. Two gliders would carry engineers of the 326th Airborne Engineer Company and a small bulldozer; two more, personnel and equipment of the 101st Airborne Signal

---

101 *A Glider Pilot's Story* by Pete Buckley.

Company, plus staff members of the divisional headquarters and another three, medical equipment and supplies of the 326th Airborne Medical Company. Because the area of responsibility for the 'Screaming Eagles' was in close proximity to 'Utah' Beach, the use of glider reinforcement was limited in scale, with most division support units transported by sea.

'Chicago' would follow the course of 'Albany' to LZ 'E' and 'Detroit' would follow the path of 'Boston'. LZ 'E' near the little French town of Hiesville and 7½ miles' inland from 'Utah' Beach was an area co-located with and slightly overlapping one of the paratroop drop zones, DZ 'C'. The area was chosen as central to the operations of the division and because a BUPs beacon was to be in place there on which the serial commander could guide using the SCR-717 search radars installed in the aircraft of flight leaders. The landing zone was a triangle-shaped area a mile in width at its mile-long base along the road connecting les Forges and Sainte-Marie-du-Mont. The zone was 1½ miles in depth and its eastern edge ran through Hiesville, the division command post two miles west of Sainte-Marie-du-Mont. In addition to its central locality, the fields within the zone were on average twice the length of most others in the vicinity. Many of the fields however were bordered by trees forty feet in height and not hedgerows, a fact that did not show up well on aerial reconnaissance photographs and their presence received little or no mention in the briefings of the glider pilots, who assumed that the borders were merely large hedges.

Aldermaston was the scene of frenzied activity on 4 and 5 June. All furloughs had been cancelled and American personnel were restricted to the base. Much of the 4th was spent loading and parking the gliders on each side of the runway in long lines The tow planes were lined up on the runway in such a manner that the lead plane could pull its glider from the line on the left, the second from the line on the right until the last glider headed down the runway behind the last tow-plane. No time would be lost in launching the aircraft. An alternating band of three white and two black stripes, each two feet wide had been hastily painted on the wings and fuselage of both tow planes and gliders to identify them to Allied ground, sea and air forces. Everything was in readiness several hours before the scheduled departure. All along the long line of aircraft small groups of men stood talking. Other groups lay sprawled under the aircraft wings, some with their eyes closed, sleeping or pretending to sleep.

On the afternoon of 5 June Flight Officer George E. 'Pete' Buckley went down to the flight line with Flight Officer 'Bill' Bruner his co-pilot to check out the CG-4A and went to meet their 81st AAA Battalion, 101st Airborne

Division passengers: Pfcs' Paul Nagelbush, Stanley Milewiski and Russell Kamp. 'We would also be carrying supplies, ammunition, their 57mm anti-tank gun, entrenching tools, a camouflage net and three boxes of rations. The total glider load was 3,750lbs. Our C-47 tow plane flight crew was pilot, 1st Lieutenant David Whitmore, co-pilot Lieutenant G. Goulding; radio operator Tech Sergeant F. Raymond and crew chief Staff Sergeant E. Harmon. Take-off was scheduled for approximately 010 on the morning of the 6th, with touchdown scheduled in enemy territory at 040 near Heisville. Our glider was No. '49' at the tail end of the 52-ship formation. 'Bill' and I then went to the mess hall for the proverbial last meal and those of us who felt the need, went to see the chaplain. A lot of us there hadn't been to church for quite some time. His tent was jammed.'[102]

The boarding order came about midnight. As the glider troops boarded the gliders the sky was dark and overcast and there were periods of intermittent rain. Shortly after arriving at their respective aircraft the glider troops had been given Dramamine tablets as a precaution against airsickness. It was expected that the circuitous two plus hours' flight would get pretty bumpy over the English Channel. They were also given a luminous button to pin under the lapel of their jackets for identification purposes and the metal crickets to be used as a means of signalling other members of their group in the darkness.

1st Lieutenant John R. Devitt, a pilot in the 73rd TCS, 434th TCG recalled: 'we mustered on the flight line sometime before midnight on the 5th, preflighting the aircraft, synchronising watches and sipping a last cup of Red Cross coffee. Aircrew were assigned specific planes when flights were organised months earlier and regarded them as personal property. Mine was 43-16052 with 'CN' painted on the nose to designate the 73rd Squadron and the letter 'O' ('Oboe') on the tail as its call sign. As we made final exterior flight checks, Lieutenant General Louis Brereton paced the flight line talking to crews, offering encouragement, wishing us 'Godspeed'.

Following Eisenhower's postponement of 'D-Day' on 4 June, Major Alvin E. Robinson and fellow crews in the 74th Troop Carrier Squadron had got set up for 6 June. 'Colonel Whitacre called me in and said he was going on the invasion drop with me. At midnight on 5/6 June we got our crew all lined up and got our final briefing of the weather that was not good at all, the ceiling over France being reported to be around 500 feet overcast and raining. The fields we were to drop our gliders in still seemed to be

_____

102 *A Glider Pilot's Story* by Pete Buckley.

clear of the posts that the Germans were busy putting in to stop the gliders. We would be towing one CG-4A glider that was lighter than the Horsa or double tow Wacos that the other ships towed on daylight flights, as our radar limited us to this. In the glider was 51-year old General Don Forrester Pratt, born 7 December 1892 at Brookfield, Missouri, the Deputy Commanding General of the 101st Airborne, Lieutenant Colonel 'Mike' Murphy the pilot and the co-pilot.'

In a last-minute change Brigadier General Don F. Pratt the assistant division commander who would have preferred to have parachuted with the first element, but was not jump qualified, so he had chosen to go in by glider, which was named *The Fighting Falcon II*. Pratt had persuaded General Maxwell Taylor, Commander of the 101st Airborne Division to let him fly in by glider so he could get into battle sooner. He sat in his jeep, which was lashed-down behind the two pilots and carried the general's command radio equipment and several extra 5-gallon Jerry cans of gasoline. His pilot was Lieutenant Colonel Michael C. 'Mike' Murphy, a native of Lafayette, Indiana and the senior US Army Air Force glider pilot in the European Theatre. This unflappable Irishman was in England on temporary duty from the States to supervise the final training of glider pilots for the Normandy invasion. He was not originally scheduled to participate in the Normandy mission, but talked Brigadier General Paul Williams, Commanding General of the Ninth Troop Carrier Command, into letting him fly the lead glider on the mission. In the co-pilot's seat beside Murphy was Second Lieutenant John M. Butler from Battle Creek, Michigan attached to the 53rd Troop Carrier Wing. At takeoff time Brigadier General Pratt was seated in the front passenger seat of his jeep reading some last minute dispatches by flashlight. He was wearing his parachute, Mae West life vest and metal helmet. Lieutenant John L. May the General's aide-de-camp was seated on the small glider jump seat behind the jeep. He was holding in his lap a briefcase full of top secret documents and maps and was heavily armed with a .30 calibre Thompson submachine gun and a .45 calibre Colt automatic.

As John Devitt boarded 'O-Oboe' he found co-pilot Tommy Foreman kneeling in silent prayer in the cabin. 'I patted his shoulder as I steeped by to the cockpit. It had been a number of years since I had any dialogue with God and I think I felt it would be hypocritical to ask for special favours now. I don't recall whether plane losses were estimated at briefing, but I did form my own estimate; five per cent as an optimistic one and 15% as pessimistic. I recall a sense of something like fear but it was overridden by the excitement of being part of the greatest military event ever. Engine start was at 0100 hours. Takeoff was at 0119 hours. The CG-4A glider mated with our aircraft was loaded with a 6lb field gun, ammunition and a three man crew. The glider crew, Flight Officer Leon C. Doelger, pilot and Flight Officer M. A. Trechak, co-pilot.'

Being the lead ship, at precisely 0119 hours Colonel William B. Whitacre and Major Alvin E. Robinson started their roll on the runway towing General Pratt's glider. On board the C-47 also was Brigadier General Maurice 'Maury' Beach, the 53rd Wing commander, born on 1 April 1903 in Caro, Michigan.

Following *The Fighting Falcon II* down the runway at thirty-second intervals were fifty-one other tow plane/glider combinations. The combined payload of the 'Chicago' glider serial' consisted of 155 airborne troops and their equipment, sixteen 57 mm (6-pounder) anti-tank guns, 25 vehicles, 25 vehicles, including a small bulldozer for the engineers, 2½ tons of ammunition and eleven tons of miscellaneous equipment and supplies including an SCR-499 radio set for the division headquarters command post. Shortly after takeoff one glider broke loose from its tow plane and landed four miles from the base. Unfortunately, the aborted glider was carrying the critical long-range command and control SCR-499 radio by which the 101st Division was to have communicated with higher headquarters. The equipment was retrieved and sent that evening in mission 'Keokuk' but together with the loss of communications personnel and equipment in 'Albany' this accident prevented the Division from communicating with other invasion forces until after link-up with the US 4th Infantry Division coming off 'Utah' Beach after noon on 'D-Day'.

The pilot of the No.2 glider, 1st Lieutenant Victor B. 'Vic' Warriner, a native of Deansboro, New York, watched Pratt's glider as it was towed down the runway and wondered why it took so long for it to become airborne. At the time the moonlight was bright despite occasional rain flurries. After what seemed like an eternity *The Fighting Falcon II* rose slowly into the air. Warriner, a member of the 72nd Troop Carrier Squadron, was not aware that the general's staff, fearful for his safety, had ordered armour plating installed beneath the general's jeep and under the pilot's and co-pilot's seats for protection against enemy flak and ground fire. Murphy would not learn of the armour plating until just before takeoff. With this considerable extra weight, plus the additional weight of the jeep radios and extra gasoline, the glider was probably over the safe load limits, but of greater import was the fact that the centre of gravity had been altered significantly. Murphy said the glider was overloaded by 1,000lbs and 'handled like a freight train'.

'Pete' Buckley's tow ship gunned its engines and started down the runway through a light rain shower, into the black of night. 'As the wheels of our glider left the ground, someone in the back yelled: 'Look out Hitler; here we come'. That helped to break the ice for the moment. After that no one said a word, as I trimmed the glider for the long flight ahead. For the next three and a half hours we would be alone with our thoughts and fears. It wasn't too bad for me because I was occupied flying the glider, but the Airborne men in back and 'Bill' Bruner had nothing to do. They must have been going through hell with their thoughts.'

Once airborne the tow plane/glider combinations circled the airfield while forming in groups of four, echelon to the right and lining up in trail. When the last combination had taken off and formed, the lead aircraft headed for St. Catherine's Point on a southern heading that took them between the Islands off the west coast of Cherbourg Peninsula. They then took an eastern heading to interdict the French coast near Barnesville. According to Colonel Whitacre the moonlight was then bright enough to see the outline of trees and fields below.[103] The weather along the route had moderated from the dense cloud bank and ground fog that had severely disrupted the parachute drops two hours earlier. Because they were in trail and not in close formation vees, the tugs and gliders were able to penetrate the clouds without losing formation. The columns drew ground fire, however and one C-47 and its glider went down near Pont l'Abbé on the Douve River, west of the landing zone. Seven transports and several gliders also incurred damage.

The Deputy Mission Commander, Major Frank W. Hansley CO of the 72nd Troop Carrier Squadron was at the controls of the third aircraft echelon to the right front. He recalled: 'The mission called for us to lead the right two columns to a different landing zone than the left two columns. We descended the entire formation down to 500 feet while flying over the English Channel. This was to better evade enemy electronic detection. We were relieved when we flew by the British Channel Islands of Guernsey, Sark and Jersey (then occupied by Germany) without any enemy response.

'As we approached the French coast, I hoped the many fires I saw ahead were a good sign that the fighters/bombers had knocked out most, if not all, enemy gun emplacements. That hope did not last long! Our lead aircraft flew a very short distance over land before streamers of tracer bullets started whizzing around the aircraft and gliders. I started telling myself,

---

103 *The Death Of General Pratt*; *A D-Day Glider Casualty* compiled by Major Leon B. Spencer USAFR Retired.

'keep the faith, keep the faith!' I then added and repeated my version of the 23rd Psalm which was 'Yea though I fly through the valley of death I fear no evil for Thou art with me.' With this true belief, it proved most calming! I am positive many others in our formation were doing much the same - all stayed the course!'

'As one string of tracers moved within inches of my aircraft, a strange question flashed through my mind – how will it feel when the bullets rip through my body? The firing stopped just before striking the aircraft!'

'I glanced around at the aircraft crew and found each of them calm and doing his job. My version of the 23rd Psalm became plural: 'Yea though we fly through the valley of death…etc.'

'I was concerned about others in our formation. If we in the lead aircraft were attracting so much enemy fire power, what is happening to those following us? There was no way of checking! We had to maintain radio silence; however, those aircraft flying off of our wings seemed to be faring well.'[104]

When Alvin Robinson had approached the French coast they could see the Germans clearing their guns as the tracers went up into the air like the tails of rockets. 'It was a pretty sight to behold if you didn't think of the fact there were bullets in those tracers. The navigator (Cauldwell) called on interphone and said we had a wrong heading as his 'Rebecca' screen showed the 'Eureka' set to be off to the left.[105] I told him to keep watching but that I had the ground in sight. I had my map marked off 'H' in two minute intervals so I could check off the check points I had picked out by which to guide myself. I knew something was wrong with the radar returns as they were not conforming to our position and heading on the ground. Colonel Whitacre was holding the wheel and he got to watching the tracers and exploding 20 mm shells around us and I looked up and he was 30° off course to the left. I told him to get back on course or I was going to take it away from him (laughing in my voice of course). He said he just could not see the instruments in the dark (he was 51 years old at that time). He reached over and turned on the blue lights on the instrument panel and I quickly had to stick my head into the window as it nearly cost me my night vision. By now the shells were bursting all around us and as we were the

---

104 *Silent Wings* (Volume 26) March 1999.

105 Although the 'Eureka' beacon set up by the pathfinders (the BUPS AN/UPN-1 beacons had been damaged in landing and were inoperable) had been placed in the placed, the 'Tee' shape formed by green Holophane marker lights was observed by pilots of the arriving C-47s.

lead ship they didn't have our speed down and didn't realize we were only making about 110 mph. I asked 'Mike' in the glider how they were doing and he said they were getting the hell shot out of them as they were missing us and going into the glider.

'Beach said on the interphone that the back end of our C-47 was also getting hit real hard. Later I found out it was just the concussions of the explosions that were making it sound like we were getting hit. Any way I had put my flak suit on the floor and had my feet on it rather than wear it. I knew they would be shooting from the ground and not from the air, so I squeezed my legs closer together just in case. The weather got worse and worse as we approached the drop zone. We were down to about 300 feet so the rest of the Group could stay under the clouds. As we crossed the last marker on my map that was a railroad just south west of Sainte-Mère Église I told 'Mike' that there was his field and if he had it in sight. He said he did and cut loose from the tow rope. Colonel Whitacre then opened the throttles up full bore and started the ship into a shallow dive. I watched the radar altimeter and when it hit fifty feet I took hold of the wheel and pulled it back and said that was as low as I was going to go. We went sailing out over the coast and there were a whole fleet of ships there. We were below the tops of some of them and so had to pull up and head back to England. We felt for the troops and glider pilots we left down there in the dark.'

'Pete' Buckley settled down on tow, holding position behind the C-47 by keeping the faint blue formation lights on top of the plane centred up in line between the faint glow of the tow plane's engine flame dampeners. 'This was not the easiest job in the world at night; the longer you stare, the more your eyes start to play tricks on you. I turned the controls over to Bruner occasionally so I could look away and get my eyes to refocus again. The added problem we faced was the extreme turbulence caused by all the planes ahead of us.'

The weather over the Cotentin was cloudy but not enough so to cause dispersion. Major Frank W. Hansley recalled: 'We came to the pre-designated point at which we would lead approximately 50% of the mission aircraft and gliders to a secondary landing zone. With the blackout, it was impossible to see good navigational landmarks as it was 4:00 am. No problem! Our aircraft had LORAN, one of the latest electronic navigational units. By automatically calculating the triangulation of three English-based radio station signals, it could indicate our location within an acceptable few yards. As we approached the LZ, we anxiously looked for the ground signals from the Pathfinder troops that had been dropped earlier by another unit. I need to commend the exceptionally well-qualified Pathfinder crew members who performed their duties with perfection during the 'Chicago' mission. We were where we were supposed to be at all times.

'As we prepared to release our gliders without that verification, their signals were activated. They were a radio beacon and the lighting of a landing tee. Those signals were wonderful assurances, but it did not relieve my great concern for the glider crews and troopers. Darkness would not give the glider pilots the visibility to select the safest landing routes. I truly regretted they had to release. The odds were very high against them.'[106]

Only one pilot straggled out of formation. He released his glider south of Carentan, about eight miles from the LZ. The other 49 pilots reached the release area, split into two columns as prescribed to avoid congestion during the landings and released their gliders from an altitude of 450 feet at 0354, six minutes ahead of schedule. The serial encountered sporadic fire, mostly from small arms, while crossing the peninsula. The enemy shot down one aircraft and glider near Pont l'Abbe and inflicted minor damage on seven aircraft. Some slight damage was also done to the gliders.

During the specified 270° left turns after release to begin heading out over the Sainte-Marcouf Islands most of the glider pilots lost sight of the 'T'. Without it in the dim light of a setting moon obscured by scattered clouds they could not recognize their landing zone. Just six landed on the LZ itself and only fifteen others in fields within a half mile. A group of ten landed in a field near les Forges west of LZ 'E'. Of the remaining eighteen, all but one landed in fields to the east within two miles. Almost all crash-landed in the smaller fields outside the LZ after overshooting to clear unexpected trees. The Waco was capable of clearing the highest trees around the zones and landing within 300 yards, but in doing so there was almost no margin for error. Pilots attempting the feat in semi-darkness were likely to overshoot and ram into a tree or ditch at the far end of field. The unexpectedness of the obstacles greatly increased the hazard. On smaller fields outside the zone a crash was inevitable and the 'T' had been misplaced somewhat west of its proper location, causing some glider pilots to mistake their position and land on unsuitable fields. German ground fire was ineffective in the dark and even though most gliders struck a tree or ditch, most loads were successfully landed without harm. Total casualties were five dead, seventeen injured and seven missing.

---

106 *Silent Wings* (Volume 26) March 1999.

John Devitt flew in absolute radio silence and without running lights in four ship flights of two ship elements. 'To maintain position in night formation, there were six low intensity blue lights on the upper surface of the wing. Our south-westerly heading took us to a point just east of Guernsey and then just outside of Jersey in the English Channel Islands. We then approached Normandy and on our LZ near Sainte-Mère-Église on an easterly heading. At landfall we encountered moderately heavy ground fire but tracers indicated it was arching ahead of the aircraft, possibly because of the much reduced speed with gliders in tow. We reached our landing zone about 0400 hours. We signalled release to the glider crew by aiming a green light through the astrodome. I silently wished my own 'Godspeed' to the occupants as they descended in the predawn light. Ten days later both glider pilots were safely recovered and back at Aldermaston, operationally ready.'

'Pete' Buckley continues: 'Shortly after we crossed the coast of France, small arms fire and heavier flak started coming up at the planes at the front of the formation and intensified the closer we got to our LZ. It looked like fluid streams of tracers zigzagging and hosing across the sky, mixed in with the heavier explosions of flak. One wondered how anything could fly through that and come out in one piece. After the front of the formation had passed over the German positions and woke them all up, we at the tail end of the line began to get hit by a heavier volume of small arms fire which sounded like corn popping, or typewriter keys banging on loose paper as it went through our glider. I tried to pull my head down into my chest to make myself as small as possible; I tucked my elbows in close to my body, pulled my knees together to protect my vital parts and was even tempted to take my feet off the rudder pedals so they wouldn't stick out so far. I really started to sweat.

'A few minutes after we had crossed the coast and before we reached our glider release point near Heisville the group ran into some low lying clouds and fog banks. All the planes in the formation started to spread out to avoid collisions and this caused many of us to land wide, short and beyond our objective when we reached the cut-off point. In a very short time - too soon for me - the moment I was dreading arrived: the green light came on in the astrodome of the tow plane, indicating that we were over the LZ and that it was time to cut off.

'At that moment I had a very strong urge to cut loose. I'm sure I wasn't the only one who felt that way on that night. It was dark; everything but the kitchen sink was coming up at us from the Germans below and that tow rope, as long as it was hooked up, was my umbilical cord. The steady pull from the tow plane signified safety and a nice ride back to England out of this mess, if I hung on. I quickly put this thought out of my mind and waited about ten seconds before I released the tow rope. It was a good thing I did because I still landed about half a mile short of the LZ. If I had cut loose at the first signal from the tow lane I would have landed in the area that had been flooded by the Germans. Many paratroopers drowned in this swampy area that night. By late afternoon, after encounters from sniper fire along the way, I arrived at the Division CP (101st) in Heisville and was assigned with other glider pilots to guard the perimeter, in case the Germans tried to infiltrate back into what we thought was a secure area. We didn't know it at the time, but they were all through the area playing possum. Some of the snipers were still in trees around the area.

'At 2030 that evening some of us were asked to go back out into the fields to meet and cover the landing of the second serial of gliders. A large group of Horsa Gliders were expected to arrive at 2100, towed again by my group, the 434th, from Aldermaston. They arrived right on time and all hell broke loose. The Germans in the fields around us who had been playing possum, opened up on them with everything they had. Their heavy AA guns outside the perimeters were firing airbursts over and into the fields while the gliders were landing. The fields in this area around Heisville were much too small for these large British gliders and those that weren't shot down crashed head on into the hedgerows. Some were fortunate and made it down in one piece; others came under heavy enemy small arms fire after they had landed and many of the glidermen and pilots were killed or captured while climbing out of their gliders. For an hour or so it was a god-awful mess and the casualties in men and equipment were heavy before the situation stabilized. After the gliders were unloaded and the casualties from the wrecks were taken care of, things settled down and I went back to the CP. to dig in for the night in an apple orchard behind a stable. While curled up in my foxhole trying to get some sleep, I suddenly recalled my boyhood days when I would get together with other kids in the neighbourhood to play war. It was always the 'Yanks' and the 'Huns' and here I was in 1944 in person, doing it for real, playing for keeps.'

Colonel Murphy said that the armada flew at 2,000 feet across the Channel, lowering to 1,500 feet as they approached the Cotentin peninsula from the west. The glider train flew between the German-occupied British Channel Islands of Guernsey and Jersey to avoid enemy fire. This was the same route taken earlier by the paratroopers. Captain Van Gorder looked out a window of his glider and marvelled at the sight. As the tow planes made wide sweeping turns he could see the blue formation lights on top of the wings stretching like a ribbon for miles. Just after passing the coastline of the peninsula the formation dropped down to 600 feet and maintained that altitude to the glider LZ. Things were quiet and peaceful until the German gunners woke up and opened up on the formation about halfway across the twenty plus mile peninsula. The formation was under fire from there to the cut-off point. Van Gorder, in the No. 2 glider, said he watched the tracers make lazy arcs in the night sky and associated them with the Independence Day fireworks displays back home. 'It was an awesome but deadly sight', he added.

As the formation continued across the peninsula Pratt's glider took some small arms hits, but no serious damage was done. Murphy said that it sounded like popcorn popping as the slugs passed through the taut glider fabric. It was learned later that the No. 2 glider, flying beside Pratt's glider, took ninety-four small arms hits in the tail section, but no one inside was hit. The sky became cloudless. As the formation passed just west of LZ 'E' Murphy saw the green release light flash on in the astrodome of Whitacre's C-47. It was about five seconds past 0400 hours; right on schedule. As Murphy hit the glider release knob he heaved a sigh of relief. He and John Butler were arm and leg weary from trying to keep the unstable glider in level flight for over two and a half hours.

The landing zone was a thousand to 1,200 feet in length, sloping downhill and surrounded by tree-studded hedgerows. The Poplar trees growing on the hedgerows were forty to sixty feet tall, not thirty to forty feet as briefed. As Murphy began his landing approach, glider No.2 was preparing to touch down just ahead and off to his right. Unplanned circumstances would result in that glider landing before Pratt's glider. In view of the heavy load it was carrying, *The Fighting Falcon II* touched down on the first third of the field at 80 mph. Murphy immediately pushed the glider down on its nose and jumped on the brakes to stop the glider quickly but the glider's forward speed did not appear to diminish at all. A fully loaded CG-4A could normally be stopped in 200 to 300 feet. *The Fighting Falcon II* continued to slide on the slick, dew covered pasture grass for about 800 feet before crashing into a hedgerow. Warriner, whose glider crashed into the same hedgerow 150 feet or so away, said that the ground literally shook when Pratt's glider slammed into the hedgerow. Miraculously, the momentum of glider No.2 was halted by a poplar tree, eighteen inches in diameter that ended up between the pilot's and co-pilot's seats, but caused no casualties.

Murphy found himself hanging half in and half out of the smashed nose section, his torso restrained by his seat belt. He looked down and saw that his lower limbs were entangled in the bent and twisted metal tubing of the glider's nose section. Murphy had sustained a compound fracture of the femur in one leg and had suffered a simple fracture of one of the bones in the lower part of the other leg. He also suffered a severe injury to his left knee. May was stunned and bruised, but was otherwise unhurt. Moments after the glider came to an abrupt halt, Murphy glanced across the cockpit and saw the badly mangled body of his co-pilot crammed into the floor section of the cockpit and knew instinctively that he was dead. The glider had struck a large hedgerow tree on that side. The impact with the immovable earthen bank had jarred every bone in Murphy's body. He was giddy for a few minutes but did not lose consciousness.

As his head cleared somewhat Murphy said he was alarmed to see several German tracked armoured reconnaissance vehicles poised just across the hedgerow, no more than fifteen feet or so away. He froze for fear that they might shine a light on him. There were German soldiers seated on the sides of the vehicles with rifles across their laps. The lead vehicle stopped in front of Murphy's glider and two soldiers jumped off. They entered his wrecked glider with flashlights, poked around for a few minutes, got back on their vehicle and hastily departed. Murphy, trapped in his seat, played dead, as did May. Several minutes after the Germans had departed he began to try and free his legs from the twisted metal tubing. The extraction was slow and painful. He tried to stand but his legs collapsed under him and he fell into a shallow ditch. While he was laying there May walked up and said that he had tried to find a pulse without success. A cursory examination revealed that the general had suffered a broken neck, very likely from whiplash. The violent forward motion of his head on impact with the hedgerow had probably severed his spinal cord. Since he was seated on his parachute his head would have been raised four or five inches. It is possible that his helmeted head had slammed into one of the metal cross members of the glider airframe breaking his neck on impact with the hedgerow. In either case he had probably died instantly. Pratt was the second American airborne general to die in combat since the war began. General Charles Keerans of the 82nd Airborne Division lost his life in Sicily. Don Pratt was first buried, wrapped in a parachute, in Normandy until the end of the war and then reinterred at Arlington National Cemetery.[107]

---

107 *The Death Of General Pratt; A D-Day Glider Casualty* compiled by Major Leon
   B. Spencer USAFR Retired.

C-47A 43-15140 (Chalk 43) in the 306th TCS, 442nd TCG which 1st Lieutenant James M. Myers flew on Mission 'Boston' (Serial 26) from Fulbeck. The aircraft has seven white squares with a cross through them for med-evac missions, painted above the first cargo area window.

'Chalk 43' (43-15140) in the 306th TCS, 442nd TCG in flight from Fulbeck.

Colonel Clayton Stiles, commanding the 314th Troop Carrier Group at Saltby seen here with President Roosevelt in the USA.

'Chalk 38' (42-100521) *Night Fright* in the 79th Squadron, 436th Troop Carrier Group, in serial 10 dropping elements of 'A' Battery of the 377th Field Artillery Battalion at 0108 hours on 6 June. The aircraft was flown by Captain Bill Watson and Lieutenant James Hardt. In the D-Day drop it received more than 200 bullet holes that took two weeks to repair.

C-47 in the 73rd TCS, 434th TCG carrying parapacks beneath its wings.

74th TCS 434th TCG personnel load a Jeep Bantam trailer onboard C-47 43-15677 at Welford airfield.

C-47s in the 83rd TCS 437th TCG at Ramsbury.

C-47s in the 434th Troop Carrier Group and Horsa gliders to carry the 101st Airborne Division at Aldermaston.

A C-47 in the 306th TCS, 442nd TCG from Fulbeck seen through the window of another C-47.

First Lieutenant Alex Bobuck checks equipment during a dry run at Exeter airfield by the 101st Airborne in front of C-47 43-15087 for Mission 'Keokuk'.

Sergeant 'Bill' Silberkleit in the 305th Troop Carrier Squadron, who was the navigator in the 442nd TCG lead ship flown by Colonel Charles M. Smith on Mission 'Boston'.

2nd Lieutenant Ted Weatherhead in the 316th TCG.

Albany C-47A 42-100558 *Buzz Buggy* in the 81st TCS, 436th TCG at Membury airfield. 2nd Lieutenant Robert Dopita, co-pilot; 1st Lieutenant Duane Smith, pilot; 2nd Lieutenant Eugene Davis Jr, navigator; Tech Sergeant Adolf Bogotch, Crew Chief; Staff Sergeant Harold Friedland, radio operator.

Captain & The Kids in the 79th TCS, 436th TCG at Membury.

C-47 pilot Clifford D. Kantz in the 100th TCS, 441st TCG at Merryfield.

Dakotas of 233 Squadron RAF lined up on the perimeter track at Blakehill Farm, Wiltshire, for an exercise with the 6th Airborne Division, 20 April 1944.

Drag-em-Oot in the 87th Troop Carrier Squadron, 438th TCG piloted by Lieutenant Orlando H. 'Bill' Allin.

C-47A 'Chalk 15' (42-100905) *Donna Mae* in the 95th TCS, 440th TCG which took off from Exeter at 2350 hours on 5 June on Mission 'Albany' and was shot down by flak while cruising at 3,000 feet, 10 kilometres south of Cherbourg. L-R: 1st Lieutenant Ray 'Ben' Pullen, pilot; 2nd Lieutenant John M. Greeley, co-pilot; Richard P. Umhoeffer: Staff Sergeant Finney W. Gordon: Staff Sergeant Sidney H. Saltzman, radio navigator. All four crew (Umhoeffer was not on board) and 18 paratroopers in the 506th PIR, 101st Airborne were killed. (Murray Lawler Collection)

Mission 'Hackensack' troopers of the 82nd Airborne Division in a CG-4A Waco glider, ready to be towed into Normandy by the 439th Group on 7 June 1944 in the assault phase of Operation 'Overlord'. The 439th dropped paratroopers in the 101st Airborne at 0108 hours on 6 June and towed glider troops of the 82nd Airborne into battle the following day. (Young)

British paratroopers preparing to go aboard their C-47.

Dakota pilot Flight Lieutenant 'Jimmy' Edwards on 271 Squadron at Down Ampney.

Main Picture: Horsa LJ135 with Flight Officer Richard Mercer and co-pilot 1st Lieutenant George Parker in the 86th Troop Carrier Squadron at the controls carried 28 men from 'Able' Company, 325th GIR. LJ135 catastrophically impacted the field, slid twenty metres breaking up in the process and ended up on its back. Sixteen troopers and Flight Officer Richard Mercer [**inset left**] were killed instantly with the rest injured. [**inset right**] The tragic end of 'Chalk 58' (42-100876) in Serial 12 flown by 1st Lieutenant Marvin M. Muir in the 439th Troop Carrier Group at Upottery.

Flight Officers Adrian R. Loving and Elmer J. Kiel in the 86th TCS who flew CG-4A 43-40197 in Mission 'Detroit'.

Major Lloyd G. Neblett in the 301st TCS, 441st TCG brought his badly damaged C-47 back after it was hit by a heavy supply bundle from another C-47 that landed squarely on his right wing.

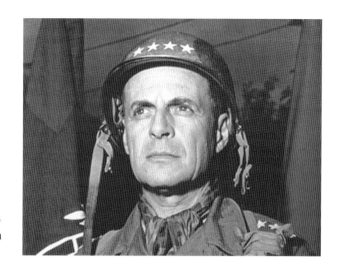

Major General Matthew Bunker Ridgway who flew in a C-47 at the rear of the 315th Troop Carrier Group formation from Spanhoe in 'Serial 19'.

1ˢᵗ Lieutenant 'Russ' C. Hennicke, pilot of the *Las Vegas Kid* in the 98ᵗʰ TCS, 440ᵗʰ TCG.

1ˢᵗ Lieutenant 'Russ' Hennicke (right) with his co-pilot Lieutenant Wilbur Leonard.

439th Glider Group briefing at Upottery.

Above: Charles E. 'Chuck' Skidmore Junior, a glider pilot in the 439th Troop Carrier Group at Upottery.

Left: 818th MAETS receiving medical evacuees from 43-15314 309th TCS at Spanhoe. The C-47s had to fly below 5,000 feet otherwise patients' chest and head wounds could start bleeding because of lack of oxygen.

Lieutenant Calvin Heinlien in the 316th TCG was killed on 7 June after an unfortunate collision with another C-47 during takeoff from Cottesmore. (Lloyd Drake Coll)

On the morning of 13 June (D+7) three RAF Dakotas on 233Squadron took off from Blakehill Farm, Wiltshire for the newly-completed B2 airstrip at Bazenvillenear Bayeux escorted by a squadron of Spitfires; thereby gaining the honour of being the first Allied transport aircraft to land in France since the invasion. After the four tons of military freight, mostly ammunition had been unloaded from each C-47, 14 casualties on stretchers and some sitting wounded were loaded aboard for an immediate return to England.

Three Women's Auxiliary Air Force (WAAF) air ambulance nurses who were flown to France to care for Allied wounded to be flown back to England were the first females to be sent into a war zone on active service by the British Government. L-R: Leading Aircraftwoman Myra Roberts of Oswestry, Shropshire, Corporal Lydia Alford of Eastleigh. Hampshire and Leading Aircraftwoman Edna Birbeck of Wellingborough, Northants. At war's end the 'Nightingales' helped treat the victims of the concentration camp at Bergen-Belsen and the Dakotas flew some of the orphaned child survivors to families in Switzerland who had volunteered to care for them.

Dakota Mark III, FZ692 *Kwitcherbitchin'* on 233 Squadron returning to the United Kingdom with wounded from Normandy in July 1944.

Major Alvin E. Robinson recalled, 'Tyson Robinson was in the tail end of our squadron and he got up into the clouds and couldn't get back into formation. He flew around France for about two and one half hours trying to find a place to drop the glider. He said he was going to just cut the glider loose but couldn't as the glider crew said they had their machine guns trained on him. The glider crew said that if he did they would shoot him down- (they had communications on the phone line wrapped around the tow rope). Well, he did finally find the coast line at 'Omaha' Beach and dropped the glider. His ship was shot up pretty bad but the Germans were reporting gliders all over North France and it probably confused them a lot. We headed back to England to prepare for the next tow.'[108]

Meanwhile, flying at the back of Serial 27 was 'Chalk 51' (43-15101) piloted by 2nd Lieutenants' Raymond C. Howard of Abilene, Texas and Eston C. Kuhn of Barbour County, West Virginia in the 71st Troop Carrier Squadron of the 434th Troop Carrier Group. It was towing the glider flown by Flight Officers' Robert J. Kile and Richard DelaGarza of the 327th Glider Infantry Regiment. The C-47 crew chief, Staff Sergeant John W. Beckley wrote: 'We were airborne by 1245 and headed for France. It was a bad night for flying as it was rainy and the air was rough. We had just dropped to 450 feet from 2000 feet when we were hit by flak. The alarm bell sounded, but at 400 feet a parachute jump was impossible. While the pilots were trying to get the plane on the ground, I took a crash position, right behind the pilot against the bulkhead. Our radio operator, Staff Sergeant Marvin C. Boetcher was in his seat and had his head down on his desk. We then bounced into a bank and lost a wing and then landed on the water again. The pilots went out through the top hatch, the radio operator and I escaped from the small front door into five feet of water. We got out of our flak suits and made it over to a road where we decided to move north. We managed to make it only ten yards when we walked into a German ambush. I received three wounds in the right side of my abdomen.'

Robert Kile recalled: 'About three minutes after landfall en-route across the peninsula the C-47 swerved to the north of the assigned course and came in contact with what appeared to be .50 calibre tracer bullets. This was approximately directly over the town of Etienville. The right motor of the tug ship caught fire and I cut loose immediately. While I was circling for a landing I noticed a brilliant flash of flame coming from the general direction of the plane and it lighted up the entire area. At the same time I could hear Lieutenant Howard 'gunning' his motors in an attempt to right

---

108 Shortly thereafter, Colonel Whitacre was made Commanding Officer of the 53rd Wing.

the plane, which was possibly going into a dive. I then picked out a field below and crash landed the glider. I did not hear or see evidence of the plane after I once fastened my gaze on the ground below in search for a landing zone. The approximate altitude at release was between 500 and 600 feet. Some paratroopers I talked with in the general vicinity the next morning said that they saw one person bail out at no more than 200 feet. No evidence of an opening parachute was observed by the paratroopers on the ground.'

The crewmembers on the C-47 were captured. On 7 June they were part of a column of prisoners that were marched a short distance and loaded onto trucks. Their truck convoy was attacked by P-47 Thunderbolt fighters, five trucks were destroyed and eighteen American soldiers and 2nd Lieutenant Eston C. Kuhn were killed in this attack. Beckley was wounded in his left leg. Howard fell into swampy ground and was not seen again. After the war he was reburied in the Normandy American Cemetery. Boetcher and Beckley spent the rest of the war in PoW camps. Kun left a widow, Bertie. Robert Kile would perish on 19 September 1944 during the 'Market-Garden' operation.

Overall, the landings in 'Chicago' were successful. Darkness minimized the amount of effectiveness of enemy fire and all but a handful of glider pilots managed to bring their craft to a stop without harming the passengers and contents, even though the gliders themselves were mostly crumpled beyond repair. Five of the airborne, including General Pratt, were killed, seventeen were injured and seven were missing.

It took time to pry equipment out of smashed gliders and more time to assemble, with occasional interruptions by rifle fire or mortar shells. A detachment sent out at dawn by the 101st Division to meet the mission at the LZ and guide the reinforcements to Hiesville did not return until noon, but when it came back it brought with it three jeeps, six anti-tank guns, 115 glider troops and 35 prisoners to boot. Because of the bad drop of the 377th FA Battalion, the division had for artillery only one 75 mm pack howitzer on the northern perimeter near Foucarville and one captured German gun at the 506th's Culoville CP, so the glider-borne antitank guns were particularly welcome. On 'D+1' and 'D+2', they provided valuable support for Colonel Sink's thrusts southward against the Germans at Sainte-Côme-du-Mont. 'Chicago' had succeeded beyond expectation.

At dawn the division command post sent out a large patrol to assist the reinforcements in removing their equipment from the crushed gliders (very few were crushed so badly that the equipment could not be removed immediately) and to guide them to Hiesville. Collecting and assembling the equipment was a lengthy process, but at noon the patrol returned with three jeeps, six anti-tank guns, 115 glider troops and 35 German prisoners. A USAF history of the airborne landings concluded that Mission 'Chicago' had 'succeeded beyond expectation'.

After the glider release 1st Lieutenant John Devitt had taken his C-47 down to near tree top level and broke out over 'Utah' Breach shortly afterward. 'The massive array of Navy craft lay silent and blacked out at that time. We headed north and home. Back at Aldermaston we were debriefed by intelligence - after a welcome shot of Scotch whiskey. Later we learned that we suffered only one aircraft loss of fifty launched. However, seven C-47s and 22 gliders were hit by ground fire. We flopped into bed to rest before a scheduled briefing for the second mission, 'Keokuk'. I found it somewhat difficult to sleep thinking of the heightened action which must then be underway in Normandy.'

Chapter 12

'Detroit'

I was plenty scared before take-off. We all were (and I could see the strain on the faces of all of the boys.) The chaplain said a prayer and then a few last minute instructions and we strapped our flak suits on, gave our last instructions to the airborne personnel and waited for the take-off signal. It was quite a thrill when I saw the Channel loom up in front of us. I remembered that if we were successful, it would be the first time in 1,000 years that a cross Channel invasion was successful. There we were over the Channel with England left quite far behind. It was an excellent evening and still daylight and all of the blunt-nosed P-47s circling overhead as protective cover gave us the assurance we needed. Then I could make out the French coast in the distance and knew it would be only a few minutes more and we would know what to expect in the way of a 'reception. As we flew over the beach I saw the greatest display of naval strength that has ever been gathered in the history of the world. And ahead of us we could see the smoke and haze, which gave us a good idea of where the battle line was. Then we all were busy trying to pick out our field. I never did see it so I picked out an alternate one.

Melville Wallace Sands, a glider pilot in the 83rd Troop Carrier Squadron describing in a V-mail dated 6 August to his wife and written from a hospital in England, flying over the Channel on 'D-Day' evening. Mel was born in Brooklyn, New York on 24 July 1916. He entered the army in January of 1942 at age 25. He chose to go into the Glider Programme and began active service 21 January 1943. He married Dolores Wollak, on 6 March 1943 and then shipped out in January 1944 to England. On 'D-Day' small arms fire shot out his flaps and brakes. The tail section hit

some trees and slowed the glider down and then it hit the ground and crashed into a hedgerow. Sands was thrown through the Plexiglas nose of the glider sustaining injuries to his ankle and a broken neck. He rolled into a ditch for cover and watched as Flight Officer Haskell Hazelwood and the two men from the 82nd Airborne in back of the glider got the 57 mm cannon and jeep out and started firing at the Germans. He received the Air Medal and the Purple Heart and left active service on 4 April 1946.

On 'D-Day' Mary Ruth Hudgens, who had been living in Homer, northern Louisiana, named for the Greek poet, was visiting her parents, Mr. and Mrs. O. L. Belcher and sister, Mrs. Robert Temple at 11044 Highland Boulevard in San Antonio. Her husband, Lieutenant Temple, a C-47 pilot in the 437th Troop Carrier Group at Ramsbury had been missing over Germany since 24 May. On 6 June Mrs. Temple was notified of her husband's death. In England, meanwhile, Mary Ruth's husband, 32-year old Colonel Cedric Elston Hudgens, the 437th TCG Commanding Officer, ignoring the medical advice of Dr. Lee Gillette the 83rd Squadron Flight Surgeon, had refused all treatment for a blocked intestine prior to 'D-Day' and had taken off from Ramsbury at 0159 hours in *Feeble Eagle* towing a Waco flown by Captain Will Evans and Flight Officer Ralph Toms. Hudgens, born on 3 May 1912 in Louisiana, had received his wings at Kelly Field in June 1935 and later was with the old 22nd Observation Squadron at Brooks Field, had served as an executive officer in England and Africa and was promoted to colonel on 14 April. His determination not to miss this momentous occasion was due to nothing more than his dedication to the 82nd Division's initial glider mission and the men he was to lead.

On 29 May the 85th TCS in the 437th TCG had departed Ramsbury in their eighteen C-47s to Membury where they were on loan to the 436th TCG. Three days later, on 1 June, Ramsbury, like every other airfield, was officially placed on lockdown status. No one, including a few local English nationals who worked on base, was to enter or depart. Many of the personnel regularly patronised the village shops and pubs in the valley below. A short truck ride to Hungerford railway station meant they could catch a train to London and whilst there many visited the American Red Cross club at Rainbow Corner. Here the homesick Yank could 'shoot pool', play jukeboxes and have his hair cut in a 'home town' barber shop. Many of the American Servicemen also enjoyed visiting dance halls and cinemas in

Swindon and Newbury. The day prior, the 82nd Airborne Division arrived at Ramsbury and was bedded down in a tent city across from the Women's Auxiliary Air Force compound. All combat crew members were also moved to the WAAF compound to further ensure operational security. As yet another measure of security, the entire WAAF compound was encircled by barbed wire and patrolled by armed guards. The crews were restricted to their compound until the final go for Operation 'Overlord' was given. On 3 June the men of the 437th TCG marched to the airfield where they began to paint those now-famous white stripes on the C-47s and gliders.

The following days were consumed with briefings and mission planning for Mission 'Detroit' to an area between the villages of Sainte-Mère-Église and Neuvill-Au-Plain to the rear of 'Utah' Beach. The area was less than ideal, with a very swampy estuary just to the west of the designated landing zone. The 437th Troop Carrier Group's C-47s towing sixty Waco gliders and eighteen Horsas would follow ten minutes after 'Chicago' and carry 'Able' and 'Baker' Batteries of the 80th Airborne Anti-Aircraft Battalion, part of the 82nd Airborne divisional staff and a signal detachment; 220 troops in all. The cargo was 22 jeeps, five trailers, sixteen 57 mm anti-tank guns and ten tons of other equipment and supplies.

1st Lieutenant Louis R. Emerson Jr. in the 83rd TCS recalled: 'Our mission briefing started about 1600 hours and lasted about an hour. First was the navigation briefing. We were supposed to navigate as intently as though we were alone, because there was always the possibility that we would be separated from our leader. Next came the weather briefing which was forecast to be clear at the drop zone with a full moon. Then there was the A-2 or intelligence briefing. We were told that the Germans did not know where our drop zone would be and they did not know the exact date of the invasion, but they did know that we were coming We were also told what to do if we were shot down and captured: Do not tell the Germans anything but name, rank and serial number Finally, there was a pep talk by the Commanding Officer, Colonel Donald French, who would be leading the Group in person He flew about every other combat mission Colonel Luke Powell, the Executive Officer, flew the others. The lead ship carried a navigator, but none of the rest of us did.

'Each Troop Carrier Group would launch a maximum effort of 72 airplanes towing 72 gliders in a column of 18 elements of four airplanes with gliders in a right echelon formation. In order to get 72 airplanes towing gliders into the air in a reasonable amount of time, they had to be pre-assembled in the proper place and sequence on the runway, packed as tightly as possible and with towropes attached and coiled so that there would be no tangle. As soon as the glider ahead of us began to move, we were to count off five seconds, take up the slack in the towrope, go to full power and take off. The headquarters squadron leading the formation was responsible for getting us to the Troop Carrier Group assembly point exactly on time. That also worked amazingly well. At the assembly point, we turned off our navigation lights and turned on the formation lights at low intensity These were hooded dim blue lights set three on each wing, could not be seen from above and could be seen from behind at no more than a 60 degree angle from the side. This was to prevent any possible sighting by German fighters.

'We could have no personal papers with us, but we were issued 100 francs of French 'invasion' money, nothing like the official French franc. We were required to wear our dog tags and we were reminded that if shot down and captured, we should reveal only our name, rank and serial number; nothing else. We could and did wear a shoulder holster with our Colt 45 automatics in it, at least until we got into the airplane. It could not be worn under the flak vest.

'On the night of 4 June, everyone was in place in the aircraft and on the ground ready to start engines when the signal came that the invasion had been postponed. A let down but not a relief. I spent some of the time in my quiet quarters writing a letter to Marilyn to be posted if I were killed. I also wrote a letter to Dick, my as-yet-unborn son for the same reason. I also wrote one to my parents. (We wrote similar letters before each combat series). All of these were gathered and picked up by headquarters for safekeeping. I then started dressing. First, underclothes of course and then flying coveralls and make sure dog tags are around the neck. Invasion money in pockets, pencils, watches - my good 21 jewel Hamilton that my parents gave me for graduation and the GI hack watch; one on each wrist - 45-calibre Colt automatic and shoulder holster. What else? I looked down into my footlocker and saw a GI magnetic pocket compass, picked it up and put it into one of the zippered pockets in my flying coveralls. Then combat boots. They were high top shoes, rough out, with buckle closed leggings attached and about eight inches high. They were not GI, but they were for sale in the PX and almost every one wore them while flying. After all was done, checked and rechecked, I lay down on my bed and tried to doze. Not a chance. I began imaging the mission. What was flak really like? What to do if hit. What to do if the glider is hit. What to do if I'm hit. Am I frightened? Like everyone else, I was sure nothing was going to happen to me, yet?

'Finally, the announcement came of the PA speaker in the hut to report to squadron operations (about a mile away) There was a 6 x 6 truck waiting in the area, we climbed in and we were taken to the squadron ready room Captain John White (squadron Commanding Officer) was waiting there. He checked everybody and everything, then we were back into the trucks and out to the airplanes and gliders which had been marshalled on the runway for about four days. Unless it was grounded for maintenance, each pilot flew the same airplane he flew across from the US for all flights. This particular night, my regular airplane, tail number 576, was grounded for maintenance and I was flying a spare. This airplane had been equipped with an experimental radar receiver called 'Rebecca Eureka'. It was a very primitive instrument by today's standards, but almost magical to us. It was a black rectangular box about eight inches square by fifteen inches long. There was a three-inch scope in the end. When turned on, there was a vertical trace across a calibrated vertical reticule. If a radar signal was being received and if we were on course toward the source, there was a cross blip with equal arms on each side of the reticule which showed the distance to the ground transmitter. If the blip was unequal on the sides, a turn toward the short side was required to get on course. It was calibrated in one-mile segments; a total of ten miles. We were told that there would be a radar transmitter on the LZ.

'Because it was fundamentally a civilian airplane, there was no escape hatch in the C-47 for the flight crew. There was no room in the seat for a parachute. We each had a parachute harness that had been custom tailored for a tight fit. If the leg straps were loose, major damage to our manhood would result when the chute opened. We wore the harness under the flak vest. The harness had large metal rings fastened to the harness shoulder straps in front and up near the shoulder. The canvas bag holding our parachute canopy was to be clipped into these harness rings. The canopy was hanging from a hook in the passenger cabin on the bulkhead between the crew compartment and the passenger cabin. To bail out, we had to get out of the cockpit seat, get to the back of the flight deck, remove the parachute from a wall rack, dip it on to our chute harness and run 65 feet back through the fuselage to the only exit door We were to do all this with the airplane out of control and throwing us all over the cabin as we tried to get back to the door. The good news was that we flew with the door removed. The bad news was that this did not help. The crew chief and radio operator might make it, but the pilots had no real chance. There is no record of any pilots able to bail out and only a few crew chiefs or radio operators made it.

'Military aircraft had self-sealing fuel tanks. That is there was a sticky coating on the inside of the tank that would fill up a flak hole if not too large and stop the leaking of fuel. Since this was a civilian aircraft, we had just plain old fuel tanks, not self-sealing. If hit in a fuel tank, there was about a 9:1 chance that we would burn. We had no armour plating around the crew seats to deflect flak. My crew chief did scrounge some armour from a crashed B-24 and welded it under my seat and the co-pilot seat. There was a Very flare pistol in a bracket in the cockpit. Under the pilot's seat were stored about a dozen Very pistol flares for signalling purposes. The end of the pistol barrel was exposed to the outside. The cartridge was about like a shotgun cartridge except about twice as big and the flares it fired were similar to Roman candle flares.

'We wore flak vests, steel helmets over our cloth helmets and goggles. The flak vest was a vest made of overlapping steel strips to give it flexibility and there was an apron over the genital area. The regular aviator goggles were to be pulled over the eyes when enemy action was encountered to protect them against flash fire.

'We waited. Waiting is the tough time. Suddenly you realize that you have not been tested. You don't know how you will react. I did not exactly feel fear, but I did have a strong sense of apprehension. Waiting in the airplane, I realized that the die was cast and that I would shortly be facing death for the first time in my life. I did not know how I would react. I kept wanting the signal to 'start engines' to be given; the longer the wait the greater the anxiety. Suddenly there was a flare shot from a jeep beside the runway. Finally, this was the signal to start engines. I worried that the engines would not start I looked at the left engine and saw crew chief Kreutter beside it with a fire extinguisher. I shouted, 'Clear left', spun up the inertia starter and engaged the starting clutch. The engine caught immediately. Kreutter moved to the right engine and we repeated the sequence. It started. Kreutter then removed the landing gear pins which prevented the landing gear from being retracted accidentally and climbed into the airplane. We were flying with the back half of the cargo door removed so that after the invasion, we could start flying combat cargo.

'One by one the aircraft came to life. Each pilot reported 'ready'. At exactly 2300 hours there was another flare and the lead ship started moving. In turn, each C-47 taxied at a moderate pace until the tow rope was tight; then full throttle and a little prayer that we would get airborne OK because that available runway was awful short. As soon as I saw the glider ahead of me begin to move, I added power quickly to take up the 300 feet of slack in the two inch diameter hemp towrope which was attached to a bridle fastened to the wings of the Horsa. As soon as I felt the tug of the glider I pushed the throttles to full open. We accelerated slowly until I felt the glider lift. Then the acceleration was much quicker. I lifted off and raised the landing gear almost the instant we were airborne so that we would accelerate more quickly and we were on our way. A lot of skill was required to be a good glider pilot. For this mission I towed a British Horsa that was actually larger than the C-47. Its wingspan was 98 feet as compared with 95 feet for the C-47. It carried almost twice as many troops as the CG-4A. Poorly flown by an unskilled pilot the Horsa could cause enough drag to keep the C-47 from taking off or if flown improperly could drag it into the ground.

'We broke ground, sucked up the gear and started our climbing turn to cut across the circle and catch up with the Group which was circling the airfield over the light ring. By turning left our wingmen could catch up. It was a slow go and it took nearly an hour to get everybody off the ground and into formation. Even at 100% power there was not more than about 95 mph available to climb and catch the group. After joining the formation we could reduce power from 52' manifold pressure and 2,700 propeller RPM to 45' and 2,500 (about 90% power), which would give us the necessary 100 mph in level flight to maintain formation. Our formation assembled without incident [the 437th had its serial in the air by 0223 with the exception of one aircraft which lost its glider, returned for a substitute and delivered it to the LZ about half an hour behind the rest] and we headed out over the English Channel. We knew there were thousands of ships under us heading to the same place. Our cruising attitude was 1,500 feet and our airspeed was 100 mph. We then headed for the assembly point. Our course was around the north end of the Normandy peninsula to the southwest coast, over the islands of Jersey and Guernsey to just northeast of Sainte- Mère-Église to the LZs.'

The weather over England and the Channel was reported as favourable with visibility over ten miles at most points. Unaffected by distant fire from Alderney and Guernsey, the formation reached 'Peoria' intact. Then, like so many of its predecessors in the paratroop missions, it ran into the cloudbank, which at that time and place extended from an altitude of about 800 feet to approximately 1,400 feet. As far as Louis Emerson was concerned, everything was going smoothly until he noticed that there was a cloud deck building under them. 'This could be a real problem if it was over Normandy. We were to pass directly over Jersey and Guernsey on a compass heading of 69 degrees, let down to 500 feet to the LZ just past

Sainte-Mère-Église. When we turned to cross over Jersey and Guernsey, we saw they were almost completely obscured by the low cloud deck. We were in our proper position, following closely behind and slightly above the flight ahead. Without warning, the flight in front of us dimmed their formation lights and as we dropped into the clouds, I lost sight of them completely. My wingmen were tucked in tightly as they should be and I turned my formation lights to bright so they could keep me in sight. At that moment, as far as I know, I was leading the rest of the invasion airborne assault!'

Colonel Hudgens and many others had climbed to 1,500 feet; went over the clouds and let down two or three minutes later through breaks in the overcast. They emerged somewhat scattered and slightly north of course. However, a substantial portion of the serial plunged into the clouds and found itself in such dense obscurity that the glider pilots could not see their own tow aircraft. Inevitably that part of the formation broke up, although most of the pilots remained approximately on course. Radio operator Donald P. Bolce in the lead plane in the second flight of nine aircraft in the 85th Troop Carrier Squadron recalled: 'After the weather began to close in and the fog started getting very thick, as we broke through the fog our wingmen, Lieutenant Melvin Fredette off our right wing and Lieutenant Eckblad on our left wing were still with us.' Bolce had wanted to be a pilot but because of a minor vision problem, he volunteered to become a radio operator on a C-47 instead. 'As we approached the Normandy coast I went back into the cabin to talk to some of the paratroopers who would soon be jumping into France. I met a young trooper from San Francisco. I was from Oakland right across from the San Francisco Bay. We exchanged names and addresses and vowed to get together after the war. While over the drop zone I watched him jump into the darkness with the other paratroopers. I later somehow lost his name and address but I can still see his face. I wonder if he made it through the war. So many, many did not.'

While in the cloudbank seven gliders broke loose, were released, or were cut loose by enemy fire. Two were later located in western Normandy, but the rest were still unaccounted for a month later. Further inland the clouds became thinner and more broken, but visibility was still bad enough to cause the premature release of seven more gliders on the west side of the Merderet. It appears that one or two pilots, catching a glimpse of the flooded valley ahead of them, mistook it for the sea and hastily gave the signal for release. Others behind them saw their gliders descending, assumed the zone had been reached and likewise released their gliders. Once out of the clouds, the serial was harassed by small-arms and machine-gun fire. One aircraft was lost, thirteen received enough damage to ground them temporarily on their return and 25 more were decorated with bullet and shell holes. The gliders, too, incurred some damage and the troops suffered a number of casualties.

Flight Officers Adrian R. Loving from Nomini Grove, Virginia and Elmer J. Kiel from Detroit, Michigan in the 86th TCS flew CG-4A 43-40197 in formation position 26 in 'Detroit', Serial 28. On board the glider were a 57mm anti-tank gun and three men from 'Able' Battery in the 80th Anti Aircraft Battalion (Corporal Paul W Buell, Pfc John H. Hunt and Private Cleon Wyman). Taking off from Ramsbury at approximately 0200 they were towed by C-47 42-92881 piloted by 2nd Lieutenant Samuel Fleming. Their route would take them through checkpoints 'Austin', 'Elko', 'Flatbush', 'Gallup', 'Hoboken' and 'Peoria' to cross the west coast of the Cherbourg peninsula and onto LZ 'O' near Sainte-Mère-Église. Three minutes after crossing the coast, Fleming, who was flying the tow plane with Loving and Kiel still in tow, began descending to the glider release altitude but entered overcast and could not see his formation leader, Captain Curtis Frisbie so he would have to navigate by himself as he had no navigator. It became increasingly difficult to remain on the correct heading as the tail of the C-47 was being pulled left and right by the glider. Upon reaching 1,000 feet the C-47 became steady again and when he reached the correct altitude he ordered his crew chief, Staff Sergeant Ferdinand Luick to check to see if the CG-4A was still in tow. It was not! They were seventeen miles from the landing zone and something had seriously gone wrong. Upon landing back at Ramsbury airfield Fleming inspected the tow rope and found that it was still in one piece with the glider release shackle intact indicating that Loving and Kiel had released from the tow plane. Nothing was heard from all onboard the CG-4A until it was found in a forest by local hunters near Le Vrétot eight months later. The decomposing remains of all five men were still inside the wreck. The loss of both glider pilots and the three passengers will remain a mystery.

The same 'Eureka' beacon and 'T' of green lights which had been provided for the paratroop drop on that zone would be used as aids for the gliders. The 'Eureka's at the checkpoints were picked up at ten to twelve miles distance and the lights at 'Gallup' and 'Hoboken' were visible from afar. About 37 pilots surmounted all difficulties and reached the vicinity of the LZ between 0401 and 0410. The 'Eureka' on LZ 'O' was functioning and had been picked up by the leaders at a distance of fifteen miles. The 'T' was not in operation and certain glider pilots who reported seeing a green

'T' south of Sainte-Mère-Église had probably sighted the one on LZ 'E'. Louis Emerson's crew had the little radar box turned on 'but' he recalls 'we were too far away to get a signal. We continued the letdown, staying exactly on 69 degrees and broke into the clear at about 800 feet, but because of the cloud cover, there was no significant moonlight. After a few more minutes my crew chief shouted that he had a signal on the radar and that the LZ was dead ahead eight miles. We were right on course, more by good luck than by good planning. As we dropped below the bottom of the overcast, suddenly the sky lighted up around us with tracer bullets. The anti-aircraft guns had found us. I shall never forget that sight. Tracers would blossom in front of us in a lazy stream like a Roman candle and then would suddenly turn directly toward us and disappear. When the radar said we were over the landing zone we spotted the Halogen signal light marking the LZ. We signalled our glider and he cut off. The other three gliders in my flight 'C' followed. He made a safe crash landing (normal in combat), as did the other three in the proper field. Neither the glider pilots nor any of the airborne was injured in my flight. We dropped our towrope, pushed the nose down and the throttles to fifty inches of manifold pressure and headed home. We were not required to maintain formation but we were to just get home as quickly as we could any way possible. I got so close to the ground at 300 mph, we nearly hit some rocks on the coast as we passed over it. We had two flak holes, both in the rear of the fuselage and both large enough to have been made by 20 mm cannon shells that did not explode!'

Loose and disorganized as the serial was, part of it did make a concerted release in two columns with the left-hand column 200 yards north of the LZ and the right-hand one heading over the centre of the zone at altitudes between 400 and 500 feet. Most of the stragglers released in that general area and at roughly the same altitude. After releasing, all aircraft dived down to about 100 feet, skimmed out over the coast through a spatter of small-arms fire and headed home. The first reached the runway at Ramsbury at 0522 and the last straggler was back by 0610.

'As we picked up the airborne Pathfinder's 'Eureka' radar signal with our 'Rebecca' set on the plane we were caught in the beams of two German searchlights. The beams were so intense that they lit up the cockpit as bright as day. Anti-aircraft fire began coming up to our plane but the German gunners were leading us too much; thus the tracers were out in front of the cockpit. Suddenly the bright searchlights went out but the tracers were still coming up at us. From the incredible noise of the antiaircraft fire we thought we were taking direct hits, but we were not. From the clear astrodome of our

C-47 I could clearly see the other eight planes in our flight behind us. The ground fire was so intense that I wasn't sure if we could make it to the DZ'.

'As Donald P. Bolce's C-47 neared the lighted 'T' of our DZ his pilot shouted, 'Green Light!' Bolce signalled with the use of his Aldis Lamp from the astrodome to all the other planes to drop their paratroopers. 'I give enormous credit to the Airborne Pathfinders who set up the 'Eureka' sets and lights on the DZ right in the middle of the Germans who were shooting at us and no doubt at them too.'

While the descent of the gliders in 'Detroit' was marked by no such confusion as had marred the big glider mission to Sicily, it was certainly not according to plan. Instead of spiralling smoothly into their appointed fields, the gliders came down by ones and by twos with each pilot following the pattern that seemed best to him. Several were under fire on their way down and one glider pilot claimed to have been attacked by an enemy fighter (probably another glider), but the main difficulty was the inability of glider pilots to identify their proper fields or, in some cases, to orient themselves at all. The railway and the town of Sainte-Mère-Église seem to have been the only landmarks that most could recognize in the dim light. Nevertheless, between seventeen and 23 managed to land on or near LZ 'O'.[109] The best concentration among these was achieved by five pilots of the 84th Troop Carrier Squadron who landed their Wacos in adjoining fields at the western end of the LZ. Nine other gliders, including two which crash-landed in Sainte-Mère-Église, were within two miles of the zone. Three, which came down near Hiesville, may have followed aids set out on LZ 'E' for 'Chicago'.

As in 'Chicago' safe landings were the exception rather than the rule. Twenty-two of the gliders were destroyed and all but about a dozen were badly smashed. Again the principal cause of crashes was the smallness of the fields and the height of the trees surrounding them, but other hazards such as swamps and the rows of posts known as 'Rommel's asparagus,' accounted for nearly half the crack-ups. One glider ran into a herd of cattle. The rough landings produced fewer casualties than might have been expected. Only three of the airborne troops were killed and 23 injured. Several jeeps broke loose and eleven of them were unusable. The guns were more durable. Of eight landed within two miles of the zone all remained intact.

One effect of the dispersion of the paratroops was to provide friendly reception committees on the spot for most of the gliders even in cases where

---

109 Interrogations of the glider pilots indicate that 23 were in the vicinity, but some of them are very vague as to their exact location.

they missed the zone by a considerable distance. Overjoyed to get artillery, these men were of great assistance in unloading. They blasted down a wall to get one gun out of an orchard in Sainte-Mère-Église and ripped another out of a Waco which had wrapped itself around a tree. By noon four of the guns were in action at la Fière and two or three others on the outskirts of Sainte-Mère-Église. Though hardly more than fifty percent effective, the mission had given the airborne troops some badly needed firepower.

Chapter 13

'Freeport' and 'Memphis'

The day after D-Day we needed to fly thousands of supplies from Cottesmore airfield back to Normandy. This was another night run with the usual blackout orders and radio silence. We were exhausted after the gruelling D-Day flight but the ground troops needed their supplies ASAP. While waiting our turn on the hangar side my group and I watched other groups' taxi into place. Each plane was signalled to take off every seven seconds like clockwork. When one of the planes accidentally got edged out of his spot and ended up with the wrong group, we noticed it was our buddy Calvin Heinlien.

We watched Calvin taxi further down where he could pull out of the way to wait for his proper group to come along. The guy behind him, however, did not realize Calvin was just moving out of the way. Instead, the pilot of the 2nd plane believed Calvin was taking off, and that he was next in line. In keeping with the seven-second rule, his engines spurt flames for takeoff. We all yelled to stop but of course with radio silence nobody heard. By the time the 2nd pilot realized Calvin wasn't moving; it was too late. Their opposing wings interlocked and spun the two pilots around, locking them face to face; wing inside wing. When that happened, the propellers of the second plane sliced right through Calvin's cockpit. We got there as fast as we could.

The propeller blades had sliced Calvin in half at the hips, cutting off both his legs. With nothing left to tie a tourniquet to, we could do nothing to save poor Calvin. Already in shock he died in our arms within minutes. Calvin's tragedy sickened everyone, but we had to shake it off and finish the supply run mission. Again I recalled my sergeant's warnings back at boot camp. Surely he knew what terrible things we would witness, but thousands depend on thousands during war. He taught us the importance of getting the job done in the midst of whatever glitches occur.

Lieutenant Julian 'Bud' Rice, C-47 pilot, 37th TCS, 316th TCG at Cottesmore.

At Saltby at 1530 hours on 6 June, following their first mission the previous evening, crews in the 314th TCG were assembled for a briefing for 'Freeport', the re-supply mission to be carried out early the next morning on 'D+1', 6/7 June by C-47s in the 52nd Wing to supply the 82nd Airborne Division. 'Memphis', the other supply parachute drop, would be conducted by the 50th Wing for the 101st Airborne Division. Under pressure of the supply needs of the airborne troops 'Freeport' had grown during May from a 185-aircraft mission to one of 196 and finally of 208 aircraft. These were drawn from the 61st, 313th, 314th and 316th Groups, each of which contributed a 52-aircraft serial. The 82nd Division had asked for 250 tons of supplies but because some items were not obtainable the mission would carry only 234 tons, about half of it ammunition, plus 22 paratroops who had been brought back on the previous night. The lead serial would carry 54 quartermaster personnel to act as dropmasters. In the other formations the crew chief and radioman would have to shove out the bundles in the aircraft. As for the bundles in the pararacks, they would salvo like bombs at the touch of a switch, providing the mechanism worked. More might have been delivered had British roller conveyers been used, but the canvas covers of American containers were apt to jam the conveyers and a decision had been made in March not to use British wicker containers.

'Freeport' was scheduled with the time of the initial drop set at 0611. Cargoes were to consist of six bundles in each aircraft and six more in pararacks in all aircraft equipped with SCR-717. The normal load thus carried was only slightly over a ton, although a C-47 could carry almost three tons. The difference lay in the need to get the cargo out within half a minute so that it would all land on the DZ. The 2nd Quartermaster Depot Supply Company, a unit of IX Air Force Service Command, was supposed to manage the loading of aircraft for aerial resupply operations and to provide dropmasters to handle the actual dropping with the assistance of crew chiefs and radio operators. That company had neither enough men nor enough training to do the job. Made up of soldiers without previous experience in supply work, it had received its first personnel on 25 April. Although it had been exposed to a two-week course in aerial resupply, only 98 of its members had qualified as supply droppers and been placed on flying status in time for 'Neptune'. Memphis', which was to be flown by two serials, each of 63 aircraft in the 440th and 442nd Groups respectively, was set up to drop at 0635, but only if specifically called for. The formations and speeds to be flown in these missions were like those in the paratroop serials, except that speed during the drops would be 120 mph instead of 110 mph. The route that would be taken was the one used by the daylight glider missions with approach and return over the Sainte-Marcouf Islands. The altitudes to be maintained were 1,500 feet over England, 1,000 feet over Portland Bill, 500 feet to the drop zone and beneath 500 feet from the zone back to 'Gallup'. If possible the zones were to be marked with panels, smoke and beacons, but it was understood these might not be available and that zones might have to be changed to suit the ground situation. At 'D+1' the element of surprise was gone but crews were told that DZ 'N', their drop zone a mile north of Picauville on the west side of the Merderet was in an area that was in Allied hands. No real difficulties were anticipated. The drops were to occur at daybreak.

At Saltby the men of the 314th returned to their Quonset barracks with the mission on their minds. In the barracks later in the evening after the briefing Staff Sergeant Mitchell W. Bacon, the radio operator on C-47 42-93605 in the 50th Squadron piloted by Captain Howard W. Sass was observed going through his barracks bags. As he began to separate items and place them in different places on his bed, a few of his barracks mates approached to ask what he was doing. It was apparent he had something in mind as he placed items in various stacks. Bacon replied that he knew he would not be returning from the mission that was to take place the next morning and was separating his personal belongs from those issued to him by the army. It would be easier, he said, for someone to send his personal items home when he failed to return the next morning. This was not the kind of talk men anticipating a combat mission wanted to hear. Others in the barracks heard the exchange. They quickly joined in the conversation.

'You can't possibly know that!' said one.

'You shouldn't even be thinking like that,' others observed.

'You're crazy, 'Mitch'. Forget that stuff' said one, half jokingly.

'Come on, man,' another suggested, 'Get that out of your head!'

By various means his friends in the barracks tried to dissuade Bacon from what he was doing but he kept at it until he had his belongings in the stacks he wanted.

'I have this premonition,' he kept replying. 'I believe my plane will not return from the mission in the morning.'

Breakfast the next morning was at 0300. As men were leaving the mess hall to board their planes, Bacon placed his arm around the shoulders of his friend, Andrew J. Kyle, a crew chief and said, 'I just want to tell you goodbye. 'Andy', I am certain I won't be returning from this mission.'

The first take-off was made by the 313th Group at 0310 after a fifteen minute delay when two of its aircraft collided as they taxied into position. Both aircraft were badly damaged and one pilot was killed. At Cottesmore at 0330 hours disaster struck as two C-47s in the leading 44th TCS were taxiing, they collided. Lieutenant Alan Wilber co-pilot in the in the lead plane flown by Lieutenant Colonel Harvey A. Berger, recalled that 'there was a 'mix-up' when we lined up for take-off. We had to taxi down one runway and turn into another because the taxiways were jammed. In the dark and without any lights someone apparently got confused and started taking off on the wrong runway causing two aircraft to collide. As our aircraft was first off, we didn't find out about it until much later.' The legs of one of the pilots, 1st Lieutenant Calvin S. Heinlein, were severed. He died later in hospital. Berger was killed on 3 April 1945 when he flew a 'milk run' carrying gasoline to Germany because he wanted to see, from the air, the town where his mother had been born. Near Cologne, his aircraft was hit by ground fire.

The other 204 aircraft chosen for the mission all took off successfully. Among them were eleven C-53s, although these had smaller doors than the C-47 and were not designed to carry cargo. There was no light of sun or moon to help the aircraft assemble and layers of heavy cloud covered the sky, the lowest being considerably less than 1,500 feet. However, the layers were broken in places and there was space enough between them at about the 1,500-foot level for the groups to form their serials. Having been assured at briefing that the weather, though unfavourable, would not require instrument flying, the troop carriers set out boldly into the murk. Instead of improving as they proceeded, the weather grew rapidly worse. Over the route for most of the 120 miles between 'Atlanta' the wing departure point and 'Elko' the command assembly point, hung a solid mass of clouds with bases as low as 300 feet and tops as high as 10,000 feet Icing conditions prevented flight over the clouds. Passage through the narrow crack between clouds and ground was hazardous, though many pilots tried it. Most flew into the clouds and attempted to continue individually on instruments. In spite of the 'Rebecca' beacons along the course a majority of these pilots lost their way at least temporarily. Radio channels to the troop carrier CP at Eastcote were swamped by requests for information and instructions. Some aircraft, particularly in the rear flights of the 316th Group, turned back under orders. Others flew around until they ran short of fuel and had to land at fields in southern England. In all, 51 aircraft failed to leave England and one other crashed, killing everyone aboard, in an attempt to land at Oxford. While some pilots took off to try again, at least fourteen were refused permission to go on.

Over southern England the weather was better and over the Channel there were only high scattered clouds, giving about 3/10ths cover at 8,000 feet. Also, by the time the first aircraft reached Portland Bill the sun was rising. It was thus possible to re-form off the south coast. This was certainly done by most of the 61st Group and by portions of later serials but many pilots failed to recover contact with any large formation and went on alone or in small bunches. From England to Normandy the mission was given the same powerful escort and fighter cover as the daylight glider missions. No enemy aircraft attempted to penetrate this screen. One straggler in the 314th Group received a blast of anti-aircraft fire from Allied shipping off the Sainte-Marcouf Islands which induced him to give up and go home. A pilot in the 313th also reported naval fire, but it stopped when he signalled his identity.

Staff Sergeant Arthur Een on Captain Greer's crew in the 314th TCG who had earlier made a night drop in Normandy recalled: 'This was the first occasion when we ever made a daylight mission over enemy territory. For the supply drop, the undersides of the planes were loaded with parapacks containing high priority supplies. These parapacks were also used when paratroopers were riding in the cabin and were released by a salvo control switch in the pilots' compartment. Inside the plane, the cabin was filled with several heavy boxes, which were rigged to parachutes attached to static lines.

'Our route was the same as for the night drop, which spearheaded the invasion. Visibility was quite good and we were greeted with the usual amount of flak and small arms fire. I could not say it was any more comforting to be able to see the crews who were putting up the flak. When it was time to push out our boxes the co-pilot came back to lend a hand as we had some very heavy ones. When all were finally jettisoned, we yelled to Captain Greer to kick the plane in the ass and get the hell out of there. This time, instead of climbing for a safer altitude he dived the plane right to the tree top level and we hedgehopped to the coast. This was an effective way to escape flak, which could not be fired effectively at low altitudes in the dark. We stayed low for most of the return and climbed to several thousand feet shortly before reaching the English coast.'[110]

'Freeport' and 'Memphis' came in over 'Utah' Beach but were nonetheless disrupted by small arms fire when they overflew German positions. 'Freeport' made landfall on the north side of the Douve estuary. The orders and briefing of the pilots had called for a drop on DZ 'N' but, as the main body of the 61st Group approached the shore, it received the prescribed signals from a 'Eureka' beacon near Sainte-Mère-Église, 2½ miles northeast of DZ 'N'. The 82nd Division, cut off from its units on the west bank of the river, had ordered the beacon to go into action on DZ 'O'. Apparently no smoke or panels were used. The 61st Group formation followed the radar signals to DZ 'O' and dropped its bundles in that general vicinity at about 0603 from between 400 and 600 feet. It reported that the dropmasters provided by the quartermaster company were for the most part awkward, timid and airsick and of little help in kicking out the bundles.[111]

After this initial drop the situation became chaotic. Stragglers and small groups, often drawn from several different flights kept arriving at irregular intervals until 0815. A few of them received the radar signals and dropped their loads on or near DZ 'O'. Elements of the 313th and 316th Groups totalling at least a dozen aircraft made their drops on LZ 'W'. Nearly half the pilots followed their maps and their instructions to DZ 'N'. Perhaps the objective seemed too obvious to require use of 'Rebecca'; perhaps the policy of restricting the use of radar to serial and flight leaders was still exercising its baneful influence; certainly a four-man crew without a dropmaster to help them would be too busy preparing to dispose of their load to tinker with a 'Rebecca' in the last minutes of their run unless it seemed necessary.

The 313th Troop Carrier Group had despatched 52 C-47s, each carrying ammunition and supplies led by Lieutenant Colonel William A. Filer, Executive Officer of the Group. This was certainly not a milk-run. Bad weather caused sixteen C-47s to abort and return to Folkingham before they left England. In the 49th Squadron 'Chalk 11' (43-15048) piloted by

---

110 *The One Man Radio Show*; Arthur Een's D-Day Communications Report.

111 There is very little evidence on the efficiency with which the supply dropping was conducted. One squadron reported that it took an average of twelve seconds per plane to get out its bundles. Others had trouble with bundles stuck in pararacks or jammed in doors, but the percentage not dropped for those reasons was very low, in the neighbourhood of 1 percent.

1st Lieutenant Edmond J. Gibala and co-pilot 1st Lieutenant George H. Ehreich crashed on approach to Edgehill in the Oxford area. Both pilots and the navigator, crew chief, radio operator and the QM dropmaster perished in the crash. 'Chalk 7' (43-15637) piloted by 1st Lieutenant Claude J. Wilson and co-pilot, 2nd Lieutenant Evert B. Reed was seriously damaged by enemy fire and was forced down on enemy territory with the bundles still in the para-racks. The C-47 landed in a shallow flooded area. Wilson tried to rescue his wounded radio operator Staff Sergeant Daniel M. Jennings under enemy fire and was eventually captured. Wilson was held at one of the German Field Hospitals for about one-and-a-half days. By that time, the Germans were forced to retreat and all bed patients, including Wilson, were left behind. He was evacuated to Southern England and his squadron buddies learnt on the 14th that he was still alive.[112] 'Chalk 2' (42-5699) flown by Kermit R. Robinson and 'Chalk 8' (43-15165) flown by Samuel M. Willis were also lost to the same squadron after they were hit and ditched in the Channel. Both crews were picked up. 'Chalk 45' (43-15632) in the 48th Squadron piloted by Edgar F. Stovall with a crew of seven was the fifth C-47 lost to German ground fire.

Despite the high abort rate, at least 148 aircraft on 'Freeport' dropped approximately 156 tons of supplies but since the Germans held DZ 'N' and most of the territory west of the Merderet, very little of what was dropped beyond the river could be collected at that time. Less than 100 tons were retrieved that day and although ultimately about 140 tons were recovered[113] the paratroops on 'D+2' were very short of food and ammunition and subsisted largely on a captured trainload of cheese.

The aircraft going to DZ 'O' passed over the Germans in the Turqueville-Fauville pocket during their approach and swung over German-held territory west of the Merderet before completing their homeward turn. Those heading for DZ 'N' had to fly for two or three miles over enemy positions. The Germans put up only moderate small arms fire with little or no anti-aircraft, but this was sufficient to bring down ten aircraft. As Lieutenant Roach's C-47 crossed the beach and headed for the DZ he kicked the rudder to put the aircraft into a skid in order to avoid the heaviest streams, but to no avail. The rounds he was taking took out one of his engines and the resulting loss of oil pressure made it impossible to feather the prop on the dead engine.

---

112 The two other members of the crew were navigator, 2nd Lieutenant John E. Bagley and crew chief, Staff Sergeant Harry G. Ossman while Major Barney Lihn the Group Surgeon flew along as observer.
113 Probably including some delivered in 'Memphis'.

The intense vibration and drag cut his speed down to just less than 90 mph as he struggled to keep the aircraft airborne while flying just above the deck. Roach, who was on only his second combat mission, managed to coax the aircraft to the Channel and was forced to ditch about ten miles north of German occupied Barfleur. Tragically, some of the bullets apparently found the radio operator, Staff Sergeant Blake and one of the life rafts. The crew managed to evacuate the aircraft to an operable raft, but Blake died before they were rescued four hours later.[114] Among those attempting to use DZ 'N' the loss rate was probably over ten percent. Of the downed aircraft, four crashed in Normandy, one was still missing a month later and five were successfully ditched off the Normandy coast. Aboard the crashed aircraft eleven troop carrier men were killed and the rest of their crews were hospitalized or missing. All of these aircraft appear to have dropped at least part of their cargoes; one was already ablaze when the bundles went out.

'Take off for 50th Squadron C-47s had been at 2338 hours' recalled Robert E. Callahan, radio operator in 1st Lieutenant Maurice R. Perreault's C-47 in the 50th Troop Carrier Squadron, 314th Troop Carrier Group. 'The skies began to clear as the planes flew south. In the bright moonlight as the formation made its way across the English Channel, a vast armada of naval vessels could be seen below. The flotilla stretched for miles and miles. Every type of vessel one could imagine, large and small, was lined up in a convoy several ships wide. To observe such a scene while flying overhead made an indelible impression upon the mind. It revealed the determination and commitment of Allied forces to place the men and materials into battle to obtain the victory.'

As the fourteen C-47s in the 50th Squadron flew inland, the C-47 piloted by Lieutenant Maurice Perreault took two hits from small arms fire. At the same time its left elevator, at the tail section of the aircraft was shot away. As the formation approached the drop zone the planes climbed to an altitude of 400 feet for the drop to be made. Switches inside the cockpit were tripped and the para-packs underneath the cabin were dropped. The time was 0615. At the same time Stanley J. Wolowski and Robert Callahan kicked para-packs out the open side door.

'At an altitude of 500 to 700 feet, the 314th Troop Carrier Group made its paratroop drop at about 0210 hours' says Callahan. 'Following the dropping of the paratroopers, the flight formation continued crossing the Cotentin Peninsula on its way out to the English Channel. All eighteen planes of the 50th Squadron would return to base. However, Lieutenant Sidney

---

114 *Blackjacks At War 53rd TCS* by Major Steven C. Franklin.

W. Dunagan, piloting one of the planes, was killed in action while making a second pass over the drop zone. Two paratroopers had fouled their rip cords as the plane passed over the drop zone and other troopers had jumped. These two were not able to exit the plane at that time. The problems quickly resolved, Dunagan circled to make a second pass over the drop zone to allow the two to jump. While making the circle, he was hit with a bullet in the left side of his chest, killing him instantly. Lieutenant Walter D. Nims, co-pilot flew the aircraft on the return flight to home base. On this mission, the 50th Squadron delivered 319 paratroopers, 1,868 lbs of ammunition and 13,935lbs of combat equipment into the drop zone.'

An echelon of three planes of the 32nd Squadron was ahead of the 50th Squadron in the larger formation on the mission. After Captain Winford D. Taylor's crew pushed the last heavy box out of the open door of the cabin and as plane was struggling to make its way back to the English Channel, Taylor was hit by bullet that entered at the upper point of his left hip bone. Lieutenant Isadore Caplan the navigator bound up Captain Taylor's wounds using the GI first aid kit nearest the bulkhead in the cabin and gave him a shot of morphine. Captain Vincent R. 'Jack' Chiodo the co-pilot took over flying the aircraft. Over the drop zone Captain Bennett, flying the aircraft on Chiodo's right was taking intense fire from the ground. It was so severe that his aircraft went out of control and into a left barrel roll while not more than 300 feet above the ground. His right wing came up and over in the roll. As it continued to roll over onto its back, his right wing came down and struck the right wing of Chiodo's C-47. Miraculously, both planes were thrown apart from the collision and pilots of both aircraft did their best to take whatever measurers seemed appropriate at the time. Bennett's plane levelled out after the roll and he belly landed it in German occupied territory. He and his crew were taken prisoner.

Lieutenant Isadore Caplan recalled: 'What is so amazing is how Captain Chiodo got control of the C-47 while occupying the right seat. He called for help as I finished assisting Taylor. I helped Chiodo to shift over to the left seat by lying down on my back between the two pilots' seats, bracing myself and placing both feet hard against the left rudder on the co-pilot's side to hold it as Chiodo made the switch to the left seat. Chiodo stepped on my stomach as he moved from the right seat to the left. For a time I got in the right seat to help Chiodo hold full left rudder and full left aileron. From the right cockpit window it appeared that ten feet of the right wing had been chopped off. We came out over the Vire River between 'Omaha' and 'Utah' beaches, flying over the battleship *Nevada*, engaged at that time in shelling 'Omaha' Beach. I have never seen so much wreckage in my life. I gave Chiodo a heading of 330 degrees to Warmwell, the emergency base. Chiodo found the compass erratic and called the emergency base for help. The compass was unreliable because of the low right wing and having to hold hard left rudder and aileron. That resulted in the plane flying somewhat off line. The pilot of a P-47 guided us to Warmwell even though we could not successfully communicate with him. We called the emergency base and the base contacted the P-47 pilot by radio. We had to deal with the P-47's prop wash while trying to gain enough altitude to clear the cliffs along the south coast of England. When the Isle of Wight came into view, Chiodo wanted Sergeant Harry D. Ray in the right seat for the good reason that the crew chief knew the hydraulic and electrical systems better than I did. Chiodo did a remarkable job of getting us back on the ground and overcoming the low right wing condition. Afterward I learned from Captain Robert L. Flory, our 32nd squadron engineering officer that a bullet had struck one of the fourteen cylinders of the right engine, pierced the piston wall but did no damage to either the piston or the push rod. But at every stroke of the push rod, the cylinder lost a small amount of oil. Under such conditions it is amazing that the right engine ran so sweetly and performed so well all the way to Warmwell, even though losing oil slowly. Captain Chiodo was awarded the DFC for his heroic performance.'

It was only on their return that the crew discovered that anti-aircraft fire had damaged the release mechanism for the para-packs and they had not released. They were still in their racks on the underside of the plane. Later Chiodo was told those packs were loaded with land mines.

'Freeport' proved to be a difficult mission on all accounts. Cloud coverage over England made formation impossible, so some formed an improvised formation while others were forced to fly singularly and several eventually weather aborted as the clouds were too thick and the traffic was too heavy for flight. The non-standard formation was led by an aircraft with 'Rebecca' equipment and dropped their bundles on a 'Eureka' which was flashing the correct code but was located about two miles east of the mapped DZ. The crews noted that intense and very accurate fire was thrown at them as they got inside the coast, coming particularly from the windows of houses.

While 'Memphis' was less costly than 'Freeport', with three C-47s shot down and another 92 damaged, it was even less successful. Virtually none of the 101st's supplies reached the division. Why it was sent at all is a mystery. The Headquarters of the 101st Division had not called for it, did not expect it and had set out no markers or beacons to guide it. No facilities for air re-supply had been established at their bases, so the mission had to stage from Welford and Membury. The aircraft were supposed to be there by 2130 on 'D-Day' for loading. The 442nd Group sent only 56 aircraft, which took off from Fulbeck with 56 aircraft between 0421 and 0428 in the dim twilight before dawn. The 440th, perhaps more confident of its ability to assemble quickly, did not take off until about twenty minutes later. One of its 63 aircraft aborted because of a flat tyre and was not replaced. A substitute had been on hand when the group left Exeter, but none was ready at Welford. The 439th had sent six to Membury to complete the serial, but through some misunderstanding those aircraft had not come properly prepared and therefore could not go on the mission. Dropmasters from the quartermaster company took part in 'Memphis', but the number involved is unspecified. Fortunately for the 442nd Group, the take-off bases lay south of the disturbance which upset 'Freeport', but the weather at the start was bad enough to make assembly difficult. An unbroken blanket of cloud covered the sky 1,500 feet up and northwest winds, blowing aloft at 27 mph, drove rain squalls across the fields. However, beyond Portland Bill weather ceased to be an obstacle. The overcast became thin and broken with bases above 2,500 feet and the wind abated. Over Normandy the clouds lay lower and thicker, but not seriously so.

The fighter protection over the Channel won, as in the other daylight missions, the enthusiastic admiration of the troop carriers. One pilot described his serial as surrounded above, below and on all sides by fighters and declared that he had never seen so many at once as during that operation. Gunners on Allied ships off the Sainte-Marcouf Islands fired at or near some aircraft in 'Memphis', but briefly and without effect.

The 440th Group encountered heavy flak, of which there was hardly any north of Sainte-Côme and dropped its load, 63 tons of ammunition, 10½ tons of rations and 21 tons of combat equipment, between 0632 and 0639. Lieutenant Myron L. Pastuhenko, navigator on C-47A-70-DL 42-100737 in the 98th Troop Carrier Squadron recalled: 'It was like flying just another routine mission until they began firing at us. When we first crossed the beach we could see puffs of smoke. Later we flew right into that stuff. Not one of us got hit, though.'

Buck Sergeant Charles Everett Bullard, a crew chief on one of the C-47s wrote: 'At 0633, we approached the French Coast and what a sight it was! From a quarter of a mile out from the beach right on to and up it, the beach ships and landing craft, as well as soldiers were everywhere! We went over those fellows at 500 feet altitude doing 120 mph, headed for the drop zone to unload their supplies. The scene down below between the beach and our furthermost troops was indescribable. We would pass over one group of men who would give us a friendly wave and then the next group of men would be shooting at us with their rifles. Our troops and the enemy troops were that close together, with those beastly hedgerows dividing the two armies. At the low altitude we were flying, we made good targets for the German soldiers over under the hedgerow on the other side of the open field next to the row we were flying over.

'After dropping our parapacks and kicking out the door packs, we made the turn and headed back for the relative safety of the English Channel. All this time we were picking up lots of rifle and machine gun fire, some of which made a few more holes in my plane. After the drop, we still ran into the waving and shooting until we got to the Channel. Here and there, pockets of troopers still had not gotten together to form a good fighting group.

'After we got out of the danger area and were headed home, I checked to make sure no ships were directly below and just could not resist the urge to fire my machine gun into the Channel. You would think that that would be a normal urge for anyone and would be perfectly OK, but I was almost written up for it. We were not to fire our weapon unless fired upon. My captain didn't turn me in nor did he care for me shooting, but some shave tail flying along beside us must have squealed on me. I am glad now I did 'cause that was the only time I ever fired my weapon while in the combat zone. We continued our return to Exeter without further incident and even though we had several holes in the fuselage, no crewmember had been wounded nor had any vital parts of the plane been penetrated. We were an exceptionally fortunate crew. My 'Guardian Angel' had pulled us through again. I don't believe my fellow flight members ever realized that no member of my flight crew had lost a drop of blood while in flight.'[115]

Staff Sergeant Arthur Een's Guardian Angel was also in evidence. 'Over the Channel, we spotted several planes, which had ditched. The crews appeared to be all right and we waved to them and noticed that launches of the British Air Sea Rescue were racing to the scene. On each occasion when we approached the English coast, I was reminded of a bunch of little chicks scampering back to the mother hen after straying a little too far away and being frightened by some unknown terror in the barnyard.

'Our landing again went off without trouble and the crews mingled on the ramp swapping the usual after mission reports. One pilot remarked that a greased straight pin could not have been driven up his butt with a sledgehammer.

---

115 *Little One and His Guardian Angel: One Man's Story of the 440th Troop Carrier Group During World War II* by Charles Everett Bullard (Williams Associates Publishing Co, 2001).

That was pretty hard to top for holding a tight rear end. I thought complexions were pretty much grey for several hours, until most of the shock wore off.'

The groups returned to their home bases, not those from which they had staged. The 440th reached Exeter at or about 0828. All C-47s of the 442nd except one, which had landed at Warmwell, were back at Fulbeck by 0905. Sixty-two aircraft of the 440th TCG dropped supplies on DZ 'E' for the 101st Airborne Division. Only one pararack pack and seven bundles, which had damaged chutes, were brought back. Most aircraft in the 440th Group probably dropped between Sainte-Côme and la Barquette. Colonel Johnson in the 501st PIR reported a supply drop at la Barquette about 0630 some distance to the west of him, most of the bundles landing in no-man's land, behind the German lines, or in the Douve marshes. Flying in from the northeast over 'Utah' Beach the 440th had only to persist on course after passing LZ 'E' to come within sighting distance of the panels Johnson had put out requesting supplies and had only to veer a few degrees to the south to reach the Douve at the point where the drop was actually made. The failure to release the supplies over Johnson's position may be explained by assuming that the leader saw the panels too late to head directly over them and chose to drop west of the signals on his first run rather than make a second pass. Some aircraft in both groups may have dropped at other points, particularly northwest of Sainte-Mère-Église near DZ 'O'. Elements of the 440th reported picking up a 'Eureka' signal and following it in, although it was poorly received. The only 'Eureka' known to have been in operation at the time was that on DZ 'O' to guide 'Freeport'. Its signals would naturally have seemed poor, since the 'Rebecca' sets of the 440th were tuned to a different channel. At DZ 'O', as at LZ 'W', such supplies as were dropped would have been picked up by the 82nd Division and if accounted for at all, would probably be credited to 'Freeport'.

The 442nd Group, which had carried 678 pararacks and bundles with a gross weight of 126 tons, dropped 652 of them about 0638 from between 500 and 1,000 feet. The rest had stuck or were damaged. One dangling parapack was pried loose by a crew chief hanging out of the aircraft with the radio operator holding his ankles. The supplies were supposed to land on LZ 'E' near Hiesville, but Headquarters, 101st Division, located in that area, asserted that it saw no drop and recovered no bundles. The 442nd Group reported that it deposited its cargoes near Blosville, 1½ miles west of Hiesville on LZ 'W'. That zone, strewn with parachutes and gliders, would seem a logical objective to anxious pilots who had received no radar signals and seen no markers. The 82nd Division, to which LZ 'W' was assigned, presumably retrieved these supplies along with those dropped there about the same time by formations in 'Freeport'. The embattled paratroops were doing very little paper work that day and probably went on the principle of all supplies gratefully received and no questions asked. The 8th Infantry may also have taken a share.

'Memphis' suffered much less from enemy action than its predecessor. The first C-47 lost occurred near 'Utah' Beach when a bomb-cluster, accidentally dropped by a P-47, hit an aircraft in the 440th Group and set off ammunition in its cargo. The pilot managed to ditch his aircraft, but the explosion had killed two crewmen, a drop-master and a correspondent. As the 440th Group turned left after its drop, flak smashed engines on two aircraft in the 97th Squadron, forcing them to ditch. The crews were rescued by PT boats that were constantly patrolling for just that purpose. From the PT boats they were transferred to the USS *Quincy* to enable the fast PT boats to stay in the area for further missions. Small arms fire at the 442nd Group just after it made its drop caused minor damage to 21 aircraft and wounded two men.

The ineffectiveness of 'Freeport' and 'Memphis' was primarily due to lack of radio contact between the airborne commanders and IX TCC. With such contact 'Memphis' would either not have been sent or would have been given adequate instructions and a zone equipped with navigational aids. With such contact the pilots in 'Freeport' would not have been dispatched to a zone which was wholly in enemy hands. The atrocious weather which broke up the formations in 'Freeport' and forced a quarter of the pilots to turn back was pure bad luck. It was also fair warning that in Western Europe operations relying on aerial resupply would have to gamble on the weather. The losses caused by enemy fire in 'Freeport' were a reminder, if one were needed, that troop carrier formations were vulnerable and that passage over alerted enemy troops could be costly.

Of about 140 aircraft which got back after being in the drop area almost all reached their bases singularly or in small groups between 0815 and 1050. Ninety-two were damaged, some very badly. Every squadron had its tale of hazardous returns. One aircraft, barely controllable and with one engine dead, had been coaxed back to Folkingham by way of the North Sea and the Wash so that it could ditch instantaneously if necessary. Between fifteen and twenty had made forced landings at Warmwell and other points in southern England. None of the damaged aircraft had to be salvaged, but many required several days' work by service units. At the end of the month casualties in 'Freeport' were listed as fifteen dead, twenty wounded and seventeen missing. It is not surprising that pilots reporting in after their return swore that second missions were jinxed.

At least there was the return of some of the glider pilots, many of whom must have been feared dead. As late as 10 June Captain Henry C. Hobbs, a glider pilot in the 93rd Troop Carrier Squadron in the 439th TCG reappeared at Greenham Common after several 'adventures' on the 'Memphis' mission. He had had a great deal of difficulty in getting his Horsa off the runway due to an excessive overload. 'Even when airborne, the controls were sluggish and the glider tended to 'mush'. I had the trim tab fully back. The trip over was uneventful, other than that.

'I didn't see the pilot's green light - the signal to cut off, but I had seen previous signals and I was well aware of the fact that I was getting near the drop area I was busy looking for landmarks The glider was so sluggish that I requested the C-47 pilot over the intercom to give us an additional 100 feet of altitude, which he did. The cut was at approximately 700 feet. I realized that we were slightly to the south of our course and I did not recognize the particular fields under me, but I sensed that the tug was commencing a left turn as briefed and knew that I had to cut. I picked out what seemed to be the best field in the vicinity. It had trees (30-40 feet) and hedges or banks (well over four feet) around it. The field was shorter than expected - probably six to seven hundred feet long and had from 2-3 feet of water. I tried to slow up my glider as much as possible but found that the stalling speed was around 110. Even at that speed I was unable to level off- the nose kept dropping. Despite my having the stick full back the glider made contact with the ground in a diving angle. As a result the nose came off and I was hurled out. Fortunately the water stopped the glider in what seemed to be about ten feet and I was not run over. None of us were seriously injured. The airborne troops got out immediately and assembled beside a hedge. There was intermittent light machine gun, mortar and 88mm artillery fire in the vicinity, but none was directed at us. I joined up with the airborne and we proceeded first to the battalion CP across fields and hit the main road south of the field. While doing so I noticed a crashed C-47 with only the tail left. The last three numbers were '605' and a flight jacket near it with the name 'Bacon' was the only identifying feature.'[116]

---

116 As the 314th TCG's C-47s were approaching the drop zone, 42-93605 piloted by Captain Howard W. Sass was set on fire by anti-aircraft fire. Just before reaching the drop zone the ship caught fire underneath the fuselage. The radio operator in another of the planes momentarily saw through the door of Sass' plane and described the crew compartment as a 'sheet of fire.' Para-packs inside the plane were seen going out the door. Pilots, witnessing Sass' plane on fire, screamed to him on their radios for the crew to bail out. No parachutes were seen departing the plane. Sass went down with his burning plane, was catapulted into a hedge when it crashed and survived with comparatively minor injuries. On 21 June Major Joseph McClure, his squadron commander, received a letter from Captain Sass. He was in the 74th General Hospital in Bristol. Wounded but somewhat improved, he was flown back to the Saltby base the next day. He could remember nothing about his miraculous escape and very little about the events leading up to his crash. He was sent home to the USA a few days later.

Chapter 14

'Elmira' and 'Keokuk'

We departed Membury at about 0840, which put us over the coast of Normandy just as dusk at about 1100 hours. It was planned for us to arrive over the landing zone just at dusk with the idea that we would be able to see our fields, but the Germans would have trouble seeing the C-47s and gliders - Wrong! The really large and heavy Horsa gliders put a strain on the C-47s; the flame dampeners were white hot making really beautiful targets against the darkening sky... Over the coast of Normandy at 400 to 500 feet above the ground and 200 mph, sitting in the left-seat of a British Horsa glider I had a million dollar seat for one hell of a show but right at the time I would have sold it for a lot less! Tracer bullets arched up toward the aircraft, curved over and fell away. We were soldiers enough to know that between each and every tracer there were five or six other equally lethal bullets. It was a sight that caused one's balls to retreat up into the body cavity and the sphincter muscles to cut leather grommets out of the seats.

Operation Elmira or my Longest Day by Gale R. Ammerman, 81st TCS, 436th TCG, who carried 7,200lbs of artillery shells that day.[117]

At Ramsbury five miles east-northeast of Marlborough in Wiltshire 1st Lieutenant Louis R. Emerson in the 83rd TCS, 437th TCG had been awakened at 1300 in the afternoon of D-Day by someone vigorously shaking him by the shoulder. Emerson had earlier flown the 'Detroit' mission; now he learned that he was to fly the 'Elmira' mission with a 1400 take off. 'This time I was to pull a CG-4A. He wrote: 'It would be flown by my friend and best man at my wedding; Flight Officer Glen McFarren of The

---

117 *An American Glider Pilot's Story* (CreateSpace Independent Publishing Platform, 2012).

279

Dells, Oregon. It seems that some of the paratroopers and glider infantry had gotten in trouble and wanted some artillery. There were to be 28 gliders on this mission flying the usual four-ship echelon to the right, totalling seven rows. Our LZ was north and east of Sainte-Mère-Église in the same general area as the morning mission. I wondered where they found a field with enough room. All open space was probably already filled with gliders.'

Between dawn and early evening on 'D-Day' the troop carriers had undertaken no further operations, but about two hours before sunset, 'Keokuk' (named after the most southerly city in Iowa) and 'Elmira' would bring in additional support for the 101st and 82nd Airborne Divisions respectively, in 208 gliders. These and subsequent missions would be heavily escorted by P-38, P-47 and P-51 fighters and their exposure to German anti-aircraft would be minimized by approaching their objectives from the east coast over the 'Utah' beachhead. Operating on British Double Summer Time both missions were scheduled to arrive before dark. In order to limit the glider columns to a defensible length and to reduce congestion during the glider landings destined for LZ 'W', 'Elmira' was split into two echelons. One, towing 76 gliders, was to be ten minutes behind 'Keokuk', the other, towing 100 gliders, would go two hours later. They were to deliver two battalions of glider artillery and 24 howitzers to support the 82nd Airborne's 507th and 508th PIRs west of the Merderet, consisted of four serials, the first pair comprising 26 C-47s in the 437th TCG towing eight Wacos and eighteen Horsas and fifty C-47s in the 438th TCG towing fourteen Wacos and 36 Horsas to LZ 'W' near les Forges, only six miles from the coast, to arrive ten minutes after 'Keokuk'. LZ 'W' was an oval about 2,800 yards long from north to south and over 2,000 yards wide on terrain much like that of LZ 'E'. The northern tip of the oval was about a mile south of Sainte-Mère-Église and the road from that town to Carentan ran through the middle of the zone. About 1,000 yards inside the southern end of the LZ, the road was intersected at les Forges by the east-west road from Sainte-Marie-du-Mont.

The second and third serials were to continue on to LZ 'O' and commence their drop two hours later at sunset. These serials comprised fifty C-47s in the 436th TCG at Membury towing two Wacos and 48 Horsas and 48 C-47s in the 435th at Welford towing a dozen Wacos and 38 Horsas (including a paratroop aircraft of the 435th, which had failed to drop its troops on the previous night). The Wacos were segregated in separate flights to reduce the problem of flying two types of glider in one formation. Within the gliders of the first echelon were 'Charlie' Battery of the 80th Airborne AA Battalion, contingents of medics, signal men and divisional headquarters personnel, a reconnaissance platoon and an air support party - 437 men in all. The cargo comprised 64 vehicles, mostly jeeps, thirteen anti-tank guns (57 mm) and 24½ tons of other supplies and equipment.

'After a short relaxing nap at the flight line, it was time to man the 32 tow planes and the English-made Horsa gliders for the 'Keokuk' mission' recalled Major Frank W. Hansley commanding the 72nd TCS in the 434th TCG at Aldermaston. 'Take off started at 6:30 pm on 6 June. As deputy mission commander, I took off in the second aircraft and flew off the lead aircraft's right wing. Lieutenant Colonel Steve Parkinson was flying the lead aircraft as mission commander.'

This was the first time that the Americans used the British gliders in an airborne operation. They were towed by thirteen C-47s in the 72nd TCS, a dozen C-47s in the 73rd TCS and seven C-47s in the 74th TCS. Of the 64 glider pilots, seventeen were from the 71st Squadron; fifteen were from 72nd; sixteen came from the 73rd Squadron and sixteen were in the 74th Squadron. Some of these glider pilots were on detached service and came originally from the 315th TCG and 438th TCG. The 73rd TCS flew twelve C-47s towing twelve Horsa gliders. With a larger load than the CG-4A any Horsas that cracked up in the small fields with hedgerows and trees would result in higher casualties than in the Waco. The mission is notable also as the first Allied daylight glider operation. The 434th's objective was again LZ 'E' near Hiesville where a detachment of glider pilots led by Lieutenant. Victor Warriner had been busy clearing and cutting down trees and the pathfinders had marked the drop zone with a yellow panel 'T' and green smoke. The platoon from the Division reserve, 3rd Battalion of 501st and the Division artillerymen, under the overall command of Colonel Sherburne, had arrived at the LZ to meet the incoming gliders. 1st Lieutenant John R. Devitt, in the 73rd TCS, 434th TCG who had towed a Waco glider on 'Chicago', recalled: 'Keokuk' launched at 1830 hours. Thirty-two C-47s towing the much larger British Horsa gliders participated. Glider L894 was mated with our plane with seven 101st crew, a truck, a 37mm field gun, radio batteries, ammunition, fuel and accessories plus the glider pilots.'

The formation carried 157 men of the medical, signal and staff personnel, forty vehicles, six guns and about nineteen tons of other equipment and supplies on what proved to be an incredibly easy mission to LZ 'E' as far as the C-47 crews were concerned. With good weather and daylight all the way everyone kept on course and in formation. The serial approached the peninsula from the east coast over the shoreline where the American amphibious forces had established their bridgehead. The Germans still had considerable forces around Turqueville, two miles north of LZ 'E' and Sainte-Côme-du-Mont, two miles south of the landing zone and had not been entirely cleared from the area between. The C-47s, coming in over 'Utah' Beach to limit exposure to ground fire, encountered no hostile action from enemy aircraft and the gliders were cut-off at 2053, seven minutes ahead of schedule. The German forces held their fire until the gliders were coming down and while they inflicted some casualties, were too distant to cause much harm. There were no casualties to power crew personnel and battle damage consisted of just a few nicks in one aircraft and the Horsas landed without serious damage.

1st Lieutenant John Devitt recalled: 'Glider release over Normandy was about 2100 hours (still bright sunlight) and the action intense. I recall the sight of one of the plywood-constructed Horsas being splintered by automatic weapons fire from nose to tail just as it completed its landing skid. Ninety per cent of the gliders were destroyed. Fourteen glider crew were killed in landing.'

The lead aircraft of the 436th took off at 2037 and that of the 435th about 2040. Glider pilot Ben Ward in the 81st TCS, 436th TCG recorded: 'My co-pilot James J. DiPietro and I went to the flight line to meet our load of glider troops. Our 'bird' was a giant glider, the British Horsa.' The great capacity of the Horsas, one of which could carry a 75 mm howitzer, a jeep and five men, enabled these serials to carry much more than those in the morning missions. The first serial carried the 319th Field Artillery Battalion and a few other artillerymen, medics and engineers, a total of 418 airborne troops. As cargo it had 31 jeeps, twelve 75 mm howitzers, 26 tons of ammunition and 25 tons of other equipment. The second serial was occupied exclusively by the 320th Field Artillery Battalion with 319 troops, twelve 105 mm howitzers, 28 jeeps, 33 tons of ammunition and 23 tons of other equipment.[118]

'We loaded up thirty troopers and their gear plus boxes of anti-tank mines which were lashed to the floor in the aisle. I glanced back down the aisle into the blackened faces of the airborne troops, all looking so competent and confident and I breathed a silent prayer. I made a last-minute check of my controls and just as we started to roll, J. J. gave me the 'thumbs up' sign. As we reached proper air speed I could feel the positive responses. Picking up speed the rushing wind sounds increased. I eased back the yoke raising the nose wheel off the runway and held it steady until reaching the 90 mph

118 According to the report of the 82nd Division, the twelve Waco gliders in that serial each carried a 105 mm howitzer.

takeoff speed. Additional back-pressure of the yoke lifted the glider and we were airborne, but the tow plane was still running on the ground. We assumed our position behind and above him and at 100 mph he lifted off and began a slow climb. At 5,000 feet we joined in line with the stream of other aircraft and headed for the English Channel.'

Flight Officer John C. Hanscom in the 89th Troop Carrier Squadron, 438th Troop Carrier Group had watched the glider-towing C-47s take off from Greenham Common on 'Albany' in the very first wave of assault on the night of 'D-Day' minus one. At a briefing on 3 June when 'D-Day' was originally scheduled, Hanscom had been excited. 'I looked at Flight Officer 'Bill' Meisburger, my chosen partner in this coming operation and my fast friend. He was pale, but his eyes were bright with suppressed excitement. He winked at me. I winked back and managed what must have been at most a thin smile. With twenty-four other glider pilots and forty power pilots we were crowded into the bare, dank interior of a Nissen hut for the purpose of being briefed on our first airborne combat mission. Major Clement Richardson, our squadron commanding officer, was standing before us waiting for the last of the stragglers to enter before commencing the briefing. When he nervously cleared his throat and began his speech, he reflected the tension prevailing in that room. 'Gentlemen', he began tremulously, 'I want you to know that the big show is about to begin and we are beginning it with a bang.'

'Major Richardson had unveiled some large maps and charts on the wall. There in a maze of lines, strings and coloured pins was a picture of the airborne invasion of Normandy He then launched into the main body of the briefing. Our C-47s would transport paratroops into Normandy. Our gliders would go in on the second wave during 'D-Day' proper. We were only a small part of the gigantic 'Overlord' operation, but to all appearances we were in the brunt of it.'

'The maps and charts revealed to us the general geography of the Cherbourg or Cotentin Peninsula which was to be the area of our destined operations. The strings and lines represented the various routes of our approach and return. From aerial photographs, much enlarged, we glider pilots studied our landing zones and planned our flight paths for landing. Another briefing for glider pilots took place in the group briefing room with Captain Orville Cawthon, our group glider operations officer. There were also three officers from the 82nd Airborne Division attempting to give us an idea of what would be expected of us on the ground after landing.'

Then there had been a twenty-four hour reprieve because of the weather but that was before. 'Now it was our turn' wrote Hanscom. 'At long last we were going into action. This time it would not be a dry run. Everyone was in a high state of excitement. The fuss and noise and hubbub and turmoil and general hullabaloo that ensued was intense. The power pilots appeared in all their combat finery including shock helmets, flak suits and Mae West life preservers. Last minute activities included the payment of gambling debts and the bidding of fond farewells. Not a soul knew what to expect on this, our first venture into actual combat and everybody acted as if nobody would ever see anybody again.

Flight Officer 'Bill' Meisburger and I solemnly flipped a coin to determine who would have the dubious privilege of acting as pilot of our glider. Among glider pilots there was no distinction between pilots and co-pilots as existed among power pilots Thus some such method as the above was used to determine who was to occupy the left seat in the pilots' compartment of the glider. 'Bill' won the toss. The die was thus cast. We shook hands; exchanged remarks of sympathy and felicitation over our mutual destiny. I had complete confidence in 'Bill's ability. We had flown many training missions together including one foolhardy venture in which we succeeded in looping a cumbersome British Horsa glider twice from an altitude of 5,000 feet. This was an unparalleled stunt for which we received proper reprimand. The Horsa was a much bigger, heavier, more unwieldy craft than the familiar American CG-4A. The eighty-foot fuselage of the Horsa was round with huge wings extending from each side about one-third of the length back from the plexiglas nose. The wing span was well over one hundred feet. A large fin and rudder assembly jutted eight or nine feet into the sky above the broad stabilizers. The top of that rudder was at least twenty feet above the ground. The landing gear was of the tricycle type and gave that big glider the appearance of a hulking bird of prey about ready to swoop. All of the Horsas we repainted a dull, dead black, suitable for such flying coffins They had the American star insignia on the upper left and under right wing tips and on each side of the fuselage in addition to broad white stripes painted around wings and body The glider was designed to hold, besides the two pilots, thirty-one airborne infantrymen with all their equipment. Our particular ship would carry fourteen 82nd Airborne troops and a trailer loaded with communications equipment. It amounted to about 10,000lbs in payload.'

Major Richardson gave his crews a short briefing. 'And then' wrote Hanscom 'we got dressed for the party. Dress included long woollen underwear, two pairs of thick woollen socks, a light woollen shirt, wool olive drab trousers and shoes impregnated against mustard gas, a field jacket with a small flag sewed onto the right sleeve and a gas detector fastened to the left shoulder, impregnated leggings, wool cap, steel helmet and liner, gas mask, ammunition belt containing 96 rounds, M-1 rifle, bayonet, trench knife, entrenching tool, first aid packet, canteen and cup, three hand grenades and a pack The pack contained a blanket, shelter half, mess kit, foot powder, matches, extra socks, two K-rations, six D-rations, two heat units for warming rations, sewing kit, another first aid kit, insect powder and halazone tablets for purifying water Over all this we wore our Mae West life preservers In our pockets we earned miscellaneous items including an escape kit containing two thousand francs in Bank of France notes, terrain maps, a small saw, compass, passport pictures, foreign language guide, whistle, flashlight, chewing gum, pencil, notebook, dog tags and more matches. The cliché 'dressed fit to kill' seemed apt. After eating an early supper at 1600, we were trucked to the flight line 'Bill' and I were assigned to glider number forty nine in a fifty ship formation. We doffed our packs and donned flak suits over our Mae Wests.'

Hanscom and Meisburger and the other glider pilots attended the roll call called by Captain Cawthon who gave them a brief pep talk. The 438th C-47s and their glider tow's took off between 1848 and 1916.

'At 1850 the first tow ship dragging its ponderous charge behind was speeding down the long runway' wrote John Hanscom. 'About 1910 our turn to takeoff came. The technique of getting a heavily loaded Horsa off the ground was at all times an exacting and hazardous undertaking for both the glider pilots and the tow ship pilots. The runway at Greenham Common was over a mile and a quarter in length and every inch of it was needed. The gliders were lined up on each side of the wide strip of concrete in alternate order with their wings inter-lapping. They formed a curious zigzag pattern when viewed from above. Each tow ship would swing onto the runway from either side immediately after the previous unit had started on its way. The two-inch, 300 foot nylon towrope had previously been attached to both the glider and tow ship.

'As the powered craft slowly eased down the runway, the rope would slither and slide from its carefully looped position like a huge endless serpent. The aft end of the rope was forked. At each end of the fork was a heavy lug which fitted into a socket on the underside of each wing about ten feet out from the fuselage. 'Bill' and I watched in fascination as that ropes lowly inched out, knocking pebbles right and left as it slid along. After what seemed an eternity, it grew taut, lifted slightly from the runway and we could feel the strain as the lugs grated in their sockets. The go-ahead signal was given and the pilot in our tow ship began easing his throttles forward. We moved slowly at first, then faster, ever faster. 'Bill' was properly holding the control wheel back so that the nose wheel of our landing gear was kept slightly off the runway surface as we gathered momentum. This was done to prevent the terrific vibration which inevitably resulted if all three wheels were kept on the ground at anything above a very slow speed. The noise of the wind about our Plexiglas enclosed compartment rose to a shriek as the air speed indicator crawled toward take off speed which would be at ninety-plus miles per hour. I shouted the speed figures for 'Bill's benefit so that he would not attempt to pull up the big ship before it gained flying speed. Reluctantly that ponderous glider left the ground. The air was warm and turbulent. That unwieldy craft wanted to do everything but remain in a straight flight path behind the tow ship. 'Bill' really wrestled with those controls. At times I helped him exert pressure on the rudder pedals to keep that yawing glider from slewing off into the ground on one wing. Now the tow ship with its tail oscillating from side to side gradually left the ground and grazed the treetops at the end of that long runway. We were off! Our first hurdle was over on that fateful 'Elmira' mission of the huge 'Overlord' operation.

'The flight was an ordeal which would live long in our memories. The air was very turbulent until we got over the sea. 'Bill' and I spelled each other at the controls in ten-minute intervals. I was wringing wet after my first stint. About twenty minutes after takeoff, I unloosened my safety belt and went back into the cargo compartment to see how our airborne troops were faring Three of them were seated on the right side in front of the trailer The remaining eleven were behind it The men in front weren't feeling very well. Their helmets were off and being put to retching functional use. They looked up with dull, listless eyes and then hung their heads back over their helmets I couldn't see what was going in back of the trailer Since the riding was even rougher back there than up front, I could well imagine, what the sight was like I went back to my seat feeling thankful that I was helping fly this winged hearse and not riding in that stuffy compartment. No matter how rough the air ever got. I had never known a glider pilot to suffer air-sickness while flying. We had telephonic connection with our tug ship and could communicate freely with our pilot, Captain Al Perry and his co-pilot. First Lieutenant John Baird. After forming we headed south and slightly to the east. The air became smooth over the water and we began to enjoy the trip a little. We were duly impressed with our heavy fighter protection. Many P-47 Thunderbolts with a few Spitfires and P-51 Mustangs were above, below and on all sides of us. They gave us a much-needed sense of security.'

At Ramsbury the 437th took off between 1907 and 1921. As the 435th circled upward to form its column of fours, one Horsa broke loose and one aircraft turned back with its generators burned out. (Both loads were towed in next morning with the 437th Group as part of 'Galveston' mission). The trip to the east coast of Normandy was uneventful. The weather was favourable and the fighter cover lavish, but, presumably because of the impending darkness, the escort turned back at the Sainte-Marcouf Islands. The troop carriers set out still unaware that the 82nd Division was marking LZ 'O' instead of LZ 'W'. They did receive a last-minute phone call from the 53rd Wing directing them to make a 180° right turn after releasing their gliders instead of the left rum prescribed in their orders. Presumably IX TCC had learned that the Germans still held the Sainte-Côme area in strength.

Climbing with the heavily laden Horsas was a slow business, but all aircraft succeeded in assembling and setting out in formation. Over England squally weather made the gliders hard to handle; they veered and pitched on their long ropes. From then on the weather was excellent with unlimited visibility and scattered clouds overhead at 3,000 feet. At Portland Bill the escort appeared. The sky seemed full of P-47s, P-51s and P-38s, an impressive array. Besides 'debusing' patrols ahead of the column, fighters were flying close cover on both sides and high cover at between 3,000 and 5,000 feet. No German aircraft appeared to challenge them and the columns flew in serenely over 'Utah' Beach.

'As soon as we in the 81st TCS planes in 'Elmira' passed over the English coast and headed south over the Channel' continues Ben Ward, 'we were presented with a sight that was almost too stunning to take in. Ships, ships and more ships of every sort, size and shape crowding in toward the beach as far as the eye could see. The bigger ships were blinking furiously to each other with signal lamps.'

1st Lieutenant Louis Emerson in the 83rd TCS, 437th TCG recalled: 'This time it was daylight and I could see the water. There were so many ships in the Channel that it seemed as though one could walk across it and not get a wet foot. I learned later that there were more than 5,000 ships involved in the Normandy landing. This time our course was to fly straight across 'Utah' Beach to the landing zone, only about ten or twelve miles inland.'

Flight Officer Elwood Harold Brindle, a Waco pilot in the 75th TCS, 435th TCG with Flight Officer Charles Neuseller as co-pilot in 'Serial 33' carried a M3 105mm light howitzer and two personnel from the 320th Glider Field Artillery Battalion. Born on 6 April 1917 where he lived in Maplewood, New Jersey, in civilian life Elwood was a clerk and after enlisting in the US Army in March 1942 he continued doing the same type of work. The Army was looking for glider pilots and he decided that this was an opportunity not to be missed. He began his glider training at Victorville Army Flying School, California as part of class WC 42-25. On 24 December 1942 he was appointed as a flight officer and began training in the CG-4A. Brindle wrote: 'It wasn't until we were winging over the Channel, bound for the Cherbourg Peninsula that the full realization struck me that our long months and years of training were over and we were finally playing for keeps. All during the final preparations - days spent in a barbed-wire enclosure undergoing detailed briefings, equipment checks, map and photo studies, lectures and pep talks - we had just the feeling that perhaps this was just another 'dry run,' but now there was no doubt that the chips were down. The air over the Channel was smooth and the sky was overcast. Down below us the swells of the Channel bore slight traces of spray. Now and then to relieve the tension somewhat we exchanged banter with the tow-plane pilot over the interphone hook-up, but I'm afraid our humour was a little corny. Before long the faint outlines of the French coast appeared. German antiaircraft and machine gun batteries were filling the sky between the coast and our LZ with an assortment of steel and lead, interspersed with red and yellow tracers which lent a Fourth of July atmosphere to the scene. Soon we were in the midst of the hailstorm in reverse. Our first reaction was surprise at the laziness with which the tracers mounted toward us in the darkness, but as bullets started to rip through the fabric of our ship we realized that their apparent sluggishness was only an illusion. It seemed the entire blackness beneath us was filled with German batteries, but suddenly we reached the area of our paratroopers, moving in ahead of us, had secured.'

Not until the release point was almost reached did ground fire begin. This rapidly increased in intensity and did considerable damage. The volume of fire was moderate, the period of exposure was short and the weapons employed were small arms and machine guns with a little 20 mm flak, but the shooting was unpleasantly accurate. Enemy troops were close to the line of flight and the mission had neither surprise nor darkness to protect it. Two aircraft were shot down after releasing their gliders, but only two or three injuries resulted. One of the two aircraft, its engines dead, dived between two trees, stripping off both wings and engines, yet skidded safely to rest. Some 37 aircraft returned to England with slight or moderate damage. Two had dead engines, one had 65 bullet holes and one limped in with the crew chief holding its shattered feed lines together. Three men had been slightly wounded.

'About 2100 I got my first glimpse of France to our right. The atmosphere was hazy and huge clouds of smoke were billowing from various burning. Villages near the shore. Everything seemed to be going smoothly and according to plan. 'At 2110 we were heading in toward the northeast beaches of the Cotentin Peninsula Below us were hundreds of naval craft of all sizes, shapes and descriptions Some C-47s were hightailing back toward England having ridded themselves of their dangerous loads. Shortly before 2130 we were crossing 'Utah' Beach and could see our proposed landing zones The formation began descending to the prescribed 800 foot release altitude I was at the controls while 'Bill' oriented himself and sought a field fit for landing Suddenly I was aware of small flashes of fire coming from the area where we had been briefed to land. Enemy defensive forces were still there! We promptly decided to hang on and look for safer refuge I could hear quite distinctly the sharp reports of rifles and machine guns below. I was not a comfortable person at that moment. Some of our gliders were landing directly into that enemy fire. Some of them never knew what hit them. 'Bill' signalled that he would take the controls. I relinquished them and seized the intercom.

'Glider to tow ship, glider to tow ship; come in tow ship' I called.

'Tow ship to glider' a metallic voice responded in my earphones.

'Looks like this is it fellas. Good luck!'

'We're cutting loose' I said. 'We'll see you later - I hope!'

'I had my hand on the big, red knob of the release lever. When 'Bill' gave the high sign I pushed the knob cutting the glider loose. I felt as if I were cutting an umbilical cord. We were freely coasting through that misty, smoke-filled, shell-ridden air. The tow ship was hightailing into the distance with our rope dangling uselessly behind it. And below us?'

LZ 'W' should have been easy to locate. The landscape was still plainly visible and some pilots saw a panel 'T' and green smoke, near which a 'Eureka' beacon was sending out signals, clearly received on the 'Rebecca' sets in the aircraft. However, because of an emergency as yet unknown to IX TCC, the 'T', smoke and radar were not on LZ 'W' but two miles northwest of it. A potential source of further confusion was the presence of the panel 'T' and green smoke set out for 'Keokuk' in the vicinity of LZ 'E', which was two miles east of les Forges. The first gliders, unaware that the LZ had been moved to DZ 'O', came under heavy ground fire from German troops who occupied part of LZ 'W'. Guided by 'Gee' and by visual identification of the terrain, the leader of the 437th Group headed straight for LZ 'W' and released his glider there at 2104 followed it appears, by almost all his serial. Ten minutes later aircraft of the 438th Group appeared over the zone and made their release, but, part of the serial had erroneously loosed their gliders over LZ 'E'. Release altitudes were generally between 500 and 750 feet. From such heights a Waco could glide more than two miles, a Horsa less than a mile. After releasing their gliders, the troop carrier pilots swung their aircraft into a 180° left turn, thereby exposing themselves to fire from the Germans around Sainte-Côme-du-Mont and headed out over 'Utah' Beach.

'Before we could catch our breath, it seemed' continues Ben Ward 'we turned to the right toward our gliders' landing zone in back of the invasion beaches. As we cut in to the Normandy coast, the Navy guns opened up - big puffs of blinding orange, followed by gushes of red on the land. LSTs (landing ships for tanks) were working on the beach. Big fires, houses burning - flashes of artillery fire along the beaches, long streams of tracers, apparently coming from a mile or so in back of the beach, arcing up into the darkening sky and in the distance the green-lit 'T' that was set up as the centre of our LZ. We were only 500 feet above the beach coming in; it was easy to see individual trucks and jeeps dashing about. Smoky black bursts of flak now seemed to be filling the sky. Practically uninterrupted arcs of tracers, red and yellow, came up toward us with fascinating deliberation and then fell away in graceful curves. We were in echelons of four to the right and our plane was an element leader. It was part of my job to signal back to the gliders with a red light four minutes out and a green light over the LZ, where they would cut off. I climbed on the wooden stool in the companionway and poked my head into the Plexiglas astrodome. To our right was the French coast coming up - still plenty visible in the gathering dark. Stretched out in front of me was an unbelievable panorama - hundreds and hundreds of ships crowding in toward the beach. Right then I wouldn't have given up my place in the astrodome for anything. Over Normandy, while the rational part of my mind was trying to take it all in, the emotional side was telling me that men were dying down there.'

Second Lieutenant Leonard L. Baer was the navigator on C-47 42-92894 in the 88th TCS, 438th TCG, which was piloted by 2nd Lieutenant Samuel S. Cromie and co-pilot 2nd Lieutenant Floyd Bennett. 'We came into LZ 'W' with no difficulty and cut our glider. I saw a C-47 burning near the centre of the LZ. As we turned we came out at 500 feet. We then went down on the deck to about 75-100 feet. Just as we hit the deck I saw the co-pilot tilt his head and duck and I heard noise in the right engine. The pilot said, 'Feather right engine!' Both the co-pilot and I slammed our hands up to feather the engine. At the time I was standing behind the pilot. Bennett opened the other engine and it immediately coughed and spluttered. He shouted to us to prepare for a crash. I turned around to Staff Sergeant John Holton the crew chief behind me and pushed both him and the radio op0-eratoir, Sergeant Joseph M. Kozik into the main cabin. I ran back with them and placed my feet against the bulkhead behind the navigator's table. Before I got flat on the floor we hit a tree and the jolt flattened us on the floor. Prior to hitting I noticed sparks coming from the right engine. We bounced off the trees and jolted three times and then slid into the ground. As soon as the plane stopped I looked back and saw daylight in the plane. The whole tail assembly was knocked off. I crawled out of the plane. The right wing was knocked off and the left was knocked off near the engine. The tail was broken off and the nose was pushed in on the co-pilot's side. I stood up and saw the pilot come out through the cabin. He immediately said that Bennett was missing. I went around to the front of the plane and saw him on a stretcher with four paratroopers. I heard a 'zing' and a paratrooper told me to keep my damned head down. They then asked us if we had any weapons on board the ship. One of the paratroopers came out of the ship with one of our Tommy guns. He thanked us for it.

'There were about twenty-five paratroopers around the ship and they were shooting into the trees at snipers. Our plane went down about two miles north of Reuville on course directly five miles from the beach at 2131.42 hours. I determined this time from my watch which was stopped. I ordered the paratroopers to destroy the plane. Upon arriving at the command post I found that all of our crew were there. We secured first aid for the co-pilot and stayed at the CP until a truck came by to take the co-pilot to the field hospital a half a mile away. The field hospital was very crowded with wounded men; many of them lying around in fields on stretchers. We were told by one of the doctors that they had over a thousand paratroop casualties. There were about a hundred wounded men out in the open. While I was lying on the ground near the hospital I saw several groups of C-47s coming in towing Horsa gliders. Three planes crashed. As far as I could observe, no plane was hit until after dropping the gliders. When the planes went to the deck they were hit by small arms fire from snipers hidden in the trees. A glider pilot near me said 'God, why doesn't someone tell those fellows to stay up high?'

No one who knew the situation on LZ 'W' at that moment would have recommended landing gliders on it. The wedge of German resistance between Turqueville and Carquebut extended across the northern part of the zone and isolated it from the territory taken by the 505th Parachute Regiment. The paratroops around Sainte-Mère-Église could not get through the belt of German territory to reconnoitre LZ 'W', let alone to set up beacons there and until late in the day General Ridgway had every reason to believe that the entire zone was in German hands. Hence he had decided to place the beacons and markers in the vicinity of LZ 'O'. He had attempted to get word of the situation to IX TCC, first by radio and later by panels laid out for a reconnaissance aircraft, but the message was not received and the panels were not observed.

The C-47s released their gliders for the original LZ, where most delivered their loads intact despite heavy damage. As a final hazard, landings had to be made in the face of obstacles greater than the other zones. Not only were there 'postage stamp' fields 200 yards long, bordered by fifty foot trees but also some of the designated fields turned out to be flooded and others were studded with poles more than five inches thick and ten feet or more in height. Trip-wires for mines had been attached to many of the poles but fortunately, the mines themselves had not been installed.

Edwin J. O'Donnell detached to the 437th TCG recalled: 'We had dropped down to about 100 feet as we crossed the beach and had climbed to between 400 and 500 feet over our 'landing zone' (really no landing zone as it was up to us to pick any field we could get into)... We made one 90° turn to the left, we passed over a glider that had already landed. It evidently had hit a mine or something; anyway the whole glider was enveloped in flames. It was then that I became aware of the enemy firing at the gliders and tow ships....James Campbell in the 86th TCS, 437th TCG wrote: 'The damn trees were about fifty feet tall (as in all the hedgerows) and I was about five feet too low to clear them. A tall limb hit my left wing about the same time as my undercarriage snagged in the tops of the trees. The left wing, catching as it did, pulled us in a turn of 90° and we stopped at the base of the trees with the left wing still tangled and the tail section twisted upside down. Not one of us got a scratch.'

The sun set a few minutes before the second wave of serials of Mission 'Elmira' had reached 'Utah' Beach and as they passed over Normandy the landscape lay in deepening shadow. The initial glider release occurred at 2255, five minutes ahead of schedule. Because no other pathfinder aids were operating, they headed for the 'Eureka' beacon on LZ 'O'. One serial released early and came down near the German lines, but the second came down on LZ 'O'. Most of the lead serial released their gliders over a mile short of LZ 'O' and six gliders were released at least five miles east of the zone.[119] The main body of the second serial was quite accurate; having loosed the first glider at 2305 but five of pilots went to LZ 'W' by mistake. Either they were not using 'Rebecca' or they trusted their briefing more than the beacon. This wave too came under severe ground fire as it passed directly over German positions. Nearly all of both battalions joined the 82nd Airborne by morning and fifteen guns were in operation on 8 June. The pathfinder troops on LZ 'E' had long since ceased operations. Un-distracted by landmarks or rival beacons, the second instalment of 'Elmira' headed for the 'Eureka' and the visual aids set up by the 82nd Division in the vicinity of LZ 'O'. To their surprise, about three miles inland the serials ran into fire bad enough to make the 435th's paratroop operation seem like a milk run. The fire grew more intense as they approached the LZ and continued during their 180° turn to the right and in some cases at least, all the way back to the coast because the course from 'Utah' to LZ 'O' passed over or just north of the German positions at Turqueville and the LZ area was within range of German forces north of Sainte-Mère-Église. A right turn after release therefore brought the C-47s directly over those forces. A wide turn or a slight deviation to the north would put a pilot over German-held territory clear to the beaches. German marksmanship was also aided by the American flame-dampeners which became white hot and shone brightly in the semidarkness.

The barrage was less deadly than it appeared. The harm it caused aboard the aircraft was proportionately about the same as that inflicted on the previous echelon. In the first serial 33 aircraft received some slight damage and two troop carrier men were wounded. In the other, three aircraft had to be ditched on the way back because of hits on engines or fuel systems. All personnel aboard them were rescued. Two aircraft had to make emergency landings in England and twenty more were damaged but readily repairable. One member of the 435th Group was killed and one wounded. Both groups scattered and returned in driblets, some arriving as late as 0300 next morning.

Glider pilot Ben Ward in the 81st TCS, 436th TCG recorded: 'Red Light!' I beamed the Aldis lamp back at my element and turned front again. I was

---

119 Some sanction to these premature releases was provided by the field orders, which prescribed release short of the zone but within gliding range of it to minimize exposure of aircraft to enemy Are.

mesmerized by the fire coming up at our planes - couldn't take my eyes off it. I could see the bullets finding the range of the leading elements. I felt right then that in a few moments I would be dead. No panic: just the mind-filling recognition of what had to be. I stood there rubbing my head with the Aldis lamp and hoping it would come painlessly and wondering how Dotty would take the news. One consolation: it seemed to me that most of the gliders from the leading elements were going to make it down near the LZ.

'Green Light!' In that very instant I could hear bullets hitting the ship, a rather dry sound like peas being dropped into a pot. Our plane lurched forward on being released from the glider and we banked sharply down and to the right, under the arcs of tracers. With the realization that we were still flying, I began to get really scared. Now that we had a chance for life I was afraid we wouldn't make it. But after that few minutes in the thick of battle all we had facing us was an uneventful, practically routine flight home.

'No yelling, no rejoicing this time when we touched down at Membury. Just a quiet, heavy sensation: 'Well, that's two out of the way.' We went outside with flashlights to check on holes in our planes. I counted four in my plane and guessed that daylight would show more; we had one mean-looking hole in the faring about ten inches from our right gas tank.'[120]

In the second 'Elmira' serial Major Francis Farley, Operations Officer of the 81st TCS was the leader of the 436th Group's second flight of nine C-47s. 'When we went through that famous cloud bank that hung over the Cherbourg peninsula, we were in a 'V-of-V's of nine planes. Colonel Brack was the leader of the other flight. As soon as Brack saw that cloud bank he went down so as to get through it; he figured he would still have enough altitude for the paratroopers underneath it.' But Farley, for some reason, thought he saw Brack turn to the left. So he also took his serial down under the cloud bank and turned the transports to the left. 'But we went too far north; and as a result we came out very near the top of the peninsula. We found ourselves only about five miles from the port of Cherbourg; and of course immediately we ran into heavy flak and other ground fire. When we started to receive AA fire we were at a rail junction ten miles south of Cherbourg.' Farley asked for a new heading to the DZ. 'When we turned to a 180° heading, we were over land; we did not fly over the coast, but sighted some burning buildings at Sainte-Mère-Église and dropped our paratroop stick. By this time only our three-ship 'V' remained; the others had lost us in the descent through the undercast.

---

120 Quoted in *Green Light! A Troop Carrier Squadron's War From Normandy To The Rhine* by Martin Wolfe.

'We had hits in our vertical stabilizer. There was a hole big enough for a man to crawl through, but fortunately none of the main controls were hit. We also took hits in one of the main gas tanks and lost a substantial portion of our fuel.'

Navigator 'Bob' MacInnes recalled: 'It was a close thing getting back to base. We were coming in with the indicator showing no fuel in the tanks. As we made our final approach Lieutenant Greg Wolf just ahead of us landed and almost immediately went up on his nose because his tyres had been shot out during the drop. We managed to pull up into the air just enough to clear his plane and immediately landed at a nearby base. When we got out the smell of gas was overpowering; it had sprayed over the entire fuselage. In addition to the big hole in the vertical stabilizer, we got our left wingtip shot off and there was a really big hole in the fuselage where the door load had been before it went out. This must have been from one of those small explosive shells the Germans were using. It sure made a mess of the floor and a part of the side wall. I also got a little piece in my wrist, but I didn't know anything about this until two days later when it began to get sore and infected. Doc Coleman dug it out with a large hypodermic needle. If those shell fragments had hit there before the door bundle went out, it would have been goodbye. The door load, all 1,100lbs of it, consisted of mortars and mortar ammunition. It had been resting on the floor directly above where the shell fragments came in.'

Crew chief, Howard 'Fat' Bowen, recalled: 'The door load and the first paratrooper went out of the door as one. Everyone else in the stick went out in seconds. Major Farley acknowledged my yell of 'All out!" and made a sharp turn to get away as I began to pull in the static lines. These were fifteen foot long tapes made of heavy webbing that were attached to the parachute rip panel and pulled open the chute when the paratrooper jumped. So there were eleven sets of static lines plus the two from the door load. Getting that sort of stuff inside the plane was not an easy thing to do. Before I got them half way in, MacInnes and 'Chick' Knight, the radio operator, had to come back and give me a hand.'

A fairly typical landing was that of the Horsa carrying Captain William W. Bates of the 53rd Wing. Unable to reach a large field, the pilot picked a small one, lowered his flaps and landed at about 70 mph. The glider bounced twice and when about ten feet off the ground on its second bounce crashed through a row of trees which stripped it of its wings and landing gear. The craft scraped to a stop ten yards behind British forward positions. There were plenty of bullet holes in the tail, but the only casualty was a soldier who suffered a broken leg as a result of leaving his safety belt unbuckled during the landing. The cargo, an ammunition trailer, was intact and was unloaded in twenty minutes. The episode illustrates the surprising degree to which the passengers and cargoes of the gliders survived crash landings. Only five Horsas landed on the LZ itself and most were released early and the distribution of the landings indicates that most of the serial had released its gliders at least a mile short of the proper point. Fourteen gliders were concentrated in a few fields about 2½ miles northeast of LZ 'E'; five were at points several hundred yards further east; eight were scattered southeast of the zone at distances up to two miles from it. Bullets and accidents combined to kill fourteen troops and cause thirty other casualties. Ten of the airborne were missing. They had been in two gliders which landed within the German lines near les Droueries.

Thanks to greater durability and their longer gliding range the Wacos made a much better safety record than the Horsas. Over half of them landed intact, while only about twenty percent of the Horsas were undamaged. Three Wacos and 21 Horsas were destroyed, but much of the destruction was caused by enemy action. Particularly in the case of landings north of les Forges, the lives of the men often depended on their jumping out of the glider and into the nearest ditch before the Germans could bring artillery, mortars or machine guns to bear on them. Unloading had to wait until nightfall or until it was clear the glider was not being used as a target. However, within a few hours most of the men and materiel which had landed in friendly territory on or near the LZ had been brought to Colonel Raff's command post on the north side of les Forges. Of the glider pilots five had been killed, four were missing and seventeen had been wounded or injured. The airborne had five killed and eighteen injured or wounded. None of them were missing for long.

The same could not be said of 1st Lieutenant Louis Emerson's crew in the 83rd TCS in the 437th TCG. 'About three miles before landfall (the beach), German 88 mm anti aircraft fire from coastal installations began exploding near us. A near miss hit us with shrapnel and ignited a fire in our right engine It quit developing power immediately. We did all the single engine things including activating the fire extinguisher on that engine, but to no avail because it continued to burn merrily. There were plastic windows along the right side of the fuselage and they began to melt from the heat of the burning engine. We were unable to feather the propeller (turn the blades so that they did not rotate in the slipstream and create a great amount of drag). With the propeller not feathered, we were able to almost maintain our altitude and 100 mph with full power on the good engine.

'There were two pilots in my glider, two airborne artillery soldiers and a 105 mm howitzer artillery piece. I knew if we cut the glider loose, it would land in the water and sink like a rock. The people in it would not be able to save themselves. I made a quick management decision and decided that we could make it to the LZ and still have about 300 feet altitude. This would give our glider a reasonable chance for a successful crash and survive and with a little luck we could get back to the coast, ditch beside a ship and if I did a good ditching job, we might not even get our feet wet. That is what we tried.

'We successfully got the glider to its landing zone. Single engine piloting protocol dictates that all turns are made toward the good engine. I started a medium turn to the left (into the good engine) around the centre of the village of Sainte-Mère-Église to head back toward the coast. I looked down the left wing and I was looking straight into a pair of machine guns on a platform on top of a building. I think it was a church. As I was looking, the gunner opened fire and his aim was excellent. His first burst knocked off most of the cowling on the good engine. His second burst knocked the cylinder heads off the engine top cylinders and his third burst knocked the dome off the propeller. Propeller pitch control was immediately lost and the blades flattened out. The engine ran away, broke and stopped turning completely. Now I was flying a glider.

'I stopped the turn, levelled the wings and set up the glide. We were over a thickly forested area, but ahead I could see two possible dear landing fields, one too dose and the other too far away and both too small. If I tried to stretch the glide to the more distant field, we would stall, the airplane would hit the ground nose first at a sharp angle and we would all be killed. A poor prospect if I tried to land in the near field. I would have too much airspeed to land and get stopped before we hit the hedgerow. I called for flaps and landing gear to slow us down, but they were not available. The hydraulic system had been destroyed by the anti-aircraft fire. At this point, I concluded there was no real chance of survival. The axiom that there are no atheists in a foxhole also applies to doomed airplane cockpits I made a quick prayer, 'Dear God, take care of my wife Marilyn and our unborn child.'

'I decided I would not give up without a fight and I went to work. I pushed the airplane down below the tops of the trees in the forest we were flying over and used the friction of the airplane striking the tree limbs as a crude brake to slow us down. I flipped the bailout bell switch to on which started a loud bell ringing and yelled, 'Prepare for crash landing!' Kreutter and Briski, who were in the cabin sat down with their backs against the bulkhead between the cabin and the flight deck. The last time I looked at the air speed, just before we crossed the border of the field, it indicated 120 mph I slammed the airplane against the ground in an effort to slow it down and it bounced. Looking ahead, I could see slightly off to the right, a break in the tree line about 25 or 30 feet wide. I dragged the right wing tip on the ground and with great good fortune was able to swing the nose (where the cockpit was) around far enough that when we hit the tree line, the nose was in the opening and was not damaged. The wings absorbed the inertia of the crash. The control wheel came back and hit me in the chest. If I had not had on the flak suit, my chest would have been crushed. As it was, ribs were broken. My seat and Gilbo's seat were broken loose from the cockpit floor. Gilbo turned sideways in his seat just before the crash and suffered a compound fracture of his upper left arm and was knocked unconscious.

'It seemed as though the crash was endless. The airplane reared like a wild horse. The sound of metal being crushed was overwhelming. Suddenly, there was complete silence. I could not see anything until I realized that my goggles were shattered and opaque. I raised them, opened the side window and looked out. There was nothing to see but shattered trees. The right side of the airplane was engulfed in flame. The Very pistol flares stowed under my seat began to explode. I could actually feel the skin on the back of my hands begin to blister. Both Kreutter and Briski had been catapulted through the bulkhead onto the flight deck. Briski reached up between our seats and opened the escape hatch above us. We got Gilbo's seat belt unlatched and pushed him up through the hatch and off the side of the fuselage. Next I went through and then Kreutter and finally Briski. We were all safely out. The airplane fuselage was broken in two pieces just aft of the door with the tail section at an angle from the rest of the fuselage. We dragged ourselves about 50 feet away from the airplane. Briski went back to the airplane, reached through the door (now at ground level) into the fuselage, located a first aid kit on the wall and brought it back. The hack watch was still on my wrist, but the Hamilton was gone forever. I looked to see what time it was and it was 21 minutes after nine. We began to assess the damage. Without warning, the entire airplane erupted in flame and we quickly retreated into a gully about 100 feet from the airplane. Up a slight incline, perhaps 100 feet away was a farmhouse. There were several people on the porch. They did not offer to help in any way. We could have used some help, even if just a drink of water. Gilbo was in great pain His arm fracture was a compound one and there was bone visible. We did not have anything from which to make a splint except a trench knife sheath. I removed my undershirt. We made bandage strips from it and used these and the knife sheath to immobilize his arm as well as we could. There was morphine in the first aid kit, but we did not want to do anything that would dull our senses. By this time, my chest was beginning to pain and I could have used a shot of morphine. The people on the porch of the farmhouse just stood and watched us.

'Why I picked up that compass in my foot locker, I'll never know but I'm glad I did. We held a council of war to decide what to do. Daylight was fading fast. Our return course, if flying, was 69 degrees. It would take us over 'Utah' Beach. Knowing that we were only about ten miles from the beach, we decided to use the compass and try to walk 69 degrees as close as we could. We stood up. As soon as we exposed ourselves, we began taking fire from a German submachine gun on the other side of the clearing. We immediately dropped back into the depression. There was nothing to do except wait until dark. The shooter could have easily captured us because all of our weapons were being destroyed in the burning airplane. He did not and for that, I am extremely grateful. While waiting for dark so we could move, I fell asleep. During the pre-mission briefing, we had been told that although there were dirt embankments and thorn trees acting as boundaries between the fields and that there would always be a gate through which farm machinery and animals could be moved from field to field. The French Underground had advised that many of these gates had been booby trapped with grenades. Since neither Gilbo nor I could climb any fences, it was going to be necessary to trust a gate each time we went from one field to another. As commander it was my responsibility to open the gates. I do not know how many gates I opened, but I do know that I expected each one to blow up It was a difficult task.

'Finally, about 1500 as we were walking along a hedgerow looking for a gate, we heard a rustling on the other side. We froze into immobility. We had been given three things to help in survival on the ground; the challenge (thunder), the countersign (welcome) and a toy noisemaker called a cricket. One cricket chirp was a challenge and an answering two chirps was the countersign. After a long moment, we heard a chirp. I immediately answered with two chirps. After a pause, a man's voice whispered 'thunder' and I replied, 'Welcome'. We had come upon an American paratrooper acting as a sentry for a group in a nearby barn. We were overjoyed.

'The paratrooper escorted us to the barn. There were about 25 enlisted paratroopers there. They had captured the building late in the afternoon and moved their wounded into it. Their corpsman dressed Gilbo's arm. He had

299

no tape, but he tightly wrapped my ribs with a gauze bandage and that eased the pain considerably. We were about five miles from the beach, but none of the invasion force had made it this far inland.

'About 1000 (this was June 7), a lone recon half-track circled through the farmyard. They were alone. The road to the beach was not secure. Regardless, we decided to try to make the beach as soon as possible. The paratroopers had captured the German equivalent of a jeep and there was a farm wagon in the farmyard. About ten wounded paratroopers were unable to sit up. We covered the floor of the wagon with straw and placed these wounded in it. We hitched the wagon to the German jeep. Kreutter, Briski and I secured folding stock carbine rifles from the bodies of dead paratroopers together with all the ammunition we could stuff into our pockets. We and the other walking wounded found places to sit on the German jeep and the wagon. Our caravan started for the beach. We were under sporadic fire and had to fight all the way to the beach; and we were late afternoon getting to it. Fortunately, none of us was wounded. There was a first aid tent on the water's edge with a Red Cross painted on it. All four of us headed for it, because Kreutter and Briski both had some serious burns on their arms and hands.

'Gilbo and I found a couple of unoccupied stretchers and gratefully lay down on them. Shortly, a corpsman brought us each a canteen cup of hot coffee, a can of C-rations (pork and beans) and four cigarettes I still remember that as one of the most welcome meals I have ever had We had not eaten since noon the day before.

'About midnight, our stretchers were loaded onto a DUKW (amphibious jeep). We were transported to a dock with an LST serving as a hospital transport anchored about 100 yards from the dock. When we came along side the LST, our stretchers were fastened to a line from an overhead crane on deck. We were lifted what seemed to be hundreds of feet into the air, swung over the side of the ship and lowered into the LST's hold. Our stretchers were placed in racks along the side of the hull.

'After about 24 hours, we arrived at Southampton and were transported to the 1st General Hospital there. I was a mess. I had not shaved in two days, all exposed skin was covered in smoke, grease, dirt and everything else and I could even smell myself. I knew that a nurse with whom I had become acquainted in North Carolina had been transferred to this unit I inquired of her. Within a half-hour, she was at my side. It was wonderful to see a friendly face. She helped me clean up. She did help me to the showers and to get a clean hospital gown. She saw to it that I got a good meal. What a relief! I was able to send an immediate message to my Commanding officer advising that all of the Very pistol flares should be relocated in some place other that the cockpit, which they were. I finally saw a doctor the next day and my chest was x-rayed. The ribs had already began to knit, so there was nothing to do but property tape my chest and send me back to my unit Two days later, I was back with my unit and ten days later I was flying re-supply missions to the beach.'

Once again small fields and enemy fire played havoc with the glider landings. The fire in some places was intense and many men were killed or wounded in the one or two minutes before their gliders reached the ground. Some pilots, despite strict orders for a slow landing, slammed their Horsas into the landing fields at 100 mph. Since the fields were short, some being only 100 yards long and since the twilight made a precise approach over the hedgerows increasingly difficult, even the most careful pilots were lucky to escape a crash.

Counting some damage done after landing by enemy fire, only thirteen of 84 Horsas were left intact and 56 of them were totally destroyed. There was a widespread feeling among the glider pilots that the Wacos, with their gentler glide and tougher frames would have done better, but none of the fourteen Wacos which were sent survived intact and eight of them were destroyed. Of 196 glider pilots ten were killed, 29 or more were wounded or injured and seven were still missing at the end of the month. The airborne had 28 killed and 106 wounded or injured, but hardly any were missing for more than two days.

Once again the occupants of most of the gliders had to take cover immediately after landing and unloading was postponed until after dark. The cargoes had come through surprisingly well. The 435th Group estimated that 39 of its 48 loads were usable and this is confirmed by estimates from glider units that 42 out of 59 jeeps, 28 out of 39 trailers and fifteen out of 24 howitzers were serviceable. However, much of the materiel could not be collected or used immediately.

The focal point of the landings of the gliders in the first serial was almost two miles northeast of LZ 'O'. This put them near to and in some cases within the German positions. A member of the divisional artillery staff, who had come with the serial, gathered about 200 men of the 319th and led them during the night into the lines of the 4th Division east of Sainte-Mère-Église. Other groups made their way back with more or less difficulty and at 1715 on 8 June the 319th Field Artillery went into action near Chef-du-Pont with almost all its men and six of its howitzers.

In the second serial, carrying the 320th Field Artillery, all gliders but the five released near LZ 'W' and one or two released a few seconds too soon northeast of Sainte-Mère-Église landed within a mile of LZ 'O'. Major Robert M. Silvey of the 320th, who had landed in 'Detroit' Mission that morning, was waiting beside the pathfinders on the zone and soon gathered slightly less than half the battalion with two usable howitzers. These began firing at 0930 on the 7th from positions 400 yards west of Sainte-Mère-Église. Thereafter patrols brought in a steady stream of troops and materiel from outlying gliders and by evening of 8 June the battalion had eight of its howitzers in action, including two landed in the vicinity of LZ 'W' and had accounted for practically all of its personnel.

'The fields were not as large as we had expected' recalled John Hanscom. 'Under conditions in which we found ourselves, they immediately assumed the proportions of medium-sized postage stamps. The trees which we had estimated to be fifteen to twenty feet in height were actually anywhere from forty to a hundred and seemed at least three hundred to us. 'Bill' made a 270 degree turn from our original flight line and approached a rectangular field on the north side of a country road. The air was filled with descending gliders. Everyone seemed intent upon getting into that field ahead of us. A glider cut in on our left and 'Bill' had to swerve to the right and do the best he could to get into the rear pasture of a farm house. That pasture was somewhat less than a hundred yards in length. It was surrounded by trees, graced with a stone bam, covered with stumps and chuckholes and traversed by a power line upheld by sturdy posts. We had arrived in the Bocage of Normandy.

'We were a trifle short for this destined haven of ours and 'Bill' had eased the big craft into a near stall with no flaps We hit a tree with our left wing. There was a terrible rending, crashing sound. Affairs were then completely out of our hands. The glider careened to the right. The ground crash shock was taken by our right wing and landing gear. The nose wheel came up through the fuselage, the skid crumpled and the floor buckled. We slewed to the right into a wall of trees and undergrowth, a good-sized tree passing by my side of the nose with inches to spare. The nose of that glider which 'Bill' and I were occupying was the only portion not completely demolished He looked at me, I looked at him and our first reaction was one of stupefied speechlessness. We mustered enough courage to look back and see how our airborne charges had fared. The three in the front section of what was left of the compartment were unhurt and were in the process of extricating themselves from the debris in preparation for action. Of the eleven men behind the trailer, one had sustained a fractured arm and another was knocked unconscious but not seriously hurt. We found out later that we had been much more fortunate than many of the others. During our landing approach I had fleetingly observed a big Horsa in the act of somersaulting over some high trees before crashing sickeningly upon its Plexiglas nose. Later we learned of the disastrous results.'

Flight Officer Elwood Harold Brindle recalls: 'The little island of American-held territory looked mighty welcome to us and at the sight of the flares sent up by our paratroopers on the ground we cut off From the towplane and wheeled around in a sweeping 270° landing turn to choose a spot for landing. A green flare shooting up from the darkness below gave me a glimmer of a field we might possibly squeeze into, so I followed the flare in. As we cleared the trees bordering the field I saw that we would have to crash-land as the field was too short for a normal approach. I set the ship down hard and we ground to a stop against a hedgerow at the far end of the field. Luckily no one was injured and the cargo was in good condition, though the glider itself was far from being in good shape. As we emerged, the paratrooper who had shot off the flare came up to us.

'Kind of a small field you picked for us, wasn't it bud?' I said to him.

'Yeah,' he agreed. 'But I wasn't expecting a big baby like this.'

'He looked admiringly at our glider; its nose nestled against the hedgerow as if it were looking for something to nibble at. Just then, a shell from a German 88 landed a short distance away and we hit the dirt. From then on, life for us consisted of digging in between artillery barrages and dodging snipers in between. As all the glider pilots were making their combat debut, new records were hung up all around for the depth and luxuriousness of foxholes. Like the fabled private who dug so deep he was charged with desertion, some of the GPs [Glider Pilots] claim to have established definitively that there are no prospects whatever of striking oil in France.'

Brindle would endure many anxious hours as he waited to be relieved and borne back to England by friendly vessels.[121] So too, John Hanscom and

---

121 Flight Officer Brindle would then continue training back at Welford and was selected to be one of the glider pilots who would be detached on a secret mission to Italy where on 15 August he flew a CG-4A glider into Southern France as part of Operation 'Dragoon'. He received a Bronze Star for his actions. He returned to Welford in late August and on 18 September he flew a combat mission to Holland as part of Operation 'Market-Garden'. On 9 December he was appointed and commissioned as a 2nd Lieutenant. For the rest of the war he would be a power glider pilot where he would regularly be a co-pilot of C-47s flying supply missions in the ETO.

'Bill' Meisburger but fate had other plans for them. Hanscom was dead tired, but not too much to note the fireworks going on all around him. 'Around 0700 a new wave of C-47s came in low. They were dropping supplies over toward the enemy from our position. We signalled by hand and smoke to entice them our way but to no avail. Shortly after that another glider mission came swooping in. Gliders began releasing over enemy ground. They were fired at with everything Jerry had. Again we began our signalling efforts and some of the towships towards the end of the formation swerved in our direction. Upon release, the gliders came in as best they could, but very few escaped crashing. One CG-4A came in apparently with its nose locked unlatched and jeep hooked up to the automatic nose lift. Upon landing, it crashed thunderously into a hedgerow; the nose flew up and the jeep catapulted out through the front end undamaged. We fully expected to find a couple of dead glider pilots but upon arriving at the wreck found them resting easily upon the grass, smoking cigarettes, shaken up a bit, but unhurt.

'About forty of us glider pilots were formed into a combat patrol; and moved up toward the enemy position under the leadership of an airborne captain. To our dismay we learned that the mission was to knock out a German field piece, a dreaded 'eighty-eight', which had been raising the devil with our tanks along the road to Sainte-Mère-Église. We soon came upon a mixed platoon of airborne and tank troops taking cover in a ditch behind a row of trees. Two Sherman tanks were lined up with their gun barrels poked through the trees aimed at the eighty-eight which was up an incline about a thousand yards in front of us. They fired on it and apparently drove the crew away. By the time we had worked our way along the hedgerows and ditches up to the emplacement, the gun was deserted. It had been hastily sabotaged. Mines and booby traps were in clear evidence. We were careful to touch nothing and to step cautiously. In the field in front of that German gun emplacement were three gliders, one Horsa and two CG-4As. One of the CGs was completely burnt. Only the skeletal structure of the steel tubing remained. The Horsa was a mess of kindling wood. The other CG had apparently made a perfect landing, but directly into the face of enemy machine gun fire. The two pilots sat stiff and cold in their seats.'

In the 436th TCG after the drop Major Francis Farley's crew had according to crew chief, 'Fat' Bowen, 'some bad moments'. 'Of course by then we were all alone. Out over the Channel I called 'Darkie' [a British direction-finding station on the coast] to get a steer home. The fix they gave me didn't seem right; but I figured they knew what they were doing. I made about a 180° turn; but pretty soon I saw all those lights and gun flashes and my God, I was damned near over Cherbourg again! So then I turned around again and headed back home. By the time I got in, they'd given us up for lost.'

The tow planes started landing at Aldermaston at 2228 hours after a 180° turn off the target and return as they had come, up over the Sainte-Marcouf islands and 'Gallup'. 'Keokuk' was not significant to the success of the 101st Airborne but the mission indicated that gliders, when not exposed to fire at close range, could be landed in daylight without excessive losses. Most of the glider pilots on 'Keokuk' had landed the Horsas with no more than moderate damage, a fact worth noting in view of what happened in Mission 'Elmira'.

Having dropped troopers on 'Albany' before returning to Greenham Common and blowing a tyre on landing, the glider tow on 'Keokuk' was Lieutenant Marvin Litke's second mission of 'D-Day'. 'The flak was very heavy and we made a tight turn and hit the deck. As we flew back across the coast I could see for the first time the mass of shipping with the big ships firing broadsides toward the shore. There were about five C-47 aircraft that had ditched near shore; the crews were standing on the wings waving at us as we flew over. I remember a pleading voice coming in over the radio asking for the aircraft to please not fly low over the beach as it caused the Navy ships to have to hold up on firing missions. I also remember being so elated (high) that I wanted to return to shore to see the grand event. For once better judgment was in gear. We had been given 'bennies' by the flight surgeon as we had been up all day and would be flying another mission the next day. These were to keep us extra alert for the period needed. In my case they kept me awake and hyper for three days before I 'crashed' and fell asleep.'[122]

Major Frank W. Hansley, summing up the mission, recalled: 'Nothing unusual happened en route. My memory flashes back to a rather open route leading over 'Utah' Beach and a trail way pretty well controlled by advancing American troops. Appreciatively, we received much less ground fire on this mission, even after we arrived over the glider landing zone area. We were later informed that the Germans saved their ammunition to use on the attacking glider men during their approach and landings. I sure saluted the glider men; they again took the brunt of the mission.'

---

122 'On 'D+3' we returned to a small strip carved out of the bluffs over 'Omaha' Beach. This time we were to pick up wounded and carried the flight nurses attached to us. We continued to fly in and out of this strip for a number of days.' *Flying With The 71ˢᵗ Troop Carrier Squadron, 434ᵗʰ Troop Carrier Group*, an autobiography by Marvin Litke.

About 0830, June the ninth, John Hanscom and 'Bill' Meisburger and many other glider pilots aboard an LST (Landing Ship Tank) landed at Portland Bill on the south coast of England to be transported by truck a short distance to Weymouth. 'There we had breakfast and waited for trucks to take us to our various bases' wrote Hanscom. 'It was a long ride to Greenham Common in our open truck and rain poured down for about half the distance. At long last about 1630 we arrived at that blessed base. Next to home, I know of no spot on earth that ever looked so wonderful.'

Everyone at Greenham Common was overjoyed to see 'Bill' Meisburger and John Hanscom, who says: 'The greater part of us had been given up for dead in the pessimistic reports given by the power pilots who had towed us into that inferno. Many of our C-47s had been hit on that mission. Two had been shot down, but not from our squadron. 'Doc' Pringle our squadron flight surgeon broke out a stock of 'Old Overholt' and we each inhaled a double shot without blinking an eye. What a bedraggled appearance we presented! Dirty, unshaven, exhausted, clothes torn and soaked with sweat, we certainly reflected that three-day ordeal of combat. We ate supper just as we were. Everyone ogled us, asked all kinds of questions and exclaimed how glad they were to have us back. The good Chaplain Lusher had tears in his eyes as he shook each of us by the hand. The mess officer saw that our plates were loaded with extra portions of everything which certainly emphasized the rarity of the occasion. We were indeed heroes for a brief spell Captain Keller, our group intelligence officer, took pictures and interrogated us briefly. 'Bill' and I took a good, long shower after all the excitement and went to bed early. It certainly felt fine to retreat into that comfortable old sack once again.

'Thus ended our first venture into airborne combat. We were indeed a sadder and wiser group of young men. Our enthusiasm for action had definitely cooled. Henceforth we would look with apprehension upon any proposed glider combat mission. Comradeship had been forged in the heat of that ordeal and a strong bond of kinship would always exist among those glider pilots who had participated. Whenever a group of them would gather, this common background of fire would furnish ample subject matter for tall tale-telling. The significance of that episode seems to gather glory as it slips farther into the recesses of our memories.'

All things considered, the glider pilots did fairly well under difficult circumstances. Only two gliders in the first serial landed on LZ 'W', but twelve came within a mile and all but one or two were within two miles of it. In the second serial all but one of the fourteen Wacos, flown by the 88th

Troop Carrier Squadron, landed on or very near the zone, nine Horsas hit the zone and six came within a mile of it. On the other hand, a dozen Horsas in that serial landed near LZ 'E' and four Horsas missed the zone by about three miles. Few, if any, followed the pathfinder aids to LZ 'O' and the 82nd Division therefore considered the release inaccurate.

The War Diary of one of the squadrons in the 434th Troop Carrier Group reported: 'Besides coming down on fields that were too small, the gliders landed in the midst of an enemy counter attack which resulted in some of the gliders either cracking up on landing or meeting heavy enemy fire from small arms and machine guns. The glider pilots in this serial received covering fire from the members of the 'Chicago' serial. From the C-47 crew point of view the mission was very successful.'

On 9 June a letter from Brigadier General James Gavin in France to a friend, General Harold L. Clark, commanding 52nd Troop Carrier Wing in England expressed his appreciation for a job 'damn well done'. In a PS he added: 'Would you please call Colonel (Joel L.) Crouch (commanding IX TCC Pathfinder) and express to him our appreciation for a job well done.'

'About a month after D-Day' concludes 1st Lieutenant Louis Emerson, 'General James Gavin held a parade with all the Troop Carrier personnel of the 1st Allied Airborne Army taking part. There I was awarded the DFC and Purple Heart. Later I was also awarded the Air Medal and one silver Oak Leaf Cluster signifying the award of five more Air Medals. We were the first crew to survive a combat crash in a C-47!'

Chapter 15

'Galveston' and 'Hackensack'

On 1 June it was time to invade Hitler's 'Fortress Europa'. We could feel the tension in the air'. Then came 3 June and we were herded into a block of barracks behind barbed wire. 'Uncle Sam' wasn't about to let any of his invasion party troops wander off downtown and give away any secrets that we might have had. And that's not to say that a single one of us knew our exact destination along the coast of France. Only 'Ike' knew the landing spots and he didn't disclose them until sealed orders were brought to commander and flight planners 24 hours in advance.

Charles E. 'Chuck' Skidmore Junior, a glider pilot in the 439th Troop Carrier Group at Upottery. Following graduation with a journalism major from Kansas University in June 1941 and holding a private pilot's licence, he enlisted in July in the aviation cadet programme, completing sixty days of primary training on Ryan Aircraft at King City, California and basic training on Vultee Trainers at Moffett Field near San Jose but he was eliminated from the flying programme in the fall of 1941 due to so called 'flying deficiency.' Finally, in July 1942 at Pittsburgh, Kansas - 16 miles from where he was born, on 17 January 1920 in Columbus, a small town in Cherokee County, just across the State line from Joplin, Missouri, 'Chuck' enlisted as a Class 'A' glider pilot. He took his dead stick training, cutting the power off and gliding back down and then it was off to basic training in gliders at Vanita, Oklahoma, 90 miles from home and advanced training on the CG-4A Waco at South Plains Army Flying School at Lubbock, Texas where he received his glider wings in April 1943 and he became a Flight

'GALVESTON' AND 'HACKENSACK'

**(Warrant) Officer. After taking his combat glider training
in North Carolina in late 1943 he went overseas on the
USS *George Washington* to England in February 1944.**

When 'D-Day' had arrived for glider pilots in England breakfast was at
0400 in the morning featuring honest-to-goodness fried eggs and a huge
piece of chocolate cake. 'Chuck' Skidmore suspected that the cook believed
that he was cooking a last meal for them and that the food glider pilots liked
most was fried eggs and cake. 'Where he got the fresh eggs, I'll never know'
said Skidmore. 'We hadn't had any in the previous four months we'd been
in England. 'The condemned ate the hearty meal,' chirped one wag. 'The
briefings for the aerial invasion of 'Utah' Beach, our particular designation,
were serious matters, but not without a little pressure-relieving levity upon
occasion. Our Chaplain, Father Whalen had probably heard about all the
profanity known to mankind because he was a prison chaplain at Joliet,
Illinois prior to volunteering for the service. So he wasn't shocked at one of
the briefings to hear some profanity which included the Lord's name. Upon
looking around his listeners, the briefer stopped to apologize to the good
Father. 'Don't worry about what I think' said Father Whalen; 'worry about
what the Lord thinks.'

'One of the briefers was our own 91st Troop Carrier Squadron's captain
named Merriman. As I listened to him, I recalled that he was a former
school teacher but quite a roughneck when he wanted to be. I remembered
that the time when he took a carbine to the shower in North Carolina to see
if its charge would penetrate the wall of wood and galvanized steel. It did.
It went clear thought, crossed half the barracks, lodged in a four by four of
hard timber. I remember hoping that the American armament would be that
good on the beach. The conclusion of the captain's briefing went something
like this: 'Glider pilots will release when the pilot of the C-47 leading the
formation starts a gradual turn to the left to return to the coast. If any C-47
pilots cuts his glider off during an invasion without sufficient reason and
there shouldn't be any, he'd better keep on going because if he comes back
here, I'll be waiting for him.' And I'll add that I never heard of any tow pilot
needlessly cutting his glider off during several invasions on the European
continent.

'Speaking of C-47s, those workhorses of World War II were actually
underpowered for many of the jobs they were called upon to do, including
pulling heavily weighted gliders. One of our C-47s carried a radio crewman
who must have weighed nearly 300lbs. Nobody knew his exact weight. But

he was heavy enough to upset the trim of the C-47 as he walked to the rear. His pilot, a Captain Anderson, joked to a buddy that he intended to tie the sergeant to the seat at the radio because he didn't want to worry about keeping his plane trimmed straight and level during the assault on 'D-Day'. My group briefing was sombre right up until the final moment.

'Sir' asked the glider pilot, what do we do after we land our gliders?'

'There was a brief period of silence, after which the briefing officer, a non-flying person, admitted, I don't know. I guess we never really thought of that.'

'Perhaps it was true. I thought then and there amid a lot of laughter, that maybe glider pilots really were originally meant to be expendable in war. The best answer to the question came from a glider pilot sitting next to me. He said, 'Run like hell.'

The mission of the 439th Troop Carrier Group (and the 441st TCG at Merryfield) was code-named 'Hackensack', the last glider mission in 'Neptune'; one of two glider missions flown just after daybreak on 7 June, to LZ 'W'; two hours after 'Galveston' the first glider mission scheduled for 'D+1'. 'Hackensack's fifty C-47s in the 439th towing twenty Wacos and thirty Horsas and fifty C-47s in the 441st towing fifty Wacos would deliver troopers, guns and vehicles in the 325th GIR to the 101st Airborne Division. 'Hackensack's lead serial carried the 2nd Battalion, 325th Glider Infantry and most of the 2nd Battalion, 401st Glider Infantry, which was attached to the 325th and acted as its third battalion. These numbered 968 troops,[123] of which Horsas carried over 800. The cargo included five vehicles, eleven tons of ammunition and ten tons of other supplies. The other serial consisted of fifty aircraft and fifty Wacos of the 441st Group from Merryfield. They carried 363 troops, mostly service personnel of the 325th and 401st and eighteen tons of equipment, including twelve 81 mm mortars, twenty jeeps, nine trailers and six tons of ammunition. A pathfinder aircraft, piloted by Colonel Julian M. Chappell, commander of the 50th Wing and Lieutenant Colonel Kershaw of the 441st, accompanied the serial to guide it to the zone.

When 'Chuck' Skidmore arrived at his glider ready for the trip to Normandy, he and the other pilot carried their parachutes onto the glider between two rows of airborne infantrymen who were already seated on either side of the glider. 'We put our parachutes in the seats, actually' wrote Skidmore 'because the seats were built low on purpose to accommodate

---

123 According to the 82nd Division, the number was 982. The operations report of the 441st Group lists 463 troops, but this figure appears to include (he pilots and co-pilots of the gliders.

a seat pack and still allow tall pilots room for their head. About that time, a burly airborne paratrooper lieutenant stuck his head in between us two pilots and said, 'There's no use in you two fastening those 'chutes. We'd never let you use them anyway.' I thought that was putting it plainly, so I didn't even bother to drape the straps over my shoulders. You didn't argue with an airborne infantry officer.'

The destination of the two missions was originally LZ 'W'. However, reports from Serial 30 of Mission 'Elmira' which had landed at 2110 on 6 June indicated that there was heavy ground fire in the vicinity of LZ 'W'. Therefore permission was obtained from the 53rd Troop Carrier Wing to change the route and landing zone to LZ 'E' about a mile west of Sainte-Marie-du-Mont. A route change over the Douve River valley would avoid the heavy ground fire of the evening before and landfall was to be made four miles south of 'Utah' Beach on the north side of the Douve estuary. The pilots were to release their gliders in the vicinity of LZ 'E' and their homeward turn after release would be made to the left, instead of the right. These changes would keep the serials out of range of the enemy north of Sainte-Mère-Église and in the Turqueville enclave.

'Galveston', whose 100 glider-tug combinations (which included two aircraft of the 435th Group towing Horsas which had aborted in 'Elmira') would carry nearly a thousand men of the 1st Battalion, 325th Glider Infantry Regiment, twenty guns and forty vehicles destined for the 82nd Division. The first serial comprised fifty C-47s in the 437th Group, 32 Wacos and eighteen Horsas. They carried the 1st Battalion of the 325th Glider Infantry and part of an engineer company; a total of 717 troops with seventeen vehicles, nine pieces of artillery and twenty tons of equipment. This would be the last time that the US used Horsa gliders in a combat operation. One Horsa in the 437th with a 1,000lb overload refused to budge. Another was accidentally released during assembly, but its tug aircraft returned and picked up a substitute. The second serial was composed of fifty C-47s in the 434th at Aldermaston towing fifty Wacos. Aboard were the headquarters of the 325th GIR, the Reconnaissance Platoon and sundry engineers and artillerymen; in all, 251 men with 24 vehicles, eleven guns, five tons of ammunition and 1½ tons of other materiel. Take-offs at Aldermaston began at 0432, more than half an hour before dawn, in conditions of poor visibility, rain and gusty wind. One glider in the 434th Group was released over the field and was replaced by a substitute. Another broke loose near Portland Bill, too far away to transfer its load.

Horsa LJ135, one of a number of gliders in the 437th Troop Carrier Group at Ramsbury that were scheduled to fly in 'Galveston' had the honour of being in glider position 1 in 'Serial 34'. The 437th TCG CO, Colonel Hudgens was flying 43-15160 the C-47 tow plane. Although not as manoeuvrable or popular as the CG-4A, the Horsa was felt to be a capable glider under the right circumstances. LJ135 with Flight Officer Richard Mercer and co-pilot 1st Lieutenant George Parker in the 86th Troop Carrier Squadron at the controls would carry 28 men from 'Able' Company, 325th GIR led by 1st Lieutenant 'Jim' A. Gayley. Mercer, a Texan, born on 27 December 1920 in Paris, Lamar County but spent his youth living in Wichita Falls. On 20 December 1941 he married Norma Jo Pierce in Muskogee, Oklahoma and having just celebrated his 21st birthday a week after his marriage, he enlisted in the US Army Air Corps on 30 December at Sheppard Field, Wichita Falls.

'Serial 34' consisted of seventeen Horsas and 32 Waco gliders in the 437th TCG and would carry 717 glider infantrymen from 1st Battalion, 325th Glider Infantry Regiment, 82nd Airborne Division and engineers from 'Able' Company, 307th Airborne Engineer Battalion. It would also carry seventeen jeeps, nine field artillery pieces and close to 20,000 lbs of ammunition and equipment. At 0439 Colonel Hudgens took his C-47-Horsa combination off; the entire formation taking 35 minutes to take to the air. One Horsa which had exceeded its maximum weight of 8,000 lbs had to abort whilst on the ground another Horsa was accidentally released over the airfield. The weather conditions over England were quite poor with low visibility, rain and gusty winds that were not ideal for a large glider tow mission to formate on each other.

Take-off for 'Hackensack', conducted from static hook-up, was begun at 0647 from Upottery and about 0717 from Merryfield. Some of the troop carriers complained that the airborne had seriously overloaded their gliders, making them difficult to handle. The sky was leaden and the air so rough that spectators on the ground could easily observe the pitching of the gliders. After England was left behind, conditions improved. The ceiling rose from 2,000 to 8,000 feet and the clouds thinned out. Over France they were scattered with bases over 3,000 feet and visibility was excellent.

The circumstances of the glider landings were not much different from those of the previous day. Over the Channel and over Normandy the weather improved. The rain gave way to thin; high, broken clouds and the visibility became excellent. The mission followed the beacons to 'Gallup', turning there and proceeding by pilotage and dead reckoning to the Sainte-Marcouf

Islands and the mouth of the Douve. Since the sun was up and the Normandy coast plainly visible most of the way after 'Gallup', navigation was not difficult. The serials passed over or near many Allied ships, but by daylight the glider formations and their identifying stripes were recognized in all cases. Some of the gliders, sluggish because of overloads, were hard to manage and some formations became scrambled. One glider pilot reported seeing C-47s above and beneath him as he approached Normandy.

The formation followed the navigational beacons of 'Flatbush' and 'Gallup' where the further south they flew, the weather began improving. The low cloud began breaking and the rain stopped, giving good visibility. Upon reaching 'Gallup' the formation turned left and the remainder of the route was flown by pilotage and dead reckoning. The sun had risen by then and the Normandy coastline was plainly visible as well as the allied naval armada which was present around 'Utah' Beach. 'Galveston' like 'Freeport' made landfall on the north side of the Douve estuary and released at 0655 hours. Small arms fire harried the first serial but did not seriously endanger it. Between the coast and the LZ both serials reported small arms fire of medium intensity, probably from German elements pushed south from the 'Utah' area on the previous day and not yet mopped up. The 437th also was fired on after its turn, which probably brought it over the German salient around Sainte-Côme. Arriving at 0655, five minutes ahead of schedule the serial came in low and released most of its gliders from between 200 and 300 feet and a few even lower. Release at such altitudes meant that the gliders could not glide much more than half a mile or stay in the air over half a minute. This decreased exposure to enemy fire but increased the chance of accidents. All but five or six of the gliders were released too soon and landed between the two southern causeways and LZ 'E', the greatest concentration being a mile northeast of Sainte-Marie-du-Mont. In the 437th's serial eight aircraft received moderate damage and eighteen in the 434th were hit, none of them seriously. Low releases however resulted in a number of accidents and 100 injuries in the 325th (seventeen fatal). The second serial hit LZ 'E' with accuracy and few injuries. 'Serial 34' arrived over the LZ at 0655, five minutes ahead of schedule, coming in low at an altitude of between 300 to 200 feet and releasing the gliders at that height, which gave the pilots only half a mile of gliding or about thirty seconds to identify a good location for landing, make the turn and getting each glider configured for landing.

The gliders landing east of LZ 'E' had only an occasional sniper or mortar shell to harass them, but suffered many accidents. No less than ten of the Horsas were destroyed and seven damaged with seventeen troops killed and 63 injured. Of the Wacos nine were destroyed and fifteen were damaged, but only 22 of their passengers were injured and none killed. The glider pilots apparently had no deaths and few injuries.

Horsa LJ135 with Mercer and Parker at the controls was released between Sainte-Marie-du-Mont and the hamlet of le Holdy. Some 200 metres from the field lay a German Artillery position with four 105mm cannons positioned to fire on 'Utah' Beach and exit causeway No. 1 which ran inland towards Pouppeville. Luckily the position had already been captured by the 101st Airborne. LJ135 catastrophically impacted the field, slid twenty metres breaking up in the process and ended up on its back. Fifteen troopers, including 1st Lieutenant Gayley plus Flight Officer Richard Mercer, were killed instantly with the rest injured. Some of the first Allied personnel to arrive at the scene were medics from 2nd battalion, 502nd PIR led by Captain George Lage the 2nd Battalion surgeon. Lage had set up an aid station at Le Holdy where his team of medics took injured personnel by jeep and trailer from the surrounding area to the 101st Airborne field hospital at Château Columbiere near Hiesville. It is unimaginable the devastation that they witnessed. Lage's medics immediately began treating the wounded as best they could where the most serious were undoubtedly transferred to the field hospital as fast as possible.

Moderate ground fire was received over the LZ and during the left hand 180° degree turn that they had to do for their return leg home but no damage was done and all the C-47s in the 437th TCG in 'Serial 34' made it safely back to Ramsbury. Colonel Hudgens, no doubt delighted to have flown two 'D-Day' missions and return safely finally succumbed to a blocked intestine. Had he accepted the treatment not only would he have lived, he would also have missed 'D-Day'. On 12 June Hudgens was buried at Madingley US Military Cemetery on the outskirts of Cambridge.

The 434th Group was flying second in 'Galveston'. Major Frank W. Hansley recalled: 'The first tow planes with gliders took off at 4:32 am., 7 June. We had rain, gusty winds and poor visibility. I was leading the 72ndTroop Carrier Squadron element, which was the third unit in our train of fifty towed CG-4A gliders. The weather cleared for much better visibility over the Channel. Unlike 'Keokuk', we received much enemy ground fire as we entered French territory. I do not remember many other details of this mission, except that some earlier gliders had landed in deep marshlands. I tried to give the glider pilots the best possible landing approach over land, yet keep them together as one fighting unit. I feel all the glider men need special recognition for carrying out so well an almost impossible assignment. The results were much more positive than was either expected or for which they were given credit for by news sources.'

The Group reached its release area at 0701, nine minutes ahead of time. Unlike the first serial it appears to have released on LZ 'W' and despite lack of beacons and markers, to have done so very accurately. The 82nd Division credited it with twenty gliders landed on the zone, nineteen within a mile of it and eight within two miles. One was 2½ miles off and one four and a half miles away. Accidents destroyed sixteen Wacos and damaged 26, but no troops were killed and only thirteen injured. Moreover, at least nineteen jeeps, six trailers and seven guns were found in usable condition. The enemy around Turqueville still kept LZ 'W' under fire, but in spite of them the gliders were unloaded in fairly good time and the glider troops assembled near les Forges.

By about 1015 all battalions of the glider regiment had reported in and were ready to support the 82nd Division. The glider men's first task was to send a battalion westward to Carquebut to deal with the Germans who had held out so stubbornly there on the previous night against the 8th Infantry. The unit arrived early in the afternoon only to find the area deserted. The Germans had fled. It then followed the rest of the 325th to Chef-du-Pont where the regiment was to report for duty as divisional reserve of the 82nd Division. That evening the 1st Battalion had 545 officers and men fit for duty, the 2nd Battalion had 624 and the 3rd had 550. Only 57 of their troops were missing, all but one of those being from the 1st Battalion. Despite the death or injury of 7.5 percent of its men during landing about ninety percent of the regiment was ready for action.

Like the daylight missions of the day before, 'Hackensack', bringing in the remainder of the 325th GIR, was accompanied from the English coast by a large escort which the troop carriers described as excellent and very reassuring.

'One C-47 pilot in our squadron was quite a comic' wrote 'Chuck' Skidmore. 'It happened he was a co-pilot on a 'Gooney bird' that pulled me into France on 'D-Day'. All we had for communication between the airplane and the glider was a telephone wire stretched along the tow rope. As we flew along the east side of the Normandy peninsula, waiting the right hand turn into the 'Utah' Beach landing area, I noticed numerous splashes in the water below us. Anderson, 'I asked on my phone, 'what's making all those splashes?'

'Those are P-51s dropping their tip tanks.'

'Anderson' I replied, 'you're a damn liar. There aren't that many tip tanks in the whole Army Air Force.' The splashes must have been German shells falling in the water.'

The approach was made by the east-coast route over the Sainte-Marcouf Islands and 'Utah' to LZ 'W'. No enemy aircraft were seen and ground fire was negligible until the LZ was reached. Even there it was directed mostly at the gliders. The lead serial began its release at 0851, nine minutes ahead of schedule, from about 600 feet and the other released its first gliders at 0859, eleven minutes early. They then turned to the right and went home as they had come except for the authorized short cut from the English coast to the wing assembly area. Meagre small-arms fire during and after the homeward turn scored some hits. Three aircraft in the 439th and eight in the 441st were damaged, but none were lost.

'Two good glider pilot buddies in my squadron were Johnny Bennett and Charlie Balfour' wrote 'Chuck' Skidmore. 'Those two were as close as friends could be, but they were forever arguing about one thing or another. One bone of contention concerned whether or not glider pilots would ever be committed to combat in Europe. Charlie said 'yes' and Johnny said 'no', right up until 'D-Day'. They asked to make the Normandy invasion together and flipped a coin to see which would fly as pilot and which as co-pilot. Bennett won the toss and along with a string of hundreds of gliders, they crossed the English Channel, flew inland over 'Utah' Beach and then Bennett released his glider from the tow and started his descent from 900 feet. They glided silently for a few seconds and then Balfour broke the silence with these words: 'Johnny, they'll never fly gliders in combat.' For several seconds, there was hilarious laughter between the pair, despite the hail of bullets that started coming up from the Germans below. The airborne troops sitting at the rear must have thought the two were slightly nutty. Luckily, all of them got on the ground unscathed.'

The 439th Group seems to have released by squadrons, rather than as a unit and since there was no marking on the zone to guide them, the glider pilots headed wherever they saw a promising spot. A dozen gliders from one squadron came down near the northern end of the zone under intense fire which killed several of the troops before they reached the ground. Most of the gliders in another squadron came down about a mile west of the zone, while a third had several land about two and a half miles east of it. The last squadron's gliders were released over the southwest side of LZ 'W' with the result that some came down in the flooded area, which at that point extended very close to the zone, if not actually into it. Of 29 Horsas accounted for, twelve landed within a mile of the zone, seven more within two miles of it, nine from two to four miles away and one nine miles off. Of the Wacos, seven were within a mile, six more within two miles and six between two and four miles away, one location being unspecified.

Small fields, high trees, flooded marshland, poles and wires set up by the Germans, debris from previous glider landings, enemy fire caused numerous accidents. No less than sixteen Horsas were destroyed and ten damaged in landing, fifteen of the troops aboard them being killed and 59 injured. Of the Wacos only four were destroyed and ten damaged, apparently without casualties. Two glider pilots in the serial were killed and ten or eleven injured.

For no obvious reason the comparatively inexperienced 441st Group did vastly better than the three preceding serials. It made a concerted release over the northern part of LZ 'W' and its gliders started down in the approved spiral pattern. The hazards and obstacles already described forced many glider pilots to zigzag about looking for a safe landing place, but by daylight in Wacos released above 600 feet they could pick and choose in an area of several square miles. At least 25 gliders in this serial hit the zone, another nineteen were within about a mile of it and the remaining six were probably not far off. Although eight Wacos were destroyed and 28 damaged, only one of the airborne occupants was killed and fifteen injured; while eighteen out of twenty jeeps and eight out of nine trailers came through unscathed. One glider pilot was killed and five injured. Highly accurate, with few casualties and with cargoes almost intact, this one serial reached the standard that glider enthusiasts had dreamed of.

The first serial, carrying all of the 2nd Battalion and most of the 2nd Battalion in the 401st GIR (the 325th's 'third battalion'), landed by squadrons in four different fields on each side of LZ 'W', one of which came down through intense fire. Fifteen troops were killed and sixty wounded, either by ground fire or by accidents caused by ground fire. The last glider serial of fifty Wacos, hauling service troops, 81 mm mortars and one company of the 401st, made a perfect group release and landed at LZ 'W' with high accuracy and virtually no casualties. By 1015 all three battalions had assembled and reported in. With ninety per cent of its men present, the 325th GIR became the division reserve at Chef-du-Pont. In general the flights held together during the return. Between about 1000 and 1038 all pilots arrived at their bases, except one who landed at Warmwell with a dead engine.

'When the other pilot and I cut ourselves free from the tow planes for the Normandy landing' wrote 'Chuck' Skidmore, 'we caught a burst of machine gun fire from the ground which missed my head by about a foot and then stitched the right wing from end to end. The first bullet - I was flying co-pilot - just missed my head as we turned our plane to the left and that why it didn't get us. If we'd gone another second farther (or a half second) it would have gotten us both in the face and we'd have probably all gone down.

'The Germans had flooded our proposed landing area so we landed in three feet of water. I went out the side of the pilot section by tearing off the canvas and tumbling in the water after first removing my flak vest. One guy didn't have the presence of mind to take off his jacket and fell into a hole where the water was over his head. Luckily for him, the other glider pilot rescued him after a series of frantic dives. It was pretty funny though to watch this big tall pilot as he dived down, came up, shook the water out of his eyes, looked around and then dived again. He must have dived down about three times before he found his little co-pilot.

'Upon landing we discovered the source of the ground fire which nearly got me. It turned out to be a bunker containing about a dozen conscripted Polish soldiers with one German in charge. After the glider infantrymen from several gliders, including ours, directed a hail of rifle fire at the bunker, the resistance ceased. There was silence in the bunker and then a single shot. Then there were shouts and laughter and the Poles emerged with their hands held high and surrendered. They weren't about to fight the Americans so they simply shot the Kraut sergeant.

'Our general instructions were to get back to the coast as best we could and get on a ship for the return to England. We landed about a mile and a half from Sainte-Mère-Église. I spent some time with some artillery guys manning a 105 cannon and some time with a communications outfit of the Army. I saw a burning C-47 on the edge of the field where I landed. I could still make out the number on the tail and I knew it had been flown by a good buddy of mine. All aboard were killed I heard later. I guess I was just lucky to get off so easy. A lot of other guys weren't so lucky.'

Epilogue

The last week prior to the invasion, we had received the order to always remain inside the house and to close the shutters - we were to remain unseen. It was the massive and noisy arrival of an elite German corps and SS officers and also the honour guards of Field Marshal Erwin Rommel. Behind the shutters we saw this small fellow with a tremendously large reputation in the front garden. He was observing Hitler's combat troops marching in review for him. Some days after, bad weather set in. The Normandy coast was hammered by rain and wind and the sea was rough. And yet it was from 11 o'clock on the evening of 5 June that we realized the coming of a great event: the Allied Invasion with bombs which caused fires dropped by RAF aircraft and hundreds of combat ready paratroopers with blackened faces. What a panic amongst the population! The Germans, surprised by the unexpected were incapable of regrouping to receive orders. Then it was a fight of one army group against another and the machineguns, at point blank range, opened up on the paratroopers that had unfortunately landed in trees, helplessly suspended there by their risers. Casualties - soldiers and civilians - began falling rapidly. At dawn the trees and smashed roofs had empty parachutes tethered to them that were blowing like cocoons in the wind. Likewise, the fields were like airfields covered with gliders from which came, all night long, soldiers, trained in England to fight immediately, which they did without hesitation.

Quickly, the small town, deserted by the fleeing Germans, was delivered by the Americans. We had the biggest joy to see them arrive in great numbers, happily, on their tanks and we placed French flags of blue, white and red out of our windows, the emblem of liberated France.

Arlette Lechevaliers, whose family lived in the village of Merville.

By noon on 7 June all major airborne missions in 'Neptune' had been completed. The glider operations had gone as well as most experts expected and vastly better than some had predicted. The predawn missions had demonstrated that gliders could deliver artillery to difficult terrain in bad weather and semidarkness and put forty to fifty percent of it in usable condition within two miles of a given point. The missions on 'D+1' had shown that by day infantry units could be landed within artillery range of an enemy and have ninety percent of their men assembled and ready for action within a couple of hours. While some felt that 'Chicago' and 'Detroit' proved the feasibility of flying glider missions at night, the general consensus was that landing in daytime or at least about sun-up had proven to be much more accurate and much less subject to accidents and that the vulnerability of gliders to ground fire had been overrated.

Many of the difficulties encountered had been unavoidable, particularly those of terrain and of weather. However, the glider pilots were convinced that they would have made better landings if provided with low-level oblique photographs plainly showing the tree-studded hedges. Also 'Detroit' would have benefitted from a warning to avoid the cloud-bank on the west coast. In 'Elmira' and 'Galveston' confusion and casualties resulted from German occupation of LZ 'W' and from the inability of the 82nd Division to inform the troop carriers of the situation. One solution proposed to avert such crises was to send an advance party with ground-air radio to talk the gliders in. Since such a party might itself fall prey to enemy action or to accident, it seems that provision might also have been made for alternate zones and for standardized visual signals to indicate that zones had been changed. As will be seen, this problem could also arise in parachute resupply missions and played a serious part in 'Market'.

American experience in Normandy indicated that the Waco was easier to fly, much easier to land and very much more durable than the Horsa. Such a conclusion was not entirely warranted since the unfamiliarity of their American pilots, the low release altitudes of the American missions and the use of fields of minimum size for landings had combined to show the Horsas in an unfavourable light. In Normandy and in other operations later the British got good results with the big gliders. The IX Troop Carrier Command was also convinced that its operations in 'Neptune' had proved the superiority of the Griswold nose, designed to protect gliders against vertical obstacles like trees and posts, as compared to the Corey nose which enabled gliders to ride up over logs or other low, horizontal obstructions. Again the verdict was premature. Had the Germans felled trees instead of erecting posts as obstacles the Corey nose might have been preferable.

The status of the glider pilots after landing was anomalous. They were troop carrier personnel. While they had been given some training in infantry tactics, it had been short and relatively sketchy, yet they constituted twenty percent of the approximately 5,000 men brought into the battle area by glider. Plans called for them to assist in the unloading of the gliders and the clearing of the landing areas, to assemble under the senior glider pilot in their vicinity and to report to the headquarters of the airborne divisions for such duties as might be required of them. It was contemplated that they would guard command posts and prisoners until a firm link-up with the amphibious forces was made and then be evacuated as soon as possible.

A majority of the glider pilots followed this pattern and on the whole did very well. While many glider pilots, particularly those landed in outlying areas, had attached themselves as individuals to airborne units and fought with them for a day or two, combat participation by the great majority was limited to a short period during unloading and assembly. There are few cases in which glider pilots were killed or wounded after leaving the vicinity of their gliders. Out of 1,030 American glider pilots reaching Normandy all but 197 had been accounted for by 13 June. What had happened to most of those missing at that time is indicated by a rise in known casualties from 28 on 13 June to 147 on 23 July. Of the latter total 25 were dead, 31 wounded and 91 injured. An additional 33 who were still missing were probably prisoners. The discipline and ground combat training of the glider pilots were criticized by the airborne and by some of their own members. However, the policy of quick evacuation had worked well in Normandy and had won general acceptance. As long as it was assumed that glider pilots could and should be quickly evacuated there was no justification for giving them extensive infantry training. It seemed much more important to improve their proficiency in tactical landings.

Of the 517 gliders used in 'Neptune', 222 were Horsas, most of which were destroyed in landing accidents or by German fire after landing. Although a majority of the 295 Waco gliders were repairable for use in future operations, the combat situation in the beachhead did not permit the introduction of troop carrier service units and 97 per cent of all gliders used by American forces in Normandy had had to be left to rot in the field. In hopes of recovering a substantial proportion of the gliders used in 'Neptune' the AAF had sent to England 108 sets of glider pick-up equipment. Essentially this apparatus was simply a hook underneath an aircraft fuselage. As the aircraft flew low over a stranded glider the hook would engage a loop of tow rope raised on a light frame and snatch the glider into the air. Since an empty Waco weighed less than 3,700 lbs, the shock of the pick-up was not excessive. The American Horsas in Normandy were practically all unflyable.[124] All but about forty of the Wacos were also found to be unserviceable or inaccessible to pick-up aircraft. Many of the remainder were damaged by vandals before they could be picked up. Some gliders in marginal condition might have been repaired on the spot or after a short flight to some base in Normandy but the troop carriers did not and could not have guards, bases or repair units in Normandy for many weeks after 'Neptune'. The ground forces, hard put to it to sustain their fighting men, opposed the landing of any unessential personnel and the few bases in the beachhead were jammed to capacity with fighters. Bad weather and the combat situation combined to delay recovery operations until 23 June. After that, fifteen gliders were picked up and flown back to England.

The feeling in IX TCC and 9th AF was that the delivery of the paratroops had been an outstanding success. Losses and aborts had been negligible. Forty-two C-47s were destroyed in two days of operations. Twenty-one of the losses were on 'D-Day' during the parachute assault, another seven while towing gliders and the remaining fourteen during parachute resupply missions. In many cases the crews survived and were returned to Allied control. Mission reports indicated that all serials had done well. Then, on 10 June General Quesada returned from a visit to Normandy with news that the paratroops had been badly scattered and that General Omar Bradley 'was much disappointed'. Bradley blamed 'pilot inexperience and anxiety' as well as weather for the failures of the paratroopers. The troop carriers had undertaken to bring 13,348 paratroops to Normandy.[125] Ten thousand men were dropped within five miles of their zones but the 101st Division had only about 1,100 troops and the 82nd Division about 1,500 troops near their

---

124 The RAF retrieved some of their Horsas late in the summer, using Dakotas with American pick-up equipment.

125 Of these, about 90 were brought back for one reason or another and eighteen were in an aircraft ditched before reaching the Continent. About 100 in 'Albany' and perhaps thirty or forty in 'Boston' were killed when the aircraft carrying them were shot down. The rest jumped. Of the jumpers over 10 percent landed on their drop zones, between 25 and 30 percent landed within a mile of their zone or pathfinder beacon and between 15 and 20 percent were from one to two miles away. At least 55 percent of the pilots made drops within two miles of their goals. About 25 percent of the troops came down between two and five miles away from their zones or beacons. With few exceptions these landed east of Pont l'Abbe and north of the Douve, seemingly within reach of the combat area. About 10 percent were from five to ten miles off the mark and four percent were scattered between ten and 25 miles from their zones. The remaining 6 percent were unaccounted for. Many were badly dropped, but some well-placed sticks went unreported because of battle losses.

divisional objectives at 'H-Hour' (0630) four hours after the end of the drop. Also, the 101st Division had only 2,500 paratroops under divisional control and the 82nd Division about 2,000 at midnight of 'D-Day'. If the troops had been able to concentrate on their zones at even the rate of one mile an hour, three-quarters of the force dispatched would have gone into action against its objectives on the morning of 'D-Day' and General Bradley would have had slight reason to complain of dispersion.

Except for slight errors in timing, troop carrier performance was almost flawless until the Normandy coast was reached and that with one exception most subsequent difficulties may be traced to three factors, clouds, enemy action and the limitations of navigational aids. Of these the cloudbank over the western Cotentin was the most damaging. At least nine of the twenty main serials had plunged into the clouds and were badly dispersed as a result. All of the six making reasonably compact drops appear to have avoided the cloudbank. Since the clouds were over a thousand feet up and less than a thousand feet in thickness it would have been easy to go over or under them with a minimum of warning. If only a weather aircraft had been sent to test conditions, if only radio silence rules had not prohibited one serial from warning those that followed, troop carrier performance would have been immensely improved. Masses of low clouds were known to be over Normandy on three June nights out of four and it must be rated as a serious planning error that no safeguard against their presence was made.

Enemy fire had considerable effect, but thanks to excellent intelligence, aircraft staying on course encountered very little flak. Thanks to effective tactical surprise and the protection of the cloud bank, fire of any sort was slight until the C-47s were within five miles of the drop zones. Even then it was wild and ineffective, causing losses of less than 2½ percent. Though pilots had been warned against evasive action many of them did it. About a fifth of them had had only a minimum of training and three-quarters of them had never been under fire before. Another adverse effect of ground fire was to interfere with navigation by distracting attention and concealing signals. A pilot whose aircraft was tossed about by a bursting shell might be a mile off course before he knew it. Light signals from formation leaders or from pathfinder troops on the ground could be hidden in a welter of flares, tracers and smoke.

The pilots were forced to rely heavily on radar because for most of their way across Normandy the clouds rendered visual navigation nearly impossible. Radar had proved to be a much less effective guide than had been supposed. It did guide aircraft to the general vicinity of their zones, but it could not be relied on to produce an accurate drop. SCR-717 was of little value in locating inland objectives. 'Gee' was successful enough, but its margin of error in Normandy averaged about a mile. Miscalculations or faulty adjustment could cause a three-mile error like that of the lead serial of the 438th Group. SCR-717 had a bad reputation for breakdowns and vulnerability to jamming. 'Gee' was 98 percent serviceable and almost unaffected by jamming in 'Neptune' but since only the pathfinders and one or two aircraft in each serial were equipped with 'Gee', it was of no help to the multitude of pilots whose formations had broken up. If all had gone according to plan, formations guided by 'Gee' or 'Rebecca' to the vicinity of their zones would have seen lighted 'T's showing them exactly where to drop. However, on four zones out of six enemy action or the nearness of enemy troops prevented display of anything but an occasional surreptitious light. At a fifth zone, DZ 'A', the 'T' was put out too late for two serials, one probably never came in sight of it and the other one tasked to use it was scattered. On DZ 'O' where 'T's were put out as planned the best drops in either 'Albany' or 'Boston' were achieved because of corrections made after the 'T's were sighted.

'Rebecca-Eureka', prescribed as the primary aid to be employed in approaching the drop zones, was so used in a majority of cases. Responses from the 'Eureka's on the zones were picked up clearly at an average distance of 16 miles, except at DZ 'A' and DZ 'N'. In the former case the beacon was turned on too late for the first one or two serials and in the latter, either because of jamming or because of malfunction, the reception was unsatisfactory. Had some beacons and some 'Rebecca' sets been turned on sooner the average reception distance might have increased to about twenty miles. As anticipated, precision dropping with 'Rebecca' proved very difficult because the blips representing aircraft and beacon merged well before the aircraft reached its zone. This may have been the main reason why so many of the pilots came within two miles of their zones, but were unable to hit them. When many beacons were used in a small area, a 'Rebecca' was likely to trigger the wrong beacon and receive its responses. Available channels were too few and too close together and the sets were insufficiently selective to prevent such reception. Many pilots in 'Neptune' are known to have picked up the wrong beacon and there is circumstantial evidence that others made drops on the wrong beacon, despite the fact that each had its own distinctive coding.

The liability of 'Rebecca-Eureka' to saturation if more than about forty sets were in use at once had resulted in it only being available to flight leaders except in case of emergency. Although used by an estimated 150 stragglers and by as many as thirty of them at one time on one beacon, the 'Rebecca' system did not become saturated. What did happen was that at least 150 pilots who needed to use it did not do so. Another handicap which especially affected the inexperienced pilots who lost contact with their formations was that only two aircraft in five carried navigators. This number, all that the tables of organization permitted, was ample for formation flying by daylight, but stragglers on a difficult flight over enemy territory at night would have benefitted by having trained men to compute their positions.

The difficulties encountered in 'Neptune' once again raised the question of whether night paratroops operations were worthwhile. Some historians have concluded that the mixed performance overall of the airborne troops in Normandy resulted from poor performance by the troop carrier pilots. Some notable writers have stated that troop carrier pilots were the least qualified in the Army Air Forces, disgruntled and castoffs.

Shortly after D-Day, two B-26 Marauder pilots were on pass in London when they encountered some Airborne troops who spotted their 9th Air Force patches and wanted to fight them on the spot. 'After calming them down' they said, 'we found that they took us to be the transport pilots who had carried them into combat. After telling them that we were in fact bomber crews, they proceeded to unload re: the quality of the pilots. According to stories we heard, they were mostly airline pilots on temporary duty who had never seen flak before and when the stuff started burning all around, they rang the bells and got rid of their loads and/or tows.' One of them added: 'Frankly I am surprised that this fiasco did not get wider publicity. I recall listening to Calais German propaganda broadcast while en route to second D-Day mission and heard about the reckless way the parachutists and gliders had been dumped in and around the Channel that morning. I put it down to propaganda, but did observe what looked like a mess down there.'[126]

The troop carrier pilots in their remembrances and histories admitted to many errors in execution of the drops but denied the aspersions on their character, citing the many factors and faulty planning assumptions. Some, such as Martin Wolfe, an enlisted radio operator with the 436th TCG, pointed out that some late drops were caused by the paratroopers, who were struggling to get their equipment out the door until their aircraft had flown by the drop zone by several miles. Others mistook drops made ahead of theirs for their own drop zones and insisted on going early.

---

126 November 2000 issue of *The Marauder Thunder* (the Marauder pilot's newsletter).

Summing up the part played by the troop carrier and glider borne operations in 'Neptune' 'Marty' Wolfe wrote: 'In spite of its intimidating complexity and the daunting obstacles it faced 'Neptune' scored many crucial successes. The time and place of the initial assault came as a complete surprise to the enemy. The Germans failed to push the seaborne infantry back down the causeways and into the sea. American paratrooper and gliderborne troops did suffer heavy losses; perhaps 2,500 killed, seriously injured, or missing but the Germans did not destroy any single paratrooper battalion or any other large airborne unit.[127] Only 41 planes and nine gliders were shot down out of a total of more than 1,500 plane and glider sorties in 'Neptune'. Only a handful of paratroopers, airsick and scared as they were, refused to jump. Our own air superiority and fighter coverage reduced the Luftwaffe to a few raids in our skytrains. Some historians point out, rather patronizingly that perhaps all the confusion on the ground in Normandy was worth the resulting losses; the Germans they say became so confused when paratroopers began dropping all over the landscape that they were kept off balance and did not throw up a major counter-attack until it was too late. This grudging pat on the head [that the airborne did well in spite of the troop carriers] grates on the nerves of troop carrier veterans.'[128]

Never again in World War II did any considerable number of Allied paratroops make a night drop.

---

127 'D-Day' casualties for the airborne divisions were calculated in August as 1,240 for the 101st Airborne Division and 1,259 for the 82nd Airborne. Of those, the 101st suffered 182 killed, 557 wounded and 501 missing. For the 82nd, the total was 156 killed, 347 wounded and 756 missing. Casualties to 30 June were reported by VII Corps as 4,670 for the 101st (546 killed, 2,217 wounded and 1,907 missing) and 4,480 for the 82nd (457 killed, 1,440 wounded and 2,583 missing). German casualties amounted to approximately 21,300 for the campaign.
128 *Green Light! A Troop Carrier Squadron's War From Normandy To The Rhine* by Martin Wolfe.

Index